Violence,
Silence, and Anger

DATE DUE

JY 15 '98			
FE 8 '01			
NO 25 03			
NO 10 04			
DE 1 04			
JE 23 08			

DEMCO 38-296

Violence, Silence, and Anger

WOMEN'S WRITING AS TRANSGRESSION

Edited by

Deirdre Lashgari

University Press of Virginia

Charlottesville and London

tle in the series
actice, Politics, Theory

THE UNIVERSITY PRESS OF VIRGINIA
Copyright © 1995 by the Rector and Visitors
of the University of Virginia

First published 1995

Library of Congress Cataloging-in-Publication Data

Violence, silence, and anger : women's writing as transgression /
edited by Dierdre Lashgari.
    p.   cm.—(Feminist issues)
    Includes bibliographical references (p.   ) and index.
    ISBN 0-8139-1492-2 (cloth).—ISBN 0-8139-1493-0 (paper)
    1. Literature—Women authors—History and criticism.   2. Violence
in literature.   3. Feminism and literature.   I. Lashgari, Deirdre.
II. Series: Feminist issues (Charlottesville, Va.).
PN471.V56   1995
809'.93355—dc20   94-38181
                                                              CIP

Printed in the United States of America

For Katherine Causey
mother and friend
who nourished me with her
vision of feminist possibility

Contents

Preface   xi

DEIRDRE LASHGARI
Introduction: To Speak the Unspeakable: Implications
of Gender, "Race," Class, and Culture   1

PART ONE
The "Knife in the Tongue": The Politics
of Speech and Silence

JANE HOOGESTRAAT
"Unnameable by Choice": Multivalent Silences
in Adrienne Rich's Time's Power   25

ANNE B. DALTON
The Devil and the Virgin: Writing Sexual Abuse in
Incidents in the Life of a Slave Girl   38

GEORGE B. HANDLEY
"It's an Unbelievable Story": Testimony and Truth in the
Work of Rosario Ferré and Rigoberta Menchú   62

KRISTI DALVEN
Native Witness, White "Translator": The Problematics of
Tran/scribing in Elsa Joubert's Poppie Nongena   80

PART TWO
Domestic Politics: Violence on the Home Front

MERRY M. PAWLOWSKI
From the Country of the Colonized: Virginia Woolf on
Growing Up Female in Victorian England   95

GISELA NORAT
The Silent Child within the Angry Woman: Exorcising Incest
in Sylvia Molloy's Certificate of Absence   111

Contents

PAMELA SMILEY
The Unspeakable: Mary Gordon and the
Angry Mother's Voices   124

RUTH O. SAXTON
Dead Angels: Are We Killing the Mother in the House?   135

PART THREE
Structures of Oppression: Subjectivity and the
Social Order

MADHUCHHANDA MITRA
Angry Eyes and Closed Lips: Forces of Revolution in Nawal
el Saadawi's *God Dies by the Nile*   147

DOROTHY DAVIS WILLS
Economic Violence in Postcolonial Senegal: Noisy Silence in
Novels by Mariama Bâ and Aminata Sow Fall   158

SHIRLEY GEOK-LIN LIM
Up against the National Canon: Women's War Memoirs
from Malaysia and Singapore   172

MICHAELA COOK
The Muslim Woman as Hero in Daneshvar's *Savushun:
A Novel about Modern Iran*   189

PART FOUR
Collective Silence, Collective Voice: Toward Community

SHERRI HALLGREN
"The Law Is the Law—and a Bad Stove Is a Bad Stove":
Subversive Justice and Layers of Collusion in
"A Jury of Her Peers"   203

ANN E. TRAPASSO
Returning to the Site of Violence:
The Restructuring of Slavery's Legacy in
Sherley Anne Williams's *Dessa Rose*   219

S. LILLIAN KREMER
The Holocaust and the Witnessing Imagination   231

Contents

VÈVÈ A. CLARK
Dangerous Admissions: Opening Stages to Violence, Anger,
and Healing in African Diaspora Theater 247

PART FIVE
Revolting Texts: Transgression (and) Transformation

ROSEANNE LUCIA QUINN
Mastectomy, Misogyny, and Media: Toward an Inclusive
Politics and Poetics of Breast Cancer 267

MADELINE CASSIDY
"Love Is a Supreme Violence":
The Deconstruction of Gendered Space in
Etel Adnan's *Sitt Marie-Rose* 282

DEIRDRE LASHGARI
Disrupting the Deadly Stillness: Janice Mirikitani's
Poetics of Violence 291

ANN E. REUMAN
"Wild Tongues Can't Be Tamed": Gloria Anzaldúa's
(R)evolution of Voice 305

Works Cited 323

Contributors 345

Index 349

Preface

This book has its roots in the feminist, antiwar, and social justice movements and the collaborative literary projects that have shaped my personal and professional consciousness over the past three decades. Many more people than I could possibly name here have influenced the development of my ideas about silence and anger and the need to speak out against violence. I thank all those I have worked with over the years who have helped me learn the life-affirming value of constructive anger, including the Comparative Literature Women's Caucus at the University of California at Berkeley, my comedics at the Berkeley Free Clinic, all those I worked with in organizing to end the war in Vietnam and protest nuclear weapons development at the U.C.-affiliated Livermore Weapons Laboratory, and my extended circle of family and friends in Iran.

Likewise, I want to thank those intellectual communities most responsible for inspiring in me a passion for collaborative work, among them Paul Piehler's graduate seminars in medieval literature; the Women's Poetry Translation Workshop; the fairy tale group, coeditors of *Scary Tales for Grown-Up Girls;* U.C. Berkeley's Strawberry Creek College (the Collegiate Seminar Program); the U.C. Peace and Conflict Studies Organizing Group; the Santa Rita Women's Jail Book Collective; my dream group and women's group allies; and my partners in the wild redwood and huckleberry haven we called "the land."

Special thanks to my coeditors of *The Other Voice* and *Women Poets of the World,* in particular to Doris Earnshaw, whose vision inspired and sustained the project to uncover, translate, and publish international poetry by women at a time when teachers of graduate courses in literature still insisted, "Women don't write poetry, women have babies"; and to Joanna Bankier, who made the journey an adventure and who continues to remind me that not everyone, fortunately, sees the world exactly as I do.

My heartfelt gratitude to the strong community of friends whose continuing practice of honest communication, including creative anger, informs this book. Thanks also to my colleagues in the English and Foreign Languages Department and across the Cal Poly campus who have sustained me with their ideas and encouragement. Special appreciation to D. D. Wills, Parvin Abyaneh, Barbara Goza, Leanne Sowande, and John

Maitino, whose collaboration in presenting workshops and forums on constructive conflict and intercultural communication has inspired me intellectually, and whose unwavering support has sustained me in all my creative work—teaching, mentoring, writing, and living. Thanks to the members of our campus Postcolonial Theory Group—especially Victorine Daigre, Liliane Fucaloro, Carola Kaplan, and D. D. Wills—who infuse our readings and discussions with the passion of intellectual discovery. And thanks also to the students in my world literature and women writers classes and in MADILA, the campus multicultural association, whose questions challenge me, whose insights inspire me, and whose courage in exploring beyond familiar territory renews my spirit.

I am particularly grateful to those whose influence has served as a direct catalyst for this book. The conference that Shirley Lim organized at the University of California at Santa Barbara on "Asian American Cultural Transformations" inspired my essay on Mirikitani, which in turn shaped my conception of the book. Ruth Saxton, who is forever pushing me off the cliff into projects I would otherwise be too busy to take on, inspired me to leap into this one as well. Carol Holder encouraged me to present the underlying concepts of this book in Cal Poly's Faculty Research Forums. Andy Moss and Jim Williams provided crucial support that made it possible for me to complete the book during a sabbatical leave.

I deeply appreciate the support of numerous friends and colleagues who read early versions of the manuscript, in part or whole, and contributed their insights and suggestions—among them Karen Berna-Hicks, VèVè Clark, Lauren Coodley, Victorine Daigre, Olivia Eielson, Nancy Gray, Cathie Carr Humphrey, Carola Kaplan, Woody Nance, Merry Pawlowski, Ruth Saxton, and D. D. Wills. I am especially grateful to my father, Ralph Eberly, for his perceptive reading of the manuscript and the encouragement that he has given me in this and all the important undertakings of my life.

Warm thanks to Nancy Essig, director of the University Press of Virginia, who nurtured this project from the beginning and has guided it through to publication. Also to the keen insights of the publisher's readers who commented on the manuscript in its early stages, and to Carol Rossi, Gerald Trett, Shirley Taylor, and all the others involved in the publishing process for their careful attention to detail. My deepest appreciation to all the contributors to this volume, without whose ideas the book would not exist, and whose dedication and good humor have made working on this project such a pleasure.

Most of all, my deep gratitude to Woody Nance, whose unfailing love and companionship have sustained me through the long haul, who reminds me not to reinscribe domination in my battles with the patriarchy and helps me remember how important humor is to all good work.

The lines from "Divisions of Labor," "Harpers Ferry," "Living Memory," "Turning," "6/21," and "Dreamwood" are reprinted from *Time's Power, Poems 1985–1988,* by Adrienne Rich, by permission of the author and W. W. Norton & Company, Inc. Copyright © 1989 by Adrienne Rich. The lines from *Shedding Silence* (San Francisco: Celestial Arts, 1987) are reprinted with the permission of the author, Janice Mirikitani.

"Up against the National Canon: Women's War Memoirs from Malaysia and Singapore," by Shirley Geok-lin Lim, was first published in the *Journal of Commonwealth Literature* and is reprinted with permission of the editor; "Disrupting the Deadly Stillness: Janice Mirikitani's Poetics of Violence," by Deirdre Lashgari, was first published in *Asian America: Journal of Culture and the Arts* 1, no. 2 (1993): 141–55, reprinted by permission of the editor; "The Holocaust and the Witnessing Imagination," by S. Lillian Kremer, first appeared under the title "The Holocaust in Our Time: Norma Rosen's *Touching Evil*," and in a different form, in *Studies in American Jewish Literature* 3 (1983): 212–22, and is reprinted with permission of the editor.

"Dead Angels: Are We Killing the Mother in the House?" is a revised version of an essay by Ruth O. Saxton that appeared in *Virginia Woolf: Themes and Variations* (New York: Pace University Press, 1993) and is reprinted with the permission of the publisher.

Violence, Silence, and Anger:

WOMEN'S WRITING AS TRANSGRESSION

DEIRDRE LASHGARI

Introduction
To Speak the Unspeakable: Implications
of Gender, "Race," Class, and Culture

> The liberatory voice . . . is characterized by opposition, by resis-
> tance. It demands that paradigms shift—that we learn to talk—
> to listen—to hear in a new way.
>
> —bell hooks

Since Tillie Olsen's provocative work "Silences" in 1965, feminist writing in the United States has taken seriously the roles of silence and
anger in the lives and literary production of women.[1] Little, however, has
been written on the specific conjunction of these issues with women's culturally shaped responses to violence. The essays in this volume engage in
a cross-cultural exploration of responses to violence in texts by writers
from twelve non-Western countries as well as the United States and
England.[2]

The contributors' discussions draw from such fields as psychoanalysis,
anthropology, political economy, and medicine as well as critical theory,
and their voices extend from the formal and academic to the highly personal and autobiographical. The range of texts discussed invites an examination of cultural and class-based differences in the nature of the violence
that women have experienced, the costs of breaking cultural taboos
against speaking out, and the strategies enabling women to violate societal
expectations without forfeiting the chance to be heard.

A writer faces contrary imperatives: to be honest, and to be heard. It
can be difficult for the writer herself to look closely into the systems that
justify and perpetuate violence, as several of the essays show. Once one
has identified the violence, it can be difficult to name it publicly, and difficult to make oneself heard. In the United States, for example, mainstream
arbiters of literary quality have often worked from assumptions uncon-

sciously rooted in gender, class, and Eurocentric culture, with a bias toward authorial distance. For a woman writing from the margins, whose work may clash with these assumptions, acceptance by the literary mainstream too often means silencing a part of what she sees and knows.[3] To write honestly may thus mean transgressing, violating the literary boundaries of the expected and accepted. This double bind is particularly strong for women writers of color, especially so if their vision is shaped by a language other than English. What is read by the dominant group as alien, rough-edged, jolting, strident, is more likely to offend when it comes from a woman. If the woman writer's root culture also has strong injunctions against "making noise," the temptation to self-silencing increases, as does the risk and necessity for breaking through. This risk often influences the way a writer shapes her work, its dramatic and narrative strategies, its language and imagery.

In addition to taboos against speaking and publishing what is regarded as unspeakable, the writer faces her audience's resistance to hearing. Paradoxically, the violence permeating the media—television, movies, newspapers—makes it more difficult, rather than easier, for us to hear. Packaged and sanitized, "violence as entertainment" can have an anaesthetizing effect that prevents us from feeling or acting. In different ways, the writers discussed in this anthology provide antidotes to this numbing. Their work calls into question our ways of keeping at arm's length what makes us uncomfortable. At its most powerful, their work often impels us to in-corporate the pain of violation, to take it into our own bodies where it can force us to respond. It implicates us, along with its characters and narrative speakers, in the struggle to give voice to the horror and the determination to end it.

Metadiscourses, or Talking about Talking Back

The multiplicity of voices talking back to each other within and among the essays in this book shapes the theoretical discourse of the volume as a whole.[4] Underlying this discourse are several concepts crucial to understanding the place of silence, anger, and transgression in women's responses to violence: decentering, heteroglossia, dialogics, and *travesía*.

Decentering, a process essential to postcolonial literary practice, redefines both subject and object of critical attention. When those who are marginal to the dominant power re-place the center, making the margin the new center of their own subjectivity, different perspectives on violence become possible. The monologic discourse of the imperial center tends to recognize as violence only what it perceives as threatening to itself. Shifting the vantage point of the subject allows one to see forms of violence that had been invisible, or to see in unfamiliar ways. When the gaze is redefined, what it encompasses changes, deconstructing the master narrative.[5]

The need for this shift away from the old center is clear in the work of such writers as Trinh T. Minh-ha and Abdul JanMohamed, who provide valuable ways of understanding and thus disrupting the binary operation of the dominant discourse. Trinh confirms the need for a "certain work of displacement," without which " 'speaking about' only partakes in the conservation of systems of binary opposition (subject / object; I / It; We / They) on which territorialized knowledge depends."[6] Also implicit in the monologic discourse of the dominant group is what JanMohamed calls its "manichaean economy," a structuring of the world along rigid us / them lines.[7] Such global binary oppositions go beyond simple nonjudgmental distinctions; inherently unstable, they tip easily onto a vertical axis: superior / inferior; better / worse. As long as the dominant hear no voices but their own, their monologic "truth" blinds them.[8] As JanMohamed shows, when the colonizer attempts to know the colonized, he generally sees not the other but only his own reversed reflection, either demonized or idealized.[9] Or, as Mary Louise Pratt shows, he sees nothing at all, only a landscape from which all human presence has been erased, containing only resources for the taking.[10]

Heteroglossia, emerging from the specifics of social context, frees the monologue from its constricting knots. When a multiplicity of voices enters the discourse, when the margins talk back to the imperial or neocolonial center, the binary structure unravels. In Rosario Ferré's novel *Sweet Diamond Dust,* when the family (national) history is retold by the household servant, the orthodox truths dissolve, other truths emerge, the shape of the story shifts, what had been presented as courage and conquest becomes violence, violation.[11]

Dialogics, the constructive discourse of conflict, becomes possible when polyvocal discourse interrupts the dominant monologue. The dialogic process is inherently confrontive, exposing discrepancies, contradictions, rifts. Thus the perceived threat: "Everything was nice and harmonious before. Now you're creating divisions." The divisions and differences were there all along but were simply whitewashed into invisibility. Dialogics allows us to begin to see.[12]

This movement toward understanding is the travesía, or crossing, which is the other side of transgression. Whatever the ground one stands on, whether center or margin, one faces in each moment an/Other ground, which is the threatening not-known. Only by violating the boundaries of the familiar and proper, risking conflict, can one reach toward connection.[13] The word, as Bakhtin says, calls forth response.[14] Conflict becomes music, or dance, exhilarating as well as dangerous.

Travesía applies not only to the unknown ground of the Other; it also means questioning what had seemed familiar, the very ground under one's own feet. The task for each of us is, as Trinh says, "to listen, to see like a stranger in one's own land; to fare like a foreigner across one's own language."[15] Particularly for readers shaped by a monologic discourse, confrontation with unfamiliar and widely differing texts and perspectives can be disconcerting. For one thing, to realize that the invisible was "not not-there," as Toni Morrison says, can be humbling.[16] It is not simply that the voices of working-class people and people of color have been stifled; they also have been unheard and rendered unhearable, aurally erased. And the dominant group, too, has been damaged in the process, deprived of access to crucial experience and ways of seeing. Polyvocal discourse can render visible the vacant spaces in what one thought was knowledge, making possible the crossing onto new ground.[17]

The Difference (Cultural) Difference Makes

As Morrison reminds us, "Cultures, whether silenced or monologistic, whether repressed or repressing, seek meaning in the language and images available to them."[18] Texts like the ones discussed in this volume, by authors writing out of culturally diverse contexts, question the reader's awareness of their cultural specificities. What sociohistorical conditions made it possible for these women to write at all? What traditions exist in their cultures of women writing? And what oppressive or liberating structures have shaped their responses to violence?

In many cultures and periods, the only women likely to have access to literacy and to a literary tradition, as well as the resources and leisure for writing, were the daughters or wives of rulers or aristocrats, or courtesans, or religious devotees. The early poetry of India, for instance, is rich with the work of women who were Buddhist nuns or, later, followers of Siva. In the Arab world and Iran, women Sufis wrote some of the earliest mystic poetry in that tradition (eighth century in Arabic, eleventh in Farsi). In certain cultures and periods, women across a broader social spectrum were actively involved in literary production. In many oral cultures, from pre-Islamic Bedouin Arabia to the twentieth-century Inuit, each member of the community was considered a potential poet, and women along with men took part in the poetic competitions and celebrations that constituted the heart of their culture.[19]

Until fairly recently, the vast majority of women in literate cultures worked too hard and were too poor to have the chance to read, much less write. Literacy has been mainly a privilege of the well-to-do, and then only in certain countries and times, and only for the fortunate. Our knowledge of women who did write has been limited by the politics of transmission: works considered important at one period could disappear in the next, in part through patriarchal bias in the institutions responsible for literary publication, distribution, and preservation.[20]

Some of the women whose work is discussed in this volume write with an awareness of a long line of literary foremothers, while others draw from ancient traditions in which "literary" composition by women has been oral rather than written. Middle Eastern women writers such as Etel Adnan and Simin Daneshvar work out of a literary heritage going back more than 4,000 years—to Enheduanna, the poet-priestess of Sumer who composed elaborate hymns to the goddess Inanna around 2300 B.C.E. and is the earliest poet known by name; and to Kubatum, another Sumerian woman, who wrote lyric poetry around 2032 B.C.E.[21]

In some cases, the relations between societies that were at differing stages of literary development created extraordinary space for women's creative work. Japan, which had no indigenous written language until around the seventh century C.E., depended for a long time on China, whose written language was nearly two thousand years older. During the 400 years of the Heian Period (794–1185), "serious" Japanese literature was written in Chinese by Japanese men educated in the foreign Chinese tradition. The young Japanese script, considered inferior and appropriate only for trivial writing, was left to the use of women—who proceeded to invent what were to become the most significant forms of subsequent Japanese literature: the tanka, the haiku, the novel.[22]

In the present century, postcolonial writers have worked in similarly complex cultural and linguistic situations. Senegalese novelists Mariama Bâ and Aminata Sow Fall, for example, inherit both a written African literary tradition, beginning with the early pharoahs of Egypt, and a rich oral tradition. Each has chosen to write in the language of the French colonizers, which is more widely accessible than their native languages. Laguna Pueblo novelist-poet Leslie Marmon Silko, who draws inspiration both from a long oral heritage and from the ancient Aztec and Maya written traditions, writes in English.[23] This increasingly wide use of English and other European languages by writers from Third World cultures has expanded the range of those languages, carrying them beyond the imperial singular to an inclusive plural—"englishes," "frenches," "spanishes" capable of embodying cultural differences.[24]

On the other hand, many writers who have chosen not to write in the dominant languages of the West have found themselves outside the West's powerful literary institutions, from publishing houses and distribution systems to the Nobel Prize and other international awards. In this country, the influence of translation on literary production has played a significant role only since the mid-1970s. Even now, widespread access in the United States to literature from lesser-known languages is dependent on the chanciness of the interest of talented translators, political visibility, and sometimes the creation of publishing houses devoted to translating work from particular cultures.[25] Twelve of the texts discussed in this volume come to us out of other languages, six translated from Caribbean, African, and Middle Eastern French, three from Spanish, and one each from Arabic, Farsi, and Afrikaans.

This opening of the doors of mainstream U.S. literature to voices outside the walls has necessarily shifted our understanding of the canon, that never clearly defined but strongly guarded fortress of "indisputable" Great Literature. Tony Morrison, discussing the startling absence of African Americans from the founding works of canonic nineteenth-century American literature, shows how deeply in fact the "presence of Afro-Americans has shaped the choices, the languages, the structure—the meaning of so much American literature" (210). Her concept of the "unspeakable things unspoken" and the "invisible things [that] are not necessarily 'not-there'" (210) is crucial to understanding silencings and erasures effected by literary institutions and by the dominant cultural ideologies that shape them.[26]

It is also important to remind ourselves that systems of domination and exclusion exist within "nondominant" cultures as well. As Shirley Lim's essay in this volume shows, societies in the process of throwing off colonial shackles nonetheless—and consequently—have a tendency to silence voices that "don't fit" in the nationalizing discourse. Lim argues that Sybil Kathigasu's memoirs from World War II, for example, have been shut out of the Malaysian national literary canon in part because of her positive treatment of British colonial influence. Similarly, Janet Lim's "Westernized" critique of gender oppression in Singapore in the 1930s and 1940s clashed with the anticolonial nationalist discourse there.

Cultural communities split by language and forced dispersion have found other ways of defining and preserving a common bond. Writers of the African diaspora, marked by widely divergent histories and cultures, see themselves as linked by the shared experience of colonization, slavery, and racist oppression as well as by the consciousness of a rich common cultural heritage in the continent of Africa. Shared oppression and culture likewise unite the peoples of other diasporas such as the Jewish, Palestinian, and Armenian.[27]

In contrast, societies encompassing disparate communities from different countries of origin have often, though not always easily, forged a new, heteroglossic identity. Malaysia, especially in such areas as Melaka, combines cultures as diverse as the Polynesian-based Malay; Tamil and Hokkien Chinese immigrants; and the Portuguese and Baba Nyonya, two groups whose unique mixed cultural and linguistic traditions derive from sixteenth-century immigrants who intermarried with Malays. Imperialism and neocolonialism work as a different sort of multicultural influence in many Third World countries, often to the detriment of women, at times to their benefit.[28]

The issue of language goes further. As several contributors to this volume show, having to learn and speak and write in the language of the oppressor can be problematic. Aside from the physical danger involved in criticizing and organizing against the dominant powers in a language they understand, speaking in a tongue not one's own requires grappling with the unspeakable in many forms. Among Rigoberta Menchú's people, the Quiché Maya of Guatemala, Indians who speak Spanish have been looked upon as traitors, sellouts. Nevertheless, realizing that without knowledge of the dominant language she could do little to protect her people from annihilation, Menchú learned Spanish in her late teens and agreed to tell her life story in this new language to Elisabeth Burgos-Debray, who edited it for publication in Spanish and later translation into English. Gaps and fissures will necessarily remain in such a multiply-translated account, especially when no words can be found in the lexicon of the second, or third, language adequate to the meanings in the first.[29] Other instances of the unspeakable in Menchú's text are cultural: rituals, concepts, experiences guarded as sacred secrets by the Maya, not to be revealed to outsiders. And in addition to the not-told against which any narrative unfolds, the teller also makes rhetorical omissions and alterations, shaping the account to a form better able to carry truth to the reluctant reader.

Culture-Based Differences in Women's Responses to Violence

What one is capable of seeing as violence depends on one's angle of vision. When Cherríe Moraga speaks of the "threat of genocide" suffered by people of color, she is referring not only to violences of overt action but also to hidden, structural violence and to the passive acquiescence that permits it to continue.[30] Women born into relative privilege, defended from racial and economic oppression, often find it hard to recognize how they stand with one foot each in the camps of the dominator and the dominated, how they have, however unconsciously, benefited from and been complicit in the oppression of others. As Peggy McIntosh points out, the heavy price paid for privilege is a peculiar blindness, the inability to see that the privilege exists. Men frequently suffer from this blindness on matters of gender, middle-class people on class, European Americans on "race."[31]

In part because of their recognition of interconnected oppressions, the writing of women of color has tended to avoid reductive oppositions between women and men. At the same time, they are often bitterly impatient with men in their communities for attacking as "disloyal to their people" women who point out connections between gender oppression and other forms of oppression. As Moraga reminds us, "To be critical of one's culture is not to betray that culture"; in fact, it is the withholding of criticism that constitutes betrayal, complicity in holding the community back.[32] There are no simple dichotomies. Men, despite the problematic advantages of gender domination, have also been scarred by patriarchy. And men are not the only oppressors. Women, whether overtly privileged or not, have frequently played a role in keeping the mechanisms of patriarchy in place, as many men have worked as allies in dismantling them.

The specificities of cultural difference reveal varying forms of resistance to oppression, and varying forms of silence and anger. Unconsciousness and acquiescence as responses to violence can be explained in terms of internalized oppression, the incorporation of the attitudes of the oppressor by the victim, or of the colonizer by the colonized.[33] Where violence is opposed, resistance may not be conscious: madness or anorexia, for instance, may be an embodied repudiation of a gendered situation that seems to allow one no other control.[34] On the other hand, conscious anger is not necessarily productive; it may simply be reactive, a lashing out harmful to self and others. When constructive, anger may not be direct. It can be explicit without being voiced: expressed nonverbally, for example, or communicated within overt politeness.

Conscious anger openly expressed may serve as a counterforce to the stultifying weight of conformist silence. Many Third World texts emphasize the necessity for such confrontive anger and action. Others portray countercommunity, empowered by shared silences, as the most effective opposition to violence. At times, in what Mary Daly has called "space on the boundary" outside the system of domination, the impact of violence can be resisted or healed through collective ritual and myth.[35] In still other cases, silence may be a means of survival, or of subversion—disguise, masking, "warrior duplicity." Examples of subversive silence appear frequently in works by nineteenth-century women writers as coded invitations to their women readers to read between the lines what could without danger be said outright.[36]

Poet Janice Mirikitani calls us to shed our debilitating silence, to "birth our rage" from the "mute grave" of patriarchal history.[37] But rage can be dangerously transgressive. Cultures differ greatly in the comfort or discomfort their members feel with overt anger or any direct expression of conflict. Anger is a form of energy that can be constructive or destructive depending on context. Aimed at the perpetrator of violence rather than at the violent act, it merely replicates the problem. As a counterforce to the wrong itself, anger is capable of transforming the opponent into a potential ally. Constructive anger is thus not something one ever "gets beyond." We can use its power to move us from unconscious passivity into clarity and the will to act. In this sense, anger is awareness amplified so it can be spoken, speech amplified so it can be heard.

But what if the hearer resists hearing, either in an effort to avoid pain, or from fear of having cherished values challenged, or from resentment of anger misread as personal attack? Any undermining of established assumptions can seem threatening. Yet, as readers, our experiences of marginalization and subordination can serve us. As adults who were once children, most of us have been members of dominated as well as dominator groups; and we can call on this remembered experience to free us from an imprisoning monologic view of the world.

The essays in this volume and the conversations opening out beyond them call on us to risk hearing, to risk seeing, and to risk the travesía, the transgressive crossing into new space.

Transgressing the Boundaries among Us:
Theoretical Implications

Trinh Minh-ha reminds us, "The challenge is thus: how can one re-create without re-circulating domination?"[38] Undoing binary structures means destabilizing not only the master narratives of the patriarchs but also our own. Women assume varying, often contradictory, positions in response to multiple hegemonies or monologisms, and as Sally Robinson points out, it is through these shifting positions that we constitute our multi-valent subjectivities.[39] At the same time, however, we may be denying the multivalent subjectivities of the Other. As Trinh puts it, Western thinkers "extol the concept of decolonization and continuously invite into their fold 'the challenge of the Third World.' Yet . . . when they confront the challenge 'in the flesh,' they . . . do not hear, do not see. They promptly reject it as they assign it to their one-place-fits-all 'other' category."[40] Similarly, in *Decolonizing Feminisms: Race, Gender, and Empire-Building*, Laura E. Donaldson argues for the need to do away with what she calls the "Miranda effect," the tendency among feminists to construct and then be trapped by a universalizing image of women's solidarity. Attempting to squeeze all women into this ideological construct, ignoring differences of history, economic class, and culture, one falls into a blindness akin to the blindness that kept Miranda from "seeing" Caliban.[41]

Strategies that displace the imperial center "defy the world of compartmentalization and the systems of dependence it engenders, while filling the shifting space of creation with a passion named wonder."[42] One metaphor for this act of displacement is that of mapping. As long as readers in the United States, for instance, assume their vantage point as the center of the universe, they may find it hard to enter into a heteroglossic discourse. The Australians' "Corrective Map of the World," with Australia at the center and everything "upside down," is not merely funny. How deeply ingrained one's seeing of the world is, how deeply forgotten the realization that on this planet there is no top or bottom, no West or Orient, unless these directions are imposed by the master discourse. Moving this center, whether on the map or in our unconscious conception of the location of imperial authority, is no easy matter—and it is crucial.

The need for this shift in vision became clear to me some years ago when I was involved in an extended collaborative project to uncover and publish international poetry by women. In the beginning, exhilarated by the connections among women from cultures as diverse as Stalinist Russia and indigenous Papua New Guinea, revolutionary Vietnam and Finland, we organized our first anthology thematically, focusing on what we as European Americans saw as the startling "universals" of women's experience. As we gathered work for the more ambitious second collection, covering 4,300 years instead of eighty, we found ourselves thrown outside our familiar ground, forced to recognize the specific cultural context in which each poet had written. This shift led us to organize the historical volume by cultural areas rather than by "common voices." Further, it disrupted our sense of geographical relationships, making it impossible to perpetuate the familiar treatment of "other cultures" as interesting additions along the banks of the U.S. or Western mainstream. Our familiar literary ground, displaced from center, became one thread among many in a shifting tapestry whose patterns were only just emerging.[43]

This multiplicity of social voices is also crucial to the concerns of this volume. For any society to get away with persistent systemic violence against those excluded from power, it must impose a monologic definition of truth, and then convince its members that any deviation would risk chaos. Yet, wherever there is a dominant discourse there are always already numerous other voices, subverting, transgressing boundaries, working to disrupt its centripetal certainties.[44] Some have argued that encouraging a multiplicity of voices carries the dangerous implication that they are all equally worthy, that everything is relative, that there is nothing we can recognize as better or more true. What, for example, about voices that are clearly speaking untruths or dangerous half-truths? The dialogics of the essays in this collection suggests that the way toward truth is not to try to build walls to shut out falsehood. Rather, as John Milton argued in "Areopagitica," destructive thinking can best be demolished through dialogue in the public marketplace, since it is more likely to wither in the light of day than if it is driven underground.[45]

This emerging play of voices in social context is, to quote Bakhtin again, "the natural orientation of any living discourse." Bakhtin defines the conflicts of difference as exhilarating, the "unrepeatable play of colors and light" as "the word encounters an alien word . . . in a living, tension-filled interaction."[46] The tensions of dialogic discourse involve risks, too, especially in what Trinh describes as a "maximal consumer society" that is "always dividing and alienating at the same time as it works at filling in blanks, holes, gaps, and cracks; rendering invisible the open wounds; evading cleverly all radical reflection upon itself."[47] Those in power tend to argue that anger is "improper" precisely because they think it is to their advantage to shut up voices that question, or might make *them* question, their dominator role.[48]

Oppression is destructive for the oppressor as well as for the oppressed, as Toni Morrison points out: "The trauma of racism is, for the racist and the victim, the severe fragmentation of the self."[49] The *curandera* in Toni Cade Bambara's novel *The Salt Eaters* challenges us in response to this fragmentation, "Can you afford to be whole?"[50] As Mary Daly and Gloria Anzaldúa show, it is always at the boundaries, the margins, the barbed-wire fences with the "no trespassing" signs that the most exciting and transformative energies lie. And the voices that have been silenced or, speaking, have not been noticed hold the missing pieces of our understanding of human community, and of ourselves.

The monologue of the dominator can deafen us to other voices. To be heard, countervoices must engage in a kind of aesthetic violence, finding new ways to make us hear. The language of creative transgression is an act of daring, a border crossing that is both "festively vertiginous" and dangerous.[51] One learns to move alertly but without fear through the borderlands, to experience the margins both as re-placed center and as cutting edge, the ground of transformation. In Trinh's words, "Whether we choose to concentrate on another culture, or on our own culture, our work will always be cross-cultural . . . because of the heterogeneous reality we all live today, in postmodern times—a reality, therefore, that is not a mere crossing from one borderline to the other or that is not merely double, but a reality that involves the crossing of an indeterminate number of borderlines."[52]

These, then, are the two sides of transgression: to violate the master's boundaries is also to affirm the possibility of the travesía, the crossing over. Not that we will get it right. In this space on and among the boundaries, our greatest advantage is the willingness to risk blowing it. Knowing we *will* blow it, and realizing it's not only okay, it's the only way through— like having to fall off the bicycle in order to learn to ride. Or like the aikido roll—"fall-down-get-up, one motion."[53]

One risk lies in the very language we use in talking of difference. In this challenging and often disconcerting period in North-South relations, when the comfortable assumptions of the dominant establishment are being called into question, the language in which these relations are discussed no longer constitutes solid ground. In many cases, we have no adequate terminology for the categories central to our conversation: old solutions have been found wanting, and new ones being proposed likewise have flaws.[54] Contributors to this volume frequently contradict each other in deciding which terms best fit the particular discourse in which they are engaged.

Part of the complication in terminology and discourse arises from changes that have occurred in accepted language as marginalized groups have reclaimed terms once considered pejorative, such as Black, Chicano, native, queer, crone. Other difficulties result from the fact that we are still immersed in the situations to which the old terms refer. In the mid-1970s, the initially invaluable term androgyny became outdated even as we still needed it. As Adrienne Rich argued, it was dangerous because it perpetuated the old assumption that certain human capacities were inherently masculine and others feminine.[55] But it was at the same time useful, not just because no other term seemed to express adequately what we meant but also because we had not yet crossed over to the new space in which such a word could apply. In order to cross over, we needed to be able to refer simultaneously to the old shore and to the new.

This shakiness of the linguistic ground beneath us becomes a metonym for the kind of reading these essays demand. Differences in language among the contributions here, like their differences in viewpoint and tone, require us to enter into dialogue with the writers, wrestling with the problems and advantages of conflicting positions. No one can be safe on this uncertain ground; each of us must negotiate our own way, with as much clarity as possible and with the continuing willingness to learn. We each confront this creative risk, repeatedly, as we seek to shape a language more appropriate to our interactions in a culturally diverse society. This process requires a critical and nonjudgmental reflectiveness, questioning our own words and the attitudes they clothe, as well as listening to the impact of our language on others, especially those to whom the language applies.

The issue, then, is not to avoid offending or making mistakes in the terms we use, since that's not possible, but rather to be willing, continually, to interrogate our own and each other's language, noticing the holes, the gaps, the distortions—and using these very fissures as passageways to clearer understanding. There is no way I can know, meeting someone for the first time, whether she will be offended by the word Chicana instead of Mexican American, or Latina, or Hispanic. But when my choice of words does offend, I can learn to hear this without defensiveness or apology and I can let this interaction help me understand the roots of this negative response in the history of the term in the Mexican-American community. I may, then, choose either to discard the term or to continue to use it, unapologetically, as the best alternative I have found so far.

As for the bugaboo of "political correctness" in general, the best response may be to undermine its illusory power with laughter.[56] My first encounter with the term was in women's groups in the 1970s, when we would humorously and affectionately call ourselves to task when we slid into self-congratulatory "rightness." Precisely because we took seriously both our differences and our interactions with each other, we knew we could not afford to trap ourselves in hostile monologisms, that no one of us owned an absolute or static truth. Laughter freed us to question our own and each other's assumptions and use of language. Language *is* loaded and has the power to kill.[57] It must be used with care—not walking on eggshells (which is also deadly), but realizing that we learn through error, through risking and falling on our faces. And we learn best when "error" is seen not as shame but as the most effective way to learn.

Once our polyvocal discourse has broken free from the strangleholds of polarization, so that those born into dominator status can stop fighting to silence the voices of the Other and those in the borderlands can stop fighting to be heard, then we can look around us and see what is to be seen, in all its disconcerting and empowering multiplicity. We can, together, get on with the business of envisioning and weaving a world conducive to human life.

Conversations: Voices in This Text

Beyond Part 1, which addresses theoretical issues involved in writing and reading female silence, the essays in this volume move from silencing toward transgressive voice, and from the isolated individual toward the possibility of empowered community. Part 5, the closing section, returns us to a focus on the strategies that writers use to speak the unspeakable, as they transgress limits, overturning the "proper" and envisioning liberatory change.

Part 1, "The 'Knife in the Tongue': The Politics of Speech and Silence," opens with Jane Hoogestraat's examination of the multiple silences in Adrienne Rich's work—experiences that cannot be named because they have been erased by dominant institutions, as well as the active silences of women struggling to find "language for pain, poverty, and violence, and then the courage to speak that language." In her discussion of *Incidents in the Life of a Slave Girl,* by Harriet Jacobs, Anne Dalton examines the author's deliberate use of silences and omissions as a way of shaping her relationship with her readers, who were predominantly female, white, middle class, and abolitionist. George Handley extends this discussion of difficulties inherent in testimonial literature, considering the methods that Rosario Ferré and Rigoberta Menchú use to negotiate the imaginative representation of pain in order to bring it into discourse. In "Native Witness, White 'Translator,'" Kristi Dalven examines the fissures in Elsa Joubert's "documentary novel" *Poppie Nongena* as examples of narrative problems that arise when a privileged Afrikaner woman attempts to speak for a Xhosa woman surviving under South African apartheid.

Part 2, "Domestic Politics: Violence on the Home Front," includes two pairs of essays dealing with related themes. The essays by Merry Pawlowski and Gisela Norat discuss attempts to retrieve deeply buried experiences of childhood sexual abuse; those by Pamela Smiley and Ruth Saxton examine problematic relationships between mothers and children, especially daughters. In all four, although the analysis focuses on family problems, it also shows how closely linked domestic violence is to larger, systemic violence: fascism, homophobia, classism, and unwitting literary misogyny on the part of women writers who confuse the destructive patriarchal ideology of the "good mother" with the capacity for nurturing in each of us.

Merry Pawlowski digs beneath the silences and gaps in Virginia Woolf's autobiographical writing to show the ways in which Woolf, through most of her life, suppressed awareness of the violence she had suffered as a child in an oppressively patriarchal household. Similarly, Gisela Norat shows how, in Sylvia Molloy's *Certificate of Absence,* the narrator's account of an abusive relationship with a woman lover overlies the deeper, more painful experience of her father's sexual and emotional abuse of her as a child.

Women unable to confront the ideology of the "perfect mother" have trouble acknowledging anger toward their own children, and this anger, unspoken, perpetuates itself. Conversely, daughters' fear of and anger at their mothers may both result from and perpetuate an exaggerated image of the mother's "goodness." As Pamela Smiley shows in her study of Mary Gordon's *Men and Angels,* the protagonist finds it hard to deal with the anger of the woman whose biography she is writing in part because she denies her own "angry mother" side. On the other hand, as Ruth Saxton argues, many women novelists transpose the idealized image of motherhood into the equally unreal image of the mother as deadly because she is "too good."

The essays in Part 3, "Structures of Oppression: Subjectivity and the Social Order," look at systems of violence on a larger scale and at the effects of this structural violence on the sense of individual identity and efficacy. Madhuchhanda Mitra discusses Nawal El Saadawi's novel *God Dies by the Nile,* which focuses on the abuse of Egyptian peasants by interlocking institutions of class, gender, government, and religion. Although the peasants as Saadawi depicts them seem incapable of effective action, protest is implicit in their ability to *see.*

The essays by Wills, Lim, and Cook reveal an increasing potential for resistance, although systemic oppression remains firmly in place. In her anthropological analysis of the novels of two Senegalese writers, Mariama Bâ and Aminata Sow Fall, Dorothy Wills shows how the female protagonists, in violating the traditional injunction against "making noise," gesture toward the possibility of undermining the interconnected systems of social oppression. Both Shirley Lim and Michaela Cook argue for the possibility of female heroism within systems of pervasive and brutalizing oppression imposed both by indigenous social and gender hierarchies and by invading colonial and neocolonial forces. Lim's essay shows the impact of imperialism, both Japanese and Western, on the narrators of two World War II memoirs, from Malaysia and Singapore, as they struggle against systematic gender oppression. Michaela Cook discusses the way Simin Daneshvar's novel *Savushun,* set in World War II Iran, displaces the conventional patriarchal hero in the process of redefining the nature of heroism itself, while also calling into question prevailing Western misapprehensions of the Muslim woman as passive and invisible.

In the essays in Part 3, resistance to oppression is only potential; in Part 4, "Collective Silence, Collective Voice: Toward Community," the movement is toward an effective dismantling of the walls of isolation, silence, and immobility. In Sherri Hallgren's essay, this movement appears, paradoxically, in the subversive and collectively empowered inaction and silence of the women in Susan Glaspell's "A Jury of Her Peers," as well as in its narrative strategy of author-reader collusion. Ann Trapasso explores, as Lillian Kremer does in the essay that follows, the troubling question of the effects of systemic racist violence on survivors of its horrors. Trapasso shows how Sherley Anne Williams in *Dessa Rose* creates a counterdiscourse to slavery by means of a kind of collective guerrilla theater, in which the use of masking and subversive laughter disguises truth in order to free it. Lillian Kremer's analysis of fiction by Cynthia Ozick and Norma Rosen points to the role of "acting" in surviving and deconstructing the violence of the Nazi holocaust, either negatively through an isolating counterdrama or positively through shared witnessing. Acting collectively becomes increasingly important in the five African American and Caribbean plays discussed by VèVè Clark, in which theater serves as an increasingly feminist and participatory medium for speaking the unspeakable.

The essays in Part 5, "Revolting Texts: Transgression (and) Transformation," show how language and strategies of representation can themselves be the site of revolt, altering our ways of seeing and being. Roseanne Quinn decodes misogynistic and universalizing discourses on breast cancer in popular and medical publications, then analyzes works by women that in acknowledging difference allow us to reclaim the power to speak and act. Madeline Cassidy's essay explores the way the dialogic structure of *Sitt Marie-Rose,* Etel Adnan's narrative of the torture and execution of a woman in Beirut in 1975, during the civil war, allows the text to point toward a "new space, a new moral ethic, that can only exist outside the framework of tribalism and factionalism, either Christian or Muslim." My own analysis of Janice Mirikitani's collection *Shedding Silence* focuses on the literary techniques by which she maneuvers the reader into hearing the unspeakable, by violating both the boundaries of normal social discourse and the personal boundaries that keep us "safe." In the final essay, Ann Reuman discusses the way Gloria Anzaldúa in *Borderlands / La Frontera* reappropriates the concept of marginalization, making it not a diminution but the mark of a "new, affirmative, feminist landscape," the cutting edge of change where "wild tongues" won't stay silenced.

"Every work materialized can be said to be a work-in-progress."[58] Inclusiveness is what this book invites the reader toward, not what it achieves. It has, as Bakhtin would say, a "joyous awareness" of its gaps and inadequacies, the holes in the fence through which it beckons the reader to explore territories and texts still waiting.[59]

May the conversations in this volume lead the reader to carry these discussions into new grounds yet to be named.

Notes

1. Tillie Olsen, "Silences in Literature"; see also Adrienne Rich, *On Lies, Secrets, and Silence.*

2. The essays in this volume consider texts by writers from African American, Asian American, Chicana, and European American traditions in the United States, and by writers from other countries including Senegal, South Africa, Egypt, Lebanon, Iran, Singapore, Malaysia, England, Guadeloupe, Jamaica, Haiti, Puerto Rico, Argentina, and Quiché Maya Guatemala.

3. For a discussion of silencing by cultural injunction and dominant literary institutions, see King-kok Cheung, "'Don't Tell'"; Yvonne Yarbro-Bejarano, "Cultural Influences: Chicana"; and Norma Alarcón, "The Theoretical Subject(s) of *This Bridge Called My Back* and Anglo-American Feminism," 363–64.

4. See bell hooks, *Talking Back,* for a provocative discussion of the dialogic process.

5. "Decentering": compare the term "re-placing" in Bill Ashcroft, Gareth Griffiths, and Helen Tiffin, *The Empire Writes Back,* and, earlier, the concept of "living on the boundaries" in Mary Daly, *Beyond God the Father,* 42–44. In *The Colonial Harem,* Malek Alloula undertakes a specific desubjectifying of the colonizer's gaze.

6. Trinh T. Minh-ha, "Cotton and Iron," in *When the Moon Waxes Red,* 12.

7. Abdul R. JanMohamed, "The Economy of Manichean Allegory." JanMohamed borrows the concept of the manichean struggle from Frantz Fanon, *The Wretched of the Earth,* 41. Sylvia Wynter provides an interesting comparison: "The pervasive cultural nationalism of the West invites as its negation an inversion of its own

presuppositions. The past has been reinvented as ideology by the West, to sustain the West's consciousness of itself as subject, a consciousness which needed the negation of the Other, the non-West" ("History, Ideology, and the Reinvention of the Past," 44).

8. See Riane Eisler, *The Chalice and the Blade,* for a valuable historical analysis of "dominator" as opposed to "partnership" forms of social organization, and their implications for gender and class relations.

9. JanMohamed, "Manichean Allegory," 83–102. For further theoretical perspectives on this process, see Michel Foucault, *The Archeology of Knowledge,* 38, and W. Lawrence Hogue's discussion of Foucault in *Discourse and the Other,* 6. Any dominant discourse includes aspects of the Other that threaten the presuppositions of that monologism. Confronted with this Other, a member of the dominant group tends to respond in one of three ways: he will, as Roland Barthes says, "blind himself, ignore and deny him [the Other], or else transform him [the Other] into himself" (*Mythologies,* 151–52).

10. Mary Louise Pratt, "Scratches on the Face of the Country." Israeli writer Amos Oz, for example, has described both polarizing and inclusive strains in the Zionist tradition: the dominant current reflected in the slogan describing Palestine as a "land without a people for a people without a land," and an important agrarian countercurrent that saw the Palestinians as long-lost brothers and sisters whom Jews would rejoin when they returned from exile (in a talk he presented at Hillel House, Berkeley, Calif., 1972).

11. For a discussion of heteroglossia and dialogism, see M. M. Bakhtin, "Discourse and the Novel." See in particular the "Glossary" explanation of heteroglossia: "that which insures the primacy of context over text," that insures "that a word uttered in that place and at that time will have a meaning different than it would have under any other conditions" (428); Bakhtin also describes heteroglossia in terms of "a multiplicity of social voices and a wide variety of their links and interrelationships," which disperse "into the rivulets and droplets of social heteroglossia . . . dialogization" (263).

12. For "dialogism," see Bakhtin's Glossary: "The living utterance, having taken meaning and shape at a particular historical moment in a socially specific environment, cannot fail to brush up against thousands of living dialogic threads, woven by socio-ideological consciousness around the given object of an utterance; it cannot fail to become an active participant in social dialogue" (276).

13. See Gloria Anzaldúa, *Borderlands / La Frontera:* "Every increment of consciousness, every step forward is a *travesía,* a crossing. I am again an alien in new territory. And again, and again" (48). Also (78–79): "At some point, on our way to a new consciousness, we will have to leave the opposite bank, the split between the two mortal combatants somehow healed so that we are on both shores at once and, at once, see through serpent and eagle eyes. . . . Or we might go another route. The possibilities are numerous once we decide to act and not react."

14. "The word in living conversation is directly, blatantly, oriented toward a future answer-word: it provokes an answer, anticipates it and structures itself in the answer's direction" (Bakhtin, "Discourse," 280).

15. Trinh, "World as Foreign Land," in *When the Moon Waxes Red,* 199. In a talk in 1991, Chela Sandoval addressed the critical importance of the dialogic process in interactions between European American feminists and American feminists of color ("U.S. Third World Feminisms"). See also her essay "Feminism and Racism."

16. Toni Morrison, "Unspeakable Things Unspoken," 210. For a powerful bringing-into-view of aspects of cultural violence that are "not not-there," see Alice Walker's polyvocal novel about clitoridectomy, *Possessing the Secret of Joy*. Like Walker, Gayatri Spivak criticizes the structural functionalist argument that if clitoridectomy "works" for a particular social structure, it must therefore be justified; see "French Feminism in an International Frame."

17. Monologic discourses about the dominant culture in any society can also erase the experiences of unacknowledged subgroups. Many European Americans, for instance, although privileged by color, have been marginalized by class, ethnicity, sexual orientation, language, immigrant status, as well as by gender, and have at times constituted a significant counterforce against the ideological hegemony of those in power.

18. Morrison, "Unspeakable," 208. The phrase "the difference (cultural) difference makes" recalls Gregory Bateson's description of communication: "the difference that makes the difference" (*Steps to an Ecology of Mind*).

19. See the introductions to cultural areas in Joanna Bankier and Deirdre Lashgari, eds., *Women Poets of the World*, esp. Stella Sandahl, "India"; Bridget Connelly, "The Arab World"; Lashgari, "Iran" and "Native American."

20. See Joanna Bankier (with Thomas D'Evelyn), "Greece of Antiquity." Sappho's poetry was all but lost during the extreme misogyny of classical Greece; a few quotations in the work of grammarians and some papyrus fragments used for packing objects in jars are all that has come down to us (136). Even in our more enlightened times, as recently as the early 1970s, the work of women writers was seldom included in English-language anthologies. Clearly, a society that assumes that women don't write will fail to see what women have written. In this case, it is not that women haven't been speaking, but that the audience has been ideologically deaf.

21. Anne Draffkorn Kilmer, "Sumero-Babylonia," in *Women Poets*.

22. Rob Swigart, "Japan," in ibid.

23. See Lashgari, "Africa" and "Native American," in ibid.

24. For extensive discussion of the literary significance of multiple englishes, see Ashcroft, Griffiths, and Tiffin, *Empire*. At its greatest stretch, writing in English by Latino authors such as Gloria Anzaldúa has incorporated extensive use of various spanishes as well, from Chicano Spanglish to untranslated passages in formal Spanish, from brief phrases noted or explained to untranslated passages in Spanish that require the monolingual English reader to make the effort to "reach across." For studies of the development of creole languages and the creole continuum, see such works as Jean Bernabé, Patrick Chamoiseau, and Raphaël Confiant, *Eloge de la créolité;* Mervyn Alleyne, *Comparative Afro-American;* and Derek Bickerton, "The Nature of a Creole Continuum."

25. For example, little from Iran had appeared in English translation until the creation in the mid-1980s of such presses as Mage and Mazda. Three Continents Press and some small presses like Waveland focus more broadly on translations from Asia, Africa, and Latin America, with smaller listings from the Middle East.

26. Morrison, "Unspeakable," 207, 210. See also Hogue, *Discourse and the Other,* especially 1–22.

27. See Trinh on the "naming of identity" as a way of "declaring solidarity among the hyphenated people of the Diaspora" ("Cotton and Iron," 14).

28. For a negative instance, see Paula Gunn Allen, *The Sacred Hoop.* Allen describes "degynocratization" as a particularly deleterious effect of the imperializing influence on women's status in indigenous American cultures. She quotes Jesuit missionary priest Father Paul Le Jeun as speaking explicitly in his reports to the French government about the concerted effort to "loosen the hold of Montagnais women on tribal policies and convince men and women that a woman's proper place was under the authority of her husband and a man's proper place under the authority of the priests" (24). As is clear in the novels of Louise Erdrich, Leslie Marmon Silko, and Paula Gunn Allen, the role of women in indigenous cultures has survived with strength despite the persistence of such attacks.

29. See also George Steiner, *After Babel.*

30. Cherríe Moraga, "From a Long Line of Vendidas": "Unlike most white people, with the exception of the Jews, Third World people have suffered the threat of genocide. . . . When they kill our boys in their own imperialist wars to gain greater profits for American corporations; when they keep us in ghettos, reservations, and barrios which ensure that our own people will be the recipients of our frustrated acts of violence; when they sterilize our women without our consent because we are unable to read the document we sign; when they prevent our families from getting decent housing, adequate child care, sufficient fuel, regular medical care; then we have reason to believe—although they may no longer technically be lynching us in Texas or our sisters and brothers in Georgia, Alabama, Mississippi—they intend to see us dead" (181).

31. Peggy McIntosh, "White Privilege." McIntosh makes the point that being born into privilege is not a fault, nor are privileges themselves bad: each of us should be free to find work based on qualifications rather than on color, or to walk through a department store without being followed by security guards. The question is what one does with the privileges one has.

32. Moraga, "Vendidas," 180.

33. See Frantz Fanon, *Black Skin, White Masks.* For a discussion of socially enforced self-silencing by teenage girls, see Lyn Mikel Brown and Carol Gilligan, "Meeting at the Crossroads." The authors describe the progressive inhibiting of voice in adolescent girls as "a kind of psychological foot-binding," which protects the "relational lies that are at the center of patriarchal cultures: subtle untruths and various forms of violation and violence that cover over or lead to women's disappearance in both the public world of history and culture and the private world of intimacy and love" (30). The girls in their study least likely to give up their voices were those who "because of color or class live in the margins" (31).

34. For example, see Charlotte Perkins Gilman's story "The Yellow Wallpaper" and Charlotte Brontë's novel *Shirley;* see also my essay "What Some Women Can't Swallow."

35. Daly, *Beyond God the Father,* 42–44.

36. See, for example, Sarah Ellis's *The Daughters of England* (1843), 90, as well as the suggestion at the end of Charlotte's Brontë's novel *Shirley* that the reader "put on spectacles" to "find the moral" (599). I discuss coded subversion in this and other works in my forthcoming study *The Agony of Leaving: Narrative Strategy in Nineteenth-Century Novels by Women.* Judith Lowder Newton's *Women, Power, and Subversion* (1981) is a valuable early work on subversive strategies in literature by women.

37. Janice Mirikitani, "Prisons of Silence," in *Shedding Silence, 8.*

38. Trinh, "Cotton and Iron," 15.

39. Sally Robinson, *Engendering the Subject.*

40. Trinh, "Cotton and Iron," 16.

41. Laura E. Donaldson, *Decolonizing Feminisms.*

42. Trinh, "Cotton and Iron," 23.

43. See Joanna Bankier et al., eds., *The Other Voice*; and Bankier and Lashgari, eds., *Women Poets of the World.*

44. Bakhtin, "Discourse," 263.

45. Our marketplace of ideas, of course, is not a free market. The human tendency toward intellectual diversity now runs up against the effects of globalization and media monopoly, which further conformity through control of information.

46. Bakhtin, "Discourse," 277, 279.

47. Trinh, "World as a Foreign Land," 196.

48. See Ronald T. Takaki, *Iron Cages.*

49. Morrison, "Unspeakable Things," 214.

50. Quoted in Moraga, "Vendidas," 180.

51. Trinh, "Cotton and Iron," 14.

52. Trinh, "A Minute Too Long," 107.

53. This is one of the lessons of the crone / bag lady in Naomi Newman's one-woman drama *Snake-Talk*. Newman is one of the founding members of A Traveling Jewish Theater, and the coauthor of *Coming from a Great Distance, Dance of Exile,* and *The Last Yiddish Poet.*

54. I refer to terms such as dominant v. minority, center v. margin, Third World, people of color, the West, race. Minority, which implies "lesser," seems inappropriate as a term for people of color, who constitute the majority of the world's population. "Third World" was invented, to refer to themselves, by representatives at the Bandung Conference of Nonaligned Nations in 1956 to distinguish themselves from the capitalist First World and the Communist Second World. Some now question its use as connoting third class. Similarly, Henry Louis Gates, Jr., has argued for placing the word "race" in quotation marks to remind ourselves that although the concept *as concept* continues to wreak havoc on social relations, it has no objective or scientific validity as a means of distinguishing groups of people ("Editor's Introduction: Writing 'Race' and the Difference It Makes," in *"Race," Writing, and Difference,* 1–20).

55. Adrienne Rich, *On Lies, Secrets, and Silence.*

56. Humor can serve us both as an antidote to our own lapses into thinking that we have found truth, and as support in confronting concerted attacks on diversity by those who want to preserve the hegemony of the dominant discourse. These opponents of cultural difference often put up linguistic smoke screens accusing multiculturalists of imposing a monologic correct line, and presenting themselves as defenders of intellectual freedom.

57. See, for example, Lorna Dee Cervantes's "Poem for the Young White Man Who Asked Me How I, an Intelligent, Well-Read Person, Could Believe in the War between Races," in her collection *Emplumada.*

58. Trinh, "Cotton and Iron," 16.

59. Bakhtin, "Introduction," *Dialogic Imagination,* xxxiii.

PART ONE

The "Knife in the Tongue": The Politics of Speech and Silence

JANE HOOGESTRAAT

"Unnameable by Choice":
Multivalent Silences in Adrienne Rich's
Time's Power

If we have learned anything in our coming to language out of silence, it is that what has been unspoken, therefore *unspeakable* in us is what is most threatening to the patriarchal order in which [some] men control, first women, then all who can be defined and exploited as "other." All silence has a meaning.

—Adrienne Rich

Adrienne Rich, perhaps the most widely read American feminist poet of the last two decades, has devoted her career to breaking the many forms of silence that have worked to oppress women. Her work is haunted by the fact that much of the experience of women has been lost to history, in part because it could not be safely spoken about or even safely seen at the time. *Time's Power* (1989), like her earlier work, undoes some silences in the very act of referring to them. In representing the communal history of violence against women, Rich refers to the silences of women who must find the language for pain, poverty, and physical violence, and then the courage to speak that language. But *Time's Power* also points to the silences that cannot be broken, to the unnameable that stands in for the losses of history that cannot be recovered.[1] Identifying what is permanently unnameable, however, often causes Rich to imagine an earlier world and, importantly, to stress a human responsibility to imagine and work toward a less violent world in the future. This distinction, between, on the one hand, what can be given voice to and, on the other hand, what can never be given voice to but must only be guessed at or imagined, is both an ethical and an epistemological imperative in Rich's poetry.

In theorizing the ways silence functions in *Time's Power*, we need to take to heart Rich's warning about the misuses of theory. "Divisions of

Labor" (1988) directly indicts much theoretical literary criticism, including political criticism with an ostensibly liberal point of view, for reducing the very real situations of impoverished women to abstractions. Rich contrasts some of the language of contemporary theory to the conditions under which many women throughout the world must work:

> The revolutions wheel, compromise, utter their statements:
> a new magazine appears, mastheaded with old names,
> an old magazine polishes up its act
> with deconstructions of the prose of Malcolm X
> The women in the back rows of politics
> are still licking thread to slip into the needle's
> eye, trading bones for plastic, splitting pods
> for necklaces to sell to the cruise-ships. . . .
>   I have seen a woman sitting
> between the stove and the stars
> her fingers singed from snuffing out the candles
> of pure theory Finger and thumb: both scorched:
> I have felt that sacred wax blister my hand.[2]

Rich reminds us that the suffering and silencing of real women can too easily drop out of poststructuralist and Marxist theoretical discourse, even when the discourse has liberation from oppression, textual and otherwise, as its professed aim.[3] The poem, then, represents a silencing in contemporary culture that Rich believes, on ethical grounds, can be overcome.

In a recent interview with David Montenegro, Rich indicated the depth of her distrust of theoretical work divorced from action when she argued that "you don't make a political movement simply out of words." She continued: "I'm thinking about grassroots women's organizations and activists who have sat through hundreds of interviews with battered or raped women telling what happened to them, and helping to empower them, and who have a knowledge about these things which is not metaphorical."[4] Both metaphor and the poststructuralist understanding of language that continues to underwrite most contemporary literary theory can further silence women in the present by discounting the reality of their experience.

Rich's poetry opposes a tendency in poststructuralist theory to overprivilege language while discounting a priori appeals to experience as naive, and often as essentialist. Andrea Nye explains the view of language, derived from a Derridean view, that I believe Rich's work contests: "Language, as a more or less ordered system of textual differences and deferrals cannot . . . be used to express any reality, feminist or other. To assert the 'presence' of a feminine experience or truth is simply to lend to one portion of the linguistic universe a superior authority, an authority that can only constitute a new, oppressive hierarchy just as dependent on the grammar of established relations."[5] But denying that language can be used to express experience is a way of further disenfranchising women, for whom official languages, as they are used, already allow very little power; it is also a way of denying any hope for meaningful expression once one has acquired a voice, thus further disenfranchising those who have historically been excluded from or silenced by public discourse.

Rich's perspective does share much with Hélène Cixous's in that Cixous acknowledges the importance of that which lies beyond language. Cixous argues that references to silence can disrupt oppressive language and logic: "Women must write through their bodies, they must invent the impregnable language that will wreck partitions, classes, and rhetorics, regulations and codes, they must submerge, cut through, get beyond the ultimate reserve-discourse, including the one that laughs at the very idea of pronouncing the word 'silence,' the one that, aiming for the impossible, stops short before the word 'impossible' and writes it as 'the end.'"[6] For Cixous, "speaking silence" can be subversive of hierarchical order; for Rich, it can also be healing, and again in a double sense. First, "speaking silence" can be the beginning of narrative, of finding a voice for one's experience; second, speaking silence also points to what is permanently missing or misnamed in received cultural and personal history.

Rich's critique of the dominant language, in contrast to Cixous's, presupposes that women can reclaim at least some areas of the dominant language to speak of their own experience and glimpse the experiences of others, that it is possible to work toward a common language. In this regard, Rich is aligned with strains in American feminism that have "pragmatically assumed that experience is separable from language and thus that women are or can be in control of language rather than controlled by it, making women capable of self-representation."[7] In this theoretical context, the silences that mark personal or cultural loss become a means of identifying women's exclusion from the dominant languages. Unlike Cixous, Rich asserts that some of what remains unspoken and silenced in the dominant discourse can be "read" and recovered, can, paradoxically, be made to speak: "Like certain other writers—Black, 'colonial,' working-class—feminists have paid attention to the processes by which silence, muteness, speechlessness, have broken into language. . . . Literacy and education have not been women's historical prerogative, even in those classes and cultures where they were open to men. And the privilege of literacy and education doesn't begin to open the doors of the taboo against lesbianism and feminist authorship and authority."[8] Rich refers again to two distinct silences I am concerned with in this essay: the silence of what we cannot know about women of the past because so few of them were able to leave written records, and the silences, now beginning to be broken, that are still imposed even on literate women in the present.

Rich's insistence on the possibility of recovering what has been silenced is complicated by the fact that learning to "read" the silenced and the unspoken is not identical to breaking silence with speech. The persistence of the "unnameable" in Rich's later work, after so many silences have been broken, attests to the complexities that emerge when a poet begins "speaking silence."[9] As Margaret Homans explains in another context, "The ambiguity entailed in the representation of unrepresentability might, then, be an instance in which French and American assumptions are equally correct—but only when taken together."[10] In simple terms, the "French" assumption is that official languages are so thoroughly male dominated that women cannot use such languages to represent female experience. The "American" assumption is that although language may have been historically male dominated, it has also been used by women and indeed can be used, in variations of existing forms, to represent the experience of women. The middle ground, directly relevant for Rich, allows for the possibility of representing silences (what Homans refers to as the representation of unrepresentability), including the silences of women who have been excluded from official languages.

Rich has been concerned throughout her career with the ethical imperative of breaking personal and cultural silences, and with the epistemological difficulties of doing so. *Time's Power* continues this dual focus, but it also marks a turning away from the documentation of violence that characterized many of the poems in *Your Native Land, Your Life* (1986), which immediately preceded *Time's Power*. The earlier volume concentrates on breaking silence about violence against women and other oppressed peoples, both as historical groups and as isolated individuals. The tone of the poems in *Time's Power* is muted, so much so that Jay Parini has noted, wrongly, I believe, that there is in the book a "sense of the poet's having partly come through her anger."[11] Anger over the oppression of women is not, for Rich, something that one "comes through" any more than one can move on after breaking silence about a particular issue only once. In *Time's Power*, Rich is drawing deeply on the past to recover, in part, both the origins of violence and oppression, and the stories, imagined and real, of the victims who, sometimes successfully and sometimes not, struggled to overcome violence or its consequences.

In the absence of written records of the experience of many women of the past, it becomes necessary, Rich implies, both to note that absence and to imagine the absent narratives. For example, in "Harpers Ferry," Rich gives voice to the *imagined* story of a white woman's escape north only to stumble on Harpers Ferry at the time of John Brown's rebellion. In the context of the poem, the escape north of black slaves has suggested to the woman that she, too, might flee abusive enslavement by brothers who have been raping her. As Rich imagines the scenario, the woman is empowered to escape by overhearing plans of the escape of black slaves, words that create a small fissure in the silence enclosing her:

> Whatever gave the girl the idea you could run away
> from a family quarrel? Displace yourself, when nothing else
> would change? It wasn't books:
> it was half-overheard, a wisp of talk:
> *escape   flight   free soil*
> sifting past her shoulder. (*TP* 39)

In this poem, epistemology, in part the study of how we know what we know, takes on a very human shape. Rich questions not only how she might imagine a story such as this one, but also how a woman like the woman in the poem would have been able to articulate, even to herself, the decision to flee.

Like certain seasonal and natural events that occur in silence, the decision to leave emerges as both silent and inevitable, even destined:

> There are things overheard and things unworded, never sung
> or pictured, things that happen silently
> as the peachtree's galactic blossoms open in mist, the frost-star
> hangs in the stubble, the decanter of moonlight pours its mournless
> liquid down
> steadily on the solstice fields. (*TP* 40)

As Rich continues her seasonal metaphor, it becomes a kind of language of the body that has been violated and of the body that has had enough:

> the cotton swells in its
> boll and you feel yourself engorged,
> unnameable
> you yourself feel encased and picked-open, you feel yourself
> unenvisaged. (*TP* 40)

29

To feel oneself both violated and "unnameable" and "unenvisaged" must, in the context of the poem, include feeling a sense of utter aloneness. Further, it would include a sense that no one else could "envision" either what one has gone through or what one is about to do.

The woman fleeing knows that she is "unenvisaged," that there is no exact precedent for her decision. At the same time, the example of the slaves is important even though her enslavement is one of gender rather than of race:

> You stop yourself listening for a word that will not be spoken:
> listening instead to the overheard
> fragments, phrases melting
> on air: *No more Many thousand go.* (TP 41)

What Rich describes here is a woman's language embodied primarily in silence combined with the fragmentary language of black runaway slaves. Later in the poem, Harriet Tubman ("Moses") does make a brief appearance, but the whispered language that the white woman appropriates is not definitively gendered. Nor is her decision to leave identical to the flight of these slaves:

> you knew they would leave
> and so could you but not with them . . .
> you could leave the house where you were daughter, sister, prey
> picked open and left to silence, you could leave alone" (*TP* 41)

Again, though the young woman has oppression in general in common with the slaves who are fleeing, she is a different sort of victim; though born "free," she has become enslaved, and silenced, by the abuse of her own family.

The silence that is a theme of "Harpers Ferry" is multivalent, conveying not only the horror of sexual violence but also the loneliness of the apparently sudden resolve to flee and the unarticulated process by which the victim arrives at her decision. The break in silence that made the other "break" possible has come from a few empowering words spoken by slaves, from fragments in their language that has become hers. In recreating this narrative, Rich breaks silence to tell the story, but she leaves intact the silences of what we cannot recover and the silences that surround the imagined character.

Rich approaches a similar theme from a more personal perspective when she moves to a Vermont landscape in "Living Memory" (1986). She begins here not with silence, but with tales that need to be retold, revised, re-remembered.

> Open the book of tales you knew by heart,
> begin driving the old roads again,
> repeating the old sentences, which have changed
> minutely from the wordings you remembered. (*TP* 46)

Rich is seeking out textual silences in this poem, listening for what she hasn't heard before, missed nuances in the language both of cultural stories and of personal memories, all that these stories and memories have obscured. As the poem develops, the landscape, including "the old roads," takes on the features of a text that needs to be read. The landscape, in turn, suggests the effaced texts of personal memory and experience: "You whose stories these farms secrete, / you whose absence these fields publish" (*TP* 47). The rereading process here includes reading for what, or more importantly, "who" is missing from received narratives.

Reading the text of the landscape, revised through personal memory and history, becomes another way both of recovering the past and of noting historical silences:

> Many guns
> turned on brains already splitting
> in silence. Where are those versions?
> Written-across like nineteenth century letters
> or secrets penned in vinegar, invisible
> till the page is held over flame. (*TP* 48)

Again, there are no literal texts that Rich can refer to here, only texts that can be inferred and imagined. The texts that come closest to telling the "versions" Rich seeks are "like nineteenth century letters," encoded or cryptic, that must be read empathetically with as much attention to what they do not say as to what they do say. We are obligated, Rich implies, to infer these texts, and to read existing texts empathetically; we are obligated to do so on behalf of those whose stories we will never know.

The most remarkable poem, to my mind, in *Time's Power* is "Turning" (1988). Here, Rich cautiously celebrates the gains that follow from "speaking silence" and transforms the notion of the unnameable as an epistemological loss or limit. In a way that her earlier work could not have predicted, Rich explores one aspect of the "unnameable" as a category of the transcendent or sacred. The poem opens with a description of droughts (surely both literal and metaphorical, perhaps spiritual) in the heartlands of various countries, and then switches to the Palestinian-Israeli conflict:

> And in that other country
> of choices made by others
> that country I never chose
> that country of terrible leavings and returnings
> in that country whose map I carry on my palm
> the forests are on fire: history is on fire. (*TP* 51)

It is not unusual for Rich to take on history and politics in her poetry, and it is not unusual for her to allude to her Jewish background. Nor is it unusual for her to find a determined hope even in the midst of historical tragedy. What is unusual, however, is the manner in which she introduces terms of Jewish mysticism, including a notion of the unnameable, into both the art and the politics of the poem.

Later in the poem, the persona is at a meeting listening to a speaker on the problem of "that other country." The poem never names the country as either Palestine or Israel; to assign either name to contested territory would be to take sides, walling out the possibility of shared discourse:

> Her subject is occupation, a promised land,
> displacement, deracination, two peoples called Semites,
> humiliation, force, women trying to speak with women,
> *the subject is how to break a mold of discourse,*
> *how little by little minds change*
> *but that they do change.* (*TP* 54, emphasis added)

Here, "breaking a mold of discourse," a goal Rich shares with Cixous and Derrida, is not intellectually abstract: the poem recognizes distinctively individual faces connected to the "minds" that change, and it insists on the "real world" significance of these changes. It matters a great deal in the poem that the speaker discussing the situation is a woman, and that her subject, in part, is the process by which women, presumably on both sides of a conflict where the sides have often refused to speak to each other, can begin speaking together about it.[12]

It also matters that the poem refers to two women listening together; as frequently happens in Rich's poetry, deeply personal issues intersect with much larger political questions. The lines quoted above are followed immediately by:

> We two have fought
> our own battles side by side, at dawn, over supper,
> our changes of mind have come
> with the stir of hairs, the sound of a cracked phrase:
> we have depended on something. (*TP* 55)

"A cracked phrase," a metaphor similar to the broken "mold of discourse," refers to a productive fissure between language and experience that marks a site for personal and political change. As in "Harpers Ferry," the language here incorporates the language of the body: "the stir of hairs" both accompanies and physically embodies the "changes of mind." Again a question of epistemology becomes a question of ethics. Realizing what a language cannot do, or what it is not doing, prepares the way for a different language, for a new manner of speaking.

The closing section of the poem proceeds, with little warning, to address an unknowable otherness, an otherness that partakes of both the secular and the sacred. It moves from "we have depended on something" to address an absent "you," in what I consider to be the most surprising "turn" in Rich's last two books of poetry:

> Whatever you are that has tracked us this far,
> I never thought you were on our side,
> I only thought you did not judge us.
>
> Yet as a cell might hallucinate
> the eye—intent, impassioned—
> behind the lens of the microscope
>
> so I have thought of you,
> whatever you are—a mindfulness—
> whatever you are: the place beyond all places,
>
> beyond boundaries, green lines,
> wire-netted walls
> the place beyond documents.
>
> Unnameable by choice.
> So why am I out here, trying
> to read your name in the illegible air?
>
> —vowel washed from a stone,
> solitude of no absence,
> forbidden face-to-face
>
> —trying to hang these wraiths
> of syllables, breath
> without echo, why? (*TP* 54–55)

Several important reviewers of Rich's work have noted the unusual metaphysical tone of these lines. Marilyn Hacker points out: "In the poem's last movement, which also ends the book, the poet/speaker is prophet in the desert again, questioning nothing less than a Prime Mover. Rich's description of this force, and her tone and stance as a questioner, are those of a Jewish metaphysical writer." [13] Robert Shaw writes of an "agnostic mysticism . . . [that] surfaces again at the end of 'Turning' in a direct address in some unknowable Other." [14] Lawrence Norfolk, reviewing *Time's Power* as a whole, remarks on Rich's skill at "unpicking and subtly altering poetic rhetoric to make it tell the stories that it originally suppressed." [15] In this poem, she "subtly alters the rhetoric" to evoke a voice inherent in it all along.

Without understanding Rich's rhetorical strategy and what is at stake here, it would be tempting to dismiss the lines that end "Turning" as a surprising and extremely uncharacteristic lapse into the rhetoric of the ineffable or the mystical. It is more useful, perhaps, to remember lines from the same volume where Rich deliberately takes a stance that counters a focus on the transcendent, as in "6/21" (1987):

> Yet it's of earth
> and nowhere else I have to speak
> Only on earth has this light taken on these swivelled meanings, only
>   on this earth
> where we are dying befouled, gritting our teeth; losing our guiding
>   stars
> has this light
> found an alphabet a mouth." (*TP* 33)

Whatever might exist that is completely outside of human language, that is completely other, can paradoxically be approached or approximated only through language.

Rich's insistence both on the powers of language and on human responsibility, and her concern with naming, demand that we take the closing stanzas of "Turning" seriously. As Elizabeth Meese explains in another context, "A writer like Rich whose thematic concerns alone have focused so unrelentingly on the complexities and ambiguities of human language (and) experience puts us on notice" to take seriously her emphasis on the limitations of language.[16] To stress, as Rich does, the "unnameableness" often attributed to the deity in differing sacred texts may be a calculated attempt to unname what multiple varieties of religious fundamentalism have named as a sanction for violence. To stress the unnameable and what is without boundaries is to remove the "logical" structures on which divisions and violence are often based. Again, in a way that Norfolk identified, Rich works from within existing rhetorical and sacred traditions, thinking through what it means to posit the existence of an unnameable power. The lines that conclude "Turning" shake the epistemological foundations used to sanction violence and division by suggesting that our knowledge of the way things must be is hardly secure.

The lines "I never thought you were on our side, / I only thought you did not judge us" raise the important question of whether the divine ground has "sides," or ever did. Rich has prepared the reader to rethink the language of division by declining to give a name to the country she writes about. By refusing to "name" the divine ground, she is implicitly deconstructing the boundary lines imposed by all forms of fundamentalism. Indeed, her criticism of boundary drawing is that such boundaries automatically proclaim an "us" as good and an "other" as bad and thus free "us" from responsibility to the other. Rich's view of an otherness without negative divisiveness requires not only a new language, far more grounded in uncertainty, but also a new logic underlying and embodied in that language.

Beyond the instruments of false division and of violence, Rich imagines the sacred as "a mindfulness": "beyond boundaries, green lines, / wire-netted walls / the place beyond documents." The place "beyond boundaries" and "beyond documents," though definitely sacred in this poem, must also be a place toward which the human imagination and human will can continue to work. Rich's whole career has shown her commitment to human responsibility and care, and the setting of the penultimate section of "Turning" ("a public meeting") only reinforces that commitment. Rich is, I believe, conducting an inquiry into a power that, if it exists at all independently of human language, is "unnameable by choice." She ends the poem with lines that question this "unnameable": "So why am I out here, trying / to read your name in the illegible air? . . . breath / without echo, why?" Whether her inquiry partakes of "agnostic mysticism" or "Jewish metaphysics," its aim is to help readers imagine what they cannot know and to work toward a world they can only imagine.

In 1979, nine years before the poem was written, Alicia Ostriker explained the need for a poem like "Turning." She cautioned that Rich, even as she continued to represent those who had been victimized, needed also to imagine a better world: "Rich's readers need to know about the female equivalent of the burning bush, the voice of the covenant, the promised land. They need to know about the goddess. Lacking the imagination's projection of a world without victims, a self unvictimized, unmastered, complete—and it is for poets to give us this, to articulate the delight that is *there*, latently, as much as women's despair is *there*—lacking this, the will to change is helplessly fettered."[17] In Ostriker's call for a poem like "Turning" and in the poem itself, the this-worldly and the otherworldly perspectives come together in a way that does not allow human beings to abdicate responsibility for this world.

The note on which *Time's Power* ends, with "Turning" the final poem in the volume, is provisional but also affirmative. The two works by Rich published since *Time's Power* continue to be haunted by the vastness of the problems of violence against women; but they also ask us to imagine "a world without victims."[18] As we document and name the problems women face, as we break silence, we are already beginning to name the alternatives. The poet's call to envision alternatives enables us to *will* to change the world in which human beings live. Poetry is not in itself change, but it can make change possible. In short, as Rich writes in "Dreamwood," it provides a "map" that allows us to:

> recognize that poetry
> isn't revolution but a way of knowing
> why it must come (*TP* 35)

Notes

1. For another definition of the term "unnaming," see Pamela Annas, "A Poetry of Survival." On the centrality of issues of language and silence in Rich's work, see Mary K. DeShazer " 'Nothing but Myself? . . . My Selves' "; Willard Spiegelman, " 'Driving to the Limits of the City of Words' "; and Joanne Feit Diehl, " 'Of Woman Born.' " Critical discussions of Rich as a political poet include Terrence des Pres, "Adrienne Rich, North America East"; Rachel Blau DuPlessis, "The Critique of Consciousness and Myth in Levertov, Rich, and Rukeyser"; and Mary Slowik, "The Friction of the Mind."

2. Adrienne Rich, *Time's Power: Poems 1985–1988*, 45. Cited hereafter by the abbreviation *TP* and the page number.

3. For positive critical readings of Rich's work in light of a poststructuralist understanding of language, see especially Elizabeth A. Meese, "Negotiating the Metalogic: (Re)Figuring Feminism in the Works of Adrienne Rich," in E. A. Meese, *(Ex)-Tensions*, 155–79; Maggie Humm, "Adrienne Rich"; Nancy K. Miller, "Changing the Subject"; and Catharine Stimpson, "Adrienne Rich and Lesbian / Feminist Poetry."

4. Adrienne Rich, interview with David Montenegro.

5. Andrea Nye, "Woman Clothed with the Sun," 671–72.

6. Hélène Cixous. "The Laugh of the Medusa," 256.

7. Margaret Homans, " 'Her Very Own Howl,' " 186.

8. Rich, "Sliding Stone from the Cave's Mouth," 15.

9. Breaking silence emerges as a complex issue in Rich also because she remains aware of the fact that neither French feminisms nor Anglo-American feminisms have adequately addressed the problem of illiteracy among women, a problem that leaves a great many women in the silent cold.

10. Homans, "Howl," 205.

11. Jay Parini, review of *Time's Power*.
12. For a discussion of some of the issues raised for Jewish feminism by the Palestinian-Israeli conflict, see Jenny Bourne, "Homelands of the Mind."
13. Marilyn Hacker, review of *Time's Power*, 466.
14. Robert Shaw, review of *Time's Power*, 167.
15. Lawrence Norfolk, review of *Time's Power*, 1000.
16. Meese, "Negotiating," 172.
17. Alicia Ostriker, "Her Cargo," 8.
18. Since *Time's Power*, Rich has published another volume of poetry, *An Atlas of the Difficult World* (1991), and another volume of prose, *What Is Found There* (1993).

ANNE B. DALTON

The Devil and the Virgin:
Writing Sexual Abuse in *Incidents in the Life of a Slave Girl*

Harriet Jacobs confronted multiple binds as she attempted to render her experiences of sexual abuse and the systematic sexual exploitation of slave women. In her 1861 narrative, she grappled with the constraints of the literary conventions of the time, while also making use of them to keep her audience's sympathy and to rally support for the abolitionist cause. In her preface, Jacobs points to absences and silences in *Incidents in the Life of a Slave Girl*.[1] She writes that her "descriptions fall far short of the facts" (xiii) and that "it would have been more pleasant to [her] to have been silent about [her] own history" (xiv). Jacobs emphasizes that it is her desire to end the suffering of the enslaved that has made her "add [her] testimony" to that of others (xiv).

Introductory comments by the editor of *Incidents,* white abolitionist Lydia Maria Child, suggest why Jacobs's prose would demonstrate such conflict as she broaches the taboo subject of sexual exploitation.[2]

> I am well aware that many will accuse me of indecorum for presenting these pages to the public; for the experiences of this intelligent and much-injured woman belong to a class which some call delicate subjects, and others indelicate; but the public ought to be made acquainted with its monstrous features, and I willingly take the responsibility of presenting them with the veil withdrawn. I do this for the sake of my sisters in bondage, *who are suffering wrongs so foul, that our ears are too delicate to listen to them.* I do it with the hope of arousing conscientious and reflecting women at the North to a sense of their duty in the exertion of moral influence on the question of Slavery, on all possible occasions. (xii, emphasis added)

Child's description that Black women "are suffering wrongs so foul that our ears [white women's] are too delicate to listen to them" implies an obverse relation between Jacobs and her audience, one in which the *more* Jacobs tries to tell, the less she may be heard by those she feels she must persuade. To be politically effective, Jacobs needed to render the material relating to sexual exploitation in a "delicate" manner, so that she would not alienate her audience from listening, while still being graphic enough to be persuasive. By using metaphorical descriptions of "foulness" Jacobs could cope with the demands of such a bind; she would be telling all, but in such a way that "too delicate" ears would not find "plain" (see xii and xiv).

In *Incidents,* "Linda Brent" was Jacobs's pseudonym as protagonist and author, and the portrayal of Dr. Flint was based on Jacobs's former master, James Norcom, a prominent physician in Edenton, North Carolina.[3] Jacobs escaped to the North in 1842 and wrote her narrative between 1853 and 1858 under conditions of physical hardship, while working as a domestic servant. During this period, Jacobs sent letters to Amy Post, a founder of the women's rights movement and a member of the New York State Anti-Slave Society. These letters reveal that Jacobs felt she was placing herself at risk when she assumed the authorial role. In one letter, composed before completing her manuscript, Jacobs tells Post that she intends to write "the whole truth" of her experiences, even though she feels that her life has had "degradation associated with it."[4] However, in a later letter, Jacobs states that she has "left out" descriptions of some of the "cruel wrongs" she suffered. Her comment that "the world might believe that a slave woman was too willing" and her request to "be judged as a woman" both emphasize the sexual nature of what she has excluded.[5] Paradoxically, even Jacobs's desire to *conceal* seems to further her effort to expose the sexual victimization. Comments such as "descriptions fall short of the facts" signal to readers the need to examine her narrative carefully in order to discover what she "might have made plainer" (xiv).

The fact that Black women at this time were stereotyped as "innately super-sexed" may well have fueled Jacobs's anxiety as author.[6] Even the images presented by leading abolitionists often played on the association of Black women with the illicit. For example, defining the dialectic often reinforced by abolitionists, Hazel Carby argues that "Garrison's sexual metaphors for black women extended from passionate whore to hapless, cringing victim."[7] Jacobs's prose, especially her apologetic tone, suggests that she was influenced by the cultural edict against Black women "assuming the independence" to give public accounts of their experience.[8] For women in general, the act of making their experience public would itself be likely to be classed as "promiscuous" or "unnatural," regardless of specific content. Because Jacobs was an African-American woman writing about sexual abuse, her authorial position was far more precarious.

Jacobs's sense of her audience seems to have posed additional difficulties for her. At several points in *Incidents,* and notably in her preface, she addresses her remarks to white females. Angela Davis comments that "white women who joined the abolitionist movement were especially outraged by the sexual assaults on Black women" and that "activists in the female anti-slave societies often related stories of brutal rapes of slave women as they appealed to white women to defend their Black sisters." [9] Jacobs may have felt it politically effective to render an account of her sexual abuse, but as Davis implies, she also had reason to fear they might read about her suffering voyeuristically. As a woman who had been brutally betrayed by her Southern white mistresses during her childhood and young adulthood, Jacobs had many reasons to feel conflicted about relating the story of her sexual exploitation to even the most sympathetic white female audience she could imagine. Her persistent efforts to write in spite of these difficulties reveals her extraordinary commitment to speaking and being heard.

Although a number of feminist critics during the last five years have provided crucial biographical information about Jacobs as well as literary and historical analyses of *Incidents,* no one has yet examined the tensions between what she literally states and metaphorically suggests about sexual exploitation. [10] To understand the range of forces Jacobs confronted as a writer, it is instructive to look at the tension she creates by describing Dr. Flint's *verbal* sexual harassment of Linda Brent through imagery that implies that he was able to molest her physically. [11] This tension is connected with several issues: the psychology of survivors of sexual abuse, the thematics of slave narratives, Jacobs's status as a Black and female narrator, her relation to her audience, and nineteenth-century concepts of ladyhood. The recent research concerning the psychology of survivors of sexual abuse provides the key to my analysis, since the meaning of the gaps, negations, and displacements in Jacobs's narrative are linked directly to her position as an adult narrator describing trauma she experienced as a child and young woman. [12]

Jacobs may have felt compelled to use the pseudonym "Linda Brent" for her narrative's author and protagonist in order to protect herself, her family, and those who helped her escape. And yet, despite this conscious masking, the narrative's subtitle, "Written by Herself," stresses the authenticity of Jacobs's account. Such juxtaposed masking and assertion of authenticity marks the language of the narrative throughout. Although

Jacobs might have used her own name if she had not feared reprisals, I am maintaining her distinction throughout my discussion. Even the most exacting and literal of autobiographers, in the process of writing, is creating a "fiction" about himself or herself. In maintaining the distinction Jacobs made, I am reminding the reader that her slave narrative is a constructed representation, while also attempting to respect her own delineations within the autobiography.[13]

In the range of critical interpretations that Jacobs's narrative has called forth, each one has stressed the degree to which Brent actively resisted Flint's abuse. Exploring the meaning of this resistance, Hazel Carby argues that although "Dr. Flint was the embodiment of the corruption of the slave system, as his prey Linda Brent was not corrupted by him, and her struggle was an aggressive refusal to be sexually used and compromised or to succumb to the will of the master."[14] Scrutinizing the conflicts between the literal and figurative meanings does not undercut the power of the resistance that Jacobs's narrative chronicles.[15] Instead, such analysis can reveal the ways in which Jacobs responded to her historical context to write "'not the life of a heroine with no degradation associated with it,' but a woman's 'true and just account of [her] own life in slavery.'"[16]

Revising Genesis: Writing the Best Kept Secret

Again and again, Jacobs shows Dr. Flint verbally harassing and following Linda Brent at all times of the day and night, as well as striking, shaking, and throwing her. She portrays his tremendous ability to violate Brent physically, but to suggest his sexual abuse she most often portrays him as a foul demon, fiend, or devil whispering in her ear. Through this imagery, which does not explicitly tell but metaphorically represents, Jacobs skillfully revises the thematics that nineteenth-century male slave narrators used, and she creates tropes through which she can tell the *female* slave's story.

In *The Best Kept Secret,* Florence Rush describes the extensive traffic in girls and women in Europe and America during the nineteenth century. Arguing that at the rare times when male abusers were prosecuted, the girls and women suffered from an equally abusive legal system and abusive publicity, Rush discusses how the widespread concept of "the sexually guilty female"—with Eve as the prototype—forced the abused female into shame and silence.[17] Jacobs's narrative suggests that she simultaneously internalized and resisted this concept.

In the opening pages of *Incidents,* Jacobs describes Brent's "fall into knowledge of evil." [18] But unlike the "falls" most male slave narrators described, which were into "the development of an awareness of what it means to be a slave," Brent's is a double one into a knowledge both of slavery and of sexual subjugation. [19] Jacobs expands the meaning of "fall," doubling it so that it relates to her position both as a slave and as a female slave. By drawing on the biblical imagery of temptation in Genesis and virgin insemination in the Gospels to show Brent's loss of her Edenic state of childhood innocence, Jacobs creates a striking counterpoint to many of the male slave narratives while also drawing on the parables and structures they often incorporated.

As male slave narrators portrayed the degradation of slavery, their role most often resembled that of an Adamic or Christ-like figure, who must "bear the slave's heavy cross." [20] In contrast to other narratives, Jacobs uses ear, demon, devil, and serpent imagery to show that Brent is parallel to both Eve and Mary. She is Eve-like because she is tempted by a foul devil, but also Mary-like as she strives desperately to resist Flint and maintain the purity that Mary personifies. It was more difficult for Jacobs to report Brent's "fall" than it was for a male narrator to portray the "fall" of an Adam-Christ figure, not only because of the Christian tradition of blaming the sexual and sexually abused woman, but also because of the strict nineteenth-century standards concerning female sexuality and respectability. In *The Madwoman in the Attic,* Sandra Gilbert and Susan Gubar analyze how nineteenth-century white women rewrote Miltonic myths, revising the story of Eve, as part of their effort to create themselves. [21] Like these women, Jacobs also revised patriarchal myths about women's sexuality, creativity, and status by telling her story from the position of an Eve figure.

Jacobs's portrayal of Dr. Flint as a demon violating Linda Brent by whispering in her ear is striking in several ways. While such imagery shows Dr. Flint's verbal sexual harassment, the image also suggests greater sexual abuse than the narrator literally reports. Jacobs first describes Flint's attempts to molest her in this passage: "But I now entered on my fifteenth year—a sad epoch in the life of a slave girl. My master began to whisper foul words in my ear. Young as I was, I could not remain ignorant of their import. I tried to treat them with indifference or contempt" (26).

There are several reasons why Jacobs might have implied the sexual abuse by describing Flint whispering in Brent's ear. In parables and folklore, the ear has traditionally been one site of the virginal woman's molestation and impregnation, as with the Christian Mary figure. [22] Also, by casting Flint as a devil-demon who whispers in Brent's ear, Jacobs retells the Genesis myth in which the serpent corrupts Eve; but in contrast to the biblical version, Jacobs's retelling emphasizes the abuser's guilt and the victim's innocence. Through this imagery, Jacobs can report what the young woman experienced while emphasizing her status as pure. Her representation of the ear as the site of sexual assault is also evocative of how a verbal attack can feel like a physical blow. Jacobs's imagery emphasizes the excruciating visceral effects that result from Flint's proximity and control: "For my master, whose restless, craving, vicious nature roved about day and night, seeking whom to devour, had just left me, with stinging, scathing words; words that scathed ear and brain like fire. O, how I despised him! I thought how glad I should be, if some day when he walked the earth, it would open and swallow him up and disencumber the world of a plague" (15–16).

With the severe injunctions women, and particularly slave women, experienced against speaking about sexual abuse, one might expect Jacobs to mask her descriptions of molestation. One such method is described by Hortense Spillers, who comments that Freud's notes articulate the "frequency with which sexual repression makes use of transpositions from a lower to an upper part of the body." She explains that Freud "specifically names the replacement of the genitals by the face as a dynamic in the symbolism of unconscious thinking."[23] Julia Kristeva, in "Stabat Mater," considers how in representations of the virginal body the ear becomes the site of the woman's sexual experience: "That the female sexual organ has become transformed into an innocent shell which serves only to receive sound may ultimately contribute to an eroticization of hearing and the voice, not to say of understanding. But by the same token sexuality is reduced to a mere implication. The female sexual experience is therefore anchored in the universality of sound."[24] Jacobs explored the correlation that Kristeva suggests among hearing, the voice, and sexuality. Her use of the woman's ear as the site of the attack is appropriate and evocative because the abused ear is parallel to the silenced mouth of the molested woman and what she cannot tell. Dr. Flint has the power to speak, but the sexually abused woman cannot name what he is "speaking," although she desperately wants to reveal the trauma: "In desperation I told him that I must and would apply to my grandmother for protection. He threatened me with death, and worse than death, if I made any complaint to her" (30). In such passages, Jacobs demonstrates Flint's extreme power not only to control who speaks, but to render others silent. Jacobs's narrative is radical because she is able to speak through her imagery even while she portrays Brent as silenced.[25]

The following passage emphasizes Flint's demonic role as he alternately tries to tempt Brent gently or to abuse her ferociously. Jacobs's choice of the verb "peopled" in describing his attacks plays on the many meanings of the word (for example, to populate), suggesting that he has succeeded in forcing the girl to imagine "unclean images" and implying that he has attempted to impregnate her. The author's references to his violation of "the most sacred commandments of nature" again stress his demonic position as he creates the hellish atmosphere in which Brent was "compelled to live": "Sometimes he had stormy, terrific ways, that made his victims tremble; sometimes he assumed a gentleness that he thought must surely subdue. Of the two, I preferred his stormy moods, although they left me trembling. He tried his utmost to corrupt the pure principles my grandmother had instilled. He peopled my young mind with unclean images, such as only a vile monster could think of. I turned from him with disgust and hatred. But he was my master. I was compelled to live under the same roof with him—where I saw a man forty years my senior daily violating the most sacred commandments of nature" (26). Through her use of the Dr. Flint-demon association, Jacobs challenges and reverses the stereotypic descriptions of Black women as lascivious. Her imagery underscores this reversal, especially since in mythology it is the demons who are sexually insatiable.[26] Recounting his repeated assaults, Jacobs describes Flint as "a restless spirit from the pit" (79), likening him to a hellish demon from the underworld.

In chapter 6, "The Jealous Mistress," Jacobs shows how Flint's wife becomes an embodiment of his own lascivious behavior; like his familiar or a succubus, she acts out his abuse by standing over Brent's bed and accosting her when she believes she is asleep: "She now took me to sleep in a room adjoining her own. . . . Sometimes I woke up, and found her bending over me. At other times she whispered in my ear, as though it was her husband who was speaking to me, and listened to hear what I would answer. If she startled me, on such occasions, she would glide stealthily away; and the next morning she would tell me I had been talking in my sleep, and ask who I was talking to. At last, I began to be fearful for my life. It had been threatened; and you can imagine, better than I can describe, what an unpleasant sensation it must produce to wake up in the dead of night and find a jealous woman bending over you" (33). Jacobs's description contrasts ironically with stereotypic portrayals of the white mistress as "pure and morally uplifted." As if she were a demon like her husband, Mrs. Flint molests the victim of her husband's "vicious roving" while she sleeps by reenacting his molestation of her. By portraying the mistress as the defiling succubus, Jacobs reveals how the master's sexual abuses infect those around him, while also refuting definitions of slave women as "lasciviously sexual" and white women as "the model of virtue."

As male slave narrators did with their protagonists, Jacobs used the Christian imagery to stress the slave woman's humanity and refined nature while revealing the inhumanity of the master and mistress. She repeatedly emphasizes the pervasiveness of Dr. Flint's abuses by stating that through them he creates an "atmosphere of hell" (40). She also characterizes Flint as a representative of "the serpent of Slavery" who has "many and poisonous fangs" (63). She shows Flint, like Satan, attempting to entrap; however, unlike conventional Christian portrayals of Eve, Brent struggles continually against his efforts to control and molest her.

In one scene, Brent questions Flint's hypocrisy in joining the church for motives of social advancement, and challenges his statement that in acquiescing to his sexual advances she should be "as virtuous as" his wife:

> His voice became hoarse with rage. "How dare you preach to me about your infernal Bible!" he exclaimed. "What right have you, who are my negro, to talk to me about what you would like? I am your master and you shall obey me."
>
> No wonder slaves sing,—
> "Ole Satan's church is here below;
> Up to God's free church I have to go." (77)

Flint behaves satanically as he curses the Bible, sets himself up as a higher authority than the Christian God, and tries to compel Brent to abandon her moral principles. In this passage, he denies Brent the right to speak, threatening that she "shall obey" him. By ending the passage with the song's refrain, Jacobs shows the extent to which those within the slave community resisted their masters' injunctions against revealing their inhumanity. They used Christian metaphor to expose their masters' stifling of Christian teachings. Through the song, Jacobs manages to highlight the fact of mass resistance in the same passage in which Flint attempts to silence Brent.

Jacobs also stresses the importance of resistance within the Black community by stating that Brent might not have survived if she had been living on a plantation or in a less populated area throughout her years as a slave (33). But despite the fact that Brent's place within a larger community buffers her to some degree, many passages detail Flint's vast power: "My master met me at every turn, reminding me that I belonged to him, and swearing by heaven and earth that he would compel me to submit to him. If I went out for a breath of fresh air, after a day of unwearied toil, his footsteps dogged me. If I knelt by my mother's grave, his dark shadow fell on me even there" (27). The image of Brent being "dogged" by Flint's footsteps until "his dark shadow fell on [her]" emphasizes how his psychological and physical impingement reinforce each other.

In "A Perilous Passage in a Slave Girl's Life," Brent enters into a sexual relationship with Mr. Sands, a white slave-owning neighbor, in an attempt to protect herself from Flint's abuse in general and, specifically, to avoid becoming pregnant with a child fathered by Flint. But after the birth of her first, and then following the birth of her second child (both fathered, the narrator reports, by Sands), the intensity of Flint's "persecutions" increases. Jacobs writes that during the first time Brent was pregnant he was the only doctor who could be called to treat her (63) and that he attended during the birth of her child. Such details once again emphasize the numerous occasions Flint had to abuse Brent and the vast extent of his power to traumatize her. By indicating that the molester attended Brent as she gave birth, Jacobs poignantly depicts the degree of her vulnerability and danger.

What No Pen Could Describe: "The Plunge into the Abyss"

Jacobs tells her readers many times that she felt she could not describe all that she had witnessed and experienced about sexual abuse within slavery. She most often stresses that she cannot completely render her experience either before or just after a passage in which she metaphorically describes Flint's sexual exploitation of slave women. For example, while recounting Flint's attempts to make the fifteen-year-old Brent his concubine, Jacobs writes, "The degradation, the wrongs, the vices, that grow out of slavery, are more than I can describe. They are greater than you would willingly believe" (26). The passage reveals an important tension: the narrator claims she is unable to describe her experience fully, and then states that the reason for her silence is her audience's inability to accept the truth of that experience. At times, however, her phrasing reveals that she confronted other forces, besides her sense of audience, that limited what she could articulate: "He came every day; and *I was subjected to such insults as no pen can describe. I would not describe them if I could; they were too low, too revolting.* I tried to keep them from my grandmother's knowledge as much as I could. I knew she had enough to sadden her life, without having my troubles to bear" (79, emphasis added). That Brent "was subjected to such insults as no pen can describe" implies that Flint abused her more harshly than *anyone* could communicate. But the passage also suggests that the narrator recoiled from recalling the trauma of the past incidents because they were too disturbing for *her* to represent. Here, the ambivalence about disclosure and concealment that marks the passage is representative of accounts by girls and women who were molested.[27]

The cultural situation Jacobs portrays is, despite many parallels, a more extreme one than contemporary researchers of sexual abuse have studied. Jacobs stresses repeatedly that she grew up in a region in which white men sexually abused Black children and women extensively. She also makes clear that Linda Brent became aware of this systematic sexual abuse when she was eleven and that she became a victim of it by the age of fifteen at the latest. Researchers have found that girls feel extreme shame, guilt, and rage as a result of abuse and often respond by defining themselves as evil.[28] They relate that the early trauma, and especially the feeling of powerlessness and stigmatization, contribute to such feelings. Jacobs profoundly resists portraying Brent as the sexually guilty female, but one can infer from her narrative that, for the slave child, the feeling of powerlessness must have been extreme. Just as victims of child abuse are often trapped into silence and powerlessness by the authority figures in their lives, Brent is abused by Dr. Flint and then by the mistress of the household.[29] Jacobs describes Brent as threatened by Flint's vengeance *if she tells,* and as subject to the mistress's abuse if she tells, does not tell, or even if the mistress *suspects* that she was sexually abused (12). Commenting on similar dynamics, Diana Russell reports that girls who were disbelieved or blamed when they revealed that they had been sexually abused often suffered the most extreme aftereffects.[30] She emphasizes that, as adults, these women had the most difficulty disclosing the fact that they had been molested, and that they felt the most guilt.[31]

Incidents suggests that because the Flints assumed the role of master and mistress to Brent, she found the sexual assaults even more disturbing than if they had occurred in a different context. In contemporary America, guardians, stepfathers and foster fathers are the ones most likely to sexually abuse girls and young women.[32] Recent research shows that molestation by an older male in the position of guardian is typically more traumatic than that by a male who is not directly responsible for the girl's safety and well-being.[33] Brent's position differs from these contemporary dynamics in an important way; she repeatedly eschews Flint's attempts to cast himself in a paternal role, rejecting as repugnant his efforts, parallel to those of many slave owners, to cast himself as fictive kin to those he has enslaved. In spite of this distinction, Brent's experience of being sexually abused by one who has absolute authority and controls the basic material necessities of life clearly contributes to the difficulty of speaking about the molestation. Contemporary studies show that even when suffering incestuous abuse, a young girl may realize that she will grow old enough to leave the household, and many girls who have been molested by a relative or acquaintance of the family leave the family at a very young age.[34] The situation of slave girls or women who suffered from the sexual abuse of white men was even more extreme because they knew that they had no legal recourse and little chance of escape, and that their status as possession was likely to be permanent. These women also had the added burden of knowing that any daughter they might bear could become subject to similar torture.

Jacobs reports that as a young child Brent learned about the doctor's power to whip and to sell slaves who spoke about his sexual abuse:

> Some said master accused him of stealing corn, others said the slave had quarrelled with his wife, in presence of the overseer, and had accused his master of being the father of her child. They were both Black and the child was very fair.
>
> I went into the work house next morning, and saw the cowhide still wet with blood, and the boards all covered with gore. The poor man lived, and continued to quarrel with his wife. A few months afterwards Dr. Flint handed them both over to a slave-trader. The guilty man put their value into his pocket, and had the satisfaction of knowing that they were out of sight and hearing. When the mother was delivered into the trader's hands, she said, "You *promised* to treat me well." To which he replied, "You have let your tongue run too far; damn you!" She had forgotten that it was a crime for a slave to tell who was the father of her child. (12)

Jacobs shows Brent's traumatic initiation, stressing that speaking about sexual abuse can destroy a slave family as well as subject individual men and women to physical torture. Early exposure to the fate of those who spoke out could have made Jacobs feel overwhelming pressure to be silent about sexual harassment and molestation during her childhood and young adulthood. The memory of such injunctions against speaking out could also have made it deeply painful for Jacobs, as a mature adult, to recall and write about her experiences in the Norcoms' household. Describing other traumatic incidents from Brent's childhood, Jacobs emphasizes that slave women who became pregnant by the white master were often greatly abused by the white mistress as well (see p. 12 for one example). Later in

Incidents Brent confronts such a nexus of abuse when Mrs. Flint repeatedly threatens to kill her, believing she is a victim of her husband's sexual assaults.

The way in which Jacobs describes Mrs. Flint forcing Brent to recount what had "passed between" herself and her master clarifies the dynamics between the two women, while once again indicating how Jacobs's sense of her audience may have silenced her.

> "If you have deceived me, beware! . . . Look me directly in the face, and tell me all that has passed between your master and you."
>
> I did as she ordered. As I went on with my account her color changed frequently, she wept, and sometimes groaned . . . but she was incapable of feeling for the condition of shame and misery in which her unfortunate, helpless slave was placed. (32)

Jacobs portrays Mrs. Flint's command and reaction specifically, but does not begin to describe what Brent said to her, even though this would have been a logical point in the narrative at which to detail the sexual abuse Jacobs had briefly described in the previous chapter. By representing what Brent said to Mrs. Flint with the gap between the first and second sentences, Jacobs suggests that communicating Flint's actions to the threatening mistress traumatized Brent and that it may also have been traumatic for Jacobs to recall and write the scene for her readers. Although the passage shows that the abusive mistress violated Brent's privacy without any intention of protecting her from Flint, through her use of the lacuna in the scene Jacobs manages to shield Brent retroactively from the mistress's probing while also protecting herself from an audience she did not trust. At the same time, the lacuna once again signals that Flint's sexual abuse is so extreme that it cannot be represented. Even though Jacobs does not disclose to her readers what Brent said about Flint, by relating that Mrs. Flint "wept" and "sometimes groaned" in response, Jacobs indicates that Brent spoke of Flint's *sexual* abuse. Descriptions of the mistress's brutality early in the narrative establish that "her color" would not have "changed frequently" while hearing reports of the master's *physical* abuse of slaves.

Jacobs further delineates the forces that silenced Brent as she depicts Linda's relationship with her grandmother, exploring both why and what Linda cannot tell her about the sexual abuse she suffered within the Flints' household.

> But Dr. Flint swore he would kill me, if I was not as silent as the grave. Then, although my grandmother was all in all to me, I feared her as well as loved her. I had been accustomed to look up to her with a

respect bordering upon awe. I was very young, and felt shamefaced
about telling her such impure things, especially as I knew her to
be very strict on such subjects. Moreover, she was a woman of a
high spirit. She was usually very quiet in her demeanor; but if her
indignation was once roused, it was not very easily quelled. I had been
told that she once chased a white gentleman with a loaded pistol,
because he insulted one of her daughters. I dreaded the consequences
of a violent outbreak; and both pride and fear kept me silent. (28)

Jacobs goes on to write that Brent "dare[d] not tell grandmother the
worst," even though the grandmother had "long suspected that all was
not right" (37), portraying Linda as a fifteen-year-old caught without recourse in a matrix of fear and shame. Linda fears the master will punish
her family or herself if she tells all; she fears that her grandmother might
endanger herself by trying to protect her, and she fears her "strict" grandmother's condemnation for revealing the "unpure" events that have tran-
spired in the Flint household. Jacobs's phrase "I dreaded the consequences
of a violent outbreak" recalls for her readers the scene she describes earlier, in which the slave man and woman who speak of the master's sexual
transgressions are tortured and then separated and sold. Several contemporary theorists on child abuse indicate that molesters consciously choose
victims who they feel have the least power to tell.[35] Dr. Flint's threat that
he would kill Linda if she "was not as silent as the grave" emphasizes the
extreme pressure slave women confronted not to disclose sexual abuse. By
this point in the narrative Jacobs had already shown readers how brutally
the doctor could enforce silence.

Later, Jacobs portrays the grandmother believing Mrs. Flint and repu-
diating Brent when she hears Mrs. Flint's false accusation that the girl has
become pregnant with the doctor's child. The grandmother's harsh response makes Brent's earlier fear about disclosure understandable. "My
grandmother . . . believed what she said. She exclaimed, 'O Linda! has it
come to this? I had rather see you dead than to see you as you now are.
You are a disgrace to your dear mother.' She tore from my fingers my
mother's wedding ring and her silver thimble. 'Go away!' she exclaimed,
'and never come to my house, again' " (57). The extreme nature of the
grandmother's reaction suggests that Jacobs may have felt pressured by
literary conventions to portray the repudiation. Perhaps Jacobs showed
her disapproval to emphasize the grandmother's "purity," so that the older
woman would appear to the audience as a sympathetic and "morally uplifted" woman. As this chapter continues, Linda attempts to explain to
her grandmother why she became pregnant; she tells her "all [she] had

been bearing for *years*" (58; emphasis added). Although Jacobs's wording does not explicitly show that she is reporting the doctor's sexual abuse, the passage strongly suggests this, since Linda is attempting to explain why she felt compelled to become pregnant by Sands. The grandmother's initial harshness, her silence, and her eventual pity and tears dramatize the difficult position of the slave mother or grandmother; like the sexually abused daughter, she, too, is caught in a matrix of forces—knowing that if the daughter is not silent, she may face torture, that if she protests her daughter's molestation, the entire family could face severe reprisals, and that both the daughter and she lack the power to escape from the white abusers without suffering.

In the course of describing Brent's relationship with the slave owner Mr. Sands, and explaining why she decided to have children with him, Jacobs clarifies the nature of the dangers Linda faced within the Flint household. Notably, the passages that assert who is responsible for Brent's relationship with Sands directly contradict each other. At first Jacobs writes that Linda became sexually involved with him deliberately and without compulsion: "*I will not try to screen myself behind the plea of compulsion from a master;* for it was not so. Neither can I plead ignorance or thoughtlessness. For years my master had done his utmost to pollute my mind with foul images, and to destroy the pure principles inculcated by my grandmother, and the good mistress of my childhood. The influences of slavery had the same effect on me that they had on other young girls; they had made me prematurely knowing, concerning the evil way of the world. *I knew what I did, and I did it with deliberate calculation*" (54, emphasis added). A few pages later, however, Jacobs writes scathingly of Flint's moralizing against Linda's "sin," her pregnancy, telling the readers that Flint's "persecutions had been the cause" of it (59). Such contradictory passages suggest that Jacobs experienced a sense of splitting. Her letters and narrative emphasize that she felt she had to demonstrate respect for concepts of ladyhood, purity, and virtue as a white audience might expect, yet her own experience had taught her that "the practice" of such a morality was impossible for a slave woman:[36] "You never knew what it is to be a slave; to be entirely unprotected by law or custom. . . . You never exhausted your ingenuity in avoiding the snares and eluding the power of the hated tyrant; you never shuddered at the sound of his footsteps, and trembled within hearing of his voice" (56).

Jacobs addresses virtuous white women throughout the chapter, detailing how the lives of slave women contrast with their own and why they could not judge Brent's decision to become sexually involved with Sands.

Jacobs reveals that Linda begins her sexual relationship with him in an effort to assert her identity and independence: "I knew nothing would enrage Dr. Flint so much as to know that I favored another; and it was something to triumph over my tyrant even in that small way" (56). But as Jacobs shows that Brent entered into the relationship with Sands as the most self-affirming choice from among her limited options, she also stresses Brent's grave danger.

The description of Brent's relationship with Sands demonstrates the extreme constraints slave women confronted in their efforts to control their own sexuality and protect themselves and their families. Jacobs relates that before Linda began the relationship, she felt a greater sense of doom than she ever had before. Historians relate that during the nineteenth century, the age of menarche was considerably later than it is today—on the average fifteen.[37] Although Jacobs is not explicit on this point, Linda's sense of impending disaster may have been related to the fact that this was the first year in which she was physically able to become pregnant.[38] Most obviously, Brent's feeling of doom stemmed from the fact that Flint was building an isolated house in which he planned to force her to live. The secluded setting would have given Flint much greater sexual access to her than he had had in the past, making it likely that Brent would become pregnant by him.[39] Not only does Jacobs make it clear that Brent is desperate to avoid such a pregnancy because she finds Flint repulsive, she also stresses that slave women who were owned by Flint, were subject to his sexual abuse, and gave birth to children he fathered, faced the gravest danger of being sold when "a new fancy took him" (see 56). In several places Jacobs reports that Flint separated such women and their offspring by selling them into the deep South.

Research concerning sexually abused girls consistently shows that, as a means of escape and of establishing an independent sexual identity, they will initiate sexual relationships at young ages. Many choose to initiate such relationships once they are capable of becoming pregnant, and do so to avoid becoming pregnant by the molester. Often, out of fear of discovery, the molester will cease to abuse a young woman when she begins another sexual relationship.[40] Jacobs does not describe Brent's sexual interactions with Sands after she "takes the plunge" and becomes pregnant. Beyond her statements about Linda's shame (which seem tailored to her "virtuous" audience), she does not detail how Linda felt about the experience (see 56). But she does show how pregnancy and motherhood at first buffers Brent to some degree from the Flints in that she is allowed to live with her grandmother after she becomes pregnant (mostly because Mrs. Flint threatens to kill her if she returns to that household).

Although Jacobs barely comments on the fact that Brent's relationship with Sands is an ongoing one, she does describe the danger she is in after she becomes pregnant by him for the second time. During this period, Flint visits the grandmother's house, attacks Linda, and searches each of the rooms at "all hours of the day and night" (62–78). Perhaps Jacobs represented Flint's continuing abuse to emphasize why Linda would need to become pregnant with another child: in order to avoid a worse pregnancy. The fact that she expresses many times the horror she felt about bearing a child who would be born into slavery suggests that she must have felt extremely compelled to have one child with Sands, let alone two. But since Jacobs barely describes the continuing relationship with Sands during this part of the narrative, one can only speculate on the events and dynamics.

Jacobs's decision to limit her descriptions of Brent's relationship with Sands was politically astute, since representing Brent's ongoing sexual involvement, which takes place outside marriage, and across race and class, would have seemed "indelicate" to many of her readers. Like other heroines of the period, such as Catherine Linton in *Wuthering Heights,* Brent has the sexual intercourse (which results in her second pregnancy) in the blank space between chapters. In one sense, Jacobs did not need to describe the sexual interactions with Sands graphically; the fact that both of Linda's children strongly resemble him adequately signifies the sexual and ongoing nature of their relationship. Because Brent does not become pregnant as a result of Flint's abuse, Jacobs needed to *signify* the molestation in another manner, as she does through her imagery.

Telling EverySlavewoman's Story and Her Own: Indicting the Hierarchy of Abusers

Shifts in focus and displacements punctuate Brent's history as Jacobs intersperses within it an almost ethnographic description of the fates of other sexually abused slave women. Many slave narrators grappled with what would be most effective politically: to focus on the experiences of the enslaved as a class, or on the heroic aspects of an individual slave, or on ways in which a particular slave's experience might represent that of many held in slavery. Discussing the development of slave narratives as a genre, Frances Foster argues: "The search for spiritual identity in the slave narratives was complicated by the desire to use incidents in the narrators' experiences as examples of the experience of many others like him. As a result, the slave narrator increasingly focused upon the effects of a dehumanizing environment upon his race rather than upon his own individuality."[41]

Jacobs seems to have had several motives for telling the story of "everywoman" who is a slave in the course of communicating her own experience; each of the stories exemplifies Angela Davis's assertion, "Slavery relied as much on routine sexual abuse as it relied on the whip and the lash."[42] Jacobs exposed the institutionalized practice of sexual abuse early in the narrative so that her readers would, from the outset, understand the slave woman's position as a sexual as well as racial commodity. She explicitly defines the vulnerable position of slave girls while describing the day her brother was sold: "He [the slave trader] said he would give any price if the handsome lad was a girl. We thanked God that he was not" (22). Also, by portraying a range of fates the abused slave women and their families might face, Jacobs charts the relation among slave women as a class. As part of this effort, Jacobs often compares Linda's position (as a skilled household manager and literate woman) with the position of the female field hand who is abused or with the position of the slave woman whom the master forcibly makes his concubine. Jacobs repeatedly shows how the white masters profit economically from the sale or labor of the children born to slave women—whom they, their white sons, or their overseers have raped—especially when the children are "too fair" (12). As Davis argues, "The right claimed by slaveowners and their agents over the bodies of female slaves was a direct expression of their presumed property rights over Black people as a whole. The license to rape emanated from and facilitated the ruthless economic domination that was the gruesome hallmark of slavery."[43]

By describing the experiences of enslaved women as a class, Jacobs emphasizes the economic relation between rape and race oppression. However, Jacobs's technique of displacing her narration of the sexual abuse Brent suffered by presenting the stories of others also serves another crucial function. When she begins to describe Flint's sexual abuse of Brent, Jacobs frequently switches from first-person narration to a generalized, third-person story of what "slave girls" have or what "the slave girl" has suffered. Sometimes, after starting to describe Linda's experience, she abruptly switches to a more concrete description of what happened to another particular slave woman or girl. Significantly, after such tangential narration, Jacobs almost never returns to narrating the incident about Linda. Consider, for example, these rhetorical shifts:

He told me that I was his property; that I must be subject to his will in all things. My soul revolted against the mean tyranny. But where could I turn for protection? No matter whether the slave girl be as black as ebony or as fair as her mistress. In either case, there is no shadow of law to protect her from insult, from violence or even from death; all these are inflicted by fiends who bear the shape of men. . . . The degradation, the wrongs, the vices that grow out of slavery are more than I can describe. . . . Even the little child, who is accustomed to wait on her mistress and her children, will learn before she is twelve years old, why it is that her mistress hates such and such among the slaves. . . . She will become prematurely knowing in evil things. Soon she will learn to tremble when she hears her master's footfall. She will be compelled to realize she is no longer a child. If God has bestowed beauty upon her, it will prove her greatest curse. That which commands admiration in the white woman only hastens the degradation of the female slave. . . . I cannot tell you how much I suffered in the presence of these wrongs, nor how I am still pained in retrospect. (26–27)

Jacobs's narrative technique of distancing herself from the trauma of sexual abuse is strongly reminiscent of the classic dissociation psychologists face when their clients mask their own problems as those of "a friend" or as problems faced by "everyone." Many survivors of sexual abuse experience some type of blocking that protects them from overwhelming memories, especially when first recalling what they suffered.[44] Jacobs's shifts to third person may have allowed her to report the molestation in masked form without actually recalling that she was the victim of molestation, or without being overwhelmed by affect that she could not endure.

Jacobs's first description of Flint's sexual abuse of Linda, tucked into a passage concerning her grandmother's kindness, the weather, and her brother's troubles, shows a similar pattern of displacement: "I was his [William's] confidant. He came to me with all his troubles. I remember one instance in particular. It was on a lovely spring morning, and when I marked the sunlight dancing here and there, its beauty seemed to mock my sadness. For my master, whose restless, craving, vicious nature roved about day and night, seeking whom to devour, had just left me, with stinging, scathing words; words that scathed ear and brain like fire. . . . So deeply was I absorbed in painful reflections afterwards, that I neither saw nor heard the entrance of any one, till the voice of William sounded close beside me" (16). The organization in this passage is striking because it suggests that Jacobs was trying to deflect attention from what is most horrifying within it. Her diction specifies that William's trials are the focus, even though the subsequent lines indicate that Linda's are more extreme than his at this point. When Jacobs writes soon after, "I remember one instance in particular," one would assume that she is referring to William's troubles, since that has been the focus in the preceding sentences. Instead, the passage digresses to reveal the young girl's anguish and danger, as if Jacobs had suddenly stopped in the middle of one thought to reveal a horrifying vision she could not repress.

In spite of the lacunae and displacements that mark the text, Jacobs reports on a wide range of sexual violence throughout *Incidents*. She indicts a hierarchy of white male sexual abusers as she describes the molestation of young girls, the rape of women, concubinage, and the sexual exploitation of male slaves by both white males and females. By stressing that slave-owning fathers corrupted their white sons, Jacobs highlighted the dynastic elements of these practices (see 51–52 for one example). Representing the dynastic reproduction of the class of sexual abusers served the political function of stressing for her readers that such oppression would continue long after her escape and after her book was published. Jacobs strove to communicate that slave women as a class had to cope with such trauma, and that even though she had suffered gravely, her position was less extreme than that of many other slave women who suffered from the "double burden" of gender and race oppressions.

In one of the saddest parts of *Incidents*, Jacobs demonstrated the ongoing, institutionalized pattern of sexual abuse, using the same imagery of "pouring vile language" into the child's ear that she used earlier to portray Flint's molestation of Linda. But here, in the case of Brent's daughter, it would have been even less likely that what took place were mere "whisperings." Her daughter's position was even more vulnerable than her mother's had been; she was isolated from all her kin and in an unfamiliar Northern community. Jacobs again shows the tremendous difficulty the child has in speaking to her mother:

> She never made any complaint about her own inconveniences and troubles; but a mother's observing eye easily perceived that she was not happy. On the occasion of one of my visits I found her unusually serious. When I asked her what was the matter, she said nothing was the matter. But I insisted upon knowing what made her look so very grave. Finally I ascertained that she felt troubled about the dissipation that was continually going on in the house. She was sent to the store very often for rum and brandy. . . . She was always desirous not to add to my troubles more than she could help, and I did not discover

till years afterwards that Mr. Thorne's intemperance was not the only annoyance she suffered from him. Though he professed too much gratitude to my grandmother to injure any of her descendants, he had poured vile language into the ears of her innocent great-grandchild. (183)

The dynamics in this scene replicate those earlier in the narrative in which Linda was unable to incriminate her abuser when her grandmother asked what was wrong. Similarly, Linda's daughter remains silent about what "made her look so grave."

Jacobs attributes the silence to the daughter's desire to spare her mother, recalling Linda's effort, as a child, to spare her grandmother. Even without detailing what the girl has suffered, Jacobs's repetition of the earlier imagery clearly conveys her meaning about sexual abuse. Through this passage, she further exposed the myth of the North as haven, showing that Linda could not prevent what she feared her daughter would experience when she was born. With crushing irony, the abuse has occurred in the "free" North where her daughter has been sent by her master-father to live as a slave.

Near the conclusion of the narrative, Linda speaks the taboo and tells her daughter of the abuses she experienced in childhood and young adulthood, overcoming the brutal silencing that both had suffered. Through phrasing that reverses the earlier images of Flint and the daughter's abuser "pour[ing] vile language" (183) into the young women's ears, Brent expresses with joy her daughter's understanding and acceptance of her story. She tells us, "my pent-up feelings had often longed to *pour themselves out to some one I could trust*" (93, emphasis added). Much as Alice Walker portrays her experience of a renewed self-love and acceptance through her daughter's vision of her mother and the world in "Beauty: When the Other Dancer is the Self," Jacobs, a hundred years earlier, portrayed Linda experiencing a similar spiritual renewal through her daughter's insight and love. Perhaps finding greater self-acceptance through her daughter's support was part of what enabled Jacobs to express herself in writing.

Jacobs's legacy to her readers is a multilayered one. Already, her text has encouraged reexamination of such subjects as forms of slave resistance, relations between Black and white women in the old South and in the abolitionist movement, and concepts and practices of mothering within slavery. But scholars might further investigate how the psychodynamics within *Incidents* relate to other works, especially those that deal specifically with the subject of sexual exploitation. Nineteenth-century African American women writers textualized sexual abuse and sexual experience in general as they were constrained by, and yet transcended, images that historically defined them as sexually insatiable, primitive, and lascivious. Study of the psychodynamics, and especially the metaphors, lacunae, and displacements within these women's texts can help scholars to understand their complex responses to rigid cultural definitions of gender, sexuality, class, and race. Further critical examination would be especially timely since contemporary novelists such as Toni Morrison, Barbara Chase-Riboud, and Sherley Anne Williams are exploring the possible meanings of these lacunae and displacements in their fictional recreations of nineteenth-century African American women's experiences within and after slavery.

Much as Linda Brent could not, as a child, tell all to her grandmother, uncle, or brother, Jacobs emphasizes that she cannot tell all to her readers. However, one of Jacobs's final assertions, after she hears of Flint's death, demonstrates her skill as an author. She offers an indictment of Flint that functions as a powerful epitaph for him, inscribed in her text, that has proved more enduring than any inscription on his headstone would have been: "There are wrongs which even the grave does not bury. The man was odious to me while he lived and his memory is odious now" (201). Writing about the sexual abuse she suffered twenty years earlier, Jacobs exposed the man who strove to make her "as silent as the grave" and, in doing so, was able to write herself out of silence.

Notes

I am grateful for having had the opportunity to present an earlier draft of this essay at the 1989 "Embodied and Engendered" conference at Claremont College and for the many suggestions offered by conference participants, especially Trudier Palmer, Willi Coleman, Eileen Wilson-Oyelaran, Richard Yarborough, and Deborah Amory. Discussions with the members of the 1990 Susan B. Anthony Faculty Research Seminar at the University of Rochester also helped me to develop my ideas. Most of all I give special thanks to Barbara Christian for her generous support and insight.

1. Harriet Jacobs, *Incidents in the Life of a Slave Girl.* All page references in the text are to the 1973 edition.
2. Minrose Gwin articulates the sense of splitting, schism, and doubleness that a Black woman was likely to feel as she wrote about her former enslavement. "In a literary remaking of her life as a slave, the black woman sees herself dually as an individual with a burgeoning sense of self and as a symbol of former powerlessness." See Minrose Gwin, *Black and White Women of the Old South,* 58–59.
3. Dorothy Sterling, *We Are Your Sisters,* 20.

4. Jean Fagin Yellin, "Text and Contexts of Harriet Jacobs' *Incidents in the Life of a Slave Girl*," 262.

5. Ibid., 269.

6. See Paula Giddings, *When and Where I Enter,* and Frances Foster, *Witnessing Slavery,* 131.

7. Hazel Carby, *Reconstructing Womanhood,* 35. Many details in *Incidents* suggest that Jacobs was familiar with abolitionists texts. She had access to a wide range of these works during 1849–50 when she helped run the antislavery reading room above the offices of Frederick Douglass's *North Star.* See Jean Fagin Yellin's recent edition of Jacobs's *Incidents in the Life of a Slave Girl,* xvi.

8. Angela Y. Davis, *Women, Race, and Class,* 41.

9. Ibid., 27.

10. Dorothy Sterling, in *We Are Your Sisters,* and Jean Fagin Yellin, in her new edition of *Incidents,* have provided much needed biographical information about Jacobs that documents the factual nature of her narrative. In *Self-Discovery and Authority in Afro-American Narrative,* Valerie Smith discusses how "both literal and figurative enclosures proliferate" within the text (30); she also points to several "narrative silences" in *Incidents* and relates them to "those aspects of her [Jacobs's] own sexuality for which the genre does not allow" (42). Hazel Carby in *Reconstructing Womanhood* focuses on the female slave narrators' responses to "the general terrain of images and stereotypes produced by antebellum sexual ideologies," and assesses how "the ideology of true womanhood . . . determined the shape of the public voice of black women writers" (40). In addition to these literary scholars, Elizabeth Fox-Genovese and Minrose Gwin have, through their merging of literary and historical methods, made valuable contributions to assessing the relations between Black and white women in the old South.

11. In her commentary on *Incidents,* Sterling characterizes Jacobs's relation to her former master by writing, "Fifteen-year-old Harriet Jacobs and Louisa Picquet fought off their masters only to say 'yes' to the next white men who approached them" (22). Gwin (in a discussion like Sterling's that conflates the author, Harriet Jacobs, and her fictionalized self-representative, Linda Brent) only comments briefly on descriptions of Flint's abuse: "At fifteen Harriet Jacobs became the mistress of a white man [Sands] quite simply to escape the clutches of her lecherous master" (57). Yellin ("Texts and Contexts," 270), the most explicit in her commentary on Flint's abuse, writes that Brent "prevents her master from raping her." Smith seems to agree with Yellin: "Her master, for some reason reluctant to force her to submit sexually, harassed her, pleaded with her, and tried to bribe her into capitulating in the manner of an importunate suitor" (*Narrative,* 36). From a substantially different point of view, Fox-Genovese makes a suggestion that can serve as a starting point for my analysis: "It stretches the limits of all credulity that Linda Brent actually eluded her master's sexual advances." See *Within the Plantation Household,* 392.

12. Throughout my consideration of Jacobs's descriptions of sexual exploitation, I use the terms "sexual abuse" and "molestation" to define a range of practices, including "any kind of exploitative sexual contact," especially that which had to be kept secret. See Diana Russell, *The Secret Trauma,* 59. Judith Lewis Herman comments: "From the psychological point of view, especially from the child's [or young adult's] point of view, the sexual motivation of the contact, and the fact that it must be kept

secret, are far more significant than the exact nature of the act itself." See Judith Lewis Herman with Lisa Hirshman, *Father-Daughter Incest,* 70. In order to distinguish physical from nonphysical assault, when I refer to sexual "harassment" I am referring solely to verbal sexual abuse.

13. The degree to which Jacobs may or may not be portraying literal details and events is not the central issue in my analysis; rather, my primary focus is on the ways in which Jacobs has constructed her literary representation of her experiences and the ways in which this representation relates to her position as a Black woman writing about sexuality and sexual abuse.

14. Carby, *Reconstructing Womanhood,* 57. Several historical sources emphasize the profound levels of the slave women's resistance to sexual exploitation. See Davis, *Women, Race, and Class,* and bell hooks, *Ain't I a Woman?*

15. Several critics have argued that Jacobs was reticent about writing because she had had a sexual relationship outside marriage and had borne children as a result. Analyzing the descriptions of Brent's relationship with Sands accounts for some of the ambivalence about disclosure in the narrative. I offer the analysis of Flint's sexual abuse of Brent as an additional explanation of Jacobs's ambivalence about disclosure, rather than as a strictly alternative one. See Yellin, Fox-Genovese, and Carby for discussions of Brent's relationship with Sands.

16. Yellin, "Text and Contexts," p. 277.

17. Florence Rush, *The Best Kept Secret,* 63.

18. Foster, *Witnessing Slavery,* 84.

19. Ibid., 85.

20. Ibid., 83–84.

21. Sandra Gilbert and Susan Gubar, *The Madwoman in the Attic.*

22. In similar terms, seventy years later, W. B. Yeats described the sexual assault on the Virgin Mary's ear in his poem "The Mother of God": "The threefold terror of love; a fallen flare / Through the hollow of an ear; / Wings beating about the room; / The terror of all terrors that I bore / The Heavens in my womb." See *The Selected Poems and Two Plays of William Butler Yeats,* ed. M. L. Rosenthal, 133. The contemporary idiom of protecting or not offending the "virgin ears" of a young female listener also characterizes the ear as a sexualized orifice.

23. Hortense Spillers, "Interstices," 97. Jacobs's portrayal of the abused ear also recalls the imagery in *Hamlet* when the ghost describes his brother as a "serpent" who "rankly abused" him by pouring poison in his ear while he was "sleeping in [his] orchard." Thus Claudius murdered the king and "won to his shameful lust / the will of [the] most seeming-virtuous queen" (1.5.35–75). The description links images of virtue, corrupt sexuality, references to Genesis, and demonic abuse with poison administered through the ear.

24. Julia Kristeva, "Stabat Mater," 142.

25. Other Black women found it difficult to describe the sexual abuse they suffered. Mary Prince's (1831) narrative was one of the earliest to portray the sexual abuse of Black women by slave owners. See *The History of Mary Prince, a West African Slave,* in Henry Louis Gates, Jr., ed., *The Classic Slave Narrative.* Elizabeth Keckley describes four years of sexual abuse in two sentences, concluding, "I do not care to dwell upon this subject because it is one that is fraught with pain." See Elizabeth Keckley, *Behind the Scenes,* 50.

26. See Barbara G. Walker, *The Woman's Encyclopedia of Myths and Secrets,* 431–33.

27. See Ellen Bass and Laura Davis, *The Courage to Heal.*

28. Ibid., 104–10.

29. See ibid., 92–103.

30. Russell, *The Secret Trauma,* 128.

31. Ibid., 33–35.

32. Ibid., pp. 256–59.

33. Herman, *Father-Daughter Incest,* 28–29; and Russell, *The Secret Trauma,* 256–59.

34. Herman, *Father-Daughter Incest,* 116–19.

35. Ibid., 131–35.

36. See Yellin, "Text and Contexts," 271, 273–74.

37. See Rush, *The Best Kept Secret,* 62–65.

38. At the time of her first pregnancy, Linda is sixteen, and Jacobs portrays Flint's sexual abuse beginning when she was fifteen. However, by referring to "all [she] had been bearing for *years*" (58, emphasis added), Jacobs implies that the doctor may have been molesting Brent for a longer period of time than she chronicles in the narrative.

39. Comparing the way Brent resists her master's plan to make her his concubine with the idealized portrayal of concubinage in Lydia Maria Child's story "The Quadroons" (1847) reveals the radical nature of *Incidents.* By incorporating much of Child's story in the various versions of *Clotel* (1853), William Wells Brown reinforced definitions of the slave concubine as a passive and tragic beauty with a "high poetic nature." See "The Quadroons," by Lydia Maria Child, in Child, *Fact and Fiction,* and Brown, *Clotel or, The President's Daughter.*

40. See Russell, *The Secret Trauma,* 166–67; and Herman, *Father-Daughter Incest,* 100. Much of the recent research on sexual abuse focuses on incest and the way in which an older family member's molestation constitutes a betrayal of a dependent child's trust; but for the slave girl who was molested by a white man, the dynamics relating to dependency and betrayal would be quite different. More sociological and psychological research is needed on the way in which race oppression changes the dynamics and effects of sexual abuse. In contrast to the lack of social science research, contemporary novelists such as Gayle Jones, Toni Morrison, Sherley Anne Williams, and Barbara Chase-Riboud have been exploring the effects of white male sexual exploitation of African American women within slavery; Jones's *Corregidora* is especially powerful because it explores the complex effects of both incestuous and transgenerational sexual abuse.

41. Foster, *Witnessing Slavery,* 5.

42. Davis, *Women, Race, and Class,* 175.

43. Ibid., 175.

44. For some examples, see Bass and Davis, *The Courage to Heal,* 54–93.

GEORGE B. HANDLEY

"It's an Unbelievable Story": Testimony and Truth in the Work of Rosario Ferré and Rigoberta Menchú

> I'll have to talk about a lot of dead bodies.
> —Rigoberta Menchú

> Everything that they relate is gossip, lies, unabashed slander, and yet it is all true.
> —Rosario Ferré

In testimonial narratives, the particular social and temporal moment in which the speaker bears witness constitutes what we might call the speaker's personality and delimits the personal nature of the truths conveyed. Historical narratives, on the other hand, have traditionally repudiated personal truths as insufficient. These narratives might not ever employ the pronoun "we" explicitly, but they do attempt to speak in the place of a larger whole in order to construct an idea of "our" history. According to Michel de Certeau, the specific time and place of the speaker of history was not deemed important until the emergence of fields that "put the subject/producer of history into question," such as ethnic studies or women's history. Previously, historiography was an "epistemology that constructed the 'truth' of the work on the foundation of the speaker's irrelevance."[1] This positioning of the voice of historical narratives ostensibly permits the articulation of a truth that is not limited to the personality either of the witnesses cited or of the author. We are therefore led to ask, by what authority can divergent and marginalized accounts of events be meaningfully included under one collective "story" of what happened to "us"? Can sufficient attention be paid to the particularity of circumstances out of which various testimonies emerge? Is a truly democratic history in danger of being an incoherent one? After exploring some of these theoretical problems, I shall discuss the epistemological conditions out of which the testimony of Rigoberta Menchú emerges and in which it has been received, looking in particular at the narrative strategies she employs. I shall then examine the tension between testimonial truth and the writing of national history represented in the novella *Sweet Diamond Dust,* by Rosario Ferré. Through these two examples, this study attempts to suggest ways of reading that will allow us to renegotiate successfully the terms on which historical truth is established.

Testimonial Language and the "Crisis of Truth"

Critical examinations of the Holocaust, although not derived from experience in plantation societies central to the work of Menchú and Ferré, provide theories of testimony and explorations of epistemology crucial to understanding these writers. Shoshana Felman and Dori Laub, in their study *Testimony,* explain that the excessive trauma of the Holocaust has caused a "crisis of truth" because "as a relation to events . . . [the victim's testimony] seems to be composed of bits and pieces of a memory that has been overwhelmed by occurrences that have not settled into understanding or remembrance, acts that cannot be constructed as knowledge or assimilated into full cognition, events in excess of our frames of reference." [2] Jean-François Lyotard, less concerned with the psychology of witnessing than with its politics, has argued that this crisis of truth is typically the result of an exercise of power, like that of the Nazis, which attempts to eliminate the possibility of any witness to its consequences. It follows, then, that some so-called historians argue that such violence never took place. Like plaintiffs in a court of law, they demand that "in order for a place to be identified as a gas chamber, the only eyewitness I will accept would be a victim of this gas chamber; now, according to my opponent, there is no victim that is not dead; otherwise, this gas chamber would not be what he or she claims it to be. There is, therefore, no gas chamber." [3] The problem here is that the question of truth has been framed according to certain rules to which the reality of the gas chambers cannot possibly correspond; hence Lyotard's term "differend," in which there is an irreconcilable incongruity in the rules of judgment. This incongruity threatens to silence the victim of terror by demanding conformity to rules that are not applicable to the victim's case; when the victim's account varies from what is verifiable according to those rules, the plaintiff can then claim that the event did not occur. "In the differend," Lyotard says, "something 'asks' to be put into phrases, and suffers from the wrong of not being able to be put into phrases right away. This is when the human beings who thought they could use language as an instrument of communication learn through the feeling of pain which accompanies silence (and of pleasure which accompanies the invention of a new idiom), that they are summoned by language . . . to recognize that what remains to be phrased exceeds what they can presently phrase, and that they must be allowed to institute idioms which do not yet exist" (13).

Elaine Scarry has similarly explained in her study *The Body in Pain* that newly invented idioms allow the victim of pain inflicted in war or by torture to remake the world that has been undone by such violence. Pain is characterized by its "unsharability"; it dismantles the victim's capacity for language and therefore the capacity to represent that pain to others. The political advantage of physical pain is that it can deconstruct speech and transform the reality of pain into a "fiction of absolute power."[4] This process is what Scarry calls the "unmaking of the world" by which political discourse and identity are forged. The task of the victim is to regain the power of self-representation by means of the imagination, which is the counterpart to pain and allows it to enter back into discourse and be represented. Self-representation through speech "becomes the final source of self-extension; so long as one is speaking, the self extends out beyond the boundaries of the body, occupies a space much larger than the body" (33). Self-representation simultaneously unveils those fictions of power that have attempted to silence the subject. As in Lyotard's schema, this reappropriation of the discourses of truth requires the employment of a new idiom that is figural in nature. According to Scarry, "the person in pain very typically moves through a handful of descriptive words to an 'as if' construction," which is a 'work of projection into metaphor'" (172).

But this new metaphorical idiom of testimony enters discourse as "at once that which cannot be denied and that [which] cannot be confirmed. . . . To have pain is certainty; to hear about pain is to have doubt."[5] Our responsibility, then, as readers of newly invented idioms that arise from the silence of pain is not to be disturbed by their elusive, unprovable quality but to see them as new languages that must say what cannot be said and that therefore operate according to rules outside the bounds of familiar discourses of truth. This is clearly the case in psychoanalysis, where we have learned to recognize, in Felman's words, that "one does not have to possess or own the truth, in order to effectively bear witness to it."[6]

Testimony may employ metaphorical language, but that is not to say that we should read an account as a metaphor. If we were to read an account by one Auschwitz survivor as a representation that stands in the stead of other possible accounts by fellow victims, we would in effect be denying the need for further witnesses. A generous metaphorical reading can thus have its own kind of silencing effect on other needed voices and can make the reconstruction of history too easy and unproblematic. Reading testimony this way would bring us back to Lyotard's courtroom scenario where one varying account is sufficient for the prosecution to claim that the event did not occur. Metonymically, then, is perhaps how we might best read the metaphorical language of a particular testimony. Doris Sommer explains that whereas metaphor provides "an identity through substitution of one (superior) signifier for another . . ., metonymy, a lateral movement of identification through relation . . ., recognizes the possible difference between 'us' as components of a decentralized whole. It is here that we can enter as readers, invited *to be with the speaker* and *not to be her.*"[7] Thus, one account only points to the possibility of, indeed the need for, further accounts rather than seeking to stand in their stead. The reconstruction of historical events, particularly those that have resulted in full or partial erasure of their own witnessing, can only take place in a slow and continual accumulation of testimonies that must be teased out of the cultural fabric. A metonymical reading helps us to appreciate our own distance from the event so that we do not assume that simply by reading a testimony we have somehow become the eyewitness ourselves.[8]

Similar dynamics between testimony and historiography exist in post-plantation society in the Americas, the society in which both Ferré and Menchú write, but for reasons different from those related to the Holocaust. Beginning with Columbus's journals, the profound silences of Native Americans, slaves, women, and others subjugated by European imperialism have haunted American historiography and impel us to read those histories for traces of what was never written. When Columbus declares that the land he sees is a marvel, we want to know with what wonder the Arawaks first see the ships land on their beaches. And this, of course, is just the smallest beginning of a crisis of truth that permeates American writing and challenges any reconstruction of these primal scenes in American history. In response to the plantocracy's attempt to render slavery's violence invisible to historians, Elizabeth Fox-Genovese has offered an example of how we might effectively confront this crisis of historical truth. She argues that Southern history can be most appropriately understood with an inclusion of experiences from within the plantation household, a space often ignored in Southern histories, where slaves and slaveholders, men and women, played their respective roles in "the decisive relations of production and reproduction," and where in the complex web of gender and race relations many events were buried in silence. Her examination of the journals of slaveholding women and the narratives of slave women gives light to some, though not all, of those silences. Each narrative shares a silence with those that were never written, and, like a metonym, suggests "dimensions of the experience of innumerable other slave women who, remaining in slavery and being unlettered, could not easily tell their own stories."⁹ An image of the plantation household emerges, when we read each testimony metonymically, as always dependent for its meaning on the possibility, or indeed the impossibility, of other witnesses.

The historical and social conditions of plantation society necessitate this sort of metonymical reading. If largely unlettered slaves, slaveholding women, or the yeomen classes (lower class, independent farmers) got a voice, they did so by speaking from within or against the master narrative, which is by its own social and historical condition metaphorical. The theoretical term "master narrative" in the context of plantation society literally refers to the political and social discourses of the slave master, what Henry Louis Gates calls the "master's tropes." Those tropes that so powerfully influence the historiography of slavery stand in opposition to the oral language of the slaves, the "vernacular," which Gates reminds us originally meant "slave born in his master's house."¹⁰ Fox-Genovese suggests that the master's language acquires its metaphorical power from labor relations over which he is lord. When the master claims that he had "ploughed [his] field," she explains that "a man with twenty or so slaves resorted to metaphor in claiming to perform his own labor," since, of course, the slaves did the actual work (128). Trauma certainly shaped language under slavery as it did in the Holocaust, but economic and gender relations in slave society additionally helped to produce the metaphorical power of the master's language and to place testimonies from the margins in a metonymical relation to one another and to the historiography of the South.¹¹

Rigoberta Menchú and the Idiom of Testimony

I, Rigoberta Menchú reminds us that the legacy of the oppressed and silenced in plantation society has not left us. Menchú describes the struggle of her people, the Quiché Indians in Guatemala, to obtain economic and cultural freedom from the ladinos, the part-Indian but white-identified landowners, who force them to labor on plantations, and from the military forces of the government that have attempted to terrorize the Indian populations into submission. The disputes over the use of her book on reading lists at various universities are only emblematic of the continuing efforts to exclude those voices from official interpretations of American history. One example is David Stoll's paper on *I, Rigoberta Menchú* presented in 1989 at the University of California at Berkeley. After having spent some time in Guatemala conducting anthropological research on the popular resistance in northern Quiché department in Guatemala, Stoll concluded that Menchú's depictions of the crimes of the military against her family were a "literary invention" if not a complete "fabrication." [12] Specifically, he claimed that in his interviews with "hundreds" of townspeople, he found little or no testimonial evidence to support Menchú's claim that her brother was tortured and burned publicly by the military along with several other Quiché Indians. He suggests that she invented the story to gain our political sympathy. Stoll's concerns, I think, are indicative of the tendency that we have of reading testimony with the expectation that it will provide us with an unmediated truth about experience, that for the testimony to be true there must be no gap between language and event.

Ironically, the publishers list the Spanish edition of Menchú's book in the genre of *historia inmediata,* falsely suggesting that we can access past events without discursive mediation of any kind. On the back cover, they also claim that in the book "we hear the voice of an entire indigenous people that has decided to liberate itself." In her prologue, Elisabeth Burgos-Debray, the Venezuelan ethnographer who edited the book from transcriptions of an eight-day interview with Menchú, states clearly, "[Rigoberta] speaks for all the Indians of the American Continent." Stoll, then, is not the only one to read this book with this expectation; we are all invited to. To read a testimonial narrative as history is to dismiss the speaker's personal accountability, to place the speaker behind the Wizard's curtain, and to read the narrative as the metaphor for all other related experience. Thus, Stoll's job is rendered both simple and facile; all he has to do is to find variance in testimony concerning the events that Menchú relates to argue that the book is not an objective or truthful account. This variance removes her from the position assigned to her by her editors as the voice of all Native America. Such expectations about how truth must be established are not unlike the expectations of the prosecutors in Lyotard's imaginary courtroom, for they are based on a set of rules to which Menchú's account cannot possibly correspond. We must not forget that we are in a differend with respect to her text, by virtue of the academic idioms commonly employed by a university reading audience, among other things. [13] Menchú's reader must resist the temptation of reading her testimony *literally*, which would deny her the capacity to represent herself *literarily* and symbolically, a capacity that her people have been denied throughout history.

Menchú herself is keenly aware that she is engaged in a struggle over language and its meanings. She relates that not knowing Spanish makes all Indian groups in Guatemala vulnerable to deception by the ladinos and impedes their ability to speak out against such deceptions or even to speak to one another. She comments, "It's a big barrier that they've sown between us, between Indian and ladino" (119). Thus an acquisition of Spanish is central to her own empowerment. But more than a linguistic barrier separates the ladino from the Indian; it is a difference of idioms and of cultural expressions that put their cultures into a differend vis-à-vis each other. A consciousness of the impossibility of adequate communication, the inevitability of translation and consequently of betrayal, even of the uselessness of witnesses, lies at the heart of her narrative.[14] She explains that "to speak with the mayor you have to get witnesses, sign papers and then give him a mordida [bribe]. . . . To speak with the Governor you need not only witnesses from the village, and money, but also lawyers or other intermediaries to talk for you. . . . he doesn't understand the language of the people."[15] The rules of papers, of lawyers, and of the Spanish language are inaccessible to the Indian.

By speaking in the language of the ladino and submitting herself to further translations and interpretations, Menchú runs the risk of failing to negotiate into that language a representation of an indigenous cultural reality. However, she manages this negotiation, paradoxically, by means of her careful use of secrets. By withholding information, she reminds us that we do not control the narrative, that she will always remain just beyond the grasp of any reading of her: "I'm still keeping my Indian identity a secret. I'm still keeping secret what I think no one should know. Not even anthropologists or intellectuals, no matter how many books they have, can find out all our secrets" (247). She refuses to allow her use of the master's language to be completely integrated into the academic idioms that have been so antagonistic toward her culture. Against our expectations that the intimacy of testimony draws us in and, in Doris Sommer's words, "shortens the distance between the writer and the reader," her references to secrets point to the impossibility of obtaining "an inviolable truth."[16] That Menchú's people use the Bible as a "principal weapon" reveals the self-consciousness with which she intentionally reads a different meaning into the stories of Christ and Moses, and with which she portrays the Indians' political struggle as a struggle over interpretation. She explains that "Christians . . . won't understand why we give the Bible a different meaning precisely because they haven't lived our reality" (134). Her language is a signification of, a pointing to, the suffering that we can never directly know; what we read cannot be a direct presentation of the events.

Although Menchú admits that she was not a witness to all that she describes, she knows that her relatives were killed, in some cases tortured, by the military. She must either remain silent or include an account of the events in order to regain that capacity for self-representation that such brutalization threatens to destroy. Her narration of the events is an act of reappropriation of that right to bear witness that has been taken from her and from her lost relatives. Concerning her father's death, she admits quite frankly, "Neither we nor any of our compañeros can say what the mere truth is because none of those who occupied the Spanish Embassy survived" (186). Nevertheless, like those who face the unprovability of the gas chambers, she creates the effect of testimony, as John Beverley argues, in order to "give an *impression of the force of the violence* that destroyed . . . the majority of her family." [17]

It is no accident that what Stoll calls "the goriest massacre in the book" is also what he claims is a "literary invention," almost a "fabrication." [18] Why would fiction and violence of such magnitude find themselves as accomplices in the same scene? Does the fiction somehow mask something that is less gory? Is it a form of exaggeration, a political ploy to pull at our heart strings? Stoll admits that there must be a "kernel of truth to it," but he finds that kernel buried beneath Menchú's inventions, rather than made apparent precisely because of them. A look at her inventions will prove my point. In her description of her brother's capture and torture, she alludes to Christ's betrayal. There was a man who "had been a compañero, a person who had always collaborated and who had been in agreement with us. But they offered him . . . fifteen dollars to turn my brother in, and so he did." [19] The public burning of the already tortured bodies of the victims is performed in front of their families as Christ was killed before Mary and the disciples. Like the water that poured from Christ's body when it was pierced in the side, their clothing was "damp from the moisture oozing out of their bodies" (177). The soldiers strip the bodies naked and cut up the clothing as did the Roman soldiers to Christ. They point to the marks on the victims' now naked bodies as symbols of the punishment that comes to those who are "subversives." But in her representation of the bodies with their marks and deformations, she reappropriates those marks, like the nail marks on Christ, as symbols of the victims' innocence and of the brutality of the government's power and of her own pain at her loss.

Menchú recounts that at an early age she recognized that "it will be my turn to talk about a lot of dead bodies [me tocará narrar muchos cadáveres]" (177). By dragging the bodies into the space of representation, she can deflate the attempt to create political power out of their objectification.[20] In the very act of narrating the disintegration of the bodies, the holes, the missing limbs, she is constructing a bond of common pain with all those involved so that the event comes to be about their plight as a people, rendering the identity of the individual families and bodies less relevant. Rather than standing in the stead of other voices, her story calls out to them by implication: "You don't think that the grief is just for yourself but for all the relatives of the others: God knows if one's relatives were found there or not! Anyway they were Indians, our brothers" (180). In this way the act of telling the story serves to break down the divisive and alienating barriers that political violence seeks to establish and maintain.

Paradoxically, Menchú's language about the suffering of others becomes an aesthetic representation of her own suffering in the passage where she most explicitly describes their pain. Bakhtin says that an ethical response to another's suffering begins when we enter into their world in order to experience their pain; but aesthetic activity begins "at the point when we return into ourselves, when we return to our own place outside the suffering person, and start to form and consummate the material we derived from projecting ourselves into the other and experiencing him from within himself."[21] We "enrich the event of [the other's] life . . . by providing a new, creative standpoint, a standpoint inaccessible to [the other]" (71). This aesthetic response is fully ethical because we can then offer "not a cry of pain, but a word" to ease the pain, an act that creates new meaning rather than merely duplicating the same pain. We have the same ethical responsibility when we read Menchú's representation of her brother's pain; we must exercise our aesthetic sensibilities so that, in Elaine Scarry's words, the text can "remake human sentience" and alter our "alive percipience."[22] George Yúdice has argued that it is this remaking of the reader's sensibilities, what he calls "concientización," that makes Menchú's testimony "ethical and aesthetic at the same time"; its aesthetic qualities draw us in so as to alter us ethically.[23]

When we listen to the words that describe her brother's torture, keeping in mind that what she relates she cannot possibly have seen herself, we see how her language points to her own imagined position outside her brother's pain and how, out of necessity and out of mourning, she has taken that pain to an aesthetic level. The continual repetition of "my her-manito" calls attention not to her brother but to her own exteriority with respect to him, not to the event but to her loss, as if this appellation calls back what is lost and yet at the same time concedes the failure to recall what is no longer retrievable. She says: "My hermanito fell, he couldn't protect his face. Immediately, the first part to begin to bleed was the face of my hermanito [Caía mi hermano, no podía defender la cara. Inmediata-mente, lo primero se empezó a sangrar fue la cara de mi hermanito]." A few lines later, in trying to understand exactly "how they died, what tor-tures they inflicted on them from start to finish," she declares, "It's an unbelievable story. . . . they took my hermanito away, bleeding from dif-ferent places on his body [Es una historia increíble. . . . llevaron a mi her-manito, quien soltaba sangre en diferentes partes de su cuerpo]." [24] The responsibility for the potential unbelievability of her narrative of this death is transferred to the violence itself; however unbelievable her story may be, it is nothing compared with the unbelievability of the violence that has forced her to narrate such things.

My own "concientización" in response to Menchú's testimony is to want to rewrite it as poetry in order to bring out the figural language that lies embedded in the rhetoric of testimony. [25] Here is an example, in two stanzas:

Le amarraban,	They tied him up,
le amarraban los testículos,	they tied his testicles,
los órganos de mi hermano,	the sexual organs of my hermanito,
atrás con un hilo	behind with a string
y le mandaban a correr.	and they forced him to run.
Y la cara, ya no veía,	And the face, it no longer saw,
en los ojos,	in the eyes,
había entrado hasta las piedras	even stones were forced
en los ojos	in the eyes
de mi hermanito.	of my hermanito. [26]

In the second stanza, the Spanish verb *veía* leaves the subject unnamed. That her brother could no longer see is confused with the fact that she also could no longer see her brother, that she is blind to the event by virtue of the violence that blinds him. The event has entered into her eyes like the *piedras* making it both invisible to her and inescapably before her eyes and part of the way she perceives the world.

Menchú's articulated grief "is a testimony to [her family] because they never exposed their lives when their grief was great too." [27] In the sense

that it implies the existence of a larger, absent whole, her pain is a metonymy of theirs. We can in this way read Menchú's work as a fragment of
the whole without pretending to know exactly what that whole is. In a
recent interview, Menchú said, "In the book there are fragments, and I
hope that one day we can redocument it so as to publish it anew, perhaps
for our grandchildren, possibly after we have included in the book a series
of other stories, testimonies, and experiences."[28] We need therefore to
hear how testimonial language bears witness to the rupture of a frame of
reference, as Felman and Laub's study has shown, and must resist reading
Menchú's testimony as something that captures in entirety the events it
describes. We can see the absurdity of complaints about her "unfactual"
and politically motivated book being on college reading lists; that there
are not more testimonies like hers available to us that can help to fill in
the innumerable unwritten chapters of American history is more worthy
of our indignation.

Testimony and Nation Making

Ernest Renan once said, "Forgetting, I would even go so far as to say
historical error, is a crucial factor in the creation of a nation."[29] The question is, what happens to national history and cultural identity when silenced or forgotten voices like Menchú's reenter the discursive framework
of those identities? Rosario Ferré's novella *Sweet Diamond Dust* (Maldito
amor) is one example of the way in which the introduction of previously
silenced voices into the national discourse can break down the opposition
between the impersonal narrative of historiography and the personal testimonials it attempts to preclude. Ferré's novella effectively enacts the unmasking effect that testimonial language can have on the writing of history. By exposing historiography's own historicity and personality, she
demonstrates that the speaker's personality will inevitably delimit in some
way what he or she claims has happened.

Rosario Ferré, who began publishing fiction in 1976, belongs to a
recent surge of women writers who have revised the national imagination
in Latin America from a postmodern feminist perspective. She and her
contemporaries have continued the revisions of national history begun
when the male writers of Latin America exploded onto the international
literary scene in the 1960s and 1970s in a movement known as the Boom.
Sweet Diamond Dust attempts to revise the master narrative of Puerto
Rico that has been heavily influenced by the hacendado class. In her introduction to the Spanish edition of the novella, Ferré chronicles the Puerto

Rican cultural imagination offered by its political leaders and novelists since the nineteenth century, a history that has idealized "the romantic life of the hacienda and its male owners," and explains that her work attempts to "parody that vision of history and of the master's life on the hacienda, to wrest from that myth its power to confer authority and identity."[30]

The narrative structure of the novella traces the social and historical changes in Puerto Rico over the past century by moving among multiple narrators from different sectors of Puerto Rican society affected by those changes. We can therefore read the work as a reflection on the conditions that helped to produce the various platforms for a Puerto Rican identity. Don Hermenegildo begins the narrative with an attempt to found a national identity on the plantation myth by writing a novel about his close friend, one of Puerto Rico's patrician statesmen and sugar mill owners, Ubaldino de la Valle. Similar to historiography generally, Hermenegildo's memorial is characterized by its attempt to speak impersonally in the name of a larger whole. The "we" of Hermenegildo's account are the possessors of a collective national memory, but by the end of the first chapter, his inclusive "we" betrays him: " 'Well-to-do families lived in elegant houses, with wood-carved lace fans. . . . At that time, Guamaneños of the upper crust all belonged to the same clan. There were blood ties among the most distant families, and *we* always gave one another financial and moral support, so as to better manage *our* sugarcane haciendas.' "[31] The impersonal and collective "we" thus quickly breaks down into a personal and particular one, that of the plantation owners. In the narratives that follow, Ferré exposes the interest of this false plurality in keeping the Diamond Dust property away from women and illegitimate children in order to legitimate the national heritage. The subsequent failure of Hermenegildo's narrative to trace the patriarchal line of legitimate authority, in what Ferré calls "the Spanish tradition of mayorazgo," is also its failure to sustain itself as history. Ironically, Hermenegildo's novel is the only narrative in quotation marks. This redaction that assigns his voice the responsibility of time and place and marks it as rhetorical rather than metaphorical reveals the rhetoric of historiography as characteristically patriarchal and nationalistic rather than objective and true.

While Hermenegildo ostensibly offers us an objective and historical point of view from outside the plantation household, Ferré provides us with a variety of testimonials from within the various spaces of the plantation household that give us a clearer appreciation of the place of Hermenegildo's narrative within that history. An examination of Titina's narrative illustrates these deconstructive powers of testimonial language. The absence of quotation marks for this narrative and the other family narratives suggests that these accounts of the family history incorporate Hermenegildo's narrative within their own boundaries rather than the other way around. As the last slave from the plantation days, Titina's intimate place in the household allows her privileged information about the family history. Titina's mother suckled Ubaldino, Titina ate from his plate and silver spoon, and she has heard most of the intimate talk between the family members. Indeed, unlike Hermenegildo, who attempts to hide his own particular time and place as a speaker, Titina refers to her intimate proximity to the speech she reports, bearing witness not just to the information she relays but to her own accountability for that information. She makes this clear, for example, in explaining his anti-American sentiments: "Ubaldino wasn't just going to let the newcomers take away what it had taken him years to rescue from the wrong hands, as he used to say to me *when I poured out his coffee in the morning.* . . . For one must be a generous host to them, he'd say to me *as I handed him his hat and his briefcase,* but one must never bed with them" (23, emphasis mine). She explains that "Manifest Destiny" and other words were "part of the vocabulary with which he damned the heavens every morning, as he shaved, washed his face, and combed his hair *before the mirror I held up to his face*" (22).

The real mirror being held up to her master's face is, of course, Titina's testimony. Her clear recollection of the master's tropes and the specificity of her personality confessed in her testimony unmask the universality of Puerto Rican patriotic rhetoric and reveal it to be the specificity of Ubaldino's personality. In an extraordinary twist, Ferré embeds the hacendado's national discourse within an account of the labor relations that make that discourse possible in the first place. Titina's speech reverses the metaphorical erasure of labor relations in the master's narrative. Just as the slave master claims "I ploughed my field," we can imagine Ubaldino, were he relating the events of that morning, saying, "I poured myself a cup of coffee," or "I got my hat and briefcase." Titina's narrative cannot be so dishonest; she cannot avoid revealing those relations, for they provide the stuff of her narrative. And once Titina suggests the possibility that Ubaldino's son, Nicolás, was murdered by someone in the family, Hermenegildo has to confess: "Every family in Guamaní hides a skeleton in the cupboard and Ubaldino's is probably no different. But it's better to forget these unhappy events, erasing them with the edifying accounts of his heroic exploits. Every country that aspires to become a nation needs its heroes, its eminent civic and moral leaders, and if it doesn't have them, it's our duty to invent them. Fortunately this is not the case with Ubaldino, who was truly a paragon of chivalrous virtue, and whose story I have already begun to relate in my book" (24–25). Ferré's fictional introduction of a previously silenced voice in the national discourse thus forces the master narrative to confess its lies, even if it does not make the truth any clearer. Like all national discourses, Hermenegildo's narrative is a careful and deliberate act of forgetting history. Titina's story evokes the need for further investigation and witnesses, and in this evocative sense we can say that Titina's narrative functions metonymically; unlike the master narrative, her story suggests other possibilities, rather than hiding them.

Hermenegildo investigates Titina's allegations, exposing himself and his reader to further versions of the family history normally marginalized in a national romance such as his own, each version informed or "slanted" relative to the positions that these characters hold in the family and in the national economy. Unlike Nicolás, the first-born who is educated abroad, the younger brother, Aristides, receives an education at home and in English. As a new Puerto Rican national, Aristides advocates an Americanized and modernized vision of his country's future and portrays Nicolás as an emasculated homosexual whose death was a suicide. He believes that his mother's will, which bequeaths the property to the mulatta Gloria, ought to be torn up because it was written out of vengeance. His mother, Laura, married into the family from a lower-class background and, as the household matron, struggles against the tradition and strength of the patriarchal order. From her we learn essential details apparently repressed in the family line: Ubaldino was not a strong leader; his father, Don Julio, was a horse tamer and a black man, a fact that undermines the family's claim to "blood purity"; and Laura allowed Gloria, who came to take care of the ailing Ubaldino, to sleep with Ubaldino so that she could shield herself from Ubaldino's venereal disease. Laura's vision of national identity is one that celebrates Puerto Rico's possibility as a gateway between North and South America, between English and Spanish heritage, and that portrays Gloria's child, named Nicolasito in honor of Laura's dead son, as the confluence of the two hemispheres, and Gloria herself as the appropriate heiress of this new mission of the island. Finally, Gloria's version of the family history represents the vengeful energy of those affected most negatively by racial, gender, and class abuses, because as a lower-class mulatta she is used by this family for their competing political purposes. Gloria declares the end of Hermenegildo's novel, rejects the will, and burns the hacienda. She insists on a narrative authority that is independent of any interest in the burden of patrimony.

Until Gloria's final narrative, the cumulative effect of these versions seems to be rhetorical; although they together cast doubt on the master narrative, no single version takes its place because no one person has access to the truth. As the testimonies accumulate so does our appreciation both of the ways in which people lie—lies being the real national heritage—and of the need that each account establishes for an additional witness to counter what has been said before. We have an increasing expectation that no matter how true one narrative appears, it will be discredited in the future. There is thus a kind of nostalgia for the truth in Ferré's novella, but, as Ellen Friedman has argued of feminine postmodernism, it is a nostalgia for the future. Friedman explains that, unlike male modernism, which tends to romanticize the past and to betray a nostalgia for the master narrative, "women's works of modernity . . . show little nostalgia for the old paternal order, little regret for the no longer presentable. The master narratives are not buried in the unconscious of these texts. . . . Although all the texts of modernity express a longing for the unpresentable, female texts often evoke the unpresentable as the not yet presented." [32]

Because Gloria usurps Hermenegildo's novel and concludes the novella, with no one following to contradict her, her testimony is the most powerfully suggestive of future, not past, possibilities. Gloria says to Titina, "Facts have a strange way of facing down fiction, Titina, and if Don Hermenegildo's aborted novel was to have been a series of stories that contradicted one another like a row of falling dominoes, our story, the one we've taken the authority to write, will eradicate them all, because it will be the only one in which word and deed will finally be loyal to each other, in which a true correspondence between them will finally be established" (82).[33] Gloria's distinction between word and deed is highly suggestive of the distinction between historiography and testimony to which I have already alluded. To record that something has happened is the intended realm of historical narrative, whereas testimonial narratives additionally record the fact that someone saw *that something* happen. This difference indicates a slippage between events and the language that reports those events, a slippage that signals the inability of historiography to recapture the past fully. If word and deed finally became "loyal to each other" in Gloria's narrative, her narrative would become History, a new master narrative, as it were, and her location in time and place would again become irrelevant. Ferré neatly avoids this epistemological trap in her apocalyptic ending to the novel. She suggests by extrapolation that when there is no need for further narrative, when we achieve the fulfillment of truth about the past and about national identity that we are looking for, then there is no longer any nation. Such a fulfillment, which would redeem a once helplessly nostalgic love of nation, can only be achieved at the cost of the end of nationhood altogether and the total erasure of history, an impossibility signified by the burning embers of the Diamond Dust hacienda. As long as we continue to draw national and cultural boundaries, love of nation will remain a bitter and cursed love, which Ferré's Spanish title, *Maldito amor,* suggests, because there will always be the need for someone new to tell someone else that something different happened. If there is to be any fulfillment of our longings for national and cultural origins, we must content ourselves with an incessant need to read yet another witness to history.

Notes

I wish to thank Julio Ramos and VèVè Clark, whose teaching inspired these ideas, Francine Masiello for her encouragement, and Mark Wrathall and Jennifer Sylvor for their help in editing. The sole responsibility for the content of the essay is mine.

1. Michel de Certeau, "History: Ethics, Science, and Fiction," 146.
2. Shoshana Felman and Dori Laub, *Testimony,* 5.
3. Jean-François Lyotard, *The Differend,* 3–4.
4. Elaine Scarry, *The Body in Pain,* 27.
5. Ibid., 13. This double-edged quality of language occurs when we attempt to represent private experience, particularly experiences of pain, according to Wittgenstein in *Philosophical Investigations* (89). When language refers only to our "immediate private sensation . . . another person cannot understand the language," but as soon as we learn to use words like "pain" to make these sensations, such as crying, more accessible to others, we fail to communicate those sensations: "The verbal expression of pain replaces crying and *does not describe it.*" Thus, the more our language strives toward communicability about private experience, the more that experience becomes inaccessible to another person.
6. Felman and Laub, *Testimony,* 15.
7. Doris Sommer, "Sin secretos," 142. Translation and emphasis mine.
8. In using the word "distance," I do not imply apathy and inaction, especially with respect to testimonies whose urgency asks a reader for sympathy or political action. My intention is simply to put the process of witnessing and responding to that witness in slow motion so that we can see what kinds of identifications with the text will be most productive and ethical. I want to insist that the tension between our identification with testimony and our own position outside it must not be collapsed into merely one or the other.
9. Elizabeth Fox-Genovese, *Within the Plantation Household,* 31.
10. Gates, *Signifying Monkey,* 52. "Master narrative" additionally refers to the acts of narration by the white male ruling class throughout the Americas that contributed to national and cultural identities based upon their positions of privilege. Ronald

Takaki's *Iron Cages* provides an example of how in the nineteenth century the master narrative was manifest in the U.S. not only in the public documents of books, editorials, speeches, and newspapers but also in the private documents of letters and diaries. By casting women and racial minorities as morally and emotionally inferior, these narrative acts attempted to preclude categorically the truth of any counternarratives.

11. Emilia Viotti da Costa emphasizes that "the concern with production and profit and the need to protect his capital imposed a limit on the slaveowner's violence that never existed in any concentration camp or prison." ("Slave Images and Realities," 300). Of course, Holocaust prisoners were also part of an economy of profit, and under some slave systems and certainly since abolition, many whites have expended considerable effort for the removal and destruction of Blacks. However, the concentration camps were specifically designed to eliminate the Jews and others, whereas in the Americas, the maintenance of the slave system for close to 400 years gave the slave-owning classes economic and social survival and has left a social legacy where "wealth, rank, color and legal status . . . generated conflicting expectations and behavior" (297).

12. David Stoll, "*I, Rigoberta Menchú* and Human Rights Reporting in Guatemala," 2.

13. Of course, a tremendous linguistic distance separates us from Menchú. In this essay, I use both the English translation by Anne Wright and my own translation, depending on which I feel is closest to the original Spanish. We must keep in mind, however, that, in either case, we are reading an edited translation of a transcription from the spoken Spanish, which is Menchú's second language, only recently learned at the time of the transcription.

14. In the Spanish edition, the title translates literally to "I call myself Rigoberta Menchú and this is how my conscience was born." The Spanish *conciencia* also implies "consciousness" or "awareness." The conscious act of employing language to name and represent herself is simultaneous with her coming to understand how the discourses around her have silenced her people.

15. Wright, trans., *I, Rigoberta Menchú*, 102.

16. Sommer, "Sin Secretos", 135.

17. John Beverley, "Introducción," 15. Translation and emphasis mine.

18. Stoll says that in the Amnesty International human rights reports there is no documentation of a public death and burning of any young men that would have included her brother. Just one week before the announcement of Menchú's Nobel Peace Prize in October 1992, Amnesty International did in fact release documentation of the death and torture of Menchú's brother, Patrocinio, that she describes. I do not believe, however, that the truth value of her representation of the event was ever at stake, nor do I think its documentation should dissuade us from appreciating her powerful use of metaphor.

19. *Me llamo Rigoberta*, (ed. Burgos-Debray), 173; my translation.

20. George Yúdice argues that hegemonic cultures often represent themselves in this "hyperreal space of death where the cadaver nourishes representation" by virtue of its disappearance, ("Testimonio y concientización," 217; my translation). It is, of course, in the same space of death that victims must be called upon to "narrar cadáveres" in order to unveil that very hegemony. Albert Camus also maintained that the role of the artist was to "demolish the deceptive image of history as an abstraction (as

an ideological or statistical, administrative picture in which death becomes invisible) by bearing witness to the body" (Felman and Laub, *Testimony,* 108).

21. M. M. Bakhtin, *Art and Answerability,* 26.

22. Scarry, *The Body in Pain,* 307.

23. Yúdice, "Testimonio," 222.

24. Burgos ed., 177; translation mine.

25. In a recent interview conducted by Alice Britton and Kenya Dworkin, Menchú explained that her political tasks at the moment outweigh the possibility of pursuing future literary projects. What interests me is how she suggests that the task of bearing testimony is not simply a political project but also an aesthetic one, that it is analogous to that of a poet. When one participates in political projects, she says, "it is very difficult to become a writer, a poet at the same time." (See Alice A. Brittin and Kenya Carmen Dworkin, "Rigoberta Menchú: 'Con quien nos comunicamos?'" 4; translation mine. The interview includes a poem by Menchú entitled "Patria abnegada," in which she aestheticizes her brother's mutilation, her mother's torture, and her father's burning.

26. *Me llamo Rigoberta;* my translation.

27. *I, Rigoberta Menchú,* 199.

28. Brittin and Dworkin, interview, 18; my translation.

29. Ernest Renan, "What Is a Nation?"

30. Rosario Ferré, *Maldito amor,* 10; translation mine.

31. Rosario Ferré, *Sweet Diamond Dust,* Ferré translation, 6; emphasis mine. All subsequent quotations in English from the novella are from this edition.

32. Ellen Friedman, "Where Are the Missing Contents?" 242.

33. This sentence does not appear in the Spanish edition of the novella. Presumably Ferré added it in her translation as a way of emphasizing the significance of Gloria's narrative coup.

KRISTI DALVEN

Native Witness, White "Translator": The Problematics of Tran/scribing in Elsa Joubert's *Poppie Nongena*

> If I have experienced the life of a black at close quarters why shouldn't I write about it? . . . You write about life as you experience it. . . . I think the blacks probably think the whites cannot write with success about them because they don't know, have not experienced their lives. But an author uses his imagination. . . . We in South Africa, we live—from childhood days—in such close proximity and we share our lives with black people. I cannot see how we cannot be allowed to write about them.
>
> —Elsa Joubert

Elsa Joubert, white South African writer, seems not to be able to escape the language of othering, of speaking gaps, polarities of "I" and "them." She seems disturbingly defensive in her assumption that she as a middle-class, privileged white Afrikaner can "know" the lives of native South Africans who have been enslaved under the conditions of apartheid. "If," she says, "I have experienced the life of a black at close quarters why shouldn't I write about it?"[1] There is an arrogance in this statement that makes me cringe, that makes me want to dismiss her as racist, not because she dares to write "the other" but because she falls into the language of us and them, leaving unacknowledged the propensity for a dominant (white) "us" to usurp the voices of an oppressed (black) "them."

But in reading Joubert's "novel" *Poppie Nongena*, I find something that is both valuable and necessary: an attempt, despite limitations, despite the blindness of apartheid, to speak toward as much truth as possible. In this richly complicated book, Joubert casts herself in the role of interviewer-researcher-documenter, and then ingenuously pretends to disengage herself, as "author," from the text, so that this purportedly "real" woman, Poppie, may speak her own story. Joubert blurs genre, claiming the work simultaneously as fiction and nonfiction. Can we be sure that this is a documentary based on actual interviews with an actual woman (whose name has been changed)? Or is the documentary mode only a novelist's ploy, much like that used in Margaret Atwood's *The Handmaid's Tale?* Though some critics have labeled the book a fiction, and others have accepted Joubert's paradoxical definition of the work as a kind of factual novel, I hope to show that the notions of Joubert as "authorially disengaged" and of Poppie as "real woman" must be questioned. For the narrative style, as I see it, invites the reader to read Poppie as a highly fictionalized amalgam: Poppie becomes teller of her tale as well as character in a story. When the "authentic" documentary qualities of *Poppie Nongena* combine with the inescapable fact of Joubert's novelizing presence, what we are left with is an important book that functions simultaneously as an act of appropriation and a complicated gesture toward a deconstruction of that appropriation.[2] In this book, Joubert reveals both the possibilities in and the dangers of mediating, of writing across toward the "other," of tran/scribing: she proffers a flawed gesture toward healing and change.

Similar in function and effect to Harriet Beecher Stowe's *Uncle Tom's Cabin,* Joubert's book, one of the few works that embodies black South African experience for a white Afrikaner audience, can be credited with having awakened the consciousness of whites to their systematic oppression of blacks, and perhaps even with having helped make possible the overturning of apartheid. In her attempt as a white Afrikaner woman to write the lives of black women (and men), to speak to the horrors of racism, Joubert enacts what Gloria Anzaldúa calls a travesía: "Every increment of consciousness, every step forward is a travesia, a crossing."[3] And yet, like the white superiority and negative racial stereotyping that mar the historically revolutionary or at least "consciousness-raising" aspects of *Uncle Tom's Cabin, Poppie Nongena* is also marked by a dangerous blindness. Anzaldúa, in *Making Face, Making Soul,* calls this phenomenon "selective reality": "Racism and internalized oppression result from the 'editing' of reality. . . . Whites not naming themselves white presume their universality; an unmarked race is a sign of Racism unaware of itself, a 'blanked-out' Racism."[4]

Poppie Nongena was originally published in Afrikaans in 1978 under the title *Die Swerfjare van Poppie Nongena* (The Long Journey of Poppie Nongena), and was translated by Joubert herself for publication in English in 1980.[5] It is the story of one woman, Poppie Nongena, as she struggles to find a place to live, to have a good marriage to a man whom she chooses for herself, to make a living, to feed and protect her family, to rear her children and send them to school so that their lives will be better than hers, and to keep the dangerous world at bay, away from her children. The narrative pattern of this "success despite hardship" story is reminiscent of the Horatio Alger myth, the pursuit of the American dream. But in this story there is a crucial difference: Poppie is an urban black Xhosa, a native South African woman born in the mid-1900s into a particular violence known as apartheid.

Poppie, "the cleverest one" of her family, was forced to drop out of school at an early age: "From her ninth year Poppie took care of the children mama had by bute Mbatane, but she never stopped reading" (48). Joubert's insertion, "but she never stopped reading," seems odd; we never actually observe Poppie reading a book. But Joubert apparently wants the readers of this "novel" to think of Poppie as someone who is not only smart but also strong and independent. Again and again, Poppie's refrain is, "I'm strong now."[6] And if it were not for such difficulties as pass laws, laws that prohibit where, when, and how Blacks can live and work, what Poppie casually and disturbingly refers to as "the pass business" (96), we would find Poppie's life in some ways parallel to that of the ultimate Cosmopolitan Woman: avid reader, money earner, homemaker, respectful follower of family traditions and customs, yet also progressive enough to "know" that in times of sickness, modern medicine is better than witch doctoring. But in Poppie's world, there are such things as pass laws. The system of apartheid allows Poppie only the pretense of independence. From this "pass business," she cannot escape.

For regardless of how strong she is, Poppie eventually comes to a painful conclusion, perhaps the most politically activist stance she takes. "I can't break the law with my hands" (185), she says, suggesting that someone could and should, somehow. But Poppie—marked with a passive fatalism that springs from a kind of Christian tolerance for suffering—is not a revolutionary or an activist. We often see Poppie in church: "Lord have mercy on her soul. She felt strength rising in her as she repeated these words, she was strong once more. Life had not defeated her, she could get up again" (172).

Poppie believes "the church is my mainstay. . . . As long as I remain true to the church, the Lord will be with me" (173). Unable to conceptualize the extent of her oppression, Poppie relies on religion to ease the burden of her life. She is strong, a worker, but her sphere is an apoliticized domestic one. The never ending struggle for a home, the struggle to educate her children, to feed her family—struggles and goals and dreams with which most white Afrikaners could identify—take precedence over any theorizing about or empathy with the revolution to abolish apartheid by the sheer force of human hands.

Some call the text a novel, and some a biography. Joubert plays with the terminology in her note "To the Reader." In this, she says that what she is setting down is a documentary-like biography-history of the "actual life story of a black woman living in South Africa today. Only her name, Poppie Rachel Nongena . . . is invented. The facts were related to me not only by Poppie, but by members of her immediate family and her extended family or clan, and they cover one family's experience over the past forty years." This might be true, but we must remember that Poppie's testimony, however "real," is only one voice, and that it is mediated. Joubert, wanting to write about the people she calls "Them," seems to have been looking for a way to represent the problems of native black women suffering under the system of apartheid when she stumbled upon "Poppie." Scholars such as Jean Marquard make the assumption that "every event in the book is authentic and as told by Poppie."[7] But Joubert, though she maintains in her note to the reader that her book is factual, actual truth, also calls her work a "novel," which implies a deliberately created, self-consciously literary invention. I believe the only way to read Poppie is to read her as a creation, as a well-researched, historically based fictional construct, a character in a story. Both Poppie and Joubert have quietly hidden, unspoken prejudices, and to speak of this text as a documentary without evaluating its many moments of racist blindness is to fail to envision the possibilities for transgressing, moving beyond apartheid mentality.

Joubert introduces herself as the interviewer of an actual Poppie Nongena, whom she is presenting to us "directly," without explicitly acknowledging the tendency of the mediator to edit, appropriate, and take exclusive possession of meaning, of reading the world. So how can I respond to Joubert both generously and critically? When the testimony of the "native" woman witness, the "original speaker"—who for a myriad of reasons has not, does not, or cannot theorize her story for herself—is transcribed by a white woman, what are the implications? How can I, as a European American feminist, respond to this mediation without ignoring and thus taking on its multiple problems?

The elements in the novel that make me want to dismiss it as an act of appropriation, as well as the elements that work to draw me in to Poppie's story, can be examined through Joubert's inventive and complex narrative techniques. The novel alternates among several different points of view. We read the formulation, "Poppie says," which implies a listener-interviewer, as often as we read "said Poppie" or the conventionally novel-istic turn of phrase, "Poppie thought." Moments of novelistic omniscience are revealed in sentence formations such as, "The pass business was some-thing quite new to Poppie" (88). The simultaneous use of these varied narrative stances—conventional first-person past tense, conventional third-person past tense, and the as-told-to interjecting third-person pres-ent tense—allows Joubert to speak in turn as the well-researched charac-ter "Poppie," (the past-situated "I"); to speak as the other-than-Poppie (the narrator, the voice that novelizes and employs such novelizing formu-lations as, "Poppie thought"); and to speak as the in-the-flesh I am Pop-pie, telling you the reader my story right now right here even as I am being novelized, and even as I novelize: here it is. This interjecting present-tense voice, which, for example, states, "I don't know what it was that year, says Poppie, but all the people's small babies died" (85), has the effect of keeping the story in the now, the still-occurring, and making the reader-listener feel as if she were in a room with Poppie, part of a community, talking forthrightly about how it is. Past and present tense mix, blurring the distinctions between oral and written narratives, and between actual lived experiences defined by Poppie and dramatized novelistic, imagined experiences defined by Joubert.

And yet however "factual" the testimony is in *Poppie Nongena,* Jou-bert's use of different points of view, especially the as-told-to narrative device, can be read not only as reportage but as an act of appropriation, of displacement, of re-presenting and usurping meaning. Joubert, though she purports to give us, as truth, the "actual" native voice, seems at the same time to want to blur the distinction between Poppie and herself as "author," thereby disguising the fact that the testimony we are reading is mediated. The lack of any quotation marks in *Poppie Nongena* further erases evidence of mediation. Paradoxically, by affecting the presence of three "different" voices and by commingling these three voices, Joubert seems to be calling attention to the fact that she is not Poppie, that the testimony is mediated.

The as-told-to device, which implies a listener and allows the reader to partake in a dialogue, also works to put the reader in a position of authority, for there is a great deal that Poppie leaves unquestioned. Position-ing the reader as more knowledgeable than the narrator is a convention of fiction, but in presumed testimony such as this, there is an inescapable po-tential for elitism. It is true that, by having the reader become more angered by the forces that beset Poppie than Poppie is herself, the narrative might politicize an Afrikaner audience into responding to the horrors of apart-heid. But this strategy is problematic in that it privileges the white reader as implicit agent for change, ignoring native movements to dismantle apartheid.

The question, then, is how are we to read Poppie? It is hard not to like her, this Ultimate Mother. And yet to read her, as Margaret Lenta does in "Independence as the Creative Choice in Two South African Fictions," as a woman with a "career," an "independent decision maker," a heroine who achieves "economic independence," as someone who has "transformed herself from a woman dependent on her group to a fully independent individual," and as one who "has been able to respond positively to the changes" (are these "changes" forced relocation? the breakup of her family? vicissitudes in the unnecessary, absolute reign of oppression?) is to leave racism unsaid.[8] Though articles written about this book support the fact that Poppie is a historically documented "real" person whose identity is protected by Joubert, Poppie's realness does not allow us to forget that her testimony is re-presented. In this book we cannot ignore the multiple problems of the not-original speaker tran/scribing the native voice. Although Lenta notes that "Poppie is finally crushed by the operations of laws which regard her and her people merely as units of the alien population, to be disposed of to the advantage of the legislating group" (47), in reading Poppie's "career" as a triumph of creative independence Lenta diminishes the very real horrors of apartheid.

In speaking both as and for the native voice, Joubert simultaneously and problematically reveals the dangerous tendency of the culturally dominant to define the world. Though her stylistic maneuvers and narrative choices suggest that Joubert means to draw attention to her novelization of Poppie—the I am her, but I am not her—when reading *Poppie Nongena* we must be aware that the words we read are mediated. There are places in *Poppie Nongena,* persistent and disturbing, where the effacing of difference by Joubert is rendered especially troublesome because we have no way of distilling the purported "real" story from Joubert's presence as novelizer, or from the silences imposed by Joubert's and "Poppie's" blanked-out racism.[9] Evidence of these difficult moments is especially apparent in Poppie's attitudes toward Blacks who speak Afrikaans, toward Bantu education, and toward "those raw people" (135) of "Kaffirland," as well as in her absolute, unwavering fatalism that is a repudiation of activism.

Mark Mathabane, in his autobiography, *Kaffir Boy,* writes:

> A million times I wondered why the sparse library at my tribal school did not carry books like *Treasure Island,* why most of the books we read had tribal points of view. I would ask teachers and would be told that under the Bantu Education law black children were supposed to acquire a solid foundation in tribal life, which would prepare them

for a productive future in their respective homelands. In this way the dream of Dr. Verwoerd, prime minister of South Africa and the architect of Bantu Education, would be realized, for he insisted that "the native child must be taught subjects which will enable him to work with and among his own people; therefore there is no use misleading him by showing him the green pastures of European society, in which he is not allowed to graze. Bantu Education should not be used to create imitation whites." How I cursed Dr. Verwoerd and his law for prescribing how I should feel and think.[10]

I quote Mathabane, not to explore his interest in Western "classics," but to show that passive respect for Bantu Education is certainly not universal among the suppressed black South African majority. Poppie seems only to care that her children get an education, untroubled by the fact that the education potentially available to black children in apartheid South Africa is legally separate and inferior. Challenging the inferiority of this education is not one of Poppie's concerns. Indeed, she seems contemptuous of everything that has to do with Black political activism against apartheid. Of the protest and massacre at Soweto, Poppie observes: "The children repeated: we don't want to be taught Afrikaans no more. When the teachers asked why they said that . . . the children said: we heard them saying that in Soweto schools and now we say it too" (307). Poppie thinks the children are, like parrots, only repeating the slogans that they have heard, slogans that apparently have no intrinsic value. We readers are privy to the things the children say, because Poppie says, "I stood listening" (307). The formulation of direct observation requires the reader to take what Poppie says (and what Joubert "reports") as "truth." Again, we must remind ourselves that this "truth" is mediated and possibly marred by its own racial blind spots.

Mathabane prefaces his memoir with a definition of the word Kaffir: "The word *Kaffir* is of Arabic origin. It means 'infidel.' In South Africa it is used disparagingly by most whites to refer to Blacks. It is the equivalent of the term *nigger*. I was called a 'Kaffir' many times" (xiii). Poppie and her family speak of Kaffirland, the tribal lands, with dread and disdain, seemingly unconcerned with the white racist implications inherent in this language of othering. When Poppie is to go to Herschel, the tribal land from which her husband comes, she says: "I was scared of the strange people and didn't look around too much, for the hut looked so dark and frightening. . . . It was a horrible place, I'm not used to such houses" (80). In fact, a disturbing fear of and plain dislike for the rural country "tribal" people is a recurring theme in the book. But when Mosie, Poppie's brother and the only other interjecting voice, says of Poppie's husband: "We didn't really know the people from Kaffirland, but we got used to them. . . . At first we were dissatisfied that our little sister should marry a man from Kaffirland. We had heard of the hardships there, but when they became fond of one another, we couldn't stand in their way" (69), and when Poppie describes Kaffirland as "the raw country" (140), then I am painfully aware of a colonialist prejudice, whether Poppie's or Joubert's, or both. For the implication of Poppie's, her family's, and Joubert's condemnation of "the raw" people from Kaffirland is that there are "good," civilized Blacks and "bad," uncivilized Blacks. This is, of course, the kind of racist rhetoric that allows racists to feel comfortable with their prejudice, like the racism of "Some of my best friends are black."

Poppie's acceptance of much that is culturally Afrikaner seems curious in one who is so fatalistic and contemptuous of revolution. On the subject of speaking Afrikaans, Poppie says: "The fact was we couldn't speak Xhosa. . . . Even now when my brothers and I are together, we speak Afrikaans, that's what we like to speak, that comes naturally, ja" (15). Poppie's brother Mosie echoes Poppie's partiality for anything that is Afrikaner: "Ag, I'm just an Afrikaner, that's all that I am, said Mosie" (297).

There is a disconcerting middle-class attitude in much of what Poppie does, says, and thinks, an acceptance of the status quo that seems to want only for things to be a little easier. Joubert presents the mediated testimony of Poppie less as a direct attack against apartheid than as a kind of biography of the Ultimate Mother, assailed and beset by legalized, political, enforced, and dehumanizing racism. In this way Joubert is perhaps able to awaken white South Africans more effectively to the horrors of apartheid, because the narrative seems to erase the distinction between black mother and white mother and in that sense to create a bridge. "You see," Joubert seems to be saying, "Poppie, this Xhosa woman, is not a radical. She is a mom, a good Christian, she is like us, and things ought to be a little easier for her." Poppie and her family regard themselves as Afrikaner, after all: "And we just had to have *Die Jongspan*, Poppie says. It was a children's newspaper; we bought it every week at the shop. It was written in Afrikaans which was our language, ja" (48). Whether or not any of this is true or representative of more than one black South African family, the implied approval of white Afrikaner culture, language, and consumerism is inescapable.

Gloria Yamamoto, in an essay entitled, "Something about the Subject Makes It Hard to Name," makes the comment, "Now, the newest form of racism that I'm hip to is unaware / self-righteous racism. The 'good white' racist attempts to shame blacks into being blacker." [11] The paradoxes circle endlessly. For when I name those places where Joubert may be appropriating or distorting "native" voices in her presentation of one woman's story, I am on shaky ground in asking that Poppie be more "political." But I can say that her voice is mediated. And I must question how far I can trust Poppie's story as it is filtered through Joubert, a white Afrikaner "transcriber," and also through me, white U.S. feminist. How do we talk about this mediation, talk all the paradoxes, talk all the problematic implications, see the potential for perpetuating distortions of the experience of South African blacks, and yet at the same time see the potential for reestablishing connections by telling a story that needs to be told? However flawed or problematic the text may be, in Joubert's very act of speaking this story, we can find, I believe, the paradox of the interstice: the possibility both for perpetuating and for traversing silenced distances.

Poppie Nongena forces the reader to engage in an active dialogue. It may be true, as Luce Irigaray says, "Who or what the other is, I never know." [12] But that does not mean that Joubert, or I, should not at least try to get to know the "other," to find a way of speaking the language of difference. Yet while trying, we must stay aware, as JanMohamed points out, that there exists the potential for arrogant appropriation and silencing when the historically dominant attempt to "know," to write, to represent the historically marginalized: "While the surface of each colonialist text purports to represent specific encounters with specific varieties of the racial Other, the subtext valorizes the superiority of European cultures, of the collective process that has mediated that representation. Such literature is essentially specular: instead of seeing the native as a bridge toward syncretic possibility, it uses him as a mirror that reflects the colonialist's self-image." [13]

For white feminists speaking of the silencing of Third World women, there may be desire for collective voice, for a respecting of plurality, for the listening to of voices not yet heard, but there is only approximation of experience. If we look closely at what is implied in JanMohamed's words, we can see that the possibility exists for the colonialist text to envision "the native as a bridge toward syncretic possibility" only if we who are readers and writers of the dominator group constantly renegotiate our stances, interrogate ourselves, acknowledge our limits, and learn to listen. To move from where we are, we must "talk back" to our own unconscious racism. Only then can we begin to create bridges that acknowledge and respect what is not spoken, either because it cannot be or because she who would speak has not yet carved the space to give her story for herself. This kind of respect will open up space and allow the possibility for genuine community.

Gayatri Spivak writes of the "larger confusion," asking the question, "Can men theorize feminism, can whites theorize racism, can the bourgeoisie theorize revolution?" Her answer is on the side of reaching for understanding: "It is when *only* the former groups theorize that the situation is politically intolerable. Therefore it is crucial that members of these groups are kept vigilant about their assigned subject-positions. . . . The position that only the subaltern can know the subaltern, only women can know women and so on, cannot be held as a theoretical presupposition. . . . Knowledge [of other as subject] is made possible and is sustained by irreducible difference, not identity."[14]

Joubert may never know the other, may never be able to tran/scribe the unmediated testimony of "Poppie Nongena"; but because the book engages us in a complex questioning of appropriation, mediation, and meaning, and because the telling of this story is still an attempt, however flawed, at writing back and talking back, and at understanding, we may yet find that this specular-colonialist text contains a gesture toward syncretic possibility, a gesture toward breaking the silence on apartheid. *Poppie Nongena* speaks to and against the horrors and waste of racial oppression, but it can only speak a partial truth. It is this aspect of the work that still disturbs me. Joubert effaces the lines and gaps between white Afrikaner and translator, between author and teller and between black African–native witness–mediated other, so as to draw in the probably white Afrikaner reader-audience-listener. But I am not able to ignore the fact that in every moment of Joubert's representation of Poppie there exists the danger of stealing and misreading the "other's" testimony. JanMohamed says of this tendency in "colonialist fiction" to efface difference, to silence: "Faced with an incomprehensible and multifaceted alterity, the European theoretically has the option of responding to the Other in terms of identity or difference. If he assumes that he and the Other are essentially identical, then he would tend to ignore the significant divergences and to judge the Other according to his own cultural values. If, on the other hand, he assumes that the Other is irremediably different, then he would have little incentive to adopt the viewpoint of that alterity."[15] Perhaps there is a third alternative, a way of respecting difference that allows for a multitude of voices. Turn dissonance inside out, for the either-or paradigm is not working.

According to Trinh, "The challenge of modifying frontiers is also that of producing a situated, shifting, and contingent difference in which the only constant is the emphasis on the irresistible to-and-fro movement across (sexual and political) boundaries: margins and centers." [16] In reading Joubert, I must be aware that she is not "the native voice," nor am I, nor for that matter is Poppie. Here, mediation is inescapable. Joubert calls attention to her presence as a novelizing force in *Poppie Nongena,* with her movement in and out of points of view. At the same time, she effaces boundaries between novelizer and novelized. The intimate as-if-in-an-interview voice of Poppie saying, "I remember" (19), and two paragraphs later "I remember. . . . This is what stays in my memory" (22), and the ubiquitous construct, "Poppie says" or "says Poppie," when mixed with an authorial voice that says, "These are the memories that are still with Poppie, of her infancy with ooma Hannie at Upington" (19), obscure the lines between mediated and mediator, even as the very complexity of such an unusual narrative technique requires the reader to theorize on the problematics of transcribing.

To tran/scribe is to try to write a bridge, to attempt to write a route over, write a way across, write beyond a limit or boundary. If we are to transgress silenced differences, when we read *Poppie Nongena* we must be aware of race, of who is writing whom, who is transcribing whom so that we do not quietly perpetuate a historical, colonialist arrogance that has valorized man over woman, white over Black, urban over tribal, transcriber over witness. The whitewashing of difference appears to create bridges where there were none by erasing gaps. But this effacing of difference means a swallowing up of her who is "other." This constitutes a quietly violent maintaining of the status quo.

Therefore, when I read *Poppie Nongena,* I must read against the tendency of the culturally dominant to usurp the "native" voice, to appropriate, redefine, and impose meaning. To read Joubert critically and generously is to name the problems inherent in her attempt at a crossing, her gesture toward community, understanding, and change. Joubert involves me, however problematically, in a dialogue; she makes me question, makes me listen, makes me respond. And by bringing me in, she involves me in the act of bridging gaps between black native and white "translator." *Poppie Nongena,* even with its many flaws, is a kind of conversation, a necessary testimony. When the text makes the reader see what Poppie does not, it places reader and author in a superior position over the original witness. But perhaps in this way Joubert prevents the white South African reader from closing off. Perhaps in this way some small part of the unspeakable can be heard.

Having wanted only to shelter her children from apartheid, Poppie in the end is reduced to someone who has "a little spittle" (353) running from her mouth. She concludes: "The children will have to look after them- selves. . . . I have found my way through everything, she thought, but through this I can find no way. Because this has been taken out of my hands, it has been given over into the hands of the children" (353). This passage echoes that earlier plea for community, for coalition. When Poppie says, "I can't break the law with my hands," it is as if we are called upon to add our hands to the task of engendering change. Our hands have been called.

Notes

1. Dieter Welz, *Writing against Apartheid*, 6.

2. Anne McClintock, " 'The Very House of Difference,' " offers another per- spective on the issues of appropriation and collaboration in *Poppie Nongena*.

3. Gloria Anzaldúa, *Borderlands / La Frontera*, 48.

4. Gloria Anzaldúa, "Haciendo caras, una entrada," introduction to Anzaldúa, ed., *Making Face, Making Soul*, xxi.

5. A more recent English edition of the novel, also translated by Joubert, has been called to my attention since the writing of this essay (*Poppie Nongena: A Novel of South Africa*, Holt, 1987). All quotations and references in the text are to the 1980 edition.

6. Throughout the text, Joubert omits quotation marks around spoken dia- logue.

7. Jean Marquard, "Poppie."

8. See Margaret Lenta, "Independence as the Creative Choice," 50, 43, 47.

9. Unconscious, blanked-out racism can permeate even well-intentioned dis- course. Neither Joubert nor "Poppie Nongena" as mediated through Joubert is free from history, from language, from the system or context of untenable state racism known as apartheid. Joubert is a "member" of the dominator group whose institution- alized racism has brutally oppressed the Black majority, and her unconscious racism distorts the retelling of Nongena's story. "I cannot see how we cannot be allowed to write about them," she says. Her privilege as a white Afrikaner allows her to write what she wishes, and allows her a kind of blindness: "I cannot see." But Poppie Non- gena's attitudes are not identical to Joubert's. Poppie's belittling, demeaning assump- tions about Blacks show that she has internalized the attitudes of the dominant group; the weight of racist oppression around her is evident in many of her ambiguous atti- tudes toward Blacks.

10. Mark Mathabane, *Kaffir Boy*, 193.

11. Gloria Yamamoto, "Something about the Subject Makes It Hard to Name," in Anzaldúa, ed., *Making Face, Making Soul*, 21.

12. Luce Irigaray, "Sexual Difference," 124.

13. Abdul R. JanMohamed, "The Economy of Manichean Allegory," 84.

14. Gayatri Chakravorty Spivak, "A Literary Representation of the Subaltern: A Woman's Text from the Third World," in *In Other Worlds*, 253–54.

15. JanMohamed, "Manichean Allegory," 83–84.

16. Trinh T. Minh-ha, *When the Moon Waxes Red*, 103.

PART TWO

Domestic Politics:
Violence on the Home Front

MERRY M. PAWLOWSKI

From the Country of the Colonized:
Virginia Woolf on Growing Up Female
in Victorian England

A record of childhood, "A Sketch of the Past," left unpublished by Virginia Woolf at the time of her death, traces a terrifying and lonely existence, compelling its readers to witness its rage at memories of abuse. We might wonder how a member of the intellectually elite British upper-middle class, a woman with every advantage and acknowledged as one of the major writers of British modernism, could have experienced the suffering of one "colonized" within the privacy of her family and home. Yet so deep were the scars of her growing up that Woolf was only able at the age of fifty-eight to confront directly, in this autobiographical prose, the sources of past oppression—her parents.[1] It was still possible for Woolf as an adolescent to love her parents with an intensity that, according to her biographers, brought on mental breakdowns after each of their deaths. I shall argue, however, that an unspeakable rage begins to find a voice in Woolf's memoir, pointing to her "colonization" as an inherently inferior female in the Victorian household as an equally important source of her recurring madness and, even more, as the key to binding together two periods of oppression in her life—the past and the present. Why else would the memory of her mother and father provoke such intensity from her sketching pen at a time at the end of the 1930s when Woolf was learning a new meaning for oppression, colonialism, and tyranny—in fascist Italy and Nazi Germany?[2] In fact, what Woolf's memoir should remind us most is that imperialist England in 1939 as in 1895 was itself fascist in its subjugation of women.

The evidence for these claims is embedded in "A Sketch of the Past," in scenes that crystallize Woolf's memories and conflate them with her fears of a present threatened by encroaching tyranny. In this memoir, Woolf creates a discursive matrix, historicized by oppressive, fascist dictatorships, where her experiences as a female growing up—including her memories of benign neglect by her mother, of violence and abuse from her father and half-brothers, and of her rage at suppression into silence— become immediate once again.[3]

What we witness as we read, however, is not only the moving childhood portrait of a lost and abused young girl as remembered by the woman she has become. This memoir is also the record of a woman's lifelong struggle for rhetorical power against domestic and social forces of domination, intolerance, and violent abuse; Woolf's memorial text, which helped give vent to her rage and organized her experiences, directs our attention beyond what is said to the struggle of what was still, for her, unsayable.

On some level, though, Woolf felt that writing was healing: "I suppose that I did for myself what psychoanalysts do for their patients," Woolf says in her memoir. "I expressed some very long and deeply felt emotion. And in expressing it I explained it and then laid it to rest."[4] Many readers would immediately question the truth of this statement, knowing what we do about Woolf's antipathy to psychoanalysis.[5] For me, the power of this passage resides more in the lie that it tells, for Woolf was not fully able to lay to rest by writing the memories that had caused her the greatest pain. The silences in "A Sketch of the Past" bear testimony to the deepest layers of Woolf's sense of colonization and oppression and to the most scarring memories that had resisted acknowledgment. In contradiction to Woolf's statement about the healing power of her self-psychoanalytic writing, the essay itself is filled with and founded upon silences, which speak as profoundly as the actual text about power, language, and weakness in Woolf's life. Here, near the end of her life, the political present floods the personal past, locking the two in a riveting discourse at once revealing and concealing one woman's oppression.

I begin with the reasons why Woolf holds her mother at a distance during the first pages of her memoir of childhood, and I find there openings for speculation far beyond what Woolf tells us. Woolf cannot bring herself to say that she does not believe that her mother loved her, or that, in fact, her mother abandoned her child to her devotion to duty as an exemplary Victorian matron. Woolf's earliest memories of pleasure and ecstasy are associated not with her mother's face, voice, or body but with other spaces—a garden, the sea—where she feels safe and enclosed in a protective cocoon. She remembers the sound of the sea at St. Ives from the safe "uterine" space of the nursery and the colors and sounds of the garden there as though she were "lying in a grape and seeing through a film of semi-transparent yellow" (65). Woolf's only memory of connection to her mother's body as she begins the memoir is that of sitting on her mother's lap in a train, traveling, perhaps, to St. Ives. Woolf is not sure about this memory, but "it is more convenient artistically to suppose that we were going to St. Ives" (64); her mother is the mere means of conveyance to Woolf's most pleasurable "safe" space. We could reasonably expect that Woolf, being so close to her mother on this first page of her narrative, would describe her; but instead what she remembers are the colors and shapes of the flowers on her dress. She does not describe seeing her mother's face or hearing her voice; indeed, she will allow her mother only a peripheral entry into the text, holding her at bay for the next fifteen pages.[6]

Woolf seems to suggest that, even though she is now a woman of fifty-eight, she must take her revenge for the child who was ignored by her mother. That revenge encompasses a textual rhetoric of distancing, partial erasure, and silencing of Woolf's earliest relation with her mother. Even as Woolf slowly begins to describe her mother as a presence in her childhood, it is a presence that is imaged as absence. Woolf's mother, Julia Stephen, managed a huge Victorian household consisting of eight children, numerous servants, and an irascible husband, and she persisted in fulfilling a lifelong dedication to and vocation for nursing, which fitted acceptably within the image of the Victorian matron's charitable duties toward the poor. The toll on her can be seen in her photographs, which show a woman grim-faced and exhausted at the age of forty-seven. Woolf says, "I see now that she was living on such an extended surface that she had not time, nor strength, to concentrate, except for a moment if one were ill or in some child's crisis, upon me, or upon anyone" (83). And although Woolf describes her as central, the image we get is that of an "absent" center to be worshiped, "in the very center of that great Cathedral space which was childhood" (81), in a childhood that was itself imaged as "vast empty spaces" (78) and a "great hall" (79).

Julia Stephen does not become a real, approachable body in her daughter's text until she is dead. Woolf's vivid memories of her mother's dying do not ignore her mother's last words to her, " 'Hold yourself straight, my little Goat' " (84), words that must have caused Woolf to wince at the mixture of love and reprimand. Woolf denies herself the ability to feel, especially now, at this most painful juncture, as is evident in the memory of her mother's dead body: "A desire to laugh came over me, and I said to myself as I have often done at moments of crisis since, 'I feel nothing whatever'. Then I stooped and kissed my mother's face. It was still warm. She [had] only died a moment before" (92). The next morning, Woolf remembers that kissing her mother's body was like kissing cold iron. These death scenes are the few times Woolf remembers being close enough to her mother to touch her, and the touch identifies the mother's dead body as radically depersonalized.

Shortly after her mother's death, Woolf suffered her first serious episode of what has been identified by her family as madness, a violent irrationality that would culminate in a suicide attempt.[7] There are no allusions to this episode in the manuscripts published posthumously as "A Sketch of the Past," but there are numerous oblique allusions to her insanity in the fiction: the mad Septimus Smith in *Mrs. Dalloway,* for example, has often been cited as an alter ego for Woolf.[8] But Woolf rarely admitted her lifelong battle with this illness in any of her autobiographical prose. I suspect that the reasons she chose not to discuss this first episode of mental illness are very complex. An earlier, rejected, draft of the manuscript memoir, in reference to the period following the death of her mother and before that of her older half-sister, Stella, contains the sentence, "This brought on, naturally, my first 'breakdown.' "[9] Even this, a reluctant admission, which insists upon enclosing the word breakdown within quotes, seems to question the breakdown and makes suspect its validity as a diagnosing term. Woolf does not elaborate, and in later versions she dropped the allusion altogether. Did she purposely choose to mute her own personal pain to reflect on the larger social picture of 1939? Were her "breakdowns" caused by more than her mourning a loss? Or were they attributable instead to rage at the tyranny of her family, of society, and of its effects on women, including her mother?[10] As we continue to examine the record of Woolf's reconstruction of the past, we find a personal account of abuse that evolves into a condemnation of the oppression of women as a whole.

An assumption that Woolf's "madness" was a response to rage is certainly bolstered by the knowledge that shortly after her mother's death, she was subjected to caresses from her elder half-brother, George, that were sexually abusive. In this memoir, Woolf reserves her sharpest accusations for Gerald, the younger Duckworth brother, muting her claims of abuse against George.[11] But Woolf's nephew and biographer, Quentin Bell, fills in some of the space left blank. On the authority of Leonard Woolf, Virginia's husband, and one of her doctors, Bell accuses George of making improper sexual advances to Virginia soon after her mother's death and of continuing at least to her father's death; and Woolf herself described the abuse in personal letters and conversations as well as other memoirs.[12]

In "A Sketch of the Past," Woolf suggests that Victorian England had deprived her of a mother who had time to attend to her needs, ultimately killing her mother with overwork within her own home and leaving her daughters defenseless against masculine violation. Woolf had already sensed that when she wrote of her mother and father: "Too much obsessed with his health, with his pleasures, she was too willing, as I think now, to sacrifice us to him . . . and so . . . she wore herself out and died at forty-nine; while he lived on, and found it very difficult, so healthy was he, to die of cancer at the age of seventy-two" (133).

As Woolf thought about her mother, she was continuing to formulate a thesis that she had introduced one year earlier in *Three Guineas*—that fascist tyranny was quite as alive in England as in Hitler's Germany or Mussolini's Italy. An important subtext of "A Sketch of the Past" is Woolf's reaction to the fascist tyrannies that were pushing war to the skies of England. "Yesterday (18th August 1940)," Woolf begins a new section of the memoir, "five German raiders passed so close over Monks House that they brushed the tree at the gate" (124). Perhaps as she wrote of her past, Woolf was making a connection for the first time—that a power very like fascism had been the governing force in her own family. While her rage at European fascism was real, the overt links between father and mother and tyranny were still very tenuous; for Woolf was understandably reluctant to indict her own parents for engaging in and complying with domestic fascism.

Reading Woolf's text as a unconscious indictment deepens our understanding of an additional element in Woolf's intensely complex relationship with her parents. Not only was she distancing herself from her mother because of her sense of childhood neglect, she was also blaming her for her complicity in the social status quo. Such blame can be more fully appreciated through a reading of the context of the memoir. Woolf wrote the words cited above sometime after September 22, 1940. She had for years been reading and gathering information on fascism, male domination, and tyranny, writing copiously in her reading notebooks. In 1937 or 1938, she copied several passages from Hilary Newitt's account of Italy and Germany under fascism, *Women Must Choose: The Position of Women in Europe Today*. Among these was a quotation from Benito Mussolini that suggests a strong parallel to the social requirements for the Victorian matron: "Woman is reserved to the family and must be a good housewife, a good wife and a good mother." [13] Another quotation echoes Woolf's memories of her parents' relationship, especially her father's dependence on her mother for approval and support: "The life of man is based on struggle ... woman's task must be to heal his wounds." [14]

The latter passage from Newitt's book is especially significant in that it comes from propaganda written by a woman, Princess Fanny Starhemberg, a high official in Nazi Austria's antifeminist government. Newitt shows how the status of women in Germany and Italy in 1937 had seriously deteriorated: women were being denied their rights, they were being ousted from jobs and professions, and they were being denied an education in an insidious reversal of the nominal gains for social freedom and suffrage that had been made earlier. Leonard and Virginia Woolf had themselves experienced the atmosphere of Nazi Germany in 1935, when they "blundered into a Nazi demonstration near Bonn." [15] Although they were not in any personal danger, Virginia found the show of hostility and the overtones of arrogance and violence a fairly shattering experience.

Woolf had read, then, about the grim reality of women oppressed by fascist rule; and, within a year or two, she would write remembering how her mother had been mastered by a strikingly similar phenomenon. Yet, unable to forgive her mother's complicity with Victorian ideology, Woolf also silenced her mother, denying her any voice or agency and insisting in an obvious inaccuracy that her mother had never written or published. As she tried to lay hold of her mother's character, she wrote in her memoir in May 1939, the following: "For what reality can remain real of a person who died forty-four years ago at the age of forty-nine, without leaving a book, or a picture, or any piece of work—apart from the three children who now survive and the memory of her that remains in their minds? There is the memory; but there is nothing to check that memory by; nothing to bring it to ground with" (85). Why did Woolf intentionally silence her mother here by claiming that she wrote no book? Julia Stephen did, indeed, write and publish a pamphlet on nursing in 1883, and she wrote several unpublished articles on the management of servants and on women agnostics. [16] But she also signed an antisuffrage manifesto, "holding that women had enough to do in their own homes without a vote" (120), clearly, in Woolf's eyes, a politically unfavorable position.

Julia Stephen's nursing pamphlet shows that she was devoted to nursing as a profession, yet was constrained by the social impossibility of pursuing her vocation beyond the acceptable boundaries of charitable bounty. Woolf regarded her mother as an accomplice with the forces of oppression. Few readers of Woolf can forget her testimony that she had to "kill" the "angel in the house" (her mother's spirit) as the embodiment of feminine self-abnegation in her fiction. [17] The angel in the house, Woolf would contend, meant death to the woman writer (one could not be both a "good" woman and a good writer), so for Woolf her mother *did not* write. Virginia Woolf would emphatically choose *not* to reproduce her mother's choices, her mother's life, her mother's definition of womanhood.

Yet putting her mother into this perspective was only half the battle against the scarring memories of the past. There remained the memory of her father. If her memories of her mother evoked neglect, those of her father recalled an overt oppression in which he had forced her to witness his violent outbursts where her only possible response was her own silent rage. "Yet he too obsessed me for years. Until I wrote it out, I would find my lips moving; I would be arguing with him; raging against him; saying to myself all that I never said to him. How deep they drove themselves into me, the things it was impossible to say aloud. They are still some of them sayable" (108). Has Woolf's pen slipped here; did she really mean to write "unsayable"? Or could she be suggesting that many things still *remain* to be said, to be written down? Indeed, as Woolf perceives, some of the cause of her rage is sayable through the very act of her writing, but much more is not. Furthermore, the realization that she can only now speak the words that would indict her father is made even more acute by the web of history in which she was caught. For, as she began to write in detail of her father, she was witnessing the fall of France to fascism. "The present. . . . June 19th 1940. The French have stopped fighting. Today the dictators dictate their terms to France. . . . I sit in my room at 37 M[ecklenburgh] S[quare] and turn to my father" (107). Woolf's most precise memories of her father recall those abusive years from the deaths of her mother and Stella to the death of her father, 1895–1904, a period when her father became increasingly tyrannical and she could not fight back.

Juggling the present and the past as she began to formulate her memories of her father, Woolf acknowledged that she had just begun to read Freud seriously for the first time. Why only now, we must ask, does Woolf begin to read Freud when the Woolfs' Hogarth Press had been publishing Freud's Collected Works for the International Psycho-Analytical Library since 1924?[18] Even more intriguing is what she was drawn to read. In December 1939 and into the first part of 1940, Woolf read *Group Psychology and the Analysis of the Ego*, probing, through her reading of Freud, the rise of fascism and its threat to civilization. In her notes, she focused on the two world wars in her experience and mused on Hitler as the epitome of masculinist attributes: "The present war is very different for now the male has also [anchored?] his attributes in Hitler, & fighting against them." [19] The irony for Woolf was that the men in her country were blind to their own domestic fascism. As she sought to find the position of woman somewhere in Freud's text or even in society, she wrote: "In the present war we are fighting for liberty. But we can only get it if we destroy the male attributes. Thus the woman part is to achieve the *emancipation of man*. In that her only hope of permanent peace" (emphasis added).[20]

Part of that emancipation might be effected, Woolf hoped, by forcing Englishmen to see themselves as participants in tyranny. To this end, Woolf had indicted her countrymen in *Three Guineas,* offering Hitler and Mussolini as the mirror images of English patriarchy: "And are we not all agreed that the dictator when we meet him abroad is a very dangerous as well as a very ugly animal? And he is here among us, raising his ugly head, spitting his poison, small still, curled up like a caterpillar on a leaf, but in the heart of England. Is it not from this egg . . . that 'the practical obliteration of [our] freedom by Fascists or Nazis' will spring? And is not the woman who has to breathe that poison and to fight that insect, secretly and without arms . . . fighting the Fascist or the Nazi as surely as those who fight him with arms in the limelight of publicity?" [21]

By June of 1940, with the fall of France, Woolf was making connections to Hitler much closer to home, much closer even than aligning Hitler's Germany with patriarchal England as a whole. She was beginning to see that her own father had been a tyrant, too. For too long, the women of Leslie Stephen's family had excused his violent temper as an expression of genius. Woolf reflected: "I think he said unconsciously as he worked himself up into one of those violent outbursts: 'This is a sign of my genius,' and he called in Carlyle to confirm him, and let himself fly" (109–10). Woolf refuses him both genius and the right to violent outbursts, naming him now what she knows him to have been then: "It was the *tyrant* father—the exacting, the violent, the histrionic, the demonstrative, the self-centered, the self pitying, the deaf, the appealing, the alternately loved and hated father—that dominated me then. It was like being shut up in the same cage with a wild beast" (116, emphasis added).[22]

Although for many years Woolf had ridiculed psychoanalysis, reading Freud had finally helped her put her father and her emotions into perspective. She could sketch her father as the tyrant she knew him to be in her personal life while facing the ambivalent emotions he caused her to feel. Yet the implications of what she could say extend far beyond into the unsaid and the unsayable: the memory of her father's irrational rages reflects the growling discourse of Hitler's ranting speeches. Woolf had written in her diary on Tuesday, September 13, 1938: "Hitler boasted &

boomed but shot no solid bolt. Mere violent rant, & then broke off. We listened in to the end. A savage howl like a person excruciated; then howls from the audience; then a more spaced & measured sentence. Then another bark. Cheering ruled by a stick. Frightening to think of the faces. & the voice was frightening."[23]

Woolf's descriptions of her father's weekly rages and her own sense of raging, silent frustration parallel the impressions she recorded after listening to Hitler. Woolf remembers with great vividness the "Greek slave" (106) years when she and Vanessa were teenagers and had to do the household accounts every week: "Then down came his fist on the account book. His veins filled; his face flushed. Then there was an inarticulate roar. Then he shouted . . . 'I am ruined.' Then he beat his breast. Then he went through an extraordinary dramatisation of self-pity, horror, anger. . . . I was speechless. Never have I felt such rage and such frustration. For not a word of what I felt—that unbounded contempt for him and of pity for Nessa—could be expressed" (144). Before she wrote these words, on November 15, 1940, she had noted in her diary several severe bombings of London and another of Hitler's speeches, making increasingly evident the interanimation of the personal and the political in her mind.[24]

Her father's rages were reserved for the women in his family, and Woolf's anger at having had to endure such brutality is still vivid: "If someone had said to him simply and straightforwardly: 'You are a brute to treat a girl like that . . .' what would he have said?" (146). Leslie Stephen thought that women's sole purpose was to serve his needs in angelic slavery; Woolf, reflecting upon her father's verbal abuse of Vanessa, wrote: "He had an illicit need for sympathy, released by the woman, stimulated; and her refusal to accept her role, part slave, part angel, exacerbated him" (145–46).

Woolf's vengeance on her father comes in the form of another denial, and she indicates what a daughter who feels robbed of power and language can do to repay such a father. While acknowledging her father's analytical abilities, Woolf would write of his lack of "creativity": "Give him a character to explain, and he is (to me) so crude, so elementary, so conventional that a child with a box of chalks could make a more subtle portrait" (146). Woolf has effectively weighed her own use of language against her father's, and she has, just as she silenced her mother earlier, virtually silenced him as well.

Leslie Stephen is to blame for far more in his daughter's eyes than simple ineptitude in the creative use of language. What would such a father have said if he had been told that his daughters had been sexually abused by his stepsons? We have to wonder if the current of his rage could have been reversed and if Gerald and George Duckworth could have become the targets of his wrath. The evidence suggests that Victorian, fascist ideology would have protected the men in Woolf's family from unpleasant recognitions, for they did not have to view their behavior from a woman's point of view. In the constructs of the Victorian family, women's servile positions left them helpless and unprotected against onslaughts such as these. What was sayable for Woolf in her autobiographical texts stands as an accusation against her father and her half-brothers for a much larger, unsayable, experience of abuse that threatened her tenuous grasp of female identity.

Furthermore, the blame for her sexual abuse seems to reach beyond the brothers who violated her to the mother who had no time for the daughters who needed her protection. Woolf was abused by both her mother's sons, by George after her mother died and by Gerald when she was very little. In the most incriminating accusation made against Gerald, Woolf wrote: "Once when I was very small Gerald Duckworth lifted me onto this [slab in the hall], and as I sat there he began to explore my body. I can remember the feel of his hand going under my clothes; going firmly and steadily lower and lower. I remember how I hoped that he would stop; how I stiffened and wiggled as his hand approached my private parts. But it did not stop. His hand explored my private parts too. I remember resenting, disliking it—what is the word for so dumb and mixed a feeling?" (69). Woolf breaks her silence to cry out in rage against a violation of women that is centuries old: "It proves that Virginia Stephen was not born on the 25th January 1882, but was born many thousands of years ago" (69).

In a house where she should have been safe, secure, protected, Woolf was, instead, neglected and verbally, psychologically, and physically assaulted. In Woolf's society (both her present and her past), women were silenced, prohibited from speaking of their abuse.[25] The terror of violation, of loss of self, that she endured in childhood as a result of abuse, neglect, and tyranny, painted powerful images in her dreams and her imagination, while leaving her outwardly speechless and powerless. However, Woolf coded in the images of her text the record of the abuse on her psyche, indicting her parents and family in the process.

One such image in Woolf's memoir is the hall mirror, for it was on a slab in the hall near this mirror that Gerald fondled her. Possibly, Woolf was not only forced to experience this violation of her body but to watch it in the mirror as well. Another memory connected with the mirror reinforces this possibility. Woolf remembers a nightmare around the same time as her sexual abuse that may point to the submerged memory of the abuser: "I dreamt that I was looking in a glass when a horrible face—the face of an animal—suddenly showed over my shoulder. I cannot be sure if this was a dream, or if it happened. . . . But I have always remembered the other face in the glass, whether it was a dream or a fact, and that it frightened me" (69).

As she continues to reflect on childhood memories, Woolf records two especially vivid "moments of being," which comment further upon the fragility of the developing ego. If we draw these two additional images into association with the mirror, we see that clusters of moments of being that began in sexual violation trace the problematic formation of female identity. Such associations include reflections that negate rather than reinforce self-images of wholeness as well as reflective surfaces that threaten to swallow or submerge the self. Woolf's memories paint a tender ego that cringes in fear at the edge of a puddle and huddles in terror in a bath: "There was the moment of the puddle in the path; when for no reason I could discover, everything suddenly became unreal; I was suspended; I could not step across the puddle; I tried to touch something . . . the whole world became unreal" (78). The cumulative impact of her childhood was taking its toll on the young Virginia Stephen; and the puddle, like the horrible face in the mirror of her nightmare, threatens her with loss of identity. Later that night, the shock of unreality and loss of agency return to Woolf with even greater force: "For that night in the bath the dumb horror came over me. Again I had that hopeless sadness; that collapse I have described before; as if I were passive under some sledge-hammer blow; exposed to a whole avalanche of meaning that had heaped itself up and discharged itself upon me, unprotected, with nothing to ward it off, so that I huddled up at my end of the bath, motionless. I could not explain it" (78).

The female body, imaged as violable, weak, powerless, and silent, inhibits the formation of identity as chronicled in this complex matrix of associations. By the end of her childhood, much damage had been done, and Woolf could only achieve feeling by splitting herself from the body that had caused her shame: "This did not prevent me from feeling ecstasies and raptures spontaneously and intensely and without any shame or the least sense of guilt, so long as they were disconnected with my own body" (68). Woolf reminds us that now reality for her resides in words: "I make it real by putting it into words" (72). But years of psychic pain and disconnection from her body leave much untold that was just as real. For ex-

ample, Woolf does not make fully explicit the connection to the juncture
in history when these memories came flooding back. On Tuesday, April
18, 1939, when Woolf began to write "A Sketch of the Past," England was
poised on the brink of war as the world waited for Hitler to attack Poland.
I would suggest once more that by allowing deeply suppressed memories
of violation to resurface at this moment, Woolf silently underscored the
parallels between a very personal oppression and the violation and suffo-
cation of all womankind, all mankind.

The record of Woolf's contribution to English letters testifies to her
ability to submerge the pain of her past in an active present. Yet, during
the years 1939–41 as she wrote her memoir, the past was reincarnating
itself in her present in a new and virulent way. Woolf was once again
feeling the crushing, numbing weight of violent oppression—much like
the oppression that had silenced her before.

Sadly, all that Woolf had once been taught about a woman's silence
and submission in her society had not been erased through time. Even at
fifty-eight, she played an old game taught to her in polite Victorian society.
It involved not coming out with all of the truth, and she admits, "The
surface manner allows one, as I have found, to slip in things that would
be inaudible if one marched straight up and spoke out loud" (150). She
plays this same game with her readers. We are invited, as this essay attempts to demonstrate, to participate in the stripping away of her polite
surface manner and to assist her in saying the unsayable. Woolf and her
sister, Vanessa, believed wrongly in the early part of the century that they
had rejected the mold of Victorian femininity because they had learned to
subvert it from within. Society's gag order for women had definitely not
been lifted by 1939, and Woolf, in her awareness of the deeply worsening
situation of women in fascist European countries and even in her own
country, had seen time folding back upon itself. She writes with painful
sarcasm of the need to continue playing the game: "We still play the game.
It is useful. It has also its beauty, for it is founded upon restraint, sympathy, unselfishness—all civilized qualities" (150).

In the past, too, she and Vanessa had seen the need to form a female
nucleus, a close conspiracy, against a world of men. Such a bonding bringing women to a common awareness might be possible in the present as
well, Woolf indicated. Just days after she dated her entry on November
15, 1940, in "A Sketch of the Past," she wrote in her diary: "I am carrying
on, while I read, the idea of women discovering, like the 19th century
rationalists, agnostics, that man is no longer God."[26]

A few short weeks later, Woolf seems to have made a truce with the past, relinquishing its pain for the immediacy of the terror of war, and she wrote lovingly and longingly of her parents: "How beautiful they were, those old people—I mean father & mother—how simple, how clear how untroubled. . . . He loved her—oh & was so candid & reasonable & transparent—& had such a fastidious delicate mind, educated, & transparent."[27] Either Woolf had exorcised the demons of the past at last or she had fled once more into rhetorical evasion. Perhaps not until this moment of writing, though, could she finally forgive them.

It would take the demons of the present—Hitler, war, chaos, madness—to silence Woolf for good. The war had robbed her of authorial agency and audience, she felt, and nothing that she wrote mattered. "It struck me that one curious feeling is, that the writing 'I' has vanished. No audience. No echo. Thats part of ones death."[28] By now, Woolf had lost the sense that there was even an "I" left to heal, if only partially, through the self-psychoanalytic action of writing. Six weeks before she took her life, she seemed to be prescient as she wrote in her diary: "Yes, I was thinking: we live without a future. Thats whats queer, with our noses pressed to a closed door."[29]

At the end of her lifelong struggle for agency and a language of her own, Woolf was confronted by a vast and insidious fascist ideology devouring Europe. Fearing that she was hearing the voices of madness once again and oppressed by a chaotic world order in which she refused to participate, she chose finally to silence herself, but not before leaving a powerfully moving record of a woman writer's search for selfhood through the reincarnation of the past in the present.

Notes

1. Virginia Woolf is the only woman to date who seems inscribed in the canon of major writers of British modernism. She is important not only for her lyrical narratives but also for her elegant, impassioned prose, which championed the cause for women and became a beacon of hope for later feminists and women writers alike. Woolf has been attacked, both during her lifetime and posthumously, as an upperclass snob who knew or cared little about the experiences of the working class or the oppression of colonized people. Yet Woolf insisted that the lowest "class" consisted of women of all social classes, especially the "daughters of educated men," a phrase she coined in her most radically feminist essay, *Three Guineas* (1938). In *Three Guineas*, Woolf was armed by her research to name fascism, in its oppression of women, as an evil that existed long before Hitler or Mussolini and that extended directly to the heart of the Victorian home. It is from this position, I argue in this essay, that we are able to view Woolf as "colonized" by a heavyhanded Victorian patriarchy most closely emblematized in her own mind by that very eminent Victorian, her father, Sir

Leslie Stephen, and by a lovely "Angel in the House," her mother, Julia Duckworth Stephen.

2. I am indebted to a number of scholars whose work has shaped my own thinking about Woolf's response to fascism. Among those works most influential for me, I would include Jane Marcus's *Art and Anger* and *Virginia Woolf and the Languages of Patriarchy,* which have compellingly advanced the seriousness of Woolf's politics, her response to history, and her feminism; Elizabeth Abel's *Virginia Woolf and the Fictions of Psychoanalysis,* which, while viewing Woolf's fiction as enmeshed in the discourses of psychoanalysis, also acknowledges the power of Woolf's response to history; Alex Zwerdling's *Virginia Woolf and the Real World,* which shows how Woolf's works are imbricated in and contextualized by history through the strength of her social vision; and Mark Hussey's recent collection, *Woolf and War,* which provides another challenge to the received notion that Woolf had no interest in or understanding of her political and social environment.

3. Woolf makes very personal what Sidonie Smith describes as the confrontation of a woman writer with the languages of man and woman as a characterizing feature of women's autobiography: "The autobiographer's confrontation with those 'maternal' and 'paternal' narratives structures the narrative and dramatic texture of her self-representation and shapes her relationship to language, image, and meaning" (*A Poetics of Women's Autobiography,* 51). Louise DeSalvo's chapter on "A Sketch of the Past," entitled "A Daughter Remembers," in *Virginia Woolf,* working from a similar assumption, provides a valuable reading of the memoir, which focuses on Woolf's abuse by the Duckworth brothers and weaves skillfully between the historical context for Woolf's writing and the causes for her depression in the past. This chapter is an important foundation for my thinking about the textual silences that cover many of these scenes of abuse, violence, and neglect.

4. Virginia Woolf, "A Sketch of the Past," in *Moments of Being,* ed. Jeanne Schulkind, 2d ed. (London: Hogarth Press, 1985), 81. Future references will be from this edition and page numbers will appear in parentheses in the text.

5. See especially Stephen Trombley, "*All That Summer She Was Mad,*" for a discussion of Woolf's doctors and their mismanagement of her treatment.

6. Critics like Shari Benstock have also noted this fact. Benstock writes: "The point is not that Woolf's mother became an 'invisible presence' after her death, but that she was always an invisible presence—too central, too close to be observed" (*The Private Self,* 27). I would add that, for Woolf, having her mother too close to be observed did not ensure against the emotional distancing she experienced as a child.

7. Quentin Bell provides what sketchy information exists on his aunt's first nervous breakdown in his authorized biography of her, *Virginia Woolf: A Biography,* 1:42.

8. See as an example, Roger Poole, *The Unknown Virginia Woolf,* chap. 9.

9. Martine Stemerick, "Virginia Woolf and Julia Stephen," 57, points out that the only account of Woolf's first breakdown in these manuscripts is in a preliminary draft for "A Sketch of the Past," *Monk's House Papers* (MH/A.5c); but even this account is largely muted. What interests me is the omission of the statement in the revised memoir.

10. These are very like questions raised by Poole in *The Unknown Virginia Woolf,* his cogent analysis of Woolf's life and work in the context of discourses about

her madness, especially those discourses of her nephew-biographer, Quentin Bell, and her husband, Leonard Woolf. Poole's work is very important for raising questions about the nature of Woolf's insanity.

11. Woolf does, however, accuse George quite directly of indecent advances in "22 Hyde Park Gate," a memoir written twenty years before "A Sketch of the Past": "Sleep had almost come to me. The room was dark. The house silent. Then, creaking stealthily, the door opened; treading gingerly, someone entered. 'Who?' I cried. 'Don't be frightened,' George whispered. 'And don't turn on the light, oh beloved. Beloved—and he flung himself on my bed, and took me in his arms" (*Moments of Being*, 155). Both Poole, *The Unknown Virginia Woolf* (28–32), and DeSalvo, *The Impact of Childhood Sexual Abuse*, argue compellingly that Woolf was subjected to more than cuddling by George.

12. *Virginia Woolf: A Biography*, 1:42–43. For Woolf's reports of her abuse, see DeSalvo, 122.

13. Benito Mussolini, "La Donna, Una Ripresa del feminismo?" *Il Nuovo Stato*, April 1935, quoted in Hilary Newitt, *Women Must Choose*, 117. Woolf cites this quote in vol. 26, p. 9, of her *Holograph Reading Notes*.

14. Quoted by Newitt, *Women Must Choose*, 130, from propaganda issued by the office of Princess Fanny Starhemberg, the Nazi Women's Leader of Austria; cited by Woolf in vol. 26, p. 9, of the *Holograph Reading Notes*.

15. Bell, *Virginia Woolf*, 2:189.

16. The writings of Julia Stephen have been collected into a volume entitled *Stories for Children: Essays for Adults*, ed. Diane F. Gillespie and Elizabeth Steele.

17. Two important references for this textual "murder" are in *A Room of One's Own* and the essay "Professions for Women," in *The Death of the Moth and Other Essays*, 236–37.

18. Elizabeth Abel notes the following about Woolf's resistance to the psychoanalytic discourse of the 1920s and 1930s: "Woolf's reticence about psychoanalysis is both characteristic and complex; interpreting it requires that we heed her own insistence on authorial silences, on what is left unsaid." *Virginia Woolf and the Fictions of Psychoanalysis*, 13.

19. *The Holograph Reading Notes*, 21:5. I found an invaluable preparation for examining the reading notes in Brenda Silver's index to the manuscripts, *Virginia Woolf's Reading Notebooks*. Silver cites this quotation in slightly different form (116): "For now the male has also [...] his attributes in Hitler, & is fighting against them."

20. *The Holograph Reading Notes* (emphasis added), vol. 21. Woolf's handwriting is not easy to make out, and I may have mistakenly transcribed "woman" for "women," but I have kept my reading as "woman" to agree with the singular pronoun in the next sentence. Woolf also neglected to make this word possessive in her notes.

21. *Three Guineas*, 53.

22. I am indebted to Elizabeth Abel's *Virginia Woolf and the Fictions of Psychoanalysis* (109), for having pointed me to this passage in Schulkind's 2d edition of *Moments of Being*. Abel uses the quote to explore Woolf's reading of Freud during her composition of *Between the Acts*.

23. *The Diary of Virginia Woolf*, vol. 5:169.

24. Ibid., 338–39.

25. See DeSalvo on Woolf as incest survivor, *The Impact of Childhood Sexual Abuse*.

26. *The Diary of Virginia Woolf,* 5:340.

27. Ibid., 345.

28. Ibid., 293.

29. Ibid., 355.

GISELA NORAT

The Silent Child within the Angry Woman: Exorcising Incest in Sylvia Molloy's *Certificate of Absence*

The nameless narrator-protagonist of *Certificate of Absence* rents and prepares a room specifically for the task of writing her personal story. Both the need and the motive for writing are expressed in the opening sentences of the novel: "She begins to write a story that will not leave her alone. She would like to forget it; she would also like to give it shape, and, in shaping it, find revenge: for herself, for her story."[1] The almost exclusive use of third-person narrative throughout the novel affords the narrator-protagonist the degree of detachment she needs to author her intimate self while concomitantly revealing the alienation she feels.

As the reader eventually learns, the reason for revenge lies in a failed love relationship, one in which the narrator was humiliated by being made to overhear a sexual encounter between her lesbian lover and another woman. The narrator seeks to inscribe the emotional pain inflicted by Vera, the woman she then loved. Recording the hurt and anger associated with the betrayal not only requires self-revelation but also compels the narrator to come to terms with her lesbian identity.

The pressure that patriarchy exerts on women to accept the heterosexual way of life as the "correct" and "normal" choice can be an overwhelming burden for those who are trying to achieve a positive lesbian self-image. The autobiographical film *Susana,* by Susana Muñoz, poignantly portrays the marginality of lesbian existence in Argentine society.[2] Populated predominantly by Spanish and Italian immigrants, as well as by a significant number of Arabs, Argentina is ethnically composed of deeply rooted patriarchal cultures. Muñoz's film depicts how both she and her family suffered through repeated attempts to self-impose conformity. The interviews with family members that are incorporated into the film consistently voice the conviction that in order to "have a future" a "nor-

mal" female shows a liking for men and for all the paraphernalia implicitly promoted to make her more appealing and marketable as a marriage
candidate. Any behavior or aspiration not fitting within the parameter of
social gender construction is labeled deviant. Rejected by a family whose
homophobic intolerance represents Argentine society at large, in *Susana*
the lesbian-identified woman seeks exile as a means of escaping Latin
American cultural conventions.

In "The Coming-Out Process: Violence against Lesbians," Ruth Baetz
describes what embracing a lesbian identity may entail for some women:
"Imagine . . . a woman beginning to realize that she is a lesbian. During
the realization process, she may have to deal with a loss in self-confidence,
self-hatred, physical illness, nervous breakdown, alcoholism, marriage attempts, realization of wasted years of trying to be someone she isn't, numerous therapy sessions, and suicide attempts. This is euphemistically
called coming out of yourself. It could more accurately be described as
waging a major battle against an invisible internal enemy that has been
culturally constructed."[3]

In this sense, *Certificate of Absence* is the testimony of a lesbian woman's "coming out."[4] The narrator acknowledges the element of risk involved in the unmasking she proposes to undertake in the text: "*Entering*
this room, or *leaving* it, implies a true act of decision on her part, a risk"
(7,emphasis added). "Entering" the room in order to record her story of
lesbian love means she is prepared to reveal her true identity; writing
means "coming out" of the closet, that is "leaving" the room, a place of
refuge from heterosexual society.[5] As the narrator suggests, the room is
also a space for introspection because in order to tell her story she will
have to search within herself and evoke a painful past: "This room . . .
has turned all of a sudden into a place of penance where she will have to
carry out alone the exorcism she plans. . . . But she is afraid to write . . .
because she knows very well how much it hurts to tell this story" (12–13).
The word "penance" connotes absolution from wrongdoing and implies
that guilt is an important element in this story that "will not leave her
alone."

In addition to the dominant discourse that reveals the narrator's struggle with a lesbian identity, "this story" also contains a muted confession
of father-daughter incest.[6] Although the adult woman is able to write the
account of her lesbian lover's treachery, the child in her cannot be as forth-
right in relating the paternal betrayal that in effect forced her to become
the object of the ultimate social taboo. When Molloy's original Spanish
text was published in Spain in 1981, Argentina's military dictatorship

(1976–83) was still in power. Keeping this cultural and historical context in mind, we can draw a parallel between the narrator's ability to write about the wounds of lesbian existence while suppressing a far more bitter incest story and the Argentine people's ability or willingness to recognize the repressive climate of their government while at the same time as a society repressing or denying institutionalized mechanisms of disappearance, torture, and extermination perpetrated against dissidents under a business-as-usual, politically constructed social façade.[7] By abusing its power in the course of imposing its will on defenseless citizens, the military regime acted much like the controlling patriarch in the incest story in Molloy's novel. Though different in degree, abduction, imprisonment, and torture are analogous to the corporal manipulation of the child at the hands of the incestuous father. Whether violated in the political or private sphere, survivors carry deep, lifelong scars.

Self-Inscribing Lesbian Identity

Let us, then, first examine the consciously evoked dominant story that, borrowing the narrator's term, "exorcises" the pain of lesbian existence. Many lesbians, aware of the risks involved in "coming out," practice selective disclosure.[8] That is, in order to cope in a heterosexual world, they may reveal their sexual identity only to certain friends and family members. "Lipstick lesbians," like their heterosexual counterparts, have not only adopted but feel perfectly comfortable with the "feminine" beauty paraphernalia, dress, and demeanor expected of females in our society. Having already internalized female socialization helps them disguise their sexual identity in a heterosexual world that cannot fathom a "feminine" lesbian. In some cases the disturbance caused by assuming such a double image may lead to internalized homophobia, in which the person comes to believe the negative attitudes that society displays toward lesbians and homosexual men.[9]

Internalized homophobia may be expressed consciously in the form of "I hate myself for being lesbian," or it may be manifested in a variety of unconscious ways.[10] In the dominant story in Molloy's novel, the narrator's recurring bouts with self-degradation suggest an unconscious need to be punished for behavior that society deems aberrant. For example, she rents the room in order to write her story in the very place where she had first been with Vera, the woman who later subjected her to "a long night of humiliation when she was . . . forced to listen . . . to the smallest details of an act of love" (6). Although deeply hurt, the narrator apparently lacked sufficient self-esteem to counter the offense: "She wanted to die, swore to avenge herself, and yet the next morning managed only to refuse the breakfast that was offered her" (6). There is also a degree of self-denigration in the facts that she becomes Renata's lover when this woman is, in turn, abandoned by Vera, and that she continues to take part in sexual encounters with Renata even after Renata has ended their relationship and has become involved with another woman. Moreover, the narrator comes to realize that Renata's renewed romantic interest is motivated by the hope of being included in the manuscript.

Besides emotional debasement, the narrator has also submitted to physical abuse: "She . . . has allowed herself to be beaten, fully conscious of what she was doing. She once saw in a pair of mirrors . . . the bruises left by a buckle. Results of one more meeting—the last—with someone who had decided to draw her out of herself" (20). The text suggests that the role of recipient in sadomasochistic relations is not new to the narrator. In fact, she expresses the desire to feel pain: "She would like to know once and for all . . . what physical pain is, something as distant and threatening to her as madness" (20). The need to be punished is manifested in the emotionally and physically abusive treatment she consistently endures. Although she finds the act of writing disturbing, by evoking and inscribing the self-degrading experiences she forces herself to come to terms with her past and her identity.

As noted earlier, Baetz lists self-hatred, physical illness, nervous breakdown, alcoholism, and suicide attempts among the ordeals a lesbian may face during her "coming out" process. The narrator of *Certificate of Absence* is familiar with all these experiences. She displays self-hatred in a variety of masochistic behaviors. On one occasion, "Renata prevailed upon her to relinquish a razor, with which she, truly beside herself, was chopping off locks of hair" (95). During periods of depression she contemplates suicide, imagining hanging herself from the cast-iron balcony outside her window. Short of suicide, she recounts deliberately injuring herself: "One night she carefully sliced open her forearm: she did not feel anything. . . . Hers is a deadened body, lacking in sensation, which nonetheless does not forget her acts of violence against it" (19).

The narrator also inscribes her inability as well as her desire to feel physical pain and illness, craving the experience as a way of reconciling her fragmented identity and her alienated body: "Today . . . she pronounces her body ill, puts it to bed, wants to take care of it and renew her contact with it" (77). Keeping in mind that society generally scorns lesbian sexuality and that incest as sexual misuse violates the victim's right to his or her own body, it makes sense that the narrator wants to reclaim and take command of her body: "She wants just to feel, to recognize herself entirely in the heavy, inert body. . . . She wants to settle in that flesh completely, as one finally settles in a place that seemed forbidden but to which one had every right" (82).

The quest to achieve an integrated identity as a lesbian also forces the narrator to contend with her procreative capacity, a matter that Mariana Valverde sums up as the lesbian's personhood-womanhood dilemma.[11] Lesbian existence, for the most part, defies patriarchy in its rejection of men as mates and in its renunciation of motherhood. This latter component of the narrator's way of life haunts her subconscious mind. In a dream, a telephone call from her dead father instructs her urgently to travel to Ephesus to visit Artemis: "She thinks of the giant statue of the goddess, of the monstrous character with the many enormous breasts. She thinks too of the pilgrims who went to see her and of the fertility with which they were no doubt rewarded" (56). Clearly, the patriarch directs her, as dutiful daughter and woman, toward the prescribed path to conception. But the narrator does not identify with a maternal role: "She prefers another Artemis, another Diana—the free huntress, not weighed down by a breastplate of fertility . . . But . . . her father did not speak to her of this elusive, virginal Diana" (57).[12] Since women's sexuality is traditionally closely associated with procreation, lesbians may unconsciously internalize society's view that they are not "real women" but pseudomales.[13]

The predicament of reconciling being a "real woman" and a lesbian is reflected in yet another dream: "More than once she has dreamed of flayings, of being flayed. For instance, she sees herself split: before her stands a sick boy, flayed from the waist down. . . . The boy in her dream has no feet, just useless stumps. He cannot walk; he falls down and cries hoarsely" (5). In the symbolic unmasking of the true lesbian identity the narrator "sees herself split." The inner conflict to accept herself as a woman produces a dream image of a male deformed "from the waist down." The pseudomale is an invalid who suffers with his impotence to move, to alter his situation. Besides pointing to a painful laying bare of the narrator's lesbian identity, the gruesome flaying imagery also suggests the helpless child whose incest ordeal becomes discernible only when the surface story is metaphorically stripped away. This brings us to the other important, but muted, "exorcism" in *Certificate of Absence*.

(Sub)scribing Childhood Incest

To inscribe the experience of incest in her story, the narrator-protagonist conceptualizes her writing as a palimpsest, in terms of layers: "A key, an ordering principle for this story. She can see only layers, strata, as in the segments of the earth's crust shown in schoolbooks" (11).[14] Significantly, however, she changes the analogy to a corporal one as a deliberate way of implicating the body: "No, more like the various layers of skin that cover muscles and bones, overlapping, in *unpleasant contact*" (11–12, emphasis added). The analogy then goes on to link the body to a childhood experience: "Who has not observed as a child, after pulling off a scab, the inner surface and the *pink sore* that goes with it—and looked at it without trembling? In that inquisitive *act of destruction* she finds the key and ordering principle for this story" (12, emphasis added). Taken a step further, since the act of destruction that leaves a pink sore could metaphorically suggest the loss of virginity, the analogy points to sexuality and childhood as key factors in the narrator's story.

An association between writing and childhood is alluded to in a scene that is an essential part of the narrator and her story, however much she tries to edit both her memories and her account: "How can she heed the prohibitions of memory when memory is alive within her. . . . Despite what she adds and scratches out—*the first letter will remain, impossible to erase*" (85, emphasis added). We see that at the core of *Certificate of Absence* lies a tale that the narrator can neither tell outright nor fully suppress. But in the latter part of the novel when the narrator shares the manuscript with a former lover, the full story that she has earlier attempted to disguise is virtually spelled out: "Renata knows full well that a story without a plot means, above all, a story whose *plot has been suppressed:* there is *a hidden figure,* like a negative, *beneath these written words*" (108, emphasis added).

Since incest is a taboo subject that has been historically denied or veiled by society, it is no wonder that the narrator circumvents the topic in her writing. Bequeathed with the Freudian legacy, for a long time the medical profession played an important role in relegating the phenomenon to virtual nonexistence. As Catherine Clément notes in *The Newly Born Woman,* Freud in his psychoanalytic work with hysterics initially accepted as fact recurrent reports by women patients of acts of seduction and perversion on the part of their fathers or other male figures, although he felt it was the child's or the daughter's unconscious desire that had led to seduction of the adult.[15] He later reinterpreted these accounts of abuse as childhood sexual fantasies, but in either case, the patient was deemed the source of the problem; she had imagined the incident or had actually brought it on.

What constitutes father-daughter incest? Eileen Starzecpyzel points out in her essay "The Persephone Complex" that lack of actual sexual contact does not rule out an incestuous relationship: "When incest is covert (in cases of intrusive voyeurism, sexually colored ridicule of a child, and sexually motivated exposure), it does not involve physical contact. However, the dynamic is always sexual misuse, both of authoritative power and of the legitimate need for closeness, over a child who is unable to resist." [16] In *Certificate of Absence* the narrator portrays her father as a voyeur whom she strongly resented for his control over her bedroom door: "She feels alone, burdened by a weight she could never shake off. Even today, she feels a knot in her stomach as she writes, finding it hard to put words together, preferring to forget and not be consumed anymore by memories. She feels that by speaking of her father, and above all by speaking of the half-open door he never let her shut, she has in turn opened up a dangerous gap in her tale" (54–55). The fact that she would rather forget this childhood memory yet needs to incorporate it in the manuscript discloses that the father's practice of keeping the door ajar was not an innocent whim. As writer, the narrator is now able to break the silence on the misuse of paternal power and, albeit symbolically, finally to take control of the door.

Characteristic of an incestuous relationship, the bedroom, which the child normally regards as a safe and personal space, becomes the scene of the frightening encounter. Incidents of physical contact are commonly initiated when the child is asleep and therefore totally vulnerable.[17] The narrator recalls, for example, how her father would enter her room every morning to kiss her and rearrange the bed linen; the unwanted contact is experienced as an assault: "When she wakes up, an hour later, she remembers that hazy good-bye as an attack, but also as an act of complicity. . . . She was afraid of having kissed him on the lips. She was troubled that her father should have taken advantage of her sleep to touch her when she did not want to be touched" (52–53). The sense of complicity discloses the burden of guilt and secrecy most incest victims bear. Moreover, the morning ritual proves especially disturbing for the child because Hispanic culture reserves kissing on the mouth exclusively for romantic liaisons.

The narrator's story does not dwell on her childhood; nevertheless, what she does inscribe of it clearly points to her growing up in a dysfunctional incestuous family. Typically the family situation where incest occurs is not a happy one despite its normal outward appearance.[18] The text confirms the false image of family bliss: "Often . . . she is struck by the idea of a broken family, although hers seemed to give the unambiguous image of union" (54). As Goldman and Wheeler have pointed out, "In most cases of incest the relationship between the incestuous father and the mother is unhappy and tense. Frequently, emotional and sexual alienation has occurred."[19] Accordingly, the narrator remembers the mother's criticisms and complaints about the father, as well as outright parental fighting.

A strained marital relationship is one factor that often leads the father, who feels misunderstood and needing nurturing, to seek the unconditional affection of a child. Frequently, consciously or unconsciously, he appropriates a daughter as a "special" child. Sibling rivalry normally ensues, and other children in the family may experience rejection or harsh paternal disciplinary action for seeking the attention and affection showered on the "special" child.[20] In the novel, the narrator's sister, Clara, is emotionally starved by the father: "He rejected the hugs and kisses of his other daughter. She sees Clara . . . climbing onto her father's knees like an eager puppy, Clara asking him for something he could not give her. He was saving it instead for her, and she did not accept it" (54). In several respects the narrator's situation is characteristic of an incestuous family. For example, she is the older daughter, she is "special" although less physically attractive than Clara, and she is a victim who cannot shake off the false position of privileged daughter.[21]

Another characteristic of an incestuous family that is present in the novel is a poor mother-daughter relationship, which undermines the daughter's ability to confide in another adult and leaves the victim with no one to go to regarding the father's behavior.[22] The narrator's description of the ritual of her mother's daily nap, where the mother expresses the wish not to reawaken, reveals the unlikelihood of seeking her as a protective figure: "Once she was in bed, their mother would ask them to sing her a lullaby: not just one, several. Then she would close her eyes and say: 'How wonderful it would be never to wake up!'" (53). In taking on the role of a child, the mother symbolically leaves her daughters motherless. Furthermore, voicing her wish not to awaken threatens the child with the real possibility of orphanhood. Indeed, the narrator checks on her mother many times during her nap, fearing she may have stopped breathing. It is reasonable to conjecture that a child who is reminded daily of the mother's death wish would not risk upsetting her with a confession of daddy's behavior and therefore endures the victimization in silence.

Studies show that years after the father's transgression, a daughter may harbor more anger and resentment toward the mother who failed to protect her than toward the perpetrator.[23] The narrator of *Certificate of Absence* does, in fact, achieve a reconciliation with her father before he dies: "They came to understand one another, free of her mother's control, shortly before he died" (53). Although she does not mention forgiving the father, the willingness, and apparently also the ability, to understand him may be linked to the hurt of unrequited love she has experienced as an adult in another type of relationship not sanctioned by society. Communication with the mother, however, can only be imagined after she is dead because there is no significant bond from which to initiate a dialogue: "Why was there so little said between us, how could we fight so often? Perhaps she will say this to her mother soon . . . although she pictures herself saying it after her death, when her mother can no longer disarm her" (115).

Eileen Starzecpyzel has labeled the incest trauma marked by "maternal loss and paternal seduction" the Persephone complex. She points out that when the father appropriates the daughter as a "special" child he severs the mother-daughter bond, leaving the child feeling unconnected to the mother.[24] Like Persephone, the child experiences herself as stolen from the mother, as motherless. According to Starzecpyzel's theory, the early alienation from the mother may lead the daughter who has been an incest survivor to seek women, emotionally and sexually, in an effort to satisfy the longing for the nurturing she was deprived of during her developmental years.

Somewhat skeptically, in the early part of the story the narrator poses the idea of a nexus between her lovers and her childhood: "She does not see the link between Vera, Renata, and her childhood very clearly; she does not believe, in the final analysis, that such a link exists. She knows only that for the moment . . . she will follow the three lines of the story, three lines that will perhaps merge later to reveal, like the layers of skin in the anatomy book, how they are connected to one another" (12). The palimpsest in the text, like layers of skin, points to incest as a possible link between childhood trauma and lesbianism. The fact that the narrator focuses the account on her adult experiences as a lesbian and interjects flashbacks of her childhood, virtually omitting adolescence, suggests the significance of the two periods.

The emotional and physical depravity tolerated by an adult lesbian woman may also be rooted in an early incest experience. One study of incest survivors showed that over 50 percent "had cut, burnt, or bruised themselves or taken poison." [25] Analogous to the narrator's almost obsessional need to feel pain, one woman in Sandra Butler's study, *Conspiracy of Silence,* tells her reason for self-injury: "When I was in sixth grade, I came to school with cigarette burns all over my left arm. I had done it because I was feeling scared that I was beginning not to feel anything. I needed to see if I was still real, if I could still hurt." [26]

The narrator's sadomasochistic liaisons could also be traced back to the childhood incest experience. In her discussion of sadomasochistic eroticism, Margaret Nichols suggests that people who engage in practices that involve shaming and humiliation could be erotically acting out frightening experiences of shame, guilt, or domination that were sexualized in childhood: "Particularly in childhood, sexual arousal is virtually indistinguishable from other arousal states, including . . . anger, or fear. . . . Thus a frightened child, or a child receiving a spanking, may also be experiencing sexual arousal, and it is quite easy to imagine a classically conditioned response to this type of stimuli becoming entrenched at an early age." [27] Besides recalling the dread she felt as a child at the thought of accidentally kissing her father on the mouth during his morning good-bye, the narrator recalls a dream in which both arousal and fear are explicitly associated with the father: "As she sits reading aloud from some text she finds tedious, something, perhaps a gesture from her father, makes her lift up her skirt, push down her underpants, and touch herself. At that moment in the dream, she experiences a pleasure such as she will seldom reach again. In great fear, she runs out . . . and rushes down the stairs" (118). Following Nichols's theory, the adult narrator's participation in sadomasochistic sexual practices could be an acting out of the shame and guilt associated with the incestuous father-daughter relationship.

The incest story, culturally shrouded in silence, is textually inscribed as a palimpsest, and the trauma also recurrently surfaces as "unvoiced" manifestations, either consciously in childhood fantasies (that is, active imagination) or subconsciously in the dream world of the adult. For example, the narrator describes how in one childhood fantasy she would transform her bed into a ship in a storm. Yet "another fantasy took place in an old bathroom. . . . She imagined herself condemned to live there forever, and thought up means of surviving: the bathtub would be a bed, she would cover herself with towels, would eat soap and toothpaste, would drink cough syrups" (7). Both the bedroom and the bathroom are places where the father had access to the child's body. He controlled the narrator's bedroom door and on occasion would bathe the two daughters together. In both fantasies the narrator imagines herself suffering through an ordeal and playing the role of survivor. Even in child's play the father is silently accused: "In games she played with her sister . . . there were never fathers or husbands: they had all died in some war or had simply never existed. Widowed mothers, maiden aunts, or orphaned sisters . . . they played at being long-suffering women who had some tragedy in their lives; whatever it was, *there were no men, no man like their father*" (56, emphasis added).

In *Certificate of Absence*, the tacit indictment against the patriarch is unmistakable. The dream in which the father instructs the daughter to visit Diana of Ephesus may well represent the lesbian's conflict between motherhood (embodied in Diana the goddess of fecundity) and womanhood (embodied in Diana the free, agile huntress), but it also yields another interpretation. The narrator admits to identifying with the angry and vengeful facet of the goddess, a Diana whose punishments symbolically reflect the desire to avenge the harm inflicted by the incestuous father: "When *one man tries to sit her on his lap, like her father*, she tears a handful of hair from his chest without a moment's hesitation. She turns *a nymph pregnant with Zeus's child*—she, the patroness of childbirth—into a bear. And she transforms *the man who dares to spy on her, when she is alone and naked* in the stream, into a stag, the better to tear him to pieces" (121, emphasis added). As these retaliatory acts of the mythical Diana reveal, the three incidents—attempted molestation, impregnation, and voyeurism—implicate the patriarch's desire. The accusation against the father is inscribed but veiled in myth, appropriately telling of how taboo the issue of incest is in society.

Let us here recall the narrator's own masking of the subject when at the beginning of the novel she implies that her motive for writing is rooted in the need to avenge an adult relationship. Whether she is conscious of it or not, the humiliating experience that originally prompted her to write is clearly not the only story clamoring for revenge in the novel. At one point in the account the narrator declares: "The story she started writing, in hopes of avenging herself, turns out to be harmless. She intended to record a lived experience, in anger; now she finds herself writing from mere habit. She deludes herself . . . because the revenge she sought has in no way altered her reality" (86). True, neither the pain related to her lesbian identity (which she openly inscribes) nor the incest trauma (subscribed in the text) can be erased; but the act of writing has transformed the narrator through catharsis. Constructively channeled into writing, the hurt and anger have induced her to break the silence. The self-reflective writing has empowered her to "exorcise" her own story and free her spirit from the burden of silence. She has taken a major step toward healing the emotional wounds by altering her self-image as victim to that of survivor.

Notes

Reprinted, with changes, from Gisela Norat, "Four Latin American Writers Liberating Taboo: Albalucía Angel, Marta Traba, Sylvia Molloy, Diamela Eltit" (Ph.D. diss., Washington University, 1991).

1. Sylvia Molloy, *Certificate of Absence*, 3. Page references in the text are to the Daniel Balderston translation, University of Texas Press, 1989. The original in Spanish is *En breve cárcel* (Barcelona: Seix Barral, 1981). The novel is Molloy's first published work of fiction. Born (1938) and raised in Buenos Aires, at twenty she went to Paris to pursue her university studies. After completing her studies in 1961, she returned to Argentina and from 1962 to 1967 taught at various institutions, including the University of Buenos Aires, Catholic University of Argentina, and the Alliance Française. In 1967 she secured a scholarship to go back to Paris and on her return trip to Argentina she came through the United States, where she has resided ever since. She has taught Spanish at the State University of New York at Buffalo, Vassar College, and Princeton University, and is presently at New York University. For biographical data see: Magdalena García Pinto, *Women Writers of Latin America* (Austin: University of Texas Press, 1991), 128–30; and Jaques Cattell Press, ed., *Directory of American Scholars*, 8th ed. (New York: R. R. Bowker, 1982) 3:360. Molloy's early work on the Argentine authors Silvina Ocampo and, especially, Jorge Luis Borges (*Las letras de Borges*), established her in the field of literary inquiry. Besides numerous critiques on various Argentine and Spanish-American authors, her more recent work includes a study of autobiographical writing in Spanish-America, *At Face Value*, and an essay in the anthology *Women's Writing in Latin America*, coauthored with Sara Castro-Klarén and Beatriz Sarlo.

2. Susana Muñoz, *Susana*, 16mm/video, 25 min., 1980, distributed by Women Make Movies, New York. Muñoz's best-known documentary feature, *Las madres de Plaza de Mayo* (1985), on the Argentine mothers who, during the military dictatorship (1976–83), organized and rallied to demand an official accounting of their sons and daughters who had disappeared, won her and coproducer Lourdes Portillo a nomination for a 1986 Academy Award and the Blue Ribbon 1986 American Film Festival Award (16mm/video, 64 min., distributed by Direct Cinema, Ltd., Los Angeles).

3. Ruth Baetz, "The Coming-Out Process," 46.

4. For a study of literary representation of gay and lesbian existence, see David William Foster, *Gay and Lesbian Themes in Latin American Writing.*

5. The narrator notes that "the room where she writes is small and dark" (Molloy, 3). *Webster's Third New International Dictionary*, 14th ed., defines "closet" in its first meaning (from MF *clos* enclosure) as "an apartment or small room for retirement or privacy."

6. Elaine Showalter in her essay "Feminist Criticism in the Wilderness," speaks of a "double-voiced" discourse in texts written by women that contain a "dominant" and a "muted" story.

7. In 1981, the same year Molloy's novel appeared, the Argentine author Marta

Traba published, in exile, *Conversación al sur,* an exposé of the Argentine government's cover-up of flagrant human rights violations. The book's brief dedication speaks to the country's traditional lack of historical memory: "To Gustavo and Elba, lest we forget." For testimony on the period known as the "dirty war," see *Las locas de Plaza de Mayo,* by Jean-Pierre Bousquet, a French correspondent for France Press in Argentina during the dictatorship. See also María del Carmen Feijoó, "The Challenge of Constructing Civilian Peace," and Gloria Bonder, "Women's Organisations in Argentina's Transition to Democracy."

8. Lee Zevy and Sahli A. Cavallaro, "Invisibility, Fantasy, and Intimacy," 88.

9. Liz Margolies, Martha Becker, and Karla Jackson-Brewer, "Internalized Homophobia," 230.

10. Ibid., 231.

11. Mariana Valverde, *Sex, Power, and Pleasure,* 57.

12. For an interpretation of the role of Diana in the novel, especially in connection with the woman as writer, see Oscar Montero, "*En breve cárcel.*

13. Christine Browning, "Changing Theories of Lesbianism," 25.

14. In regard to the use of the palimpsest, Sandra M. Gilbert and Susan Gubar, in *The Madwoman in the Attic,* 73, discuss the long tradition of women's literary works "whose surface designs conceal or obscure deeper, less accessible (and less socially acceptable) levels of meaning." Francine R. Masiello in "En breve cárcel" refers to the use of the palimpsest as response to the established male writing canon.

15. Hélène Cixous and Catherine Clément, *The Newly Born Woman,* 40–47.

16. Eileen Starzecpyzel, "The Persephone Complex," 262.

17. Louise Armstrong, *Kiss Daddy Goodnight,* 23, 25, 59, 150.

18. Judith Herman with Lisa Hirschman, "Father-Daughter Incest," 745.

19. Renitta L. Goldman and Virginia R. Wheeler, *Silent Shame,* 24.

20. Ibid., 37.

21. See ibid., 34–35; and Herman and Hirschman, "Father-Daughter Incest," 743.

22. Goldman and Wheeler, *Silent Shame,* 30.

23. Ibid., 35; Herman and Hirschman, "Father-Daughter Incest," 747.

24. Starzecpyzel, "The Persephone Complex," 266, 268.

25. Goldman and Wheeler, *Silent Shame,* 40–41.

26. Sandra Butler, *Conspiracy of Silence,* 45.

27. Margaret Nichols, "Lesbian Sexuality," 111.

PAMELA SMILEY

The Unspeakable: Mary Gordon
and the Angry Mother's Voices

The image of a mother lovingly crooning her child to sleep with soft lullabies is such a cliché that it is almost ubiquitous in our culture: appearing on embossed Christmas cards, in Mrs. Ramsay's bedtime stories to James and Cam in *To the Lighthouse,* in ads for life insurance. Such an image has the power to define lives by making the unspoken argument that it is this image of mother that is "natural." If one is a mother, then one must by definition feel as loving and nurturing and patient as those silently beautiful images with which we are surrounded. But what of the other image of mother, the one that is not shown? What of the Janus-face of the loving madonna—the mother's face strained in anger at her child? What of those mothers? Are they mothers? What if a woman recognizes herself more in the angry mother than in the madonna?

This dialogue with images of the loving mother and the angry mother informs Mary Gordon's novel *Men and Angels.*[1] The protagonist, Anne, is caught between the two images: she seeks the ideal mother for herself, and she seeks to be the ideal mother for her two children while denying the angry mother. Each of Anne's relationships in the novel is a variation on this mother-child configuration, and in each case, with the exception of the one that ends the novel, she represses any recognition of the validity of the angry mother.

At the onset of *Men and Angels,* Anne's life seems to be following the happy-ever-after formula. Although she, the bright daughter, has been rejected by her mother in favor of her more conventional sister, she is her father's favorite. She has been married for several years to a man named Michael but then takes a job that separates her from her husband. The job involves writing a biography of the artist Caroline Watson by interviewing Caroline's daughter-in-law, Jane. Anne's love for Caroline and Jane, two magnificent figures of female authority who give Anne the love her own

mother denied her, is counterbalanced by Anne's growing antipathy to
Laura, Anne's children's au pair. Laura represents both Anne's angry self
and the child she cannot love. When Anne finally fires Laura and Laura
commits suicide, Anne is forced to accept the anger she has projected on
Laura as her own anger.

On the most obvious level, the dialogue with images of the mother
begins by positing the naturalness of the madonna: Anne is a madonna;
the love she finds in Caroline and Jane is the ideal mother's love; mothers
who are not like Anne or the like Caroline and Jane in their mothering of
Anne are flawed because of selfishness, class, or fate. Anne appears, and
presumes herself to be, the ideal mother: again and again, she refers to
motherhood as primary to her self-definition. The name she shares with
the mother of the mother of Jesus links her to an unbroken narrative of
ideal mothers. Laura's description of Anne's photograph positions her as
a madonna: "She sat holding her babies and her face was golden, the face
of light" (249).[2] Michael's friend describes her as the Angel of the House:
"But what a genius you have for family life. I cannot imagine you would
want to work. It is for people that your gift is" (225). Feminist theory
such as Julia Kristeva's "Stabat Mater" makes predictions about Anne's
"mother voice." Kristeva describes her communication with her own child
as being outside of language, and she foresees that the "mother's voice"
will exceed and disrupt language, recentering signification in the semiotic,
the body, the metaphorical.[3] Anne's orientation away from the symbolic
should signal a flowing toward wholeness, a resisting of abstraction, and
a rootedness in the body. But because Anne represses her anger, which is
a crucial part of herself, she is imprisoned by what she denies and is unable
to attain the wholeness that Kristeva predicts.

Anne plays the part of the madonna with so much conviction that she
dis-covers the gaps in the patriarchal narrative of maternity even as she
covers them. Patriarchal celebration of mother love is simultaneous with
the subordination of it to the Law of the Father with its distrust of human
connection. By placing mother love at the center, in the position reserved
for justice, faith, morality, and passion in the world of men, Anne subverts
the Law. Mother love constitutes her standard of justice and moral decision: "Justice, what a small part it played in her life. Like most women,
she feared it. Justice in her life conjured up the implacable God of Moses
depriving his servants of the promised land because of the rock struck
twice. . . . Whatever moral considerations Anne owed to the rest of hu-
mankind was dwarfed by her first duty: to keep her children safe" (353).
Mother love is also Anne's "ruling passion" (336): "No one told her [be-

ing a mother] would be like the way she loved her children. . . . How I love you she always wanted to say, and you can never know it. I would die for you without a thought. You have given my life its sheerest, its profoundest pleasure" (22–23).

Anne's pleasure in the world similarly resists symbolism and remains rooted in the body. Money, for example, is not an index of power, but "a nice thing [because] . . . it said, you can have this, and this, and this. This you can put against your skin, that in your mouth, and on your feet boots that make you swoon with pleasure" (314). Money's value lies in sensual gratification, and one of the most distinctive characteristics of Gordon's heroines is their sensuality.

This very sensuality, part of the visceral connectedness that defines the madonna, attracts Anne to the paintings of Caroline Watson and initiates her into a daughterly relationship with the dead Caroline and her daughter-in-law, Jane. Anne describes her love for her children as a semiotic flow; she remembers that "when they were babies she ached for them if she were away from them. . . . They had lived in the curve of her body when she nursed them. . . . Flesh of my flesh" (216–17). The same desire for wholeness compels her when she looks at Caroline's paintings: "Seeing those paintings, something grew in Anne, something she'd lived with since but hadn't known before, a push or a desire like hunger for a definite, but hard-to-come-by food. The painting made her greedy to be with them, to speak of them: they belonged to her" (35). Anne's response to the paintings is not limited to an intellectual evaluation. She explains her understanding in terms of the body: hunger, desire, the stuff of appetite and physical need. These semiotic responses disrupt the symbolic divisions and order of intellectual language in a primal urge toward wholeness. Her understanding echoes the "mother's voice" predicted by Kristeva as it escapes the Lacanian signifier's determinism by reverting to the prelinguistic chora.

Given these echoes, it is not surprising that Anne describes Caroline Watson's oeuvre in pre-Oedipal terms—a nostalgic reference back to a time before separation, when meaning was not contingent on difference or on the substitution of symbolic language for the presence of the desired one. Writing a catalogue of Watson's art, Anne interprets Caroline's Cassatt-like images into words: "a universe exclusively female. . . . a summer world of women left in the country with their children" (71). Such a woman-centered community of mothers and children, devoid of fathers, destabilizes cultural narratives by foregrounding women's realities and including the mother's voice.

The rightness of Anne's adopting Caroline Watson as her mother is indirectly justified by Anne's response to Caroline's daughter-in-law, Jane. Anne brings her children for a weekend at Jane's home. Even the look of Jane's home, with its old china and understated elegance, makes Anne feel that she has "come home" in a way that has been impossible for her in her relationship with her own mother. She feels a sense of return and wholeness. Coming back from a brisk walk in the cool fall air, she wanted to say, "'I missed you' . . . placing her cool cheek against Jane's, which was warm and dryish. But that was absurd: she knew Jane only slightly, she had left her only an hour before" (167).

With the long-dead Caroline Watson and Jane, her living representative, Anne senses a primacy of connection in which the boundaries between self and (m)other are indistinct: "We are connected. In the bone. This woman whom I know and do not know at all, is a part of my life like my own children" (80). This feeling of physical and emotional belonging is the need that informs the ubiquitous image of the ideal mother that haunts us in images on greeting cards and in the media.

Anne and Caroline-Jane are depicted as ideal mothers. But *Men and Angels* is a work filled with mothers, most of whom are not ideal. Anne is not blind to the presence of these flawed mothers, but she rationalizes their behavior as accidents of selfishness or class. Anne's own mother, for example, prefers her sister—a reaction Anne credits to jealousy. Anne feels that the withholding of maternal love is the price she pays for her father's favor: "Her mother would never forgive her, and perhaps she was right. Her father preferred her, he always had" (385).

Her mother is also flawed by her middle-class identity and her physical lack of substance. Anne responds to the luxury and sensuality of Jane's Thanksgiving dinner by recognizing that it "was a table her [Anne's] mother couldn't have set in thousands of years" (167). While Anne admits that the dinner and Jane's home were "all that Anne felt she had not been born to," there is the unspoken implication that Anne feels she *should* have been born into a wealthier class because of the sense of coming home she feels with Jane and Jane's world. In a mixed tone of relief and self-justification Anne compares her birth mother with Jane: "Anne put her arms around Jane and embraced her. How pleasant it was to feel Jane's large bones, her firm flesh. She had always been afraid to embrace her mother too robustly. Her mother was so much smaller than she; her bones were light and delicate. Anne felt for years that she had loomed above her mother, that she could hurt her with her sheer physical size. Jane smoothed Anne's hair and kissed her on the forehead. . . . [Anne] would sleep well; she was very happy. Jane had taken her in" (173–74). Just as Jane's world matches Anne's aesthetic one, so does Jane's body match her physical size and her sense of her own substantiality. In a single stroke, Anne identifies her mother's flaws as an issue of class and separates herself from identification with them.

Other less than ideal mothers are found lacking for similar reasons. Mrs. Post, the mother of Anne's children's au pair, Laura, says of her daughter: "She never meant anything to me, not from the minute I saw her. She was ugly. She tried to make me miserable. She always hated me, whatever bullshit she said, she always hated me. . . . watching me, making me feel like a piece of shit for breathing" (380–81). Anne finds Mrs. Post a "monster" because she has the "face of hatred, not contorted, not grotesque, but smooth and distant, like a face on television. That woman [who] had said she hated her daughter since the moment she was born" (382). How does Anne account for such monstrousness? Anne, who defines motherhood as "a place where hate could not enter," explains Mrs. Post's unmotherly hatred in the same way she explains her own mother's inadequacies: selfishness and class. As Anne drives through Mrs. Post's neighborhood, she notes evidence of the "bleak testimony of a place down on its luck, of bad times, no jobs, and no money" (376). Similarly, she sees Mrs. Post as flawed by working-class values: "Obviously she had some ideal of beauty clear in her own mind, but Anne had trouble placing it. Her hair was a flat gold color, cut into a style called a wedge, a style inspired by an ice-skater, which had been slightly out of fashion for five years. Her fingernails were long and polished reddish black; her toenails were the same color. . . . [She was] obviously in costume; [she was] trying to play some part" (378). That "part," as Anne sees it, constitutes Mrs. Post's selfish and futile attempt to deny her working-class limitations and escape the results of becoming pregnant with Laura at seventeen: "You know how old I was when [Laura] was born? Seventeen. It was the end of my life" (380).

On the first and most obvious level, then, *Men and Angels* seems to confirm the good-mother angry-mother dichotomy by setting up extreme examples of each: Anne and Caroline-Jane as good mothers; Anne's birth mother and Mrs. Post as angry mothers. On a less obvious level, however, *Men and Angels* blurs these divisions. "Ideal" Anne and Caroline-Jane are clearly also angry, despite Anne's attempts to repress her recognition of this fact.

Traces of the anger first surface in Anne's research on Caroline Watson as a painter. In her hunger to know Caroline, she reads the artist's journals and letters. Anne imagines herself the protector of Caroline and her inter-preter to the world: "What she had to do was build a house for a woman she loved. Like a pioneer husband claiming the forest, she must clear through the wilderness. She must build the house entire. . . . Without the house that she would build, the woman she loved, dead forty-five years, unknown to almost everyone, could not be made to live" (80–81). As Virginia Woolf advises women writers in *A Room of One's Own*, Anne looks back through Caroline, recovering evidence of the painter's life and art that satisfy a "hunger that [Anne] felt, that women felt, to know the details: where women stood in relation to their families, as daughters, sisters, mothers" (82).

Because daughterly "hunger to know" often reads a mother's life ac-cording to what the daughter finds important, it can result in an appropri-ation of the mother that silences her as effectively as patriarchal idealiza-tion. But despite Anne's personal need to resurrect Caroline as the ideal mother, she is unable to repress entirely the traces of anger that she detects in Watson's art and her relationship with her son, Stephen. Caroline Watson's paintings seem to celebrate an idyllic pre-Oedipal world, "un-troubled, suggesting life was good, [for] mothers and their children" (292). Anne is drawn to Caroline's nostalgic evocations of a world of sen-sual and physical connection between mothers and children. Yet even as she responds, she recognizes a small note of discord. The mothers and children in the paintings "looked as if they didn't like one another" (112). And Anne finds that Caroline in her journal angrily describes her son, Stephen, as a child who "dulls everything, muddles everything. His unhap-piness poisons the house. . . . [I] despise my son for his slowness, his mis-ery. My son, I know where he is. He sits outside my door, waiting for me to finish. I can hear his breath through walls a foot thick. His breath steals mine and blinds me" (204).

Anne can deal with Caroline's ambivalent pictorial images of mothers and children because she can distance herself from them with the analyti-cal language of art criticism. She imagines herself describing these paint-ings with phrases such as " 'It should be noted,' and 'The style demands.' Hard words, formed words, white stones that she could hold and sepa-rate" (400). But without such carefully controlled language and symbolic distance Anne cannot process maternal anger and dislike; she admits that Caroline's feelings toward her son were "a barrier between us that was as profound as one of language" (113).

Anne attempts to repress her recognition of Caroline's anger because her own self-definition requires walling anger out. Because she is unable to tolerate contradiction, she denies the complexity of Caroline's maternal response. She rationalizes that Caroline's mother love might have been vulnerable to the psychological trauma of culturally enforced self-sacrifice; Stephen is for Caroline a "bad accident born of the body, fathered in secret by a stranger whose name no one knew" (166). But even as Anne recognizes the continual self-sacrifice demanded to sustain the good-mother angry-mother division and the mother's necessary "pushing away" of the child who threatens to consume her, she still diminishes her vision by refusing to account for the creative and self-protective aspects of anger. Anne counters, "a child didn't have to earn its mother's love. . . . You loved them simply because they were. And because they were yours" (166).

Another way in which Anne attempts to rationalize Caroline's ambivalence is by doing a feminist reading of her own reaction to Caroline's negative feelings toward her son. Anne realizes that "no one would have pored through a male artist's letters to his children as she had through Caroline's and Stephen's. It was that Caroline was a woman and had a child and had created art; because the three could not be connected in some sort of grammar" (114).

But these rationalizations do not set to rest Anne's nagging suspicion that Caroline's ambivalence toward her son is not a minor, discrete flaw, but "some deficiency of spirit, some inexcusable coldness at the center that cast doubt on the rest of her life" (165). Unlike Caroline, Anne feels able to integrate without ambivalence the demands of mother and artist; she finds that the process of the one enhances the joys of the other: "She would take her mind, sharpen it, make it single; she would take the facts she had learned, the words that there were for them, join them together. . . . And then, refreshed, she could dive down to the dense underworld, to her children and say 'this is life. What shall we make of it? For it is terrible, and shining, and our hearts are sore'" (400).

But even as Anne claims her artistry and her motherhood to be integrated, she still recognizes in herself some maternal imperfections. She admits that her power comes from her children's "dependence . . . and their trusts; it was their weakness, after all, that gave her strength" (117). She also recognizes her own powerlessness to "influence the course of things determined so much by their natures and their fates" (26). The all-powerful mother, who according to Kristeva protects men from death, is only a child's fantasy.

As the novel progresses, it is Anne's relationship with Laura that forces her to admit her own maternal anger. Anne, positioned as mother by Laura's need of her, dislikes Laura more with every passing day: "It was unbearable, the things Laura made her feel. She could have gone her whole life without feeling them. It was Laura's presence with her in the house, it was the life she had to live beside her that made these antipathies so brutish and so real" (203). Here Anne attempts to distance herself from her own dislike of Laura by claiming that her anger is Laura's fault.

Anne's self-definition is shaped and contained by patriarchal definitions of the good mother that hide the possibility of maternal rejection by shutting out anger. Without an image of motherhood that could articulate a wider range of emotional states, Anne must continue to deny negative emotions such as violence, ambivalence, rejection, and anger.

Unwilling to recognize anger in herself, Anne describes it as uncharacteristic: "Anger was an emotion Anne had rarely; when it came she felt it in a way she felt a headache, a sensation unusual but not entirely unfamiliar" (127). Even when she feels herself to be absolutely justified in her anger, as when she fires Laura on the grounds that Laura has jeopardized the children's lives, Anne separates herself from her anger by describing it as a bird: "She had become the wings, the beak, she could feel her body whirring, she could feel her limbs grow long and pointed, ready to swoop, ready to strike. Her movement across the snow felt like heavy flight" (340). Haunted by the conflicting demands of being a woman, a mother, and a writer, Anne represses recognition of her own limitations (her anger at Laura, her mother's rejection of her), and mystifies the parallel limitations she cannot ignore in Caroline Watson.

It is Jane, positioned outside the conventional narratives of maternal love (since she has no real children, only her symbolic child, Anne), who finally demystifies Caroline's maternal role. First Jane problematizes the presumption that there is a fixed meaning to the words "mother love": "Mother love. I haven't the vaguest idea what it means. All those children claiming that their mothers didn't love them, and all those mothers saying they'd die for their children. Even women who beat up their children say they love them, they can't live without them, they wouldn't dream of giving them up. What does it mean 'I love my child'?" (163).

Then Jane takes the term "mother love" and springs it from its patriarchal context as defined by the needs of fathers and children. Instead, Jane locates mother love in the chosen mother-daughter dyad created by women not related by blood: "Caroline was a perfectly murderous mother to Stephen, but to me she was a mother made in heaven. Whereas I feel no more for my own mother than I felt for a rather distant cousin" (279). And lastly, Jane disconnects mother love from judgments of Caroline's worth: "She was marvelous. What she said about herself was right. She was often unkind, impatient and unjust. She was terrifically self-absorbed. But she was loyal and honest and courageous. She was a great painter. She had only to open a door to make life come into a room. In her presence despair was impossible, depression the invention of the Russians or the English or someone in a country far away from where you were" (335).

As Jane defines her, Caroline bursts through the binary paradigm of "good" and "bad" mother and becomes simply human, valued for her creativity, her energy, her art, and her passion as well as for her admittedly flawed capacity to mother. Caroline thereby becomes an example of what Marianne Hirsch calls maternal "double-voicedness." Uncontained by her role in the father and child narratives, the double-voiced mother is "tolerant and generous even as she is angry; a mother who can feel and express her anger without doing any devastating damage; a mother who is able to combine anger with attentive love."[4]

But if it is possible to cite Caroline as an example of maternal double-voicedness, it is not true of Anne. To the very end of *Men and Angels* Anne is caught in a recurring pattern of recognition and repression of her own anger and passions. For example, she admits, and then immediately represses, her recognition of the impulse behind child abuse: "One could easily see why it happened all the time. In the three years when she had been home all day with the children, her own frustrations had shocked her; the boredom that led to irritation at the smallest thing. But . . . you did not hurt your children. You kept them from harm. That is what you did if you were a mother" (215).

Anne's final reverie, the conclusion of *Men and Angels* and its closing statement on mother love, admits the existence of mothers who are angry and who hate:

> There were mothers who loved their children in a way that cut their
> children's breath and stopped their hearts; there were mothers who, in
> a passion of love, took their children and pressed them to their bosoms
> and in the next moment threw the children screaming from them,
> covered with blows. There were mothers for whom the sight of their
> children meant nothing: no love stirred, no part of the heart lifted.
> There were mothers who hated their children from the moments of
> their births, who hated the first touch of flesh on flesh and went on
> hating. There were mothers who loved their children but could not
> love them, for they bent to kiss the child's flesh and felt the flesh
> stop up their mouth and make them fear for their next breath. And
> children throve or starved, and no one knew why, or what killed or
> saved. (399)

Like a litany to the Virgin, Anne acknowledges the multiple, often nega-tive, expressions of mother love. But despite Anne's experience with Caro-line, she still sees these mothers as "other." She defines herself as different from them, not because of self-sacrifice or genius but because of luck: "Some grew in the face of sorrow, and some were undone. Some opened and enlarged, and some were ground to dust. Some became, only in sor-row, truly human; some were turned to animals who bit and snarled and lay in wait, who killed the weaker in contempt, for nourishment and from natural obedience to force" (398). Anne decides that whether one is a good or a bad mother is a matter of fate. Maternal anger is therefore an individual failing and not a cultural problem; and without a recognition of societal causes, the personal can never become political.

By denying her own anger, Anne closes out the possibility of a collec-tive anger that might translate the full range of maternal feelings into a political resource. As Peter Lyman argues: "A psychology of suffering would have to understand guilt, anxiety, depression or hysteria as re-pressed social relations. Psychology without this sense of social relations 'mythologizes' human suffering, treating it as essentially individual and a problem of 'personality.' Psychology serves the interests of hegemony when it strips human experience of its collective and active character and conceals oppression by blaming victims for their symptoms."[5] This indi-vidualizing of motherhood is what makes Anne's final reverie so dis-turbing. Although she has managed to accept the possibility of alterna-tives to the patriarchal idealization of motherhood, she is not yet able to see herself in these terms, not able to translate this alterity into political choices. Why?

Any view of the mother that exposes the traditional split between "bad" and "good" is risky both to the mother and to the child. The femi-nist daughter who names her mother's anger may find herself on the re-ceiving end of that anger, and recognizing the difference between the ideal and the real makes a daughter no better prepared for maternal rejection. For the mother, it can be painful to acknowledge the maternal double-voicedness that makes her only human, a considerable loss of power from the semidivine status of the "good" mother.

But most interesting, particularly in *Men and Angels,* is the risk in-volved in linking the image of the "good" mother with the issue of class and therefore with female privilege. Throughout the novel the mothers Anne views as "good" tend to be upper class. Anne identifies with Jane's class and distances herself from her real-mother's class; she sees herself and Jane as good mothers, her own mother as bad. Mrs. Post, decidedly working class, is a bad mother. That Caroline Watson, upper class, is both a good mother (to Jane) and a bad mother (to Stephen), is the puzzle that Anne struggles to define.

The link between maternal anger and class identity is one that Gordon herself makes. In an interview with Annie Milhaven, Gordon described her own mother, a disabled woman who worked to support her family, as "tough" and "aggressive." She likewise described her grandmother as "very tough and strong. Not a nice woman. Not a tender woman." She went on to add that women who live in economically precarious situations tend to be very different from the maternal ideal; immigrant women (like those in Gordon's family) "could not afford to be too understanding because their life was very hard." [6]

Although Gordon identifies herself as one of the line of strong women in her family, she clearly also identifies with the learning, the formality, and the ritual of her Roman Catholic childhood and her early life with her father. Like Anne and the main character in another novel, *Final Payments,* Gordon seems drawn to the trappings of education and privilege as a way of separating herself from the impotence of maternal anger and the vulnerability of being judged for that anger as bad. Recognition of that impotence is reflected in her admission that immigrant mothers say to their children, "Life is very hard. Better be ready to stand up for it and protect your flanks. Because they'll get you." [7] The tragedy of personalizing and distancing oneself from such maternal anger, instead of politicizing it by identifying it as collective and justified, is that it perpetuates the necessity of such cautions. As long as anger is linked to class and separated from the collective, the privilege of some women will be maintained only at the expense of all women.

Notes

1. Mary Gordon has written such novels about women's lives as *Final Payments, The Company of Women,* and *Temporary Shelter.*

2. Mary Gordon, *Men and Angels.* Page references to this work will appear parenthetically in the text.

3. Julia Kristeva, "Stabat Mater."

4. Marianne Hirsch, *The Mother-Daughter Plot,* 191.

5. Peter Lyman, "The Politics of Anger," 58–59.

6. Annie Lally Milhaven, "Interview with Mary Gordon," 112.

7. Ibid.

RUTH O. SAXTON

Dead Angels: Are We Killing the
Mother in the House?

Angels have hovered in and out of my consciousness for many years. Just when I have begun to take them for granted, they shift their shapes. As a little girl who memorized biblical texts before I understood many of their words, I repeated the Twenty-third Psalm over and over again. For longer than I care to admit, I basked in the delightful knowledge that three female angels—Shirley, Goodness, and Mercy—were following me around, looking out for my well-being. As an adult woman who reads and teaches literature by women I now talk about the Angel in the House, that phantom killed by Virginia Woolf in self-defense. And just as I once confused qualities with angels, I think women may sometimes confuse mothers with angels, mistakenly thinking that if we would be writers, we must kill not only the Angel in the House but the mother as well.

According to Virginia Woolf, "A woman writing thinks back through her mothers."[1] In *The Madwoman in the Attic,* Sandra Gilbert and Susan Gubar agree with Woolf, arguing that women writers, unlike men, celebrate their foremothers and do not experience Bloomian anxiety of influence. They argue that because historically so few women have become writers, the woman writer, rather than rebelling against her literary foremothers, is instead searching for a literary maternal lineage to validate her own identity. Yet, as I survey the landscape of fiction by women, it is strewn with the corpses of dead mothers. I have begun to feel a bit two-faced, hydralike, as I cite theories of female development to my classes of women college students by scholars such as Nancy Chodorow and Carol Gilligan, theories that celebrate permeable boundaries between mothers and daughters as the source of women's intimacy, while at the same time teaching novels by women that express rage at the mother.

Writing about mothers who are writers is "almost a taboo topic," according to Ursula Le Guin, because women have been told that if they try to do both, "both the kids and the books will pay—because it can't be done—because it is unnatural."[2] In this *New York Times* essay in which Le Guin argues that literature is impoverished by such a narrow, misogynist view, she nevertheless claims that "the greatest enabler for me was always, is always, Virginia Woolf." At times I think every woman writer of my generation traces her literary lineage to Woolf, and until recently I would have agreed with Le Guin, unconditionally claiming Woolf as my foremother. Why do I now feel constricted by the paradigm implicit in Woolf's writings, particularly in *A Room of One's Own* and *To the Lighthouse?* Unconditionally to claim Woolf as my foremother requires too much sleight of hand. To be subject rather than object in her texts, I must remain forever identified as a daughter, for she reinscribes the essentialist dichotomy between procreation and creation, mother and writer.

For twenty years I have taught women students *A Room of One's Own* and *To the Lighthouse.* Seven years ago I gave the first of my annual lectures on the Angel in the House. Citing Woolf's essay "Professions for Women," I pointed out the need to slay the angel that is memorialized in Coventry Patmore's famous nineteenth-century poem about his short-lived wife, and I noted the many angel women in Victorian fiction: Dickens' Esther Summerson, Rose Maylie, Little Dorrit, and Little Nell, Thackeray's long-suffering Amelia, Elizabeth Gaskell's Mary Barton, George Eliot's Dorothea Brooke and Maggie, to mention only a few. I included Tillie Olsen's cautionary essay of twenty years ago, "One Out of Twelve: Writers Who Are Women in Our Century," in which she recognizes the importance of class differences and urges us not to mistakenly equate the Angel in the House with that essential angel "who must assume the physical responsibilities for daily living."[3] I mentioned Alice Walker's 1974 essay "In Search of Our Mothers' Gardens" in which she extends Woolf's and Olsen's description of the Angel to include African American female ancestors who may have been mistakenly misidentified as "saints" instead of "artists."[4] Olsen and Walker, while recognizing the specter of the angel, that martyred woman who looms as a model for women in the pages of literature, take care not to blur differences such as those of class and race among actual women. They point with gratitude and respect to foremothers who faced the daily demands of hard lives and were protective of their daughters, and they insist that those "angelic" foremothers were necessary in a racist, sexist, class-divided society and must not be mistaken for the well-to-do angel of Woolf's essay. Sitting in a draft is conspicuous self-abasement compared with the sacrifices of a mother who goes without food to feed her hungry child or works for a "Miss Ann" so that her daughter may one day receive an education. That selfless angel who torments Woolf does, however, cast her shadow on living women in neighborhoods far from upper-class England. Even if we choose neither to identify with her nor to be perceived as her opposite, she persists symbolically for us as an ideal. As Woolf insisted so long ago, "It is far harder to kill a phantom than a reality."[5]

Woolf in her essay "Professions for Women" sets forth two tasks for any woman who would be a writer: (1) she must kill the Angel in the House, and (2) she must be herself, that is, figure out what a woman is and tell the truth about her own experience(s) as a body. Let me refresh your image of that Angel in the House: "She was intensely sympathetic. She was immensely charming. She was utterly unselfish. . . . She sacrificed herself daily. If there was chicken, she took the leg; if there was a draught she sat in it . . . she was so constituted that she never had a mind or a wish of her own."[6] While it is easy to laugh at the caricature of the martyr who sits in drafts and takes the least desirable piece of chicken, that angel bears an uncanny resemblance to Mrs. Ramsay, the most celebrated mother of Woolf's fiction, whose death is the precondition that makes it possible for the surrogate daughter, Lily Briscoe, to create. I come away from *To the Lighthouse* feeling as if I have inhabited the consciousness of Mrs. Ramsay—the mother, the angel—assuming I know her from the inside, when, in fact, I have inhabited the surrogate daughter's consciousness of the mother.[7] It is quite valid to see the mother as she is experienced by the daughter or the surrogate daughter. However, the conduit through which we read the mother, not only in *To the Lighthouse* but in other novels by women through which women readers and writers trace their matrilineage, is virtually always the conduit of the daughter. We have access to the inside of Mrs. Ramsay's head through the daughter's imagination: the primary narrative consciousness of the text is therefore that of the daughter.

Mrs. Ramsay has become the prototype of the ideal mother. She creates a mood of community and connectedness over and against the darkness without; for example, at the dinner party she weaves a connection between the disparate and separate guests, drawing out the socially inept Mr. Tansley, soothing the widowed Mr. Bankes, smiling on the young couple whose engagement has come about at least partly because of her, understanding and communicating silently with her well-meaning but abrupt husband, drawing her daughters into her circle of nurture and welcoming them into her fecundity and beauty. She cushions the horrors of life by wrapping her shawl around the boar's skull nailed to the wall of her children's bedroom when her young daughter can't sleep, and simultaneously acknowledges its importance to her son while softening its shadows on the night wall. Mrs. Ramsay, weaving a word picture about the shawl-wrapped skull, telling "how lovely it looked now; how the fairies would love it; it was like a bird's nest; it was like a beautiful mountain," allows her daughter to contain its horrors in language, in story, in romance.[8] Mrs. Ramsey calls into being the artistry of the surrogate daughter, Lily, who is compelled by Mrs. Ramsay's very being to perfect her painting and who wishes she could somehow absorb Mrs. Ramsay's wisdom and be united with her. Lily imagines "how in the chambers of the mind and heart of the woman . . . were stood, like the treasures in the tombs of kings, tablets bearing sacred inscriptions, which if one could spell them out would teach one everything," and yet what she wants is "nothing that could be written in any language known to men, but intimacy itself, which is knowledge."[9]

As reading daughters, though we are aware of the mother's stern fierceness, we still expect that unconditional love, that mitigation of the horrors of life. Yet as daughters, the implication is that we must finally kill this mother angel if we are to survive as more than a shell spent for others. We must kill her, the Angel, the ideal mother, if we are to avoid becoming like her. We may appreciate her selflessness on our behalf and recognize that it may have protected us and that that protection itself may have made possible visions of a life quite unlike hers, yet we are furious at its incredible cost. Who might she have been had she not sacrificed herself? We feel guilt at her sacrifice and we feel guilt if we reject her identity in becoming other than like her. Her motherly qualities, the very ones we most value, leave her spent without the possibility of becoming anything else beyond mother, certainly no possibility of painting or writing—of art.

When Woolf writes about the angel, I see the idealized mother. In violent language, Woolf insists on both the difficulty and the necessity of murdering the angel: "I turned upon her and caught her by the throat. I acted in self-defense. Had I not killed her she would have killed me. She would have plucked the heart out of my writing." Woolf equates plucking the heart out of her writing with the murder of her self. The act must be repeated, for the phantom angel does not easily die: "Whenever I felt the shadow of her wing or the radiance of her halo upon my page, I took up the inkpot and flung it at her." Though Woolf flatters herself that she "killed her in the end," she implies that this murder is not only an occupational hazard of the woman writer of her generation, but that it must be committed anew and repeatedly by each woman who would be a writer.[10]

When we read about that deadly angel in the house, I believe many of us conjure up images of a being much like Mrs. Ramsay. Yet as I consider Mrs. Ramsay, I realize it is dishonest not to admit that I share some of her qualities. For quite a while, as I led discussions in which my women student readers fought against her values, I disowned any such identification. Obviously, any maternal or angel aspects that lingered in my late twentieth-century feminist consciousness must be hidden; or, if acknowledged, they must be condemned as remnants of prefeminist development. Lately, however, I have wanted to differentiate between "excelling in the difficult arts of family life" and "sacrificing oneself daily."[11] Excelling as a mother, as a member of a family, does not necessarily mean being without career or profession, sacrificing oneself to eight children and a needful, demanding Mr. Ramsay. I want to point out to my students that being sympathetic or compassionate or kind is not at all the same as daily self-sacrifice and certainly not identical to having no mind or wish of one's own.

As I have grown older and my daughters have grown into women, my response to Mrs. Ramsay has become more complicated than it once was. Killing the mother-angel, becoming a corpse on the field myself, no longer appeals to me. I wonder if, in recognizing our own anger at the mother as well as at the patriarchal father and feeling collective relief that Woolf has dared to voice women's anger, we have unintentionally colluded in the misogynist view that woman can be either a mother or a writer but not both.

Why are women so angry at their mothers? Is it that "mother" is a term defined entirely by woman's physical status, that one is no longer defined as self but as mater-ial? Is it that daughters so fiercely love their mothers and then are forced to separate in a way much more complicated and unacknowledged than the separation of the sons? Do we see the mother as both good mother and bad mother and see ourselves as the social evidence of the success or failures of her mothering? If we, like her, capitulate to the angel role, do we validate her life? At what cost to ourselves? If we reject her capitulation, do we invalidate her life?

Woolf, whose own mother died at forty-nine, writes of the freedom she only later experienced in creating for herself a life quite different from that of her mother. Yet she missed her mother desperately. She puts into *To the Lighthouse*'s fictive portrayal of Julia Stephen the powerful love and sympathy and sense of loss she experienced when she was deprived of her mother as a young adolescent. She portrays her own mother lovingly at the same time that she recognizes the danger inherent in the role her mother played. Her anger at the position of the mother is subtle and is not an open attack on the mother herself. Yet, in the shadow of her own angelic mother, she herself fought for inner freedom to express herself in writing that calls into question the very underpinnings of her mother's being.[12] It is as if Virginia as daughter adored her mother but as an aspiring writer was appalled at the expectation that she should follow in her angelic footsteps. Perhaps because her mother's death prevented her from experiencing normal adolescent arguments with and separation from her mother, she continued to be haunted by the myth of her mother, the angelic specter, the internalized notions of appropriate womanliness. That set of expectations that she fictively represents in *To the Lighthouse,* she, the writer, must strangle in her essay "Professions for Women."

As a mother and writer I have become uncomfortably aware that the two women writers who have most influenced my intellectual life, Virginia Woolf and Doris Lessing, both write as daughters who view their mothers as dangerously powerful beings. In their narrative voices, both writers create fictional mothers who represent something against which daughters must rebel. Mrs. Ramsay's daughters dream of a life different, more free, less man-pleasing than that of their mother. Martha Quest, protagonist of the five-volume Children of Violence series, does not resolve her conflicts with her mother until after her mother's death, and even then feels as if she never really knew her. Mothers in both Woolf and Lessing are defined by overassociation with the female body, and both writers see the female body as a trap. Lessing, whose female characters are sexually active whether or not they bear children, sees the body as primarily a container for the mind, and, problematic at best, never to be confused with the self. Woolf's characters escape the inevitable and self-stifling identification with the feminine that motherhood brings only by remaining childless. The mother with her idealized but taboo body is seen as the locus of discomfort for the daughter who must be violently separated from the mother-daughter bond if she is to become a writer.

I once taught seminars on women writers whose novels seemed invariably to include dead or nonfunctional mothers and to end with heroine's madness, death, or unbelievable marriage, and I searched for novels with more open endings. Delighted by two novels written by women colleagues whose fictive heroines survive, I began to include them on my reading list. These more open-ended novels allow their heroines to live, to grow, to experience lives quite unlike those of their mothers. But then I realized that here the heroines' mothers die in both texts. Even my contemporary friends and colleagues, mothers themselves, narrate their novels from the perspective of daughters who cannot succeed until their mothers have died. Diana O Hehir's *I Wish This War Were Over* and Sheila Ballantyne's *Imaginary Crimes* both have female protagonists who avoid madness, death, and unlikely marriages; but the mothers still float dead on the ceiling in their surviving daughters' dreams. My early pleasure in tracing the development of daughters who survive was undercut by the recognition that their mothers do not. What's a mother to do?

This spring I taught a special topics course in which we explored representations of mothers and daughters in selected fiction by twentieth-century women writers. We read texts by Woolf, Lessing, Katherine Mansfield, Jean Rhys, Jamaica Kincaid, Maxine Hong Kingston, Toni Morrison, and Paule Marshall. Following an initial discussion of Woolf's "Professions for Women" and an explanation of my thesis about the privileging of the daughter's point of view in virtually all novels by women, especially in canonical works by white women, we talked about our expectations of mothers in the fiction we read, our classifications of fictional mothers into those we consider "good mothers" and those we consider "bad mothers." We listed all those foolish mothers and wicked stepmothers who populate the novels we love: the ineffectual Mrs. Bennet of *Pride and Prejudice,* Jane Eyre's wicked "stepmother," Mrs. Reed, and the missing or dead mothers of the many orphaned heroines. It's not easy to think of a good mother in a novel who lives into old age or a mother who is herself an artist. I asked whether the paradigm I see in white Anglo women writers operates in novels by women of color. To what extent do working-class novels by women kill off the mother? Does the angel hover over fictional creations by writers who are themselves mothers? The class was intended as an inquiry. Because I thought it focused almost exclusively on the point of view of daughters, I was a bit worried about the responses I would get from older women students who were themselves mothers. Would they feel vilified by the texts, the class, the point of view with which I opened the course? Would women of color find validation of themselves in any of the stories told by Kingston, Kincaid, or Marshall? What would the class do with Morrison's *Beloved* in a context that foregrounded mothers and daughters rather than slavery? Would mothers in the class feel vulnerable as mothers to the murderous anger of the fictional daughters?

Women students nearly all responded in rage, not only at the fictional mothers, but also at their own mothers, and at me as surrogate mother. As I pointed out the perspective in a work as that of a daughter, women readers saw larger than life representations of mothers, and the classroom was filled with rage, guilt, fear. For example, in our discussion of Doris Lessing's *The Four-Gated City,* whereas I focused attention on Martha's intensive working out of her feelings with her own mother, students saw Martha primarily as a mother who not only abandoned her own daughter but never apologized for that abandonment. Rage permeated one student response, a middle-aged mother of an adult daughter, who nevertheless read the text from her point of view as an abandoned daughter, and confronted my text selection as if I, too, had abandoned her. She spoke with intense feeling of being betrayed by me into plowing through more than 600 pages of a novel in which the protagonist doesn't ever apologize to her abandoned daughter. How could I possibly credit such a fictional character with working through anything? Of what use was the analysis of a character who tries to understand her own mother but never communicates her regret or apologies to her own daughter? The Martha of the novel was read only as a bad mother by a forty-five-year-old mother whose reading response was that of deprived daughter.

Discussion among the students repeatedly circled back to questions of good and bad mothering, as they attempted to differentiate between their deeply felt opinions about the qualifications of even a "good enough mother" and their profound discomfort at the prospect of being confined to such a role themselves.[13] Students who criticized Mrs. Ramsay's angelic qualities in *To the Lighthouse* wanted Jane Somers of Lessing's *The Diaries of Jane Somers* to take the dying Maudie into her flat and care for her although Jane had a high-powered editorial position and was already more than a good neighbor to the aged Maudie. Abstract ideas about woman's rights battled with internalized notions about familial and womanly duties. Jean Rhys's Antoinette was left emotionally vulnerable because of the inability of Annette to provide adequate mothering; Jamaica Kincaid's Annie John needed to escape excessive mothering. Always the class felt sympathy for the daughter and criticized the mother, who, no matter what her own difficulties might be, loomed large and negative in the fictive daughter's life. The more good a mother was, the more her qualities would be experienced as obstructions by would-be self-actualized daughters.

As the course came to a close, we reflected on what we had learned. After a semester of difficult discussions, uncomfortable silences, and a reluctance to examine the mutually exclusive expectations of women in their roles as daughters and as mothers, one student quietly remarked that as a result of the class, "I saw my mother as another woman for the first time." The rest of us sat uncharacteristically quiet as the import of her words sunk in. No longer larger than life, angel or monster, the mother began to assume human size.

Think back for a moment to "Professions for Women" and to Woolf's questions: What is a woman? What does it mean for a woman to be herself? She says that she herself has not yet solved the problem of telling the truth about her own experiences as a body. She stresses the importance of discussing the many phantoms and obstacles looming in a woman's path, and she suggests that we won't know how to define woman until woman has expressed herself in all the arts and professions open to human skill. I would add Mother to Woolf's list of arts and professions, and would suggest that until mothers of many races, ethnicities, classes, ages, and sexual orientations write their multiple truths, including anger at the daughter but also pleasure, desire, and joy, we as readers will continue to internalize distorted reflections of mothers and limited choices for women.

I have always loved Woolf's looking-glass image in which woman reflects man at twice his natural size. Only recently have I begun to suspect that in the novels I teach, daughters have been reflecting mothers at twice their natural size, and that that helps to explain why mothers like Mrs. Ramsay and Mrs. Quest loom so large as angels or monsters, and why they give me such satisfaction as daughter and so little as mother.

As my daughter remarked at the age of twelve, when I had returned to school and teaching, "It was great having the kind of mother you used to be, but I would hate to grow up to be one."[14] If mothers begin to tell the truth, to write from inside their own experience, the fictive portrayals of mothers just may shrink to human size, allowing daughters to tell their truths, and to write without committing matricide.

Notes

1. Virginia Woolf, *A Room of One's Own*, 101.
2. Ursula Le Guin, "The Hand That Rocks the Cradle Writes the Book."
3. Tillie Olsen, "One Out of Twelve," 32.
4. Alice Walker, "In Search of Our Mothers' Gardens," in *In Search of Our Mothers' Gardens*, 231–43. Walker also extends Woolf's ideas about a woman's telling the truth about her experiences as a body in her discussion of Phillis Wheatley and Judith Shakespeare.
5. Virginia Woolf, "Professions for Women," in *The Death of the Moth*, 238.
6. Ibid., 237.
7. See Elizabeth Abel's "Spatial Relations" for a discussion of Lily Briscoe's

painting and its meaning in the novel (Abel, *Virginia Woolf and the Fictions of Psycho-analysis,* 68–83).

8. Virginia Woolf, *To the Lighthouse,* 172.

9. Ibid., 79.

10. Woolf, "Professions," 237–38.

11. Ibid., 237.

12. For background on the autobiographical elements of *To the Lighthouse,* I recommend Lyndall Gordon's *Virginia Woolf: A Writer's Life,* and Phyllis Rose's *Woman of Letters: A Life of Virginia Woolf.*

13. We read Carolyn Steedman's *Landscape for a Good Woman* and discussed the difference between a "good woman" and the "good enough mother" as described by D. W. Winnicott in *Home Is Where We Start From.*

14. Kirsten T. Saxton is now writing her doctoral dissertation in English at the University of California, Davis. She has become one of my best readers, critics, and allies.

PART THREE

Structures of Oppression:
Subjectivity and the Social Order

MADHUCHHANDA MITRA

Angry Eyes and Closed Lips: Forces of Revolution in Nawal el Saadawi's *God Dies by the Nile*

The peasants of Kafr El Teen in Nawal el Saadawi's novel *God Dies by the Nile* silently endure the oppressive conditions of their marginal existence.[1] "Be patient and pray [to] Allah" (6), Kafrawi tells his sister Zakeya early in the novel, silencing her anxieties about the disappearance of her young niece. Presumably, the villagers voice their concerns in their prayers, but we do not hear them. We do hear, periodically, Sheikh Hamzawi's calls to prayer rending the terrible silence that afflicts the village. The novel opens with the clockwork motions of Zakeya working in her field, her "lips tightly closed," while nothing, not even the Nile, appears to stir: the air is "hushed and silent," the mud huts sit "huddled in rows, their tiny windows closed," and a "dark, slimy, oozing layer" of decaying matter chokes the stream that runs at one end of the village (1–2). The daytime silence of the village passes unchanged into the stifling and inert darkness of the night. Chapter 1 ends with Zakeya and Kafrawi sitting "immobile as the mud huts buried in the dark," enveloped in a silence "heavier than the thick cloak of darkness around them" (7).

But, like the powerful currents that run beneath the calm surface of the Nile, the silent villagers harbor a deep discontent that appears in occasional and quickly stifled flashes in their eyes. Zakeya's "large, wide-open eyes," for example, express "an angry defiance" (1). Kafrawi's eyes, like Zakeya's, are "large, black and also full of anger," but "mingling in their depths with despair, and expressing a profound humiliation" (6). His daughter Nefissa has proud and angry eyes, overlaid with "a cloud of anxiety, as though she was lost and afraid of what lay ahead of her" (18). It is as though the institutions that control the villagers' lives have effectively silenced them, but cannot forcibly close their eyes, which reflect the unvoiced story of their collective suffering, the sparks of suppressed anger signaling their potential for bringing about change. Nawal el Saadawi, a medical doctor specializing in women's health, has written at length about the physical and psychological oppression of women.[2] In this novel, she draws attention to the systemic brutalization of the Egyptian peasantry; she also demonstrates the importance of claiming the body as a site of resistance against oppression. The angry eyes and the closed lips of the peasants signify their protest against a system that strictly censors their voice.[3]

Zakeya's "wide-open eyes" guide us through the novel: they not only enable us to perceive the inertia that presently afflicts the village, they take us on a journey backward and inward, and, through a series of dreamlike recollections, weave a history of the village that is fraught with deprivation, violence, and bloodshed. Zakeya's "silent" story (its crucial features reinforced by the remarkably similar recollections of Nefissa and Fatheya) parallels the "told" one in the novel about power struggles, rapes, and murders in Kafr El Teen. This essay examines the apparent disjunction between these two levels of action: while one—Zakeya's assassination of the tyrannical village Mayor (137)—impels revolutionary action, the other folds back into the deathly silence with which the novel began: "The dark night had by now enveloped Kafr El Teen in its heavy cloak, and the air hardly moved over the surface of the river. The sombre mud huts and the winding lanes seemed to sink into a silence as still and profound as the silence of death, as the end of all movement" (128). The revolutionary impact of Zakeya's hoe that kills the Mayor does not seem to touch the village. Zakeya goes to prison, the novel ends, and Kafr El Teen remains consigned to its "silence of death." But the ending also leaves us with the profound irony of the phrase "the end of all movement," forcing us to acknowledge the radical potential of stillness and silence. True, Zakeya's act is an isolated gesture of rebellion in a village that appears to have accepted its miserable fate, but it does transform our perception of the silence that permeates the village. We realize, as the Mayor presumably does just before Zakeya strikes him, that stillness does not signal passivity but unrealized action.

The novel emphasizes the difference between meaningful action and mere motion. Despite its appearance of immobility, Kafr El Teen teems with activities. Peasants go about their daily agricultural and cultural rituals; sometimes the frustrations of their daily existence erupt into frenzied and violent conflicts that lead to diminished rather than strengthened communal ties. For instance, the villagers eagerly gather to watch the police chase and arrest Kafrawi for a trumped-up murder (60). They know that Kafrawi is innocent, and they hate the police with "the hidden ancient hatred of peasants for their government" (60); but they nevertheless enjoy the spectacle of the chase. Similarly, they enjoy watching Sheikh Hamzawi, who has fallen out of the Mayor's favor, being beaten up: "They forgot almost everything else at the sight of the quarrel. They stood there enjoying the spectacle of men fighting, not caring who was doing the beating and who was being beaten" (109–10). This is not mere apathy; rather, having turned their own misery into an enjoyable spectacle, the villagers have managed to objectify themselves.

Juxtaposed against such moments of frenetic motion is Zakeya's vigilant and impregnable silence. After Kafrawi's arrest, she withdraws from the normal village activities—even stops working in her field. With lips "tightly closed" and eyes "wide-open," Zakeya nurtures her silent vigilance through her introspective explorations of the past—her murdered mother, her brutal husband, her dead infant children, her son Galal taken away to fight in the Sinai war, her brother Kafrawi taken away to prison, and, always, looming large in her memory, the massive iron gates of the Mayor's mansion. Her reflections lead her finally to a profound and momentous recognition of the cause of her problems: "I know who it is. . . . It is Allah" (135). Her assassination of the Mayor, the "Allah" who controls the villagers' destiny, is the logical next step. Zakeya's act, therefore, is rooted in a process of politicization that involves a refiguring of the past to understand and address present problems.

Zakeya discovers the source of the injustice her family has been subjected to and strikes at it. Her development in the novel corresponds to Saadawi's notion of the creative process. Addressing a seminar on "Creative women in changing societies" (Oslo, July 1980), Saadawi defined creativity as "the mobilisation of the potential of all peoples to improve life." A crucial part of the creative process, she claims, is "reflection, meditation and contemplation of the past" that enables "the individual to live through reality once more, yet in a way which is different." The aim of creativity is "the development of new ideas and feelings which help people attain a more complete understanding of themselves . . . so that their hopes and determination in the struggle for freedom and justice, their anger and rebellion against all forms of oppression and injustice . . . are strengthened."[4]

The novel locates the creative impulse not only in acts that bring about political transformation but also in everyday activities that engage the body in productive work. Creativity, as Saadawi defines it, resides in the "optimum use . . . of bodily force to achieve a given objective."[5] The creativity of the peasants in this novel is etched in their bodies and in the way they work on the land. Saadawi draws attention to their work-roughened hands "with a groove made in the middle [of the palm] by the hoe," and their bare feet, "their toes big and flat, their heels dark and cracked" (88). We notice the vitality and power with which Zakeya plies her hoe: "Now her hoe could be heard, thudding out over the neighbouring fields with a steady sound, as it cut deep into the ground. The muscles in her arms stood out, and below the black *galabeya* knotted tightly around her waist, the long powerful legs showed naked and brown in the morning light" (2). We notice too the graceful dignity of Zeinab's walk as she balances a jar of water: "She held herself upright, balancing the earthenware jar on her head. Her tall figure swayed from side to side, and her large black eyes were raised and carried [an] expression of pride" (14).

But the novel also makes it clear that the creativity of peasants that is evident in their ability to adapt and survive is perceived as a threat by the feudal establishment that rules Kafr El Teen and uses all the ideological forces at its command to undermine the peasants' potency. For instance, Elwau's reclusive silence, his preference for plowing his field on Fridays rather than praying at the mosque, arouses the Mayor's deep suspicion; he puts an end to Elwau's disturbing presence first by identifying him as Nefissa's secret lover (Nefissa, impregnated by the Mayor, has fled the village), and then by having him killed, ostensibly by a revenge-seeking Kafrawi, Nefissa's father (42, 48). The bonus in this plot is that it also gets rid of Kafrawi, another "honest" and "proud" peasant.

Peasant women are particularly vulnerable before the ideological constraints that seek to limit their movements. While the reader is invited to notice Zeinab's proud carriage as she balances the jar of water on her head, the Mayor also watches her, and his description ascribes to her body a blatant and inviting sexuality: "[The Mayor's] eyes followed the tall lithe figure of Zeinab as she walked along the river bank. He could see her firm, rounded buttocks pressing up against the long *galabeya* from behind. Her pointed breasts moved up and down with each step. Beneath the tail of her *galabeya* two rosy, rounded heels peeped out" (14). The integrity of Zeinab's body falls apart as the Mayor's objectifying gaze picks out only the sexually overdetermined parts of her body: her buttocks, her breasts, and the alluringly peeping "rosy" heels. This body seems to "speak" for itself; the Mayor interprets the language of this body, and Zeinab's voice becomes superfluous. By the end of this chapter, the Mayor and his men have established the "brazenness" of all the women in Zeinab's family, and it is only a matter of time before Zeinab is delivered into the Mayor's "service."

But the female peasant body can also subvert the very basis of its patriarchal appropriation. Long before she kills the Mayor, Zakeya's "wide-open eyes"—eyes that remain literally open till the end of the novel—and her "tightly closed" lips register her silent defiance of the established order. Her eyes (and those of her nieces) are the subject of lewd jokes among the Mayor and his cronies: "It's a well-known fact that the womenfolk in the Kafrawi family have their eyes wide open and are quite brazen," Sheikh Hamzawi informs the Mayor (17). But the joke is an uneasy one, for the "open eyes" of oppressed people are potentially dangerous for the oppressor. Besides, no one is quite sure what Zakeya's angry eyes see; she does not speak—her lips are "tightly closed." Zakeya reappropriates her body and claims her silence as a prerogative, thus defeating a traditional patriarchal strategy of imposing control.

Zakeya's silence is all the more disturbing because it resists interpretation. At one point in the novel her stony silence, broken only by her questioning of Allah's mercy, is diagnosed as the possession of her soul by an evil spirit.[6] The villagers gather around her, performing the necessary rituals to drive away the spirit. What follows is a significant reversal of the roles assigned by folk traditions; and it is the only scene in the novel that comes close to a vision of communal healing. While the villagers chant prayers and dance around Zakeya, Zakeya begins to move inward and backward, reliving the past horrors of her life. As the frenzy of the ritual mounts, the two separate movements converge, but it is not Zakeya who is reclaimed by the healers; rather, *they* join Zakeya in confronting their collective suffering:

> Now they were all screaming at the top of their voices. Zakeya and
> Om Saber, Nafoussa and Zeinab, Sheikh Metwalli and all the men and
> women of Kafr El Teen who were gathered around. Their voices joined
> in a high-pitched wail, as long as the length of their lives, reaching
> back to those moments in time when they had been born, and bitten
> and beaten and burnt under the soles of their feet, and in the walls of
> their stomach, since the bitterness flowed with their bile, and death
> snatched their sons and their daughters, one after the other in a line.
> (76)

The string of passive constructions—"born, and bitten and beaten and burnt"—casts the villagers as victims of an inexorable system of oppression, almost cosmic in its all-encompassing reach. The ritual fails to cure

Zakeya; the systemic source of her illness, fleetingly revealed in the repertory of brutalities suffered by the peasants, hides in the ideological configuration of the villagers' plight: the belief that it is their destiny to suffer.
The fact that Zakeya remains "possessed" and the others subside into
their usual passivity suggests that such custom-honored and ritualized expressions of anger and discontent dissipate rather than reinforce the villagers' potential as a political force.

The revolutionary force of Zakeya's act must be located in the political
and ideological horizons of the novel. The situation in Kafr El Teen is
fairly typical of small villages in the so-called Third World where colonial
exploitation, with its emphasis on profitable cash crops, severely impoverished the existing rural agrarian economy.[7] Political independence, often
only a transfer of the same economic structure to "native" hands, did not
free the peasants from the crippling grip of an extortionist system that
barely allows them to subsist by cultivating their land. Modernization
measures often exacerbate this condition, thereby increasing the gulf
between "backward" villages and "modern" cities. As we see in the novel,
Kafr El Teen does not seem to have much contact with modern Egypt.
Here, the Mayor rules like an autocratic feudal chief and represents for
the villagers the "government" they pay their taxes to. His henchmen
boast that the government of Misr (Egypt) has little control over their
administration. "Who would dare deny that we are just as much of a
government ourselves?" the chief of the Village Guard brags (9). All civil
and clerical appointments depend on the Mayor's favor. As for the villagers, their very existence hinges on the Mayor's approval: he routinely rapes
the women of the village, and blatantly exploits the peasants; to cover his
tracks, he confiscates their land, has them arrested on trumped-up
charges, even has them murdered. It is with good reason that the villagers
admit their enslavement to the Mayor: "We are God's slaves when it's time
to say our prayers. But we are the Mayor's slaves all the time" (53).[8]

The novel explores in some detail the specific implications of this exploitative system for peasant women. Zakeya and her nieces suffer because they are poor and because they are women; their labor and their
sexuality are exploited by the Mayor and other men in the village. Saadawi's insistence on the inseparability of class and gender needs to be
taken seriously: she makes it clear that the Mayor's feudal rule exploits all
the peasants, both men and women; but she also points out that women
suffer additionally because they are forced to submit to harrassment, rape,
and prostitution *because* they are poor.[9] Furthermore, poor and uneducated peasant women are shut out from the official channels of redress.

Having no access to the institution of impersonal and bureaucratic rule of law, they are forced to depend on men. Zeinab's experience in trying to track down her imprisoned husband is a case in point. She manages to find the prison only to be told that she needs a written permit to visit her husband. Then, "after the man explained [how to get a permit] she walked back along the same way, took a train and managed to get back to Bab El Hadeed. There she found a tram which dropped her in front of a huge building full of people, and desks, and papers. She entered the building and was swallowed up with the other people. Inside she went from room to room until it was time to leave. And this went on for several days. She felt she was going round and round in an endless journey" (133). Zeinab emerges from this bureaucratic maze only to be led away into prostitution.

The simultaneous operation of class and gender in determining the experience of oppression is further emphasized by the presence of the Mayor's wife in the novel: in keeping with her class position, she speaks a language that echoes the rhetoric of Western feminism, protesting the sexual double standard practiced by men and the burden of morality placed on women (39). She is certainly aware of the prejudices that sustain the injustices against women, but her understanding of "sexism" is necessarily shaped by her class perspective. She knows that her husband and son routinely abuse the village women, and she ridicules their sanctimonious hypocrisy. But her rhetoric of sexual inequality excludes the experience of women who are forced to exchange sexual favors for their material survival. Nor does she fully grasp the complex structure of patriarchal domination that implicates her in its exploitative moves. Declaring that "these peasants never calm down unless they wreak vengeance on whoever is the cause" (40), she simultaneously asserts her distance from "these peasants" and disclaims responsibility for whatever is about to happen. Her understanding of the oppression of women is limited by her lack of understanding of class conflict. Saadawi makes this point in an interview with *Race and Class,* where she urges Western feminists (not unlike the Mayor's wife) to "look deeper" for the cause of women's oppression: "Quite a lot of Western women say [the enemy] is the man, and even want to dispense with him totally, but we must remember that men too are the victims of . . . the same patriarchal society" ("Arab Women," 178). In this novel, Kafrawi forces his resisting daughter Nefissa to go into the Mayor's "service" when his authority in his household is questioned (21). Fatheya recounts a similar incident in her life, using nearly identical language (31). In both cases, the men respond to the pressures of an ascribed manhood dictated from above by forcing their women into unwanted situations. In other words, they compensate their economic powerlessness by claiming the "classless" privileges of patriarchy. The novel insists on locating patriarchal oppression within the larger economic structure.[10]

Besides class and gender, the other ideological complex that determines social relations in Kafr El Teen is, of course, religion. Here, too, the novel draws attention to the way women are affected. Saadawi, like many other Arab feminists, attacks the Western notion that Islam is primarily responsible for the oppression of Arab women. "Islam is not the enemy of women," she claims, "but it has been and is being used by patriarchal systems so that its most repressive and reactionary aspects are emphasized."[11] Again, Saadawi insists on the connection between economic oppression and religious exploitation.[12] The blindness of the villagers' faith is always set alongside the manipulative moves of the clergy and the Mayor's henchmen. This novel exposes the collusion of secular and religious patriarchy most clearly in the person of the Mayor. He is not the Allah the villagers pray to, but, the novel suggests, he might as well be, for he controls not only the material life of the villagers but also the religious institution. His emissaries invoke Allah's commands to trick Zeinab into accepting his offer of "employment," which she had continually refused to do. Men and women alike are victims of the ruling power's appropriation of religion. The clearest statement of the corruption of Islam, the corrupting force being the Mayor's invincibility, comes significantly from Sheikh Hamzawi, the village Imam. " 'In their hearts [the villagers] don't fear God,' " he tells his wife. " 'What they really fear is the Mayor.' " Hamzawi explains the situation: "[The Mayor] holds their daily bread in his hands and if he wants, he can deprive them of it. If he gets angry their debts double. . . . He is a dangerous man and fears no one, not even Allah. He can do injustice to people and put them in gaol when they have done nothing to merit it. He can even murder innocent people' " (106). Zakeya's killing of the Mayor and her claim that she has "buried [Allah] there on the bank of the Nile" (138) thus constitute a protest against the corruption of religion by secular institutions of power.[13]

Zakeya's gesture of rebellion cuts through all the intersecting structures of domination and oppression. She is the poorest of the poor: a peasant woman who, by the end of the novel, has no family left and no buffalo (without which, of course, she cannot till her land, which will soon be confiscated anyway). She literally has nothing more to lose when she picks up her hoe and strikes the Mayor, the king-god who represents all the controlling institutions of her existence. Significantly, the novel places the agency of revolutionary change in a woman who has receded so far from the margins of the socioeconomic matrix that she has ceased to matter. She literally comes out of an unrelieved darkness to kill the Mayor.

The vision of revolution embodied in this novel, limited though it may be in scope, is significant. Saadawi has often been accused, mainly by readers and critics in Egypt, of telling her Western readers what they want to hear about the nature of the treatment of women in a Muslim culture.[14] As a non-Egyptian, non-Muslim reader, I acknowledge my limitation in recognizing this posture. But as a non-Western woman academic who lives and works in the United States, I welcome all efforts to locate women's struggles within class conflicts, as Saadawi does in this novel. Western feminist discourses typically ignore the class dimension in women's movements—a serious deficiency that is only beginning to be addressed.

Notes

1. The original Arabic edition of *God Dies by the Nile* was first published in Beirut in 1974, under the title *Mawt al-rajul al-wahid ala al-ard* (The Death of the Only Man on Earth). Sherif Hetata's English translation was published in London by Zed Books in 1985. All subsequent quotations are from this edition.

2. Among Saadawi's best known nonfictional works on the subject are *The Hidden Face of Eve* and *Al-Marah Wa-al-jins* (Women and Sex). Her novels include *Woman at Point Zero, Two Women in One, Memoirs of a Woman Doctor,* and *The Fall of the Imam.*

3. The struggle against silence and censorship informs Saadawi's writing in important ways. *God Dies by the Nile,* like all the books she wrote in the 1970s, had to be published in Lebanon because she could not publish in Egypt. Attempts to silence Saadawi began following the publication of *Women and Sex,* when she was dismissed from her position as the director-general of the Ministry of Health. Her books were banned in Egypt for eleven years under Anwar Sadat. On September 6, 1981, Saadawi was arrested by the Sadat government, placed in solitary confinement, and threatened with a political inquest. In an introduction to her play *Al-Insan* (The People), she speaks of Sadat as a paranoid despot, who "decided to finish all his opposition and to silence all voices which did not agree with his" (Rachel Shteir, "Breaking the Silence," 48).

4. Nawal el Saadawi, "Creative Women in Changing Societies," 160–63.

5. Ibid., 160.

6. The villagers seem to believe that Zakeya is suffering from *'uzr.* For a useful analysis of folk attitudes toward this illness, see Soheir A. Morsy, "Sex Differences and Folk Illness in an Egyptian Village."

7. For an extensive discussion of the impact of colonial economy in Africa, see Walter Rodney, *How Europe Underdeveloped Africa.* Pages 149–69 discuss the effects of cash-crop farming.

8. The half-English, blue-eyed Mayor is, as Bharati Mukherjee points out, a

"coded allusion . . . to [Egypt's] colonial legacy as well as to the Sadats" ("Betrayed by Blind Faith"). In an interview with George Lerner in *The Progressive* in 1992, Saadawi claimed, "All my characters are real." Speaking of the Imam in *The Fall of the Imam,* she said, "He may be Sadat, Khomeini, Reagan, Bush, Kennedy, or anyone who uses God and politics."

9. In their introduction to *Women and Class in Africa,* Claire Robertson and Iris Berger emphasize the importance of the relationship of gender and class for women in Africa. The colonial economy, they assert, introduced new class differences and reinforced existing gender differences: "Cash cropping was introduced mainly to men, who also found more numerous opportunities for wage labour. Pressured by the need to pay taxes, virtually everyone was brought directly or indirectly into the nexus of a commercial economy. As European sexism was added to patriarchal elements in indigenous cultures, sex roles changed to the detriment of women, and they lost political power. While women retained responsibility for feeding their families, the prevalence of male labour migration in many areas left them to do even more of the agricultural work" (6). The continued economic subordination of "independent" African countries under neocolonialism has only worsened the situation for women. Soha Abdel Kader discusses the adverse effects of Sadat's open-door economic policies on the lives of women: "The reshuffling of the production structure to fulfill the needs of an economy open to uncontrolled market forces and the free flow of foreign capital and imports reinforced and even exacerbated the subordination of women by reducing their employment opportunities and increasing the levels of their absolute and relative poverty" (*Egyptian Women in a Changing Society,* 126).

10. Saadawi continues to insist on the vital connection between the liberation of women in the Third World and the liberation of the Third World economies from neocolonial domination. Along with Fatima Mernissi and Mallica Vajarathon, Saadawi wrote a critique of the 1976 Conference on Women and Development held at Wellesley College, pointing out the lack of a global perspective in the discussions of Third World women's problems in the West: "The women from industrially developed countries focussed their attention on the oppressive conditions of women in developing countries; the causes of oppression became secondary. For example, discussion about the so-called effects of 'development' and 'modernization' on the degrading economic conditions of women in developing countries was not linked to economic/political factors such as the role of the multi-national corporations" ("A Critical Look at the Wellesley Conference," 103). Saadawi points out the same deficiency in a 1983 conference entitled "Common Differences: Third World Women and Feminist Perspectives," held at the University of Illinois in Urbana-Champaign: "Women who claim to be discussing the liberation of women [at this conference] are, in a sense, doing exactly what the society at large does—that is, separating the sexuality of women from their political reality. Therefore, their solution is not a political solution but a social and personal solution. There's an incredible reluctance to discuss the question of capitalism and the role of capitalism in a sexist/racist state and its impact on women in the Third World" (Tiffany R. Patterson and Angela M. Gilliam, "Out of Egypt," 193).

11. Saadawi, "Arab Women and Western feminism," 176. In the same interview, Saadawi claims that like all new religions, Islam began as a protest religion that took up the cause of oppressed groups like women and slaves. But, once it became part of

the established order, it was used in the service of the state and the ruling class. See also George Lerner's interview of Nawal el-Saadawi in *The Progressive,* 33.

12. Saadawi claims that the colonial powers maintained "a schizophrenic split" between civil and religious laws, in order to "modernize some sectors of the society at the cost of others, to open the upper classes to the civilization of the West, and to lock the overwhelming majority—especially the rural population—into the ancient heritage." This division, she asserts, persists in the neocolonial phase: the public laws are constantly changed to suit the systems of production, while the family laws (rooted in Islam) "sow in people's inner selves a passive indifference, an attitude of submission, a tendency to resort to the past or to spiritual powers to solve their financial crises" ("The Political Challenges Facing Arab Women," 12).

13. In the interview with George Lerner (33), Saadawi affirms that the liberation of women must involve a progressive reinterpretation of Islam: "We are always linking religion to politics, to sex. We are talking about the three taboos: religion, sex, and politics. This to us is feminism or women's liberation, the unveiling of the mind."

14. Sabry Hafez, for example, questions the basis of Saadawi's fame in the West: "Why is there a gap between [Saadawi's] standing in the West and that in her own culture? Is it because her writing is simpler and appeals to a wider public? Or is it because there is something in her writing that makes it appeal more to the Western reader than to the Arab? Do her views tell the Western reader what he or she wants to hear about the nature of the treatment of women in a Muslim culture? Has she attained her fame because she vindicates the main tenets of the traditional orientalist discourse on the position of women in Arab society, and confirms many of the prevalent stereotypes about Arab women and men? ("Intentions and Realization in the Narratives of Nawal El Saadawi," 189). See Patterson and Gilliam, "Out of Egypt," for Saadawi's explanation of this perception.

DOROTHY DAVIS WILLS

Economic Violence in Postcolonial Senegal: Noisy Silence in Novels by Mariama Bâ and Aminata Sow Fall

The voice in Aminata Sow Fall's *The Beggars' Strike* seems to come from the context in which the characters are developed rather than from any narrative personality in particular. It is the voice of the baobabs, the cooking pot, the courtyard children. The voice of Mariama Bâ's *Such a Long Letter,* in contrast, is the historically situated, socially constructed, intensely self-aware personality of the letter writer. Both are Senegalese voices.

The two works first appeared in the same year, 1979, in French.[1] The colonial language has been the medium through which a few African and Afro-Caribbean male scholars and writers have been able to gain entrée to the rarefied and inward-turned world of French letters. Such figures as Léopold Sédar Senghor and Aimé Césaire in the 1930s, through the Négritude movement, carved a tiny space for African writing on the edge of the French-speaking elite circle. This "space" was self-defined as one of feeling.[2] Négritude was later felt to be yet another permutation of European thought, despite its assertion of the greatness of African civilization, because it embraced the European preoccupation with dichotomies of reason and emotion, white and black. Eventually, it yielded to subsequent generations of African writers not given to essentialism, dichotomization, or implicit acceptance of the social order (Madubuike and others allude to the assimilationist tendency of some Senegalese literature).[3] Such men as Camara Laye, Birago Diop, Ferdinand Oyono, Cheikh Hamidou Kane, David Diop, Ousmane Sembène, writing in French, spoke to local and global issues from traditional and postmodern African perspectives. Their critique of Senegalese assimilationist tendencies is as harsh as that of French racism.[4]

But there were no African women's voices in French print until Bâ and

Fall.[5] *Such a Long Letter* received the Noma Award for literature in 1980; Bâ's second novel, *Un chant écarlate,* published in 1981 shortly after her tragic death, created a stir in the African critical and feminist worlds. Fall's work has received comparable attention, especially as an indictment both of the postcolonial social organization and of elements of tradition, which she believes exploit and oppress people more patently and viciously in the modern context than they seem to have historically.[6] Bâ and Fall continue the scathing critique of Senegalese social institutions and behavior best exemplified by Sembène's novels and films, and expand its range to include patriarchy and polygyny.

Seen as ethnography, the two novels considered here take as their object the structure of Senegalese social categories. Their subjects arise from the interplay of these categories as the constitutive mode of political economic transition in this "developing" country.[7] The following summary of the substance of the novels is intended to provide a foundation for an ethnographic analysis, based also on extensive research on Senegalese life, culture, languages, and social history.

The story of *The Beggars' Strike* depicts the efforts of Mour Ndiaye, director of public health and hygiene, to rid the capital city, Dakar, of its legion of beggars. Mour epitomizes and caricatures the modern Senegalese man, full of ambition for appointment to high office and yet enslaved by the seemingly whimsical instructions of his marabouts.[8] Happily married and the father of several children, including a daughter in law school, he nonetheless takes a seventeen-year-old girl as a second wife. His long-suffering first wife is astonished and humiliated. She vilifies him, but stays. The beggars are forced by Mour and his staff from their habitual activities and haunts and driven to the outskirts of town where they are housed in a suburban compound by a woman who has come to be their informal leader, Salla Niang. She had gone into begging following the birth of twins and had prospered in this endeavor and eventually married well, but she continued begging at her post outside the city hospital as a way of supplementing the household income.[9]

Mour discovers that in chasing the beggars from Dakar he has broken the balance of the ritual clock of charity. That balance comes from the blessing that is exchanged for the gift, a blessing the well-off are always in need of, which cannot be bestowed except by the pure and poor. Mour, desirous of being named vice president by His Excellency the president, seeks the counsel of a marabout, who tells him to sacrifice an ox and donate the meat to the poor all over the city. Finding no beggars within the city limits, he cannot comply. He goes to Salla Niang's compound to persuade them to return to their places. The beggars, well paid and fed by handouts from city dwellers who have sought them out there, decide to go on strike after he leaves: to cease begging. Mour fails to achieve his ambition. He mistakenly interpreted their inaction for compliance with his pleas to go back to begging.

Such a Long Letter focuses on two characters. The letter is that of Ramatoulaye, a fifty-year-old Senegalese woman, to her lifelong friend Aissatou. It recounts events from their youth and education, focusing on their courtships and married lives. The heart of the story is the betrayal of both by their much loved and believed-to-be loving husbands. Aissatou's husband is pressured by his mother, a proud noble who despises the blacksmith caste into which Aissatou was born, into a second marriage with a cousin. Aissatou leaves her husband rather than accept a cowife. Ramatoulaye's middle-aged husband marries a companion of their school-age daughter and surrounds her and her greedy family with the things that mark the modern Dakar bourgeoisie: imported cars, a suburban townhouse, nightclub outings, Western clothes. He also runs up a huge debt, which Ramatoulaye learns of only after he dies of a heart attack. Against the pleading of her eldest daughter, a feminist, she had stayed with him after his second marriage. After his death, she rejects two subsequent offers of marriage, one from her husband's brother and one from a disappointed suitor from her youth, and goes on with her twelve children to find other solutions to life's problems.[10]

The Novelist as Ethnographer

Are women beggars? Is the violence of purging Dakar of the poor analogous to pushing aside the old wife for the new? In their ethnographies of Senegalese society, the authors weigh the oppressions of tradition with those of modernization and seem to find a balance.

Each novel articulates, by very different stylistic means, a fundamental problem: does the replacement, or displacement, of traditional social structural categories and their relations into the contemporary socioeconomic context substitute for their dialectical, polycentric, reflexive, processual nature a singularity, a constant? That is to say, there are limitations on the actions of persons in the traditional society by virtue of their membership in social groups (especially women and lower castes), but these may be lifted or transformed in other contexts.[11] In the postcolonial society, this social tradition prefigures yet cannot recover its flexibility from the asymmetrical distribution of resources and power, the engine of economic violence. Once introduced to a society from outside, violently, the money-driven, monopolistic, expansionist, centralized colonial system subverts while leaving superficially intact the precolonial social configuration, perhaps at every stage of revolution from independence movement to the incomplete transformation of society from within.[12] This is the driving force of neoimperialism. It freezes what was fluid, closes what was open. The precolonial endless, dyadic, contextualized game of status and opportunity, which certainly disadvantaged women and lower castes in many settings, had no absolutes, no finalists. Even the oldest male nobles had their betters: their marabouts. And even the marabouts had their mothers and their mothers-in-law. Any imbalance was temporary.

The novels set up a series of homologies, based on their "ethnography" of Senegalese society:[13]

Husband	Men	Older	Noble	Affines	Senior kin
Wife	Women	Younger	Nyényo (casted)	Ego	Ego

Very broadly, husbands are superior to wives as men are to women, as older people are to younger, as nobles are to nonnobles (the castes and slaves), as in-laws (affines) are to the person having married into the family, and as your senior kin are to you (e.g., elder brother, grandparent, maternal uncle, mother's brother's children, etc.). The fact that everyone participates in more than one category means that everyone has superiors, inferiors, and peers. Hence, women, subordinates in some senses, have access to status through caste, kinship, and age. In earlier times, poverty and hardship were equally available to all (except perhaps for the monarchs now gone), making these conditions unremarkable. Today, poverty and hardship are unequally distributed both as a result of the unequal participation of Senegal in the global economic system and of the unequal participation of Senegalese in Senegal's tiny portion of it.

This economic inequality constitutes violence, defined as the use of force with no appeal to reason or feeling. Pushed by colonial mercantilism, then capitalism, from productive subsistence into a wage economy, the Senegalese have been deprived of the possibility of resorting to traditional culture as a palliative for their postcolonial situation. The loss of choice and freedom experienced by all Senegalese under the colonial regime is, ironically, exacerbated by the vitality of dyadic, complementary relations from within the traditional society itself. The native patron-client system, once assimilated to the imported hierarchical, racist, and sexist colonial system, has produced a social milieu that bears the worst features of both. The economic violence produced by colonial commercial expansionism, forced cash cropping, and resource stripping has been perpetuated in the postcolonial context of unchecked economic exploitation. Inegalitarian social traditions of Senegalese society lend themselves to neocolonial oppression.

The Culture of Silence

In Senegalese culture, silence is not golden (in fact, noise from griots brings them riches), but it is noble. The articulation of the noble-nyényo opposition is made in terms of the distribution of religious piety, social status, land tenure, and activity. Speech is classed as action. Activity, noise, aggressiveness, demands, loudness, talk, are the domain of the nyényo; the superior status of the noble is signified by quiet, little speech, submission to God's will, contemplation. The noble acts through others. Thus, to speak much, to complain, indicates nonnobility. To assert one's rights is to violate one's claim to status.

The women in the novels of Bâ and Fall equivocate this set of relations between speech and action: Lolli, Mour's wife, speaks out as she insults her husband, but she does not act; Salli, the mother of twins, makes little response to Mour's pleas to the beggars to return to their posts, but she takes action to deny him his goal; Aissatou leaves her husband without a word; Ramatoulaye withholds both language and action. In the transitional society of today, in which most people are oppressed from without and some also from within, women are cracking apart the equivalencies of speech and action, of silence and submission, of silent submission and status. They may have to be willing to commit class suicide, to borrow Trotsky's term from an entirely different frame of reference (that is, they may have to abandon the privileges of nobility). But they are finding that, in the modern situation of aggressive economic violence, the traditional system of compensatory status guarantees them neither the respect of their husbands, nor food for the family, nor schooling for the children, nor any of the other material supports their silence would have earned them in other times.

Thus, in traditional affairs, women were not compelled to acquiesce to marital or familial arrangements that disadvantaged them personally; no compulsion was necessary: if they complained, they lost status and were returned ignominiously to the supervision of their fathers or brothers. Traditionally, however, women had resort to other sources of status than gender or speech behavior—their own positions in the kin group, eventually their age, or their caste. The violence of limited choice and power was muted by a reciprocal restoration of choice and power in a different context. Women who agreed to enter into or remain in a disagreeable marriage were assured their livelihood (even the worst philanderer of a husband was expected to maintain his wives and children as comfortably as possible). Women could expect to grow in influence and authority in their own lineages and in their affinal networks with the birth of children and with increasing age. Their devotion to a troublesome husband would be praised; they would be considered deeply religious and honorable.

The background of postcolonial economic violence renders the whole society noisy, busy, demanding, in relation to the external powers. Nothing mediates this relation. Considerations such as privilege of birth, kin category, age, are irrelevant. The colonization of the traditional social structure relegates women's many places and voices within it to one position, one possible language. Their traditional silence and submission are the sign of a certain voice that can no longer be heard. Now, not to speak and not to act have begun to mean simply that you can be taken advantage of.

Fall's broad ethnography of her culture examines social categories in addition to women. Beggars and their mistreatment have been used elsewhere to signify the corruption of modern life in Senegal, for instance by Ousmane Sembène in his recent novel *Xala*.[14] The poor, like griots, speak or act to gain their livelihood, in requesting alms and praying for the deliverance of the donor; they exchange their blessing for money. The modernization of poverty and the enrichment of the elite disturb the traditional mutuality of their dependency. The elite begin to hoard their wealth, the poor grow too numerous to support. In fiction, at least, they have their vengeance. The role of women in Bâ's and Fall's novels is comparable: like the poor, they are the miners' canary. When they are fallen low, the ability of the society to sustain itself fails. When speech and silence both do them disservice, only violation remains, of tradition and of people's hope for justice.

Whatever inequality between male and female existed precolonially in Africa, it has been exacerbated and compounded by the imposition of European patriarchal sexism. The European evolutionist concept of the Great Chain of Being that ranked the races also consigns women to the lowest rung of cultural and intellectual development.[15] Like racism, the new opposition of men and women obscures the masked opposition of ruling class and oppressed. In the same way that the modernization of poverty moves beggars to revolt against the new order (as Fall describes in her novel), the displacement of women from their locus as the site of cultural transmission and the repository of family prestige may have dire consequences. The perceived cacophony of their voices and angry action fictionally entails the destruction of the indigenous code of power, by which high-status women were rewarded for silence.

Women's Complaints

In both traditional and modern, transitional Senegal, society has found it necessary to control women's behavior in order to perpetuate itself and the status quo. Marital and reproductive life are the key to this control. Though he was not concerned with polygyny or endogamy, Bourdieu's discussion of "marriage strategies" as strategies for social reproduction is apt.[16] Extending his approach, we see that the one-sided freedom of men to marry multiple wives and the stricture placed on men and, more tightly, on women to marry within their caste, constitute a recipe for the continuity of the status code. (Men who wish to marry outside their caste can do so either by making a "good marriage" first or by becoming so old, so high in status, that no one will dare say anything to them about it. Women have no such hopes.) Modern women are ambivalent about these, as about other forms of marital violence (the arranged marriage, which men either instigate with the father of a woman they have chosen, or which men may not be confined by if they are able to make a "love match" later as well; and the levirate discussed in note 10). Madubuike discusses the corruption of the traditional bride-price exchange by the money economy.[17] Women's ambivalence stems from the problem of the signification of silence and submission: that is, to be noble, to be good, to be pious, is to be compliant. In traditional times, there was no contradiction in accession to this formula. Women who submitted were rewarded through their key role in social reproduction and the boost to their status. The women characters in *The Beggars' Strike* and *Une si longue lettre* live the contradiction without any reward.

Another matter, not spoken of in these novels, is female circumcision, usually taking the form of clitoridectomy in West Africa.[18] The sexual violence of rape was probably unknown in precolonial Africa, but ritual mutilation of various kinds was widespread. Clitoridectomy has persisted, though it is drawing increasing fire from foreign and African feminists.[19]

A good many African people, including women and feminists, resent the tendency of foreign feminists to give this matter priority over political and economic parity or the health and schooling of children.

Though clitoridectomy is not widely practiced in Senegal today, it is well known to Senegalese people and is another kind of deprivation about which women have mixed feelings. Awa Thiam, a Senegalese, was among the first scholars to focus on the meaning of this custom, along with Nawal el Saadawi, the feminist Egyptian physician.[20] Thiam's study is principally of language and discourse in relation to sexuality and gender. She links clitoridectomy and polygyny to the discourse of deviance that defines women as by nature defiled, unwhole, unwell, and potentially unholy (witches and adultresses). The custom is thus another form of silencing to which women submit because they are placed in an ideological quandary. Not to be circumcised is to be unmarked as a member of one's group. Not to be circumcised is to proclaim loudly your independence of family and future husband, your willful and ignoble indulgence of self (that is, not to be a good, ritually pure woman). Not to be circumcised is, paradoxically, also to be a child, with the child's corresponding low status and lack of freedom. Furthermore, ritual initiations are in general not enacted as an opposition of genders, though they have the effect of separating the men from the boys, the men from the women, and the women from the girls. They are more a conspiracy of the elders to control the young and maintain the social order than an oppression of women by men. (The clitoridectomy operation itself and the accompanying ceremony are performed by older kinswomen and female ritual proficients.) Of course, in the case of clitoridectomy, the explicitly sexual implications and usual rationale (to promote chastity and marital fidelity) put it in the domain of sexual violence.

Traditional practice would seem to give women sufficient cause for complaint against the organizing principles of custom. Colonialism gave them greater cause. The few occasions of women's rebellion against colonial administrations in Africa produced a sort of shock among colonials and local men alike. A famous incident, the Aba women's riots of 1929 in Nigeria, was a threat to the view of reality held by the English and their local flunkies: the invisible became visible, the mute spoke out.[21] Not only are women writers often drawn into the struggle of the underprivileged, but also the metonymical relation of all women to the poor, victims of a kindred violence, puts them on the same path to rebellion.[22] The least likely—the silent, submissive mothers and daughters of society—become the most dangerous. What other means of change is possible, when women are told they have the right to speak but must speak without making a sound?

The Textualization of African Women's Voices

The evocation of genuine African women's voices in fiction (and elsewhere) involves a number of stylistic and theoretical problems. Principal among these are (1) the problem of the person (subject) in a collectivist society, (2) the problem of the deconstruction of narrative, dialogue, and historical context through oral tradition (the unwritten word), a rich tradition that has dominated Senegalese verbal art, mythology, science, history, and other language-based communicative forms, and (3) the key cultural and social role of "griottes," women praise singers, genealogists, and verbal specialists.[23] It is not my intention, nor is it within my capability, to explain these matters in any definitive way, but we must at least briefly consider how they influence our reading of Bâ, Fall, and any other African women who speak out.

As noted by many authors, the epistemological and ideological difficulties of distinguishing the distinctively African from the generally postcolonial or from the fundamentally human make postmodern literary criticism noisier than it used to be.[24] Furthermore, Bâ and Fall speak very differently, Bâ in the nuanced rhythm of a literary conversation, Fall in the allusive cadence of Wolof verbal art. Their characters are individuals. To insist on any univocality or unity of theme and purpose in African novels is to trivialize the historical and existing diversity and vigor of indigenous culture. The unifying thread in African experience is drawn from the political economic sphere, not from the cultural sphere, that is, the asymmetrical colonial and postcolonial relations between South and North. This single thread is, of course, of consuming interest in many African works, but it is not the only interest. Senegalese writers, Bâ and Fall included, are also absorbed by the contradictions and continuities of their own internally varied and changing, yet in many ways stable, society.

Thus, there is no peculiarly African subject embodied in these, or any, novels. There are many African and Senegalese subjects, many female and male subjects, some self-seeking, others more socially conscious. Journeys of self-realization, generally considered to be a European literary preoccupation, are staples of the African epic tale and emerge in modern literature as well, in *Such a Long Letter,* for example.[25] The collectivist social forms of traditional West Africa do not suppress or constrain the dramatic expression of the individual subject, but they do place it in a different context, which must be approached anew with each reading and each work.

The new, feminist social and cultural critique conducted in *The Beggars' Strike* is played out in native, collective categories, as in the following culminating scene. Mour, the observer here, sees the assembled beggars not as a group of individuals but as a mass defect, and he sees Salla, too, not as a person or woman but as an invention, an artifice. People become abstractions in three senses: to him, literally, as a self-interested government official, persons are pawns or numbers; in a hopeless and violent world, people are benumbed by others' and even their own desperation to the extent of being abstracted from each other; and in Sow's creative transformation of conventional categories, persons can represent or embody such abstractions as justice or will:

> He has never seen, as if simultaneously projected onto a screen, the
> image of so many physical defects, so much physical decrepitude and
> human disintegration from which, it is true, some patches of light
> stand out, like this Salla Niang whose face gleams like a bronze bust,
> fashioned by a master sculptor. (80)
>
> . . . . . .
>
> "I'd like to speak to the master of the house."
> "I'm in charge here."
> A clarion-call of a voice, clear and crystalline like a stream of molten
> silver. Mour is silent for a moment, then begins to wonder what kinds
> of links there might be between this lady and these beggars. (81)

The links are those forged between all groups and individuals—here, women and the poor—by their resistance to economic violence and their common oppression.

Griots as a group are also linked to women by their low status and by the signification of this status differential in terms of relative noisiness. Sufficient attention has begun to be addressed to the issues of orality and griots' performance to develop a theoretical framework for the relations between these genres and contemporary African written literary forms.[26] I am not prepared to elaborate this framework in this essay, but as an anthropologist interested in the full range of human communication, I find the differences between Senegalese oral tradition and Senegalese modern novels, between griots' art and behavior and the writers' crafts, more compelling than their similarities. They constitute different tools and involve different speakers and receivers. Sometimes their messages and codes overlap, sometimes not. The semiotic of griots' art establishes a different range of relationships between the performer, the audience, the song or story, the manner and occasion of the performance, and its meanings. Writers can draw upon this range, can work within it, but they can also operate beyond it in a semiotic range of their own. Griots themselves signify a set of meanings quite different from those that exist in the persons and activities of writers. Senegalese reading novels do not think to themselves, "This is or is like the performance of a griot." They may react to certain characters in terms of caste judgment, however: "She is acting like a griot."

Bâ and Fall draw meaning from this heritage in their novels. Without diminishing the rich sources of oral tradition, they complement it with the textured experience of contemporary Senegalese people speaking through their writing. There is no evolutionary direction of orature to literature, nor is there any necessary artistic direction the other way. The forms are distinct, though available to each other as enactive devices. The trace of oral culture in literary works by Africans can be tracked through the use of proverbs, ritual incantations, verbal art, and so on. Griots themselves as individual characters or as a class, where they exist as such, can call forth oral (spoken-heard) devices into a written-read communication.

The griotte character in *Such a Long Letter* acts as a counselor to Ramatoulaye; she is the faithful family retainer giving conservative advice—to remain, to remarry, to sharply restrain her errant daughters. Griots, of course, and griottes especially, embody the ambiguity of status in traditional Senegal; they have a freedom and a voice that most others do not, yet have the lowest status of all castes, apart from *jaam,* the descendents of slaves. They are the living representatives and reservoir of the past, yet in their loud and feared expression they are a continual challenge to the status quo. Ramatoulaye chooses to be self-reliant and to let her daughters become themselves. The griotte in this case acts as the voice of tradition, not the path of departure Ramatoulaye seeks; the griotte's own role remains to support and defend her mistress.

The new women of Senegal have no guides to follow in their questioning exploration, but Bâ, and Fall as well, seem to say that Senegalese women will continue to be the conservators of personal and familial relationships, while supporting one another. Bâ's main character concludes that there is no contradiction in accepting tradition while struggling for change: "Ce sont toutes les familles, riches ou pauvres, unies ou déchirées, conscientes ou irréfléchies qui constituent la Nation. La réussite d'une nation passe donc irrémédiablement par la famille" (130). (It is all families, rich or poor, united or torn apart, aware or irreflective who constitute the

Nation. The success of a nation thus is passed on unavoidably through the family.)

The textualization of the voices of women and beggars in *The Beggars' Strike* also arises dialectically from the hedged play of status in Senegal. The exploited and oppressed of society cannot be done without: the rich and privileged would not exist without them; from this ironic perspective, women and beggars, however troublesome, are necessary to the continuity and prosperity of all. Viewed thus, the problem of poverty is the problem of wealth, the problem of restriction is that of privilege. The dialectic turns on the associated themes of individual-group and modern-traditional (the latter represented in *Beggars* by Mour's healer and in *Letter* by the griotte). The deemphasis on narrative personality in Fall's novel makes the individual personalities of the women characters and beggars more vivid, and it also makes almost epic their common language of deliverance. Acceptance of tradition no longer means silence or submission for either author. It means to sow the seed of transformation in the brutalized postcolonial soil.

Notes

1. For this essay, I use the English translation (1981) by Dorothy Blair of Aminata Sow Fall, *The Beggars' Strike*. Mariama Bâ's *Une si longue lettre* has been translated into English with the title *So Long a Letter*, which I find less idiomatic than my preferred translation, "Such a Long Letter." Readers may take their pick.

2. Henry Louis Gates, Jr., "Introduction: Writing 'Race' and the Difference It Makes," in Gates, ed., *"Race," Writing, and Difference*, 13.

3. See, for example, Ihechukwu Madubuike, *The Senegalese Novel*.

4. Cf. Shirley Geok-Lin Lim and Norman A. Spencer, eds., *One World of Literature*.

5. Dorothy S. Blair, *Senegalese Literature*.

6. Fall's latest work, *Le Jujubier du patriarche* (1993), also exemplifies an ethnographic approach.

7. Although anthropologists began to include works of fiction and poetry in their ethnographic analyses of particular cultures more than thirty years ago, only recently have they begun to view such works as incorporations of cultural analyses carried out by the authors, as, in effect, ethnographies by natives. An interesting example of this approach is Richard Handler and Daniel Segal, *Jane Austen and the Fiction of Culture*.

8. *Marabout,* a French term designating Islamic religious proficients of the West African mystical tradition, is more accurate and less loaded than "sorcerer," *imam,* "witch doctor," religious cleric, or any number of other more familiar English terms. A marabout may be, though is not necessarily, a healer, a teacher, a diviner, a preacher. Usually he is a man, always a sage and ritual specialist. Women are well represented

in other religious roles less closely associated with Islam, such as priestesses of possession cults and fortune-tellers.

9. Categories of people eligible to request alms include lepers, the blind, disabled, fools (the deranged), mothers of twins (who represent a liminal ontological category, human and divine), mutes, and of course the destitute. In order to be destitute in Senegalese society, one's family must be entirely deceased or severely poor, since the extended family and lineage are considered an honorable source of support in any kind of difficulty.

10. The levirate, or widow inheritance, is a common practice in Senegal, especially where older women or young widows who have not yet borne children are involved. In a society where women do not customarily live alone, single women and widows are nominally in the custody of their fathers or brothers. In the case of the older women, a marriage of convenience, often in name only, to a kinsman of the deceased husband may be preferable to their returning to their natal household or to that of some other male relative. Because a childless widow has not yet fulfilled her part of the marital contract, bearing children, her family will have to repay the bride-price they have received for her if she comes back to them. Hence, both families may find it desirable to marry her to a man in the dead man's patriline. The Senegalese women with whom I have discussed this custom indicated that women are consulted when these circumstances arise and are not generally compelled to accept the marriage if they refuse. However, the ideal of the Senegalese wife is one who subordinates her personal wishes to those of her husband, his family, and her family, and who endures without complaint whatever choices they make for her. This contradiction is clearly depicted in Bâ's and Fall's women characters' contemplations of their dilemmas: from outrage to acquiescence, from submission to rupture, or from silence to vengeance, the "good wife" and the true heart vie.

11. Several of the ethnic groups whose tongues are classified in the West Atlantic language family of the Niger-Kordofanian phylum of African languages have social stratifications best described as caste systems. In Senegal, this includes the Wolof, Peul, Toucouleur, Serer, and Diola people, who are the majority groups. The basic division is between noble and nonnoble (/géer/ and /nyényo/ to use the Wolof appellations). Within the nyényo are five occupationally defined, ranked, endogamous castes: woodworkers, leatherworkers, blacksmiths, griots or praise singers, and descendents of slaves, in descending order of status.

12. Ibrahim James, "The Four-Stage Revolution."

13. I have used the anthropological designation "ego," common in kinship diagramming, to refer to the person from whose point of view one identifies a relationship: one is subordinate to one's in-laws (affines) and chronologically and genealogically senior relatives, for most purposes.

14. Sembène uses a strike by railroad workers to evoke the opposition of European and African, elite and oppressed, in his 1960 novel, *Les Bouts de bois de dieu: Banty Mam Yalla* (God's Bits of Wood). *Xala* (1973) uses traditional healers as well as beggars in its critique of the Senegalese bourgeoisie.

15. See Rosaline Ekpenyong, "Women's Role in the New Age."

16. Pierre Bourdieu, "Marriage Strategies as Strategies of Social Reproduction."

17. Madubuike *Senegalese Novel,* 51.

18. Other forms include labiectomy and infibulation, or "Pharaonic circumci-

sion," in which the girl's vaginal opening is stitched together, allowing only room for the flow of menses until her wedding night, when the husband or sage woman–midwife removes the stitches. Unless carried out under sterile conditions, these operations may lead to infection, peritonitis, infertility, and death. Also, of course, they render the woman incapable of enjoying sexual relations, though they do nothing to prevent her from experiencing love or sexual attraction, which is thought to be the purpose. One commonly cited goal for performing clitoridectomy on young women is the assurance of their premarital chastity and marital fidelity. Others include the removal of any abstract masculine principle from their personalities (the Dogon), and the promotion of fertility.

19. The IIDA, a Somali women's relief group based in Mogadishu, plans a campaign against female circumcision in that country, but it has so far been ignored by the U.N.–U.S. Joint Task Force in meetings that decide Somalia's political future. This issue is taken up by Halima Ismaym Ibrahim, quoted in Andrew Cohen, "Some Scenes from an Intervention," 164. The effectiveness of grassroots and nongovernmental organizations in dealing with local affairs has often been overlooked by outsiders.

20. See Awa Thiam, *La Parole aux négresses* (1978).

21. See Michèle Fielaux, " 'Femmes invisibles' et 'femmes muettes' "; and Evelyn Rich, *Memorandum on the Aba Women's Riot.*

22. See John D. Ajala, *"The Beggars' Strike,"* and Susan Z. Andrade, "Rewriting History, Motherhood, and Rebellion."

23. For background on the oral tradition and griottes, see Bill Ashcroft, Gareth Griffiths, and Helen Tiffin, *The Empire Writes Back,* and Lloyd W. Brown, *Women Writers in Black Africa.* The anthropological literature on Africa contains numerous studies of griots as a social structural phenomenon. Folklorists have recorded their tales, "ethno"-musicologists have taped their music, and now comparative literature is considering whether their traditions may be a literary source. Griots in Senegal are especially interesting because of the status code of silence. They are the ultimate noise makers—loud, importunate, verbally artful, visible everywhere, hence active, and therefore low status. Yet, like women, they are essential for the continuity of the society. They are the link to its past, whereas women are the link to its future.

24. On this point, see Daniel Segal's Introduction in Segal, ed., *Crossing Cultures.*

25. See Mildred Mortimer, *Journeys through the French African Novel.*

26. See Eileen Julien, *African Novels and the Question of Orality.*

SHIRLEY GEOK-LIN LIM

Up against the National Canon:
Women's War Memoirs from Malaysia
and Singapore

Every emerging literature has its pioneering women writers. If their number has been small, this has resulted usually from the unfavorable conditions under which they wrote: absence of encouragement for their "unwomanly" efforts, lack of publishing opportunities, and the burden of domestic work and marital responsibilities.[1] As many critics have noted, pioneer women writers tended to write in forms not traditionally considered literature, such as diaries, letters, journals, stories for children, and autobiographies, and because the subjects and content of their writing tended to fall outside areas assumed to be significant, their themes have frequently been dismissed as subjective, personal, or sentimental.[2] Indeed, because many women generally have not been present in the halls of political power and decision making, their work has been perceived as extraneous to a national literature.[3] In colonial and postcolonial societies, women writers may face additional forces rising from the gendered or patriarchal shape of national ideologies that exclude them. Even when they do publish, their works are located outside the perspectives of critics and cultural historians of these newly emerging nation-states who are themselves involved in articulating ideologies of nationalism to counter their colonial past. The authors of *Toward the Decolonization of African Literature,* for example, argue for an Afrocentric literature that resists European and other nonnative influences and revives a pure and original tradition, leading to the corollary that value can only be attributed to works that in some way carry a family or national identity.[4] Many examples of women's writing therefore have not been collected or even noticed, laboring as many critics do under assumed values of what constitutes a "significant" or "national" literature.

Malaysian-Singapore women writing in English today still face the problem the 1958 *Litmus One* editors complained of, that is, the "lack of a common local and long-standing tradition."[5] The major difficulty in attempting to recover neglected texts and to inscribe the names of Singapore and Malaysian women writers who do not appear in the national canons is that there is little information or material on them. Their works are usually out of print and may not be found in libraries, even in special collections. They may not appear in editions of *Who's Who*, newspaper reviews, or biographies. Defining and assessing their contribution to cultural history is difficult given this absence or scarcity of materials.[6]

This essay attempts to map a tradition of women's writing, to light up an area of invisibility, as it were. The trope of uncharted territory is closely related, moreover, to that of territory that has no legal status, that needs as yet to be "chartered." Bearing in mind the significance of the Women's Charter Bill of 1961, which secured legal, professional, and economic rights for Singaporean women, the term "unchartered" has a special aptness for the women who were writing in the region before the 1961 bill.[7] My study suggests that the works of early women writers from Malaysia and Singapore, in particular Sybil Kathigasu and Janet Lim, have been neglected partly because their status as individuals in newly formed nation-states was legalistically unclear and undefined, and outside hegemonic national definitions.[8] Alix Kate Shulman has pointed out that such women writers, writing within the context of rapid identity changes fostered by cultural and language policies shaped by ideologies of nation building, manifest lives of "uprootedness, social displacement, even exile" that are characteristic of a number of international women writers. "The phenomenon of displacement," she notes, is the cause for the obscurity of many international women writers; their lives and the fate of their books reflect "the political upheavals, class warfare, and social turbulence that have characterized our century."[9]

Male writers in Third World countries have by and large not suffered from such neglect. Take the case of Wang Gungwu, born in Indonesia and educated for many years in China, who wrote a slim volume of poems (*Pulse*) and two critical essays on Malayan writing in the 1950s before moving on to make his career as a historian. Although Wang removed himself from identification with the nationalistic politics of Malaysia and Singapore by emigrating to Australia in the 1960s, *Pulse* is generally referred to as marking the beginning of Malayan writing in English.[10] His two essays on the use of English in creating a Malayan literature are also cited as formative contributions to the evolution of a Malaysian-Singapore literature in English.[11] Wang's contribution is still recognized today, perhaps for the very reason that his involvement in Malayan writing some forty years ago was of a dogmatic nature in that it helped formulate a nationalist ideology consistent with contemporary nation-building ideals.[12]

The continued usefulness of Wang's texts to contemporary cultural commentators demonstrates how ideological considerations play a role in the construction of a national canon. This is not to say that texts are appropriated as propagandistic instruments to serve the authority of powerful established agencies. Literary texts and readers, after all, have their own evasive, subversive linguistic discourse strategies that resist political appropriation. But in the constructions of national canons, works that diverge from or take issue with the accepted ideology of national identity can be expected to be marginalized or excluded.[13]

Colonialism, Nationalism, and Gender: Locating Female Heroism

Despite the charge that women writers have been too subjective to be of interest to national movements directly involved in shaping a national literary canon, the evidence of political consciousness and a public imagination in Malaysian-Singaporean women's writing before 1970 is substantial.[14] Indeed, political consciousness is foregrounded in the early autobiographies, *No Dram of Mercy* by Sybil Kathigasu and Janet Lim's *Sold for Silver*. Kathigasu's memoir represents the author herself as a heroine, a woman warrior, and an upholder of Western values such as individual liberty and free speech: "I have never been held back by fear of the consequences from saying what I think is right, and I refused to deprive myself of the liberty of expressing my true feelings about the Japanese" (44). Kathigasu was a well-known and well-loved community figure, a midwife and nurse, who during the war risked her life and her family's safety by giving medical assistance to the Malayan People's Anti-Japanese Army (MPAJA). Throughout the memoir she refers to the resistance group as guerrillas; they were later labeled Communists.[15] As a result of this resistance work, she was arrested by the Japanese and imprisoned.

The first part of the memoir describes the Japanese occupation of Malaya as a particularly brutal suppression of the Chinese population: "Their rule was based on terror, and this was particularly so in respect of the Chinese. . . . They feared the Chinese, and gave expression to their fear in savage persecution and constant spying. . . . Hence the public executions which were a barbarous feature of Japanese rule" (52). The author's documentation of "savage" and "barbaric" sexual assaults, looting, and kill-ings of innocent civilians bears searing witness to a recent history that has been suppressed by Japanese nationals and the interests of corporate capital.

Three ideological aspects introduced in the opening section make the memoir especially problematic from a nationalist perspective: the author's unswerving pro-British stance, her sympathetic view of the MPAJA, and her Catholic faith. As a part-Irish Eurasian, born Sybil Daly, and married to a doctor, Kathigasu was a privileged woman in a colonized society and counted white male professionals and white women among her friends. As revealed in her memoir, her personal traits—generous treatment of poor patients, devotion to the ill, idealism in helping the guerrillas, and extraordinary courage—explain the sympathy and furtive support she re-ceived from her non-Japanese captors and guards (35). She frequently seems to ignore the fact that the prison guards are collaborators, and inter-prets their support as an expression of covert pro-British loyalties: "Our guards made no secret of their hatred for the Japanese regime and their longing for the return of the British" (150). One incident describes Kathi-gasu's reply to a Japanese officer who orders her to "address a Japanese as Tuan [master]." Boldly, she declares, "I speak English . . . and I never used 'Tuan' to the British so why should I to you?" (142). Here Kathigasu appeals to English as the language of democratic egalitarianism. The Brit-ish, according to her account, operate outside the frame of fascist domina-tion, unlike the Japanese colonizers who insist on their superior position. We glimpse how deep an ideological gulf there is between Kathigasu and the ordinary Malayan people, who were treated as racial inferiors by the Japanese and the British alike. British colonialism has historically meant domination over and suppression of non-British peoples, albeit in a pater-nalistic manner in contrast to the Japanese colonizers' violent militarism. Kathigasu's Anglophilia emerges again and again in her memoir: "I re-minded the guard of what Malaya owed to Britain, and of the amount of talent, labour, money and material which had gone to make Malaya the happiest and most advanced country in the East" (162).

Kathigasu's perspective contrasts sharply with that of Janet Lim, whose war memoir expresses disenchantment. Lim, unlike Kathigasu, was not a privileged colonial subject, but rather an impoverished China-born orphan, an unmarried nurse having no class or race privileges and there-fore no stake in British rule. Lim approached the Japanese displacement of British colonial rule with a certain optimism: "I thought that war would solve some of our problems, especially that of the colour bar, which was

very marked in those days. For instance, during the early campaign of
Malaya, someone wrote to the local press asking the Government to supply a special bus for Europeans only, as the Asians were filthy" (104).
Kathigasu's white-privileged, procolonial admiration for British paternalistic rule thus creates a problem if we try to interpret her work as Malaysian national literature when "national" is constituted as unambivalently
oppositional to colonialist culture.

Similarly, Kathigasu's sympathetic account of MPAJA military activities, which describes the resistance movement as chiefly Chinese (58), and
the portraits of informers and collaborators, willing or unwilling, do not
fit in with the accepted version of official Malaysian national history. In
Kathigasu's memoir, Chinese resistance fighters are national patriots.
These "patriots," however, have been demonized in postwar British colonial history; and this view persists in contemporary histories of Malaysia,
which condemn them as Communist insurgents and murderous sympa-
thizers of the People's Republic of China.[16] Kathigasu's memoir reminds
the reader that the MPAJA was an ally of "Britain and America in the
fight against the Axis" (99). Her portraits of idealistic young Chinese men
such as Berani, Don Juan, and Moru contradict the stereotype of the killer
jungle squads popularized in the sensationalist nonfiction accounts by ex-
British administrators. In the struggle for the minds and hearts of the
people that characterized the postwar years in Malaysia, Kathigasu's
memoir stands apart from the prevailing British colonial ideology and also
the Malay-dominant state ideology of nationalism in which Malay political practice was seen as central and the Chinese were viewed as opportu-
nistic economic sojourners.[17]

Finally, Kathigasu's memoir testifies to her Catholic faith. Borrowing
images from a long tradition of Christian martyr narratives, the text constructs her heroism and courage under unendurable torture as Christian
martyrdom and offers a literal representation of her religious beliefs: "It
was during the early hours of the morning that I awoke, feeling a gentle
tap on my feet. As I opened my eyes I was dazzled by a vision of the Sacred
Heart before me. . . . And His voice said to me: 'My child, you must be
ready to pay the supreme sacrifice, for the glory that is to come'" (40).
Even if constructed as a fictional narrative, this passage is difficult to place
in a national ideology that is strictly secular in Singapore and Islamic in
Malaysia.[18] John Clammer, in his study of culture and society in Singapore, notes that religion in Singapore "stands in a rather uneasy alliance
with the secular powers: both are competing for control of the dominant
symbolic system of the society."[19] In Malaysia, although Christianity is

tolerated, the state has promulgated national culture as one that is Malay in customs and cultural values and Islamic in religion. Presented as a motivational and dramatic feature in a professed "true" story, the Catholicism in Kathigasu's memoir complicates, if not makes impossible, the figure of the woman as (secular or Islamic) nationalist heroine. These aspects of the hegemony of Singapore and Malaysian secular and Islamic, anti-Communist, and decolonizing nationalisms would continue to raise difficulties in teaching Kathigasu's book in the region.

Yet *No Dram of Mercy* is a powerfully, if simply, written war memoir, which in addition to its vivid and unrelenting descriptions of brutality and corresponding courage reveals the sources of the protagonist's survival and grace. Kathigasu may attribute her strength to her God, but the frank, straightforward narration testifies to a belief in communal sharing, communication, and interdependence in the face of physical barbarities that helped preserve her from degradation, insanity, and death. Kathigasu is a Western-informed observer, motivated by the ethos of Western-style democracy—liberty, equality, and fraternity. The highly risky effort to keep a forbidden short-wave radio in order to listen to BBC reports on the war is one instance of her resistance against the prohibition on free communication: "[The BBC news] was a constant reminder that we were not alone—that the world we knew still existed though we were temporarily cut off from it. This knowledge fortified our faith in the ultimate victory of truth and right" (51). Kathigasu made her clinic a clearinghouse for information, including information on Japanese troop movements that helped the guerrillas, despite the threat of punishment that would follow on discovery. In prison, she continued to pass on information, using Samy, an Indian Sanitary Board laborer, to carry messages to her husband and family.

Her actions, based on these principles, provoked her Japanese captors' ill-treatment. But her drive toward democratic and communal free speech, to break the oppressive silence imposed by the Japanese military, also liberated her from her imprisoned isolation. Her belief in freedom of speech led to actions that saved her from the machinations of the Kempetai (Japanese Military Intelligence). More significantly, the memoir constructs a relation between Western liberal ideology and spiritual resources that preserves the individual in the face of physical torture and Eastern (Japanese) totalitarianism.

The narrative of torture and imprisonment is illuminated throughout by the counterinsurgent drama of "speech": "It became almost an obsession with me to make contact with as many different people and to pick up as many scraps of information as I could. . . . I took every opportunity of engaging the other prisoners in conversation and picking up from them even the slightest item of gossip" (129). The power of communication, of "free" speech practiced under murderous conditions, motivates and saves Kathigasu's life and spirit. This theme gives her memoir a dimension of significant language that takes it beyond the level of simple sociopolitical documentation and into the realm of textuality.

Kathigasu died a few years after the war from septicemia in her jaw, which was broken by her Japanese jailer. Her memoir, besides its value as a historical document, also presents us with a female figure whose life and writing provide an exemplar of the Asian woman as agent in the most urgent of sociopolitical circumstances, under conditions of war.

Countering "National" History: A Feminist Memoir

Leong Liew Geok, one of the few critics to examine women's memoirs from the Malayasia-Singapore region, has pointed out that Janet Lim's *Sold for Silver* is more an autobiography than Kathigasu's memoir, for it covers the entire life of the protagonist up to the end of the war in the Pacific.[20] Writing a war memoir offered Lim a pretext for writing her life. Yet to read *Sold for Silver* simply as a life story is to misread it. Lim's war experiences can be seen as the centerpiece of her autobiography, but the life story as a whole is a feminist text that indicts not just her Japanese captors but a broad patriarchal world, both Asian and European. Lim says in the preface that she wrote the book in two parts, the section dealing with wartime Singapore between 1949 and 1950, and the earlier part, treating her childhood, in 1955—that is, the feminist indictments, which are almost solely confined to the first half of the book, were written almost ten years after the war ended, when Lim was older and had more distance and control over her materials.

The autobiography opens with the eight-year-old Chui Mei's arrival in Singapore, then steps back to narrate the events leading to her abandoned and indentured position. Very quickly, a larger family and communal narrative is established. We learn that one of Chui Mei's sisters "was given away to a convent," and that when a brother "was born a year later . . . there was great rejoicing" (15). These details delineate the particular experience of life in a society in which value, property, and lines of descent were assigned to males: "In China, women were not entitled to inherit property; everything went to sons or, if there were no sons, to brothers and nephews" (26). In the patriarchal society, women were generally restricted to domestic roles and positions: "Occupied in housework . . . Chinese wives lived almost separate from their husbands. . . . [My mother] seldom went beyond the high walls of the village" (19). For women, marriage, which offered them their only means to social position, was also an institution that secluded and oppressed them: "A village girl enjoyed great freedom before her marriage; but after a marriage had been arranged she was strictly forbidden to go out alone" (19). Thus constrained, women frequently chose the desperate way out: a cousin's wife hanged herself three months after the wedding (19).[21]

The patriarchal construction of women's identities was also perpetuated by women who, having passed through the social systems, accepted the low status of women and their marginalization in the domestic sphere. "Cooking, sewing and looking after the house formed a girl's passport to marriage and some strict prospective mothers-in-law insisted on investigating a girl's work before they would accept her" (19). The narrator's mother, "like most village women, was convinced that daughters were of little value" (20). Lim's observations of traditional Chinese patriarchal structures are not new, but together they introduce the major motif of the autobiography, the fate of women as epitomized in the life of one woman in an oppressively patriarchal society.[22]

Although Lim's description of life in China is highly gender-differentiated, and the details are structured in terms of the asymmetrical relation between male and female roles, status, and valuations, there is no overt moral judgment: she sets down observations, not propositions. The narrative avoids a polemical feminist dimension, making it easy to overlook the fact that the asymmetrical construction of female identity already predicates a moral dimension. Lim's narrative, moreover, does not single out men as responsible for gender inequalities and sexist and sexual oppressions. If conditions of women's lives in China (and Singapore) were unequal, narrow, and restrictive, the patriarchy that maintained these conditions was not solely identified as male and evil. Lim's relations with her parents illustrate the ironies in women's social enslavement. Her father "was very gentle, patient and affectionate" (20), and willed "his whole estate" to her (27). In contrast, her mother embodied the attitudes of rejection and insistence on female inferiority associated with the worst of patriarchal structures: "Mother was a very strict woman and never showed her love for me. Nor did she answer my endless questions; instead, I received slaps on the face for being too talkative. . . . My mother often complained that I was the ugliest child in the family" (20). On her father's death, her mother remarries and betroths the child Chui Mei to her second husband's younger nephew (33). After further unhappy wanderings, her mother and stepfather finally abandon her in a town near Swatow: "Mother gave me twenty-five cents and told me to be good and promised they would soon come back for me. . . . That was the last I ever saw of them" (36).

The structural irony of the maternal as figure for patriarchal attitudes and behavior is unconscious on the part of the narrator, however, and it becomes increasingly complex in the later part of the book when the adult Chui Mei, now known by her anglicized name, Janet Lim, expresses her deep psychological bonds to a vision of the maternal quite unrecognizable as the mother of her childhood. The chief hurt in the protagonist's life is her orphaned or "unmothered" and "homeless" condition. After she is rescued by British women missionaries from her *mui tsai* (slave girl) position and from the sexual assaults of her elderly master, Janet is happy as a resident in the girls' home except during the holidays: "Perhaps it was when I saw the boarders go away with their parents that I felt most lost, unwanted and homeless" (71).[23] Just before turning sixteen years old, she follows the advice of her beloved Miss Kilgour and takes up nursing. What troubles her is that she had to stay always in the hospital, "whereas most nurses could go back to their own homes when off-duty. . . . This emphasized my lack of real home and of the loving care of parents" (85). But she says that she was motivated to complete her nursing training "so that I could afford to go back to China and look for my mother, of whom I had never stopped thinking" (95). After she is adopted unofficially by a daughterless family, she feels that she at least has a home: "I always refer to Mrs. Chan as my 'adopted mother.' . . . I no longer had that sense of loneliness, that feeling of not being wanted, for I too could say: 'I am going home'" (96).

But she still has a feeling of being motherless and abandoned. In the two situations when she is closest to death, she has a vision of "my real mother's face": "She spoke to me and I could hear her solemn voice saying: 'Child, don't be afraid; I am always with you'" (128). The profound irony of such an ever present maternal love—"always with you"—against the truth of having been abandoned suggests multiple psychosocial interpretations, among them the failure of the daughter to separate herself from her mother. As the vision disappears, however, she recognizes "the stark reality of her [mother's] death." In the displacement of the unacknowledged maternal abandonment to an acknowledged maternal death, the daughter receives psychological comfort and "was (able) to hang on grimly to life" (129).

Similarly, when she attempts to hang herself in the cell after she is captured by the Japanese, "I dreamt of my real mother. She came towards me with outstretched arms. . . . I said, 'Mama, you must not leave me again, I am very lonely and everybody hates me.' But to my dismay she began to recede, growing smaller and smaller until her face became so blurred that I could see her no longer" (215). This occasion, when the experience of maternal abandonment is played out in her imagination, signals the point when her "separation anxiety" is finally internalized and integrated into the personality. Though it marks her breakdown, the lowest point of her struggle against her captors, it also marks the point when the theme of search for her mother ends. After this revision of maternal abandonment, an independent Janet is able to work as housemaid and nurse with the Japanese, who leave her virtue intact.

The narrative of Janet Lim's struggles to preserve her virginity from the Japanese officers forms the most gripping part of the book, but it is only a continuum of the larger narrative of women's experiences in a society that treated women as objects, "a slave, to be bargained for and sold like merchandise, to suffer shame and the whips of one's master and mistress" (42). In 1932, at the age of eight, she had been sold for $250 to a Chinese family in Singapore. As is explained to the girl, her master "preferred very young (girls)"; his second wife "had suggested to him to 'import' a few girls. . . . I was to be his concubine and his slave" (46). At eight, Chui Mei learns to defend her virginity: "I cannot express my terror when I heard his footsteps. I crawled anywhere, inside cupboards, under the beds, outside the windows, anywhere, as long as I could get out of his reach" (42). Chui Mei's mistress beats her for refusing to sleep with the old man. The girl's terror of violation under a Chinese roof within a social economic system with legislative standing in the Straits Settlements is perhaps more terrifying than the grown woman's flight from Japanese rapists, for it was sanctioned by men and women from her own community.

Lim's life story of female subjugation is legitimized and made more objective by the narrative strategy of historicizing the subjective discourse of autobiography. The personal story is placed in the context of a larger social history, and the intervention of this larger dimension into the young girl's life radically changes it. The girl's life is "rescued" and altered by external agencies; so also the autobiography is "rescued" and altered by history. The memoir suggests that where individual rights do not matter or even exist, the story of the individual needs to be mediated by the story of society, that is, by history. Memoir, not autobiography, is produced when the value of the individual is weighted against social narratives.

Lim's memoir crosses into social history at the point when the South Seas Chinese world encounters British colonial agency, when what is personally known is taken over by the colonial unknown: "Unknown to me, changes were then taking place in Singapore which were to have a great effect on my life" (49). In 1932, the Straits Settlement Government passed the Mui Tsai Ordinance to control the trade in girl slaves (49). Under the ordinance, a new, Westernized, Christian influence enters Chui Mei's life. Significantly, it is European women, part of a countertradition of Victorian missionaries, who rescue her from sexual and physical abuse. Mrs. Winters is a colonial figure whose position as Lady Assistant Protector of Chinese underlines one ideological problem in many narratives of Asian women's struggles for human rights. Mrs. Winters's "rescue" of Chui Mei is, after all, a willful intervention into an "indigenous" social practice. Such Western intervention, in the context of nationalist struggle, can be and has been criticized as an act of colonial oppression, resulting in the destruction of the colonized culture. But a feminist reconstruction of Asian women's life stories, as in Lim's memoir, may suggest a more complicated interpretation of colonial interventions, one less readily oppositional and less able to be appropriated for nationalistic purposes. Chui Mei is taken away from her owners to the Poh Leung Kuk Home, at that time a residence for between 200 and 300 girls, "slaves, orphans, and prostitutes" (54). Mrs. Winters, we are told, "had been the saviour of many hundred of girls" (57). The missionary women, chiefly spinsters and educators, nurtured her: "they not only gave me my education, but also a home, security, affection and personal guidance" (61).

In bearing witness to the horrors of indigenous patriarchal societies and to the history of colonial women in effecting changes in the conditions of women in Asia, Lim's memoir interrogates a national ideology that is based on the dualistic opposition of the good indigenous culture and the bad colonial exploiters, and suggests a different feminist ideology that illuminates the patriarchal aspects of indigenous culture and can therefore be appropriated as a defense of colonialism's "civilizing" mission. In portraying political evil as indigenously patriarchal and political good as colonial agency, and in emphasizing oppression as patriarchy rather than as colonialism, a feminist work like Lim's contradicts, subverts, and refuses to support the hegemony of nationalism, which is constructed on the polarization of bad colonialism versus good nationalism and on the coercive power of national identity formation. Feminist accounts of colonial experience may therefore be construed as marginal if not oppositional to a dominant nationalist discourse, and they are thus more difficult to include in a canon of national literatures, when "national" is the governing term for a hegemonic state-articulated "culture" rationalized to support control of its citizens.

The women's movement in Singapore in the nineteenth and early twentieth centuries was chiefly motivated by Christian missionaries. Lim's memoir traces the source of Chui Mei's rescue to 1842, "when two European women . . . saw mothers forced by poverty to sell their daughters. They got permission from the Governor to start a home for such children" (60). In much of Asia, a chief attraction of Christianity for native women was its message of gender equality and human rights for women. In Korea, for example, the earliest converts and Korean missionaries came from the ranks of women who found in the Christian credo a liberationist message from the Confucianist seclusion and degradation of their sex.[24]

The missionaries' recognition of the value of women explains why it is that the authors of oral and written memoirs such as those by Lim and Kathigasu are Christianized Southeast Asian women. Until recently, a missionary education was the only formal education available to women in Malaysia and Singapore. Such an education gave these women the English language, which enabled them to record their experiences for an English-educated audience. More importantly, taught by missionary, frequently spinster, teachers, the young women received models of independence, professionalism, and self-respect that offered them other visions for selfhood and life than the traditional models of wife, mother, domestic, and unvalued slave that the first chapter of Lim's autobiography so graphically describes. Even the positive portrayal of the traditional positions of women by Mrs. Lee Chin Koon, mother of Mr. Lee Kuan Yew, once Prime Minister of Singapore, cannot obviate women's subordinate and dependent status: The Straits-born Chinese, she says, "did not like their daughters to be educated in schools. It was felt that education would make daughters independent and difficult to control, and they would, therefore, have trouble with their mothers-in-law when they married. The daughter-in-law would have to live with her husband's family and obey and serve her mother-in-law, the head of the household. . . . And do not think that because most of us did not go to school we were not trained. No! We were being prepared for marriage at a very young age."[25] In contrast to this traditional Straits Chinese female role, the eventual line of Janet Lim's life is non-Asian and Westernized. The narrator portrays herself as unsubmissive, resistant, scornful of the compromises of marriage, family, and domestic service that traditionally secure women's positions in her society. She resists surrender of body and self to male-dominated decisions on the place of the female in society even as her women friends succumb to what appear to be easy solutions to their vulnerabilities and weaknesses. Mao, the Siamese widow who, like Chui Mei, is taken away to the Yamato Hotel by Japanese officers, withdraws into madness (169), and later happily becomes "the fifth wife of the old jeweler who tried to make me his fourth wife" (225).

The memoir details numerous instances when women who place their welfare in the hands of male protectors are betrayed. Even physical beauty does not ensure male loyalty. An "unusually pretty" woman who had given birth to a baby girl "feared her husband might sell the girl when she died" (92). In order to escape the air raids in Indareong, Lim's friend Doris marries a Chinese farmer who later kills her and then is told that "if he behaved well he would only have to serve one year's sentence" (251). Lily, Lim's Indian friend, worries that her husband, whom she had married three days before her flight from Singapore, would take another woman (231). Even as Hashimoto Tada and Inou free her from her cell and find her a safe position as an unpaid housemaid in the house of a high Japanese official, Lim says, "I do not trust any men, especially men like you, with your sweet talk" (220). The dynamic of female-male relations, the memoir relentlessly asserts, is that of trust and betrayal, innocence and violation. The narrator's experiences as a victim of patriarchy lead eventually to totalizing hatred: "I hated God and all men and most of all I hated myself" (218).

In this bleak self-reflexive recoil from patriarchal tyranny, even the women missionaries are not spared. They also have been constructed by patriarchy to observe and mystify its power. To the missionary women, "men were considered superior to women. . . . We girls were told not to associate with them in any way. We were even told not to sit down on a seat recently vacated by a man since if we did so we might get a baby" (79). Even though they rescued Asian women from the abuse of prostitution and slavery, these missionary women still accepted the paternalistic objectification of women as exchange value, as practiced in seemingly less abusive arranged marriage systems. "From its earliest days the school had provided wives for Chinese converts and it was a normal procedure . . . for a man to come to the school to get a young wife" (75). Following "the traditional Chinese arranged-marriage system" (82), the "girls were lined up and walked one by one past the office and the man pointed to the girl he wanted. She had to accept or refuse on the spot. Usually it was considered worth getting married in order to get out of the home" (83). Lim's representation of European missionary activity demonstrates that while as a colonial agency it intervened to correct abuse of women, it was itself an agent of patriarchal values.

The memoir concludes with the victory of the Allies over the Japanese and Lim's personal triumph over tremendous injustices, practiced by both men and women, and by Asians and Europeans alike. The autobiographical heroine is last seen unmarried, virtue intact, nursing career in place. Surely this is a text that should have pride of place as a cultural document in the evolution of a national culture. Yet if Christian subjects and Western-influenced feminist themes are perceived as "non-Asian," and if nationalism, itself a European-based political notion, is framed as an Asian-based cultural identity, these subjects drawn from Malaysian-Singapore women's histories and war memoirs can be seen as falling outside the national canon-deciding criteria. As John Clammer argues, the idea of "Asian values" as the base of Singapore's culture, expressed in the concept of "cultural ballast," the idea of the fundamental opposition between Asian and Western values, and the notion of Western values as polluting an idealized and pure Asian society, pervades Singapore's political ideology and also the Malay-dominant ideology of the Malaysian state.[26] A recuperation of such women's writing as contributing to a national canon must assume as its corollary the rehistoricizing of national culture as less clearly Asian in base—as mixed, ambiguous, discontinuous, disruptive, questioning the value of indigenous social institutions, not easily assimilable to constructions of mono-Asian cultural identities. These women's contributions cannot be read simply or transparently, for they occur against a sociopolitical backdrop that has also historically privileged male cultural products and relegated women's writing to an inferior position. Kathigasu's and Lim's memoirs are strong political voices, which assert that women, in spite of condescension, persecution, and torture, hold ideological views with consequences for themselves and for their society. Although we may speculate on the reasons for their neglect, we will do even better to read them carefully. As committed women in Asian societies that have paid little attention to the tradition of women's writing, these authors can tell us much about the function of gender, class, and race in their multiethnic societies and about the dangers of marginalization for women whose struggles for identity fall outside or resist a unitary, "true" national identity—itself contingent and provisional—constructed by state power.

Notes

1. In Third World countries until very recently, literature was visibly male-dominated, reflecting among other things women's limited access to the discourse of nationalism that has taken central stage in this literature. See the essay by Neil Lazarus, "Africa"; also Lloyd W. Brown, "Introduction," *Women Writers in Black Africa*. Simi-

lar questions about the absence of women in literary discourse were raised by Virginia Woolf, *A Room of One's Own;* by Alice Walker, *In Search of Our Mothers' Gardens;* and by Lawrence Lipking, "Aristotle's Sister."

2. Lucy M. Friebert and Barbara A. White, for example, make a case for including in the American canon writing disparaged as sentimental literature; see the preface to *Hidden Hands*. Nina Baym gives a convincing explanation for the dismissal of women's writing from the evolving canon of American literature by male interests and concerns in "Melodramas of Beset Manhood."

3. The discourse of nationalism has proceeded together with racialist and patriarchal discourses. See S. J. Smith, "Social Geography—Patriarchy, Racism, Nationalism."

4. *Toward the Decolonization of African Literature,* ed. Chinweizu, Onwuchekwa Jemie, and Ihechukwu Madubuike, is a classic postcolonial critical work that regards African literature as "an autonomous entity separate and apart from all other literatures" (4). Its Afrocentric and separatist position, though it is significant as part of the process of decolonization, threatens to shape another hegemony that dictates acceptable and unacceptable styles based on ideological considerations that come close to a tribalist argument: "An *extensional definition* in which *family resemblances* are pragmatically employed to decide which of any doubtful or borderline cases should be included with the indisputable canon of African literature" (308, my emphasis).

5. *Litmus One (Selected University Verse, 1949–57),* 17. For an opening effort to retrieve such a body of women's writing, see Koh Tai Ann, "Biographical and Literary Writings and Plays in English by Women from Malaysia and Singapore."

6. I should point out that, beginning with the Portuguese (1511), the territories that make up twentieth-century Malaysia and Singapore were progressively colonized by a series of European naval powers. Japanese forces invaded the Malayan peninsula in December 1941, and British forces did not return till September 1945. Malaya became independent of Britain in 1957, and Singapore received home rule in 1959. In 1965, Singapore became a separate state after an attempt at shared governance as part of the nation-state of Malaysia failed.

7. Vivienne Wee, "The Ups and Downs of Women's Status in Singapore."

8. Sybil Kathigasu's *No Dram of Mercy* was first published in 1954. Janet Lim's *Sold for Silver* was first published in 1958. Both are war memoirs. Citations to these books will be from the Oxford University Press editions (1983 and 1985).

9. Alix Kate Shulman, "Lost Women Writers II," 18.

10. See two works by Anne Brewster, *Toward a Semiotic of Post-colonial Discourse,* and "Post-colonial and Ethnic Minority Literatures in Singapore and Malaysia"; and Shirley Lim's "The English-Language Writer in Singapore."

11. Wang Gungwu, "Trial and Error in Malayan Poetry," and "Some Suggestions for Malayan Verse Written in English."

12. Wang Gungwu is now Chancellor of Hong Kong University, in which position he speaks as a scholar and representative of diasporic Chinese.

13. See Wendell Harris's essay "Canonicity" for a comprehensive discussion of the various forms of canons that apply in our cultural construction of national literatures.

14. See Edwin Thumboo's "Introduction" to *The Second Tongue.*

15. For an analysis of the history of the communist insurgency in Malaysia and Singapore, see Lucien Pye, *Guerrilla Communism in Malaya.*

16. Aside from Pye, much of the literature on the MPAJA that appeared during and after the course of the insurgency depicted the MPAJA as less concerned with anti-Japanese activities than with post war political ambitions. According to Edgar O'Ballance, "The MPAJA avoided Japanese troops and took practically no action against them at all. [The policy was] to collect arms, win local support or dominate the population by terror, and wait for the allies to win the war" (*Malaya,* 58–59). Harry Miller (*Menace in Malaya*), calls the MPAJA "overbearing, arrogant, insolent, and insulting" terrorists (51), whose brutalities led to a "hatred of the Chinese": "The Malay Governments felt the Chinese were nothing but saboteurs. . . . Even some senior British Civil Service officers, steeped in the pro-Malay tradition, developed a dislike of the Chinese. This feeling remains among some of them to this day" (57–58). After the Japanese surrender, the MPAJA was absorbed into the MCP (Malayan Communist Party), whose strike activities and later armed insurgency became conflated with the Cold War global struggle between the United States and the Soviet Union. Anthony Short says, "There is, however, a widespread belief that the order for an insurrection came from Moscow; that it was obeyed in Malaya; and that it formed part of an integral Soviet pattern of insurrection in South-east Asia" ("Communism and the Emergency," 152). In this context, Kathigasu's praise of the MPAJA is now seen as politically "incorrect." In contrast to official interpretations provided between the 1950s and 1970s, it asserts an oppositional interpretation of MPAJA activities, one that locates them first as "nationalists" rather than as antinationalist tools of the then-feared Soviet Union.

17. This sort of stereotyping of Chinese immigrants is discussed in Bedlington: "[The British] saw the Chinese as unscrupulous merchants whose word was less than their bond. . . . Malays generally share most of these stereotypes (adding some of their own)," viewing the Chinese as "unreliable in interpersonal transactions, as exploiters of the Malay peasantry, as materialistic sybarites, and significantly, as alien transients whose loyalty is directed outward toward a Communist China" (Stanley S. Bedlington, *Malaysia and Singapore,* 126).

18. Malaysia and Singapore, despite intertwined colonial histories and shared indigenous and immigrant populations, have arrived at different national cultural policies. Malaysia, asserting the special status of the Malays as "sons of the soil," maintains a national language (Malay) and Malay-dominant national culture, whereas Singapore is officially multiracial, multicultural, and bilingual (English and the mother tongue, whether Chinese, Malay, or Tamil). See Lloyd Fernando, *Cultures in Conflict,* for a discussion of the shift from an English-language-dominant British colonialist society to a Malay-language, Malay-dominant society.

19. John Clammer, *Singapore: Ideology, Society, Culture,* 47.

20. Leong Liew Geok, "Literature from History."

21. See Margery Wolf, "Women and Suicide in China," for an anthropological description of effects of oppressive patriarchal value systems on Chinese women.

22. For a study of the patriarchal structure of traditional Chinese society and the participation of women in its asymmetrical constructions of gender roles and status, see Kay Johnson, *Women, the Family and Peasant Revolution in China.*

23. The injustices perpetrated by *mui-tsai* system are also recorded by Ong Song Siang: "The case in which a Chinese woman was sentenced in February 1907 to four months imprisonment for inhuman treatment of a girl of 16, who had been bought

for $230 by her husband, exemplifies the view still held by some Chinese people here as to the rights possessed by them over 'bought' maidservants. . . . Her life was no better than the slaves whose escape from the Sultan's harem was mentioned in the *Hikayat Abdullah*"; see *One Hundred Years' History of the Chinese in Singapore*, 412–13.

24. More work needs to be done in the area of European missionary "rescue" of women. An archival resource is the publication of the Wesleyan Methodist Missionary Society Archive (London), *China: Women's Work Collection*. In the introduction to Mary Paik Lee's autobiography, *Quiet Odyssey*, Sucheng Chan discusses the "profound impact" of Protestant missionaries on the "extremely excluded" lives of Korean women; widows, for example, "accorded no rights whatsoever [found] a place in the new community of believers" (xxvi, xxviii).

25. Lee Chin Koon, *Mrs. Lee's Cookbook*.

26. Clammer, *Singapore*, 22. For an example of the kind of continuous public discourse that establishes the polarity between Asian and Western identities encouraged by the state, see the unsigned article, "Major Long-term Aim: To Preserve Asianness," *Straits Times*. Oct. 6, 1990, 9.

MICHAELA COOK

The Muslim Woman as Hero in Daneshvar's *Savushun: A Novel about Modern Iran*

I have often recalled an incident that took place after one of my seminars in graduate school. I was with a classmate who was discussing ways to focus her studies on a wider range of culturally diverse texts. In the seminar that evening, she had given an excellent presentation on Toni Morrison's "mythmaking" in *Song of Solomon*. After class, in the restroom, talking about Morrison's healthy revision of female "beauty" with characters like Eva and Hannah Peace and Pilate, she suddenly hissed, "Those damn Muslim women always mess up the restroom on Fridays with their filthy feet washing. I wish they would go to hell." I was stunned. It was a Tuesday night, and there was nothing I could see in the restroom that could have triggered such anger.

A few weeks later in the same seminar, again out of the blue and this time citing Marilyn French, my classmate announced that *all* Muslim women undergo clitoridectomy and infibulation, which they perform on one another. Here I intervened and corrected her, explaining that female mutilation is not part of the teachings of Islam but is a tradition that, where practiced, comes from culture rather than religion. As Fernea and Bezirgan explain, the "central paradox" of Middle Eastern Muslim societies "may best be understood if one thinks of a straight line as representing that society. At one extreme end of the line stands the Koran, the codification of the word of God and the ideal touchstone to which all actions of life are to be conformed and related," and which many Muslim women would argue is liberating. "At the other extreme end of the line lie the forces of tribal and family custom (the word of men)."[1]

Once home, I checked my classmate's source, and indeed, in the 640-page *Beyond Power*, French devotes six pages to a formal discussion of Islam. But in one paragraph I can cite several instances of erroneous or

misleading information. "Under Islam," French says, "women are secluded in a back section of a house and may not come into public rooms
if there are male visitors."[2] French perhaps is ill-informed or unfamiliar
with the many Muslim women in Indonesia, the United Kingdom, Paki-
stan, Sweden, India, the United States, all over the world who do not
follow this cultural practice. She goes on to say, citing Naila Minai, that
a daughter is entitled to only half the inheritance of her brother. She fails
to mention that in much of the Middle East before the birth of Islam, girl
babies were buried alive and women had few rights. She also omits Naila
Minai's explanation of the liberatory intent of the Koranic doctrine of
female inheritance: upon marriage a man pays his bride a dowry that will
remain her own nest egg and protection against abuse. In case of divorce,
she takes the dowry with her. When a woman works, she is entitled to
keep and spend all her earnings, whereas the husband is financially responsible for maintaining the family (including a wage-earning wife) and
the home. A woman inherits property from her husband, although less
than her children because of her assurance of being supported by her sons
in widowhood. According to Minai, "Her inheritance from her father [is]
half her brother's: her husband [supports] her, whereas her brother . . .
[supports] his wife."[3] French then goes on to say, also incorrectly, that
"under Islam," "the worst suffering undergone by Moslem women [is]
clitoridectomy and infibulation" (255), again as if the practice were universal or widespread among Muslims or inscribed in the Koran. In the
next paragraph, she further misleads by citing Nawal el Saadawi, whose
research on female "circumcision" recorded in *The Hidden Face of Eve*
not once mentions Islam as the directive for female genital mutilation.

Westerners, especially feminists, need to understand a bit more of the
complexities and diversity of Muslim histories and societies in this time
of broadening interest in inclusion and multiculturality. If we understood
Muslim peoples better, we might be less likely to support the bombing of
civilian Baghdad or to applaud plots for assassinations and the imposition
of new world orders on the peoples of the Middle East. Simply put, we
need to take on the task of learning something real about Muslim people,
who have been the targets of the "most malicious campaign of defamation
in human history," beginning with anti-Muslim propaganda during the
Crusades and continuing through the great Western literary tradition and
into today's evening news.[4] As non-Muslim women seek out and listen to
Muslim women, as some of our false images shatter, we are sure to hear
echoes of our own struggles.

Simin Daneshvar's *Savushun: A Novel about Modern Iran* (1990), the

first novel published by an Iranian woman, is an effective antidote to Western ignorance about Iran, which, like other Muslim societies, has been
misrepresented and feared in the West. In her fictional history, Daneshvar
gives us new ways to think about the women of her culture and their
silencing and liberation by showing that the situation for Iranian women
has been lashed to broad historical and political conditions that reach
beyond national borders. Daneshvar shows why freedom and peace are
elusive for women whose husbands, sons, mothers, and sisters are being
brutalized by foreign military powers. As the author creates her female
hero and the variety of female figures that color her text, she restores the
shapes of diverse human individuals to the blank images of passivity and
inertia imposed by the West on Iranian women, veiled women, Muslim
women en masse.

Savushun, a poetically evocative and suggestive work, sustains several
levels of meaning, prompts numerous and various readings, and resists
neat closure as it lays bare the atrocities of the Western occupation of Iran
during World War II and explores the impact of traditional patriarchal
culture on modern women in particular. Focusing on her often silenced
heroine, Zahra Khan (Zari), Daneshvar illuminates how national and international affairs violate human rights, tangle individual lives, and para-
lyze potential heros. Through her newsreel of violent images, we see, as
foreign occupation rends a community, how families bind tightly together
and ultimately bequeath to a new generation strategies of resistance. The
brilliant play of images that brings this work to life shows what it takes
for a woman in Daneshvar's war zone, when pushed even to the brink of
madness, to reassess her courage and emerge as a hero from the shadows
of one more brand of patriarchy.

The wedding that opens the story becomes a backdrop for the violence
that ensues, embodying the impact of the actions of the United Kingdom
and Russia in chopping up a country on their maps and starving the
people for oil and access to the Persian Gulf. Most of the Westerners at
the wedding, some of them men dressed up in military uniforms and dec-
orated with medals and ribbons, are arrogant, avaricious, and uncomprehending of Iranian culture. They are treated to a spread of delicious food
and drink by a boot-licking governor who is eager to accommodate them
even as his own people starve, making the wedding a ridiculous sham for
foreign eyes. The music that follows the wedding march sounds to Zari
like battle drums and reflects the state of the city, which has become a war
zone. The occupation has splintered the people into factions and has in-
cited violence. In the neighborhoods, heads are found severed and bodies

cut to pieces. The siphoning of the city's food to feed British troops, who are on Iranian soil to defend British interests against Hitler, has caused a tremendous food shortage. The people also accuse the British of contaminating the fresh water and bringing their diseases to Iran.

Shiraz, the place Daneshvar takes us, the city of poets and flowers, has become a graveyard. The greed and the butchery, engendered by foreign occupation, have extinguished the fires of poetry, emasculated some men and driven others to a senseless bravado: one man is "prepared to swallow dynamite" or to set himself on fire with gasoline (247). Tricked by the slick talk, the hard cash, and the weapons cynically being sold by the British, who are determined to divide and conquer, some men are returning to their tribes, rekindling ancient intertribal hatreds. The British provoke the internal chaos and keep their own hands clean while they gloat from the sidelines. With the "stranger's" story of chapter 17, Daneshvar shows us young conscripts to the tribal conflicts who are forced to defend themselves with guns they have not been taught to shoot. With their one bullet apiece, these defenseless young men are themselves blown to bits by neighbors or cousins, or they are forced to watch as their brothers are ripped open by "enemy fire" as they defecate or vomit in their trenches. There is no room in the hospitals for the sick and dying. Corpses litter the halls and reception rooms. Patients are all teeth, hair, and bones. Typhus is rampant. Doctors and nurses themselves are sick and dropping dead. The hypocritical Christian missionary hospital will not take the citizens of Shiraz. Its beds are full of the British officers, men "fair-skinned and blond," some who appear to have nothing wrong with them (198). Zari will come to say of Western paternalistic charity, " 'Obviously, they built the hospital for the day they would need it themselves' " (195).

To challenge systematic oppression effectively, "a person must be armed either with money, or authority, or masculinity, or legal backing, or age. If deprived of all such weapons," one will surely be crushed.[5] Thus, to contend with the danger in this occupied state, Daneshvar needs a "hero" who has some power in the patriarchal community, who will be listened to by other men and be heard, someone who knows the world. Zari's husband, Yusof Khan, is such a man. Yusof has been, as Audre Lorde expresses it, a "watcher" of the oppressor.[6] He is a landowner who has been educated in Europe and knows the Europeans and the Western world, and he has a reputation in his community for self-restraint and wisdom.

Although Yusof functions overtly as the novel's hero, Zari, who will emerge as the real hero, is the lens through which we see both the devastating occupation and the limitations for women in this patriarchal society. While exposing the atrocities of occupation, Daneshvar is no less interested in the violence that is built into the patriarchal culture of Iran, a country that, as in the cultural landscape of the West, has historically tied the hands of women, silenced them, and deprived them of work outside the home. Daneshvar is concerned about legal and social structures that diminish women, waste talents, and stunt lives, and about women like Zari, who, in refusing to accept these structures of oppression, become heroes in spite of the odds.

We come to know Zari's courage as we watch her walk through the dangerous streets, face strangers at her door, nurse the sick who end up in her home. Although we admire or question Yusof from a distance, and often, like Zari, miss out on his most important stratagems for resistance, we are close to Zari, within earshot of her soliloquies, inside her hallucinations. We are close enough to scrutinize through her the undervaluation of women, and to understand how her outer and inner worlds clash because of culturally sanctioned gender bias.

Zari, who has internalized the patriarchal definition of the good woman, says at first that she wants nothing more than a peaceful environment for her children. We witness her courage in her narrow world of "home," where her perceived duty is first of all biological. The job of producing her husband's children has twice taken her to what she describes as the "'brink of death'" (174). Her fear of pregnancy is real—her hips are narrow and she is small. Now she is expecting another child, and, although she has paid a visit to the midwife for an abortion, she decides that she will take the knife again and give her husband another child, a decision her husband and son applaud. We know that often under patriarchy, giving birth is not seen as heroic. Even life-threatening childbirth is often merely a "female danger" lumped with rape and wife beating. Like incalculable numbers of other women who have lived without full participation under the rules of husbands and fathers, Zari has no "real ownership of her own body," for it is "the property of the capitalist and feudal classes which reign over society," of which her husband is a part.[7]

Zari's faithful execution of her religious vows of charity, which she has kept for a decade and which take her every Thursday into dangerous streets, is another testimony to her courage. Zari has made these vows to protect her through the dangers of childbirth and for the health and long life of her children. Her vows take her to the prison and insane asylum where she carries fresh fruit, home-baked bread, cigarettes, shoes, and newspapers to prisoners and patients, and expose her not only to obscene gestures and threats from soldiers on the streets, and to typhus and other diseases, but also to the frightening life within the walls of the institutions. Patients are starving. Some are kept in chains and speak gibberish. Howling obscenities at Zari, a crippled woman accuses her of poisoning the dates. Other women call Zari slut, whore, motherfucker. One woman blames Zari for her paralysis. When she returns to her home after dark, after feeding and offering comfort to the starving rejects of the world, Zari's head is splitting. Yusof accurately blames the familiar headache on the weekly nightmare from which she has just taken leave.

As we follow Zari through the streets into the insane asylum, we see not only her courage but another instance of the "female invalidism" so prevalent among women who attempt to embody the seductively perfect image of the angel of mercy.[8] Daneshvar says the roles open to women—housewife and mother, nurse, teacher, prostitute, although all potentially compassionate, caregiving roles, are limited and limiting. And Yusof does little to help matters, branding Zari's devotion and work as useless, " 'rotten from the core' " (149). As we watch Zari doing what little she can to make life more comfortable for others, and as she continues to idolize her husband and begins to blame herself, we spot Yusof's flaws. We come to know him as the sometimes tender husband who both loves his wife and robs her of her confidence.

By branding traditional female work as useless and defining her as always wrong and helpless, Yusof and other male authorities drain Zari of her strength and courage. Writers as diverse as Harriet Beecher Stowe, Virginia Woolf, Anzia Yezierska, and Etel Adnan have challenged this double bind, which on the one hand restricts women with no money to bed and broom as unpaid cooks, caregivers, cleaning ladies, concubines, and at the same time defines these roles as valueless. Meanwhile, the men are free to roam the "dangerous" real world to do the real work: heroic deeds that the women later hear about and marvel at. Zari is one of these familiar female figures "trapped—even buried—in the architecture of a patriarchal society." [9] According to the men, Zari should be content to play her culture's version of Penelope at her magic loom or of Dorigen wringing her miserable, waiting hands as she stumbles around her black rocks. Like Daneshvar, we who have been seduced by and then weaned from these dangerous images of female passivity and patience know the paralyzing underside of the seductive ideology. In Zari's home, even her ten-year-old son, Khosrow, has more freedom of movement than his mother, and Yusof is often away from home for weeks at a time. But for Zari, home and family are defined as her world. Her weekly trips to the prison and insane asylum are not exceptions, only a temporary stretching of the walls and rules of "home." Zari herself calls her home her "city," her "country"—and echoing Elizabeth Barrett Browning, also her "prison." As she feels more threatened and silenced within her walls, Zari comes to believe that it is criminal that her world is so small.

Zari sees herself as the peacemaker, but her home and its extensions are at first the only places in which she can begin to create the peace she craves. And there, she must face her male opponents with their arsenal of words before she can dare challenge anyone outside on issues, no matter how domestic and small. Zari was a virtual orphan when she married at sixteen the older, educated landowner, Yusof. Looking up to him as she does, she can never win the domestic war of words, even when she is right, but must always defer to the so-called wisdom of men, and then suffer patiently while they ridicule her efforts at creating peace and accuse her of getting the family into messes, while they with their weapons gamble with lives. At one point, Yusof slaps his wife, accusing her of being spineless in his absence. Her brother-in-law (whom she refers to as her executioner) teaches Khosrow not to listen to his young mother because women are all "cowards and liars." He also reminds Zari that after her husband, he is ruler over her and her children. Khosrow has learned from both father and uncle that women keep boys from becoming men.

Zari soaks up these cultural lessons and Yusof's complaints, which live inside her and give rise to self-doubts that begin to erode her mental health and isolate her. These messages from the men insist to Zari that she is nothing but a scatterbrained coward fit only for the cookstove and the sewing machine. Initially paralyzed by her doubts, she is obsessed with her wish to do something that someone will at least notice if not praise. She comes to believe that her efforts are nothing and that she turns for others like a wheel, producing what no one can see. She scrutinizes her every act for evidence of courage or cowardice. She knows she cannot, like Yusof, ride out to the pastures alone, or stay away from home for weeks at a time, or carry a weapon, or plot a war. She cannot even join the political discussions in her home where the men dismiss her or hush her up before she can give voice to a thought, as if she were a stranger to the violence, danger, and death around her. She is finally numbed into concluding that with three children to care for and one on the way, "it would be impossible for her to engage in anything that would disrupt the

normal flow of life" (247). The only "brave thing" she can do is "not keep
the others from being brave and let *them* . . . do something" (248). In
other words, she decides she must keep still.

As the tension in the family and community grows, Zari surrenders
her powers and waits, swatting flies, spilling beads, vomiting. To keep
peace in her home, she turns her anger on herself, allows herself to be
pushed around, and stays quiet. Her job is to take off her husband's boots,
bring him his hookah, and sit at his feet, or wander the empty rooms of
his house until he needs her to be his comfort. She feels powerless as her
husband's leadership of the resistance movement takes him closer to danger. She begs him not to be the one to sacrifice himself. But only in her
private thoughts does she criticize the men: "O, God, what kind of people
are these men? They know it is useless, but to prove their existence, their
manhood, and courage, and for their children not to later spit on their
graves . . . they dig. . . . God forbid" (252).

Although her focus is on Zari, Daneshvar gives us many other women
to think about. Beneath the apparent main text dealing with the male
characters' reactions to the devastation of occupation—the secret meetings, their hushed conversations and hunting trips, the trial of the horse,
the stranger's story, Kolu's illness and conversion to Christianity—is the
key subtext in which the novel uncovers the evil of female subordination
and the suffering it causes in the lives of all the women we meet. With this
collage of female tragedies, Daneshvar is digging at that "piece of the
oppressor which is planted deep within." [10] The storm of female voices in
the novel adds up to a powerful protest against the accumulated ridicule,
scorn, and inequities that have kept the women in Daneshvar's culture—
in any culture—bruised and stunted beings. With the other female characters and their stories, we begin to see how subtly and tightly the restrictive
social order has bound them through economic dependence and the power
of tradition: polygamy, prostitution, veiling, widowhood, confinement.

While telling these stories within her story, which both expose and
criticize the subordinate stature of women and help us to see Muslim
women more accurately in all their multiplicities, Daneshvar continually
shows the problems of women as inseparable from broader political and
economic questions. Daneshvar knows that the struggle for individual
freedom, whether male or female, works into the larger struggle against
foreign domination. Yet in this problematic place, a real and unromanti-
cized Shiraz, Zari finally puts self-doubt and fear aside to emerge as the
hero only after the death of Yusof, when Daneshvar yokes Zari's wish for
personal peace to a wish for the liberation of her people.

The last time Yusof goes away to the pastures, he plans to distribute the surplus food to the peasants rather than turn it over to the British. While he is away, Zari's nightmares portend danger. She becomes sure Yusof will never return alive, and when the men bring him home, she knows he is dead. She is paralyzed with grief. During her vigil, violent impressions whirl in her mind, until by morning, she feels she is on the brink of insanity. Zari emerges finally with a new, more courageous voice. She begins to speak boldly to Yusof's followers of her regret that she was ever afraid, confessing that she had tried to make her brave husband afraid. She asks, now that Yusof is dead, what is there to fear? " 'I for one have gone beyond all that' " (363).

Zari comes out of her long state of domestic numbness by expressing publically a healthy anger—here a positive emotion that gives her the energy to survive and carry on what Yusof has begun. Moving beyond the paralysis of self-doubt and fear, away from the brink of madness, Zari uses the courage that, despite *her* doubts, we have seen was hers all along. She will be brave, she says, " 'while alive and for the living,' " and she will also weep when the brave are killed (364). The grieving widow can finally stand up to her brother-in-law, whom she has loathed but could never face honestly. She opposes him openly, supporting the people's wish to carry Yusof's coffin through the streets to the center of the city and bury her husband as a martyr, even at the risk of a bloody riot. She says the people of Shiraz who have been exploited have the right to assemble to honor their hero. She is fed up both with her brother-in-law's hypocrisy and with her fears.

Daneshvar has shown us Zari's heroic acts throughout her text, even in flashbacks to Zari's childhood. However, when Yusof is returned to his wife with a bullet in his head, Zari undergoes the necessary inner transformation that saves her from her deadening self-doubts and broadens and deepens her courage. Within a few hours, she has not only reclaimed her voice and gained the healing energy of her anger, she has also experienced a piece of her culture that had eluded her in the British-run schools where as a child she studied Christian heros and memorized Milton. Several times in the novel, Zari has been told by various people the story of Siyavesh. After Yusof's death, after she has gone through the night of the violent images, she returns in her mind to the afternoon in the pastures when she walked with a peasant woman who explained to her the meaning of the day and evening of Savushun, which commemorates the death of Siyavesh, the "dear one," the hero who, like Yusof, fought so many enemies alone, carrying no weapons, the hero who did not cry out even when he was tortured and killed. Finally, Zari comprehends the meaning of this harvest ritual, this collective mourning in which villagers through-out Iran have taken part for centuries, grieving for the fallen hero who passed on to his people his courage and desire for justice and independence.

To move beyond just "mother of the house" to public activist, Zari has had to understand that her courage will grow as she joins collectively with others to liberate her people from foreign oppression. She does not fear the violence in the streets, the riot and the bloodshed. She quotes her husband, "'A city must not be completely without men,'" or people—male and female—who will bind together for the sake of justice (376). As Zari buries her husband and bandages the wounded, she feels compassion for all those in the world who must fight for justice and human rights. No longer constrained by timidity, her narrow world has widened and her city and country reach beyond her garden walls.

We in the West can get from *Savushun* a new angle on what Western powers will do for oil and thus make some sense of the anti-Western re-actions of the people of Iran when Mohammad Reza Shah Pahlavi was dethroned in 1979 during the Islamic revolution. We can learn from the violent images and the anger in *Savushun* that people under occupation are all victims, and we can begin to understand how strategies for resis-tance can be passed to new generations. In the novel, men and women alike have suffered under Western occupation and political and economic exploitation. The contributions of the Iranian people to the world have been held in check by the continuing effects of the West's veiled neocolo-nialism: the violence in the streets, the censorship, the fear, the poverty.

Within this larger context of Western occupation, Daneshvar exam-ines the overt and covert violence directed at women in the 1940s and today, who are too often excluded from public life and are poorly re-warded for the important contributions they make to family and home, the building blocks of their society and culture. Daneshvar shows that women in her culture, as in ours, have been oppressed by powerful tradi-tions insidious enough to pit women against each other. But under the boot of foreign domination and in the midst of violence and war, eliminat-ing gender inequalities may not be possible. Political and economic inde-pendence is the necessary first step to solving other human rights prob-lems, and general liberation requires the free and equal contribution of both men and women.

For all its pain and violence, *Savushun* is nonetheless a healing text. This fictional history points to the British as ultimately responsible for the chaos and violence, but the text does not permit its characters or readers to blame everything conveniently on "the other." In the same way that Iranian men and women are oppressed by the British, Iranian women are oppressed by the patriarchal structures within their own culture. We see the inseparability of the two areas of liberation in Zari's growing authority and heroism. Yet she is not simply taking on a patriarchal mantle. Her "feminine" and "domestic" qualities, such as her compassionate quest for harmony and her commitment to life, are part of her heroism; they are embodied in recurring images of living, growing, nourishing things—the pools of water, the fresh bread, the tree of independence that will flourish. These images frame the novel's moments of hope and the determination and courage of people, who in spite of the obstacles at home, in spite of the starvation, war, and death, are participating in the complex and confusing struggle for liberation and the right of all human beings to live freely.

Simin Daneshvar's evocation of modern history, an antiwar, human rights, women's rights narrative, is, as Barbara Christian says of the work of many Third World writers, "a written figure which is both sensual and abstract, both beautiful and communicative. . . . a necessary nourishment for [her] people and one way by which they come to understand their lives better." [11] *Savushun: A Novel about Modern Iran* has sold a half-million copies in Farsi. We in the West can profit too from the translation—we who have had too few lessons from Middle Easterners and Muslims who are writing for their own people, not for our gaze. *Savushun* and its author are laying the "foundations for a future of change, a bridge across our fears of what has never been before." [12]

Notes

1. Elizabeth Warnock Fernea and Basima Qattan Bezirgan, eds., *Middle Eastern Muslim Women Speak*, xix.

2. Marilyn French, *Beyond Power*, 255.

3. Naila Minai, "Women in Early Islam," 353.

4. Muhsin Mahdi, Foreword to *Middle Eastern Muslim Women Speak*, ed. Fernea and Bezirgan, xi.

5. Nawal el Saadawi, *The Hidden Face of Eve*, 49.

6. Audre Lorde, "Age, Race, Class, and Sex," in *Sister Outsider*, 114.

7. El Saadawi, *Hidden*, 64.

8. Sandra M. Gilbert and Susan Gubar, *The Madwoman in the Attic*, 54.

9. Ibid., 313.

10. Lorde, "Age," p. 123.

11. Barbara Christian, "The Race for Theory," 336.

12. Lorde, "Age," 37.

PART FOUR

Collective Silence, Collective Voice: Toward Community

SHERRI HALLGREN

"The Law Is the Law—and a Bad Stove Is a Bad Stove": Subversive Justice and Layers of Collusion in "A Jury of Her Peers"

Susan Glaspell's 1917 short story "A Jury of Her Peers" has been quietly stunning women readers since its reappearance in a feminist anthology nearly twenty years ago. A novelist and playwright who won a Pulitzer Prize in 1931 for her novel *Alison's House,* Glaspell had been all but forgotten until her story was reprinted in Lee R. Edwards and Arlyn Diamond's *American Voices, American Women.* On the surface a detective story about two Iowa women who unintentionally solve a crime right under the noses of their officious husbands, who cannot see the very clues they're searching for, the plot of "A Jury of Her Peers" is an in-joke among women, who recognize the narrative's clues.

When the story opens, a farm woman, Martha Hale, is being called from her bread baking to accompany her husband, John, along with the sheriff and his wife and the county attorney, on a trip to the neighboring farmhouse where Minnie Foster Wright has been arrested for the murder of her husband. When John Hale had gone to see Wright the day before, Minnie had said her husband could not speak to him " 'cause he's dead,'" and explained further that "he died of a rope around his neck." [1] Today the small party that has come to Minnie's house to investigate the crime consists of three men and two women: Sheriff Peters, Mr. Henderson the county attorney, and John Hale, along with Mrs. Peters, who has come to get some things for Minnie, who is being held in the county jail, and Mrs. Hale, who has come to keep Mrs. Peters company. The men are looking for the crucial piece of evidence: "the motive—the thing that shows anger or sudden feeling."

While the men search the barn and the upstairs bedroom where Wright was found hanging, the women are left to themselves in the kitchen and the parlor. Nervously waiting, they discover their own bits of evidence to solve the crime that has taken place. Essentially, Minnie Foster Wright has killed her husband because he has strangled her canary. At the end of the story the women hide the dead bird—the piece of evidence that would certainly convict Minnie Wright—from their husbands, the law. These are the "facts" of the story. In one sense, then, the story functions as a "who done it" battle between the sexes, and its initial delight comes from seeing the "little women" outsmart—outintuit—the sheriff and their husbands.

Critics have noted the qualities of feminist mystery writing obvious in the text. Sandra Gilbert and Susan Gubar place this story in a tradition continued by Agatha Christie's Miss Jane Marple, in that the women "understand the crime even while they implicitly vindicate the woman who committed it." [2] Annette Kolodny suggests that "the intended emphasis [in "Jury"] is the inaccessibility of female meaning to male interpretation," pointing out that the men in the story lack the "proper interpretive strategies" to unravel the motive. [3] She terms this blindness to a set of details "sex-coding," and suggests that "lacking familiarity with the women's imaginative universe, that universe within which their acts are signs, the men in these stories can neither read nor comprehend the meaning of the women closest to them—and this in spite of a common language." [4]

It's Lucy and Ethel triumphing over Ricky and Fred, and their solving the murder and then not telling is wickedly satisfying. [5] Kolodny calls it a happy ending. But it's not a secret shopping spree that is at stake here; a woman has murdered her husband and will get away with it. This initial imbalance—that the life of a man, a woman's husband, even, could be equal to that of a pet bird—increases what should be the social outrage at the crime they cover up. At its core, this story is radically subversive in all it implies about the different experiences, modes of interpretation, and potential for power in men and women. As the title suggests, what Glaspell explores in "A Jury of Her Peers" is a parallel system of justice, one in which women can be judged according to context and truly by their peers. It is in this way an exploration into female ethics. Even more subversive, though, it reveals a vigilante form of justice, one enacted in secret, in unspoken collusion between members of a group who speak the same language in a way that eschews language. But it is not simply the plot that makes this story compelling. Its subversive power comes, even more importantly, from what Glaspell does with the narrative, which enacts between the narrator-Glaspell and her readers the same collusion she depicts between her characters.

The first scene in the Wrights' home sets up the differing perspectives of the women and the men in the story. The three men who represent the prosecuting forces of law—Sheriff Peters, who arrested Minnie and will conduct this investigation; Mr. Henderson, the county attorney who will prosecute; and John Hale, the testifying witness—investigate the scene of the crime. Glaspell sets these men up as figures of authority and expertise—Sheriff Peters "made it plain he knew the difference between criminals and non-criminals" (360)—only to undermine them. They don't see, don't understand, don't know. They come into the story only briefly at the beginning, at the end, and once in the middle, to stroll through the kitchen chitchatting pieces of legality and patronizing the women, saying there's "nothing here but kitchen things," and giving "a little laugh for the insignificance of kitchen things" (365). That they are looking specifically for female anger, the clue to the motive for murder, and are completely unable to see it, is the story's biggest and most resonant joke.

The county attorney, more derisive than dismissive, complains, "Dirty towels! not much of a housekeeper, would you say, ladies?" (366), and, with a disdainful and aggressive gesture that will contrast with the women's treatment of the objects in Minnie's house, he kicks some pans under the sink. In the same way that the man of law assumes he has an infallible sense of who is and isn't a criminal, this prosecutor presumes to judge Minnie, acting as an arbiter of excellence in the realm that is appropriately hers. (Elaine Hedges's research on the circumstances of female farm life and work, documenting the hours of labor required of a farmwife to produce among other items in the week's laundry, one clean towel, makes even clearer to modern readers what the impact of this identification would have been for the farmwives, pointing out the enormity of the oversight, as well as of the insult and ignorance, of the sheriff's comment.)[6] His remark invites the other two housewives to collude with him in his estimate, but they remain silent.

When Mrs. Hale remembers that Minnie had worried the evening before about her fruit, Mr. Hale, the expert witness exclaims, "Well, can you beat the woman! Held for murder and worrying about her preserves!" With "good-natured superiority," he says, "women are used to worrying over trifles" (365). Whether arrogant, hostile, or patronizing, the men clearly feel they are in control and that the women's presence on this mission is superfluous.

As they leave the kitchen, Henderson says it will be all right to leave the women unattended because "of course Mrs. Peters is one of us"; he cautions her to keep her "eye out . . . for anything that might be of use. No telling; you women might come upon a clue to the motive—and that's the thing we need." As he leaves, Mr. Hale musingly says, "but would the women know a clue if they did come upon it?" (367).

The women, as it turns out, do keep their eyes open and it is with their eyes that they conduct their own investigation and carry out a sentence; the result, however, will be a collaboration with rather than a condemnation of Minnie's revolt, as they too betray their husbands. When the men leave, the narrator stays with Martha Hale and Mrs. Peters, in the territory that is Minnie's: the kitchen and the parlor. Without meaning to, and only because they unavoidably find themselves literally in Minnie Foster's place, the two women come to understand the crime, find the clues, including the dead canary, the all-important piece of evidence that supplies the motive for the killing, and come to their own verdict, reading the details of Minnie's life that tell her story.

In the same way that the house is its own separate world from the world of the barn, the system of those who live in the house is different from that of the world of the men. The sheriff and his men are interlopers in this territory, and their methods do not help them understand what happened and why. Because they cannot "see" the significance of the women's lives, they do not look for clues in Mrs. Wright's life, and therefore they literally cannot see the clues to the motive for the killing—the one crucial detail needed for a murder conviction in their legal system. The women's method is intuitive and empathetic. Martha Hale's first comment after the men have left is, "I'd hate to have men comin' into my kitchen . . . snoopin' round and criticizin' " (367). She recognizes the signs of "things half done," in a sugar bucket with its lid off and a half-filled bag beside it, and thinks of her own kitchen, her own task interrupted. What the men interpret as inept housekeeping Mrs. Hale is able to discern as a process interrupted, as her own process of bread baking has been interrupted to come on this mission. Her identification with (as opposed to Henderson's judgment of) Minnie's activity tells her something.

Later she finds an erratically stitched quilt block and feels "queer, as if the distracted thoughts of the woman who had perhaps turned to it to try to quiet herself were communicating themselves to her" (373). This is passive investigation, possible only by someone who not only can understand sewing but also can get into the mind of the woman who sews. This whole scene is filled with examples of the two women's indulging in the pathetic fallacy as they read Minnie's life. The dingy red rocker "didn't look in the least like Minnie Foster" (363); the house itself looks "lonesome this cold March morning . . . and the poplar trees around it were lonesome-looking trees" (360). Mrs. Hale remembers Minnie Foster, "kind of like a bird herself" (375), "singing in the choir" (369).

Unlike Mrs. Hale, Mrs. Peters is not moved by memories of Minnie Foster, nor is she disturbed by the physical disorder of the house. What ties her to Minnie is similar experience, thinking of the work gone to waste when the preserve jars break. Mrs. Peters decides to take quilt blocks for Minnie to work on in jail, and it is this gesture of kindness to the other woman, and not the legal investigation with the intent to convict, that turns up the telling evidence of motive, for in the sewing box they find a dead bird, its neck broken, lovingly wrapped in silk and placed in a pretty box. Mrs. Peters, horrified, remembers "When I was a girl . . . my kitten—there was a boy took a hatchet, and before my eyes—before I could get there . . . If they hadn't held me back I would have . . . hurt him" (377), conjuring both the specter of violence in even a small boy and her own potential for violent retribution.

All along, Mrs. Peters, wife of the sheriff, has reminded Mrs. Hale that "the law is the law.' It is not until she identifies with Minnie that she has the resolve to join with Mrs. Hale in covering up the crime. When Mrs. Hale suggests how still it would have been "if there had been years and years of—nothing, then a bird to sing to you, it would be awful—still—after the bird was still" (377), Glaspell notes that "it was as if something within her not herself had spoken, and it found in Mrs. Peters something she did not know as herself" (378). That something in women that finds itself in other women is making the case, without saying it outright, that Minnie's crime is justifiable.

Mrs. Peters responds with a memory of her isolation on a homestead in Dakota, when her baby died. Although she falters at this point in her reverie, saying, "The law has got to punish crime, Mrs. Hale," what has been building for her as well as for Martha Hale is a sense of unity with Minnie. In identifying with Minnie Foster, they break the principle of objectivity in crime detection. They are slowly allowing their values of what constitutes life to enter into their judgment. At one point Mrs. Hale says, "It seems kind of sneaking: locking her up in town and coming out here to get her own house to turn against her!" again personifying a housewife's house; and Mrs. Peters counters, "But Mrs. Hale, the law is the law." The subtext to the entire conversation is a debate about the ethics of murder, a question that in this case is not abstract; they are verging on being accomplices.

Caught in a moment of trying to work Minnie's stove (the meaning here is probably heightened if we think of March in Iowa before central heating), Mrs. Hale responds, "The law is the law—and a bad stove is a bad stove." Again without saying so explicitly, she proposes an equality of values and perspectives: the patriarchal, abstract system of justice that the men in the room above them represent, and the system into which the women themselves are slowly, literally feeling their way.

At this point, they put on trial John Wright and the life-draining barrenness of living with him. When Mrs. Peters observes that the townfolk considered Wright a "good man," Mrs. Hale grimly concedes that "he didn't drink, and kept his word as well as most . . . and paid his debts. But he was a hard man . . . like a raw wind that gets to the bone" (375). For these wives, a husband is indeed the climate in which they must live. She notes that he wouldn't have liked the bird, "a thing that sang. She used to sing. He killed that too" (377). At this moment, when Mrs. Hale superimposes the image of Minnie onto that of the strangled bird, she names what Wright, in his enforced silence and poverty, has done to Minnie—"killed"—thus indicting not her crime but his. Seen in this way, Minnie's act is not only retribution for the twisted neck of her bird but also revenge for the loss of the one thing that brought contact to her life.

Essentially, "A Jury of Her Peers" asks us to understand and to condone the murder of a man for the murder of a canary; or at least these are the "facts" as the sheriff and county attorney would see them. These are certainly what the facts would be in a court of law, and, as Mrs. Peters has remembered her husband saying, things don't look good for Minnie Foster Wright. More specifically, we are to see how these two deaths are equivalent—that of a husband and that of a pet.

While the official police investigation has been going on in the upstairs bedroom and out in the barn, literally and figuratively both above and beyond the scope of the women's concerns, the narrative point of view has stayed with the women in the shabby and cold farmhouse kitchen, as alienated as these farmwives from the men who have appeared only once to joke about the quilt blocks, asking if they thought Minnie had intended to "knot it or quilt it." Because the narrative voice has kept the reader in the same room with these women, moving as close as possible to their unspoken thoughts, the reader has done the same sympathetic exploration of Minnie's wretched, lonely life. The legal case the story makes is the same as the women's, and it is presented seductively rather than ironically, persuading us to become part of the sympathetic jury of Minnie Foster Wright's peers.

And yet, in real legal terms, the truth is that a woman has killed her husband and may not be prosecuted. In contemplating their cover-up, Mrs. Hale and Mrs. Peters are about to overturn the system not simply of justice but of conventional values, instituting a female system of ethics for that of the patriarchy.

Carol Gilligan's work on women's morality suggests that women handle the inevitable aggression in the world very differently from the system of laws and regulations our patriarchal society has created. Gilligan proposes that "if aggression is tied, as women perceive, to the fracture of human connection, then the activities of care . . . are the activities that make the social world safe, by avoiding isolation and preventing aggression rather than by seeking rules to limit its extent." "In this light," she argues, "aggression appears no longer as an unruly impulse that must be contained but rather as a signal of a fracture of connection, the sign of a failure of relationship." [7]

Mrs. Peters and Mrs. Hale, then, in their empathy and their desire to help Minnie Wright—their "activities of care"—are doing more to "make the social world safe" than are the sheriff and attorney who seek to see Minnie punished. Also, if fracture of connection is the dangerous activity, then Wright's "crime" in this female version of an ordered and safe world is, first, his isolation and emotional abandonment of his wife, and, finally, his destruction of what did constitute her connection with something that would communicate with her—her canary. When Wright kills "the singing" in Minnie, he has fractured connection, which, according to Gilligan, is what makes life meaningful and safe for women; in this system of values, then, this is indeed a heinous crime: Wright is clearly wrong.

Gilligan also studies the ways in which women judge others. In describing the reactions and justifications of one participant in her study as she makes a moral choice, Gilligan says, "She ties morality to the understanding that arises from the experience of relationship, since she considers the capacity to 'understand what someone else is experiencing' as the prerequisite for moral response" (57). In generalizing about women's ability to judge, she cites studies indicating that "the moral judgments of women differ from those of men in the greater extent to which women's judgments are tied to feelings of empathy and compassion and are concerned with the resolution of real as opposed to hypothetical dilemmas" (69). For Mrs. Hale, the law may be the law, but in Minnie Foster Wright's case, that rocker and that bad stove, not to mention her bird, are the real facts of the case and the details that guide her judgment.

Mrs. Hale and Mrs. Peters don't stop in their indictment of Minnie's husband; they judge themselves as well. Gilligan explains that "although independent assertion in judgment and action is considered to be the hall-mark of adulthood, it is rather in their care and concern for others that women have both judged themselves and been judges" (70). Each time Mrs. Hale uncovers another aspect of Minnie's dismal life she is pained by the thought that she had not come to visit her more often; perhaps if Minnie had been less lonely she might also have been less desperate. Her guilt overcomes her when she invokes the young Minnie Foster, "when she wore a white dress with blue ribbons, and stood up there in the choir and sang." Glaspell continues the narrative to explain: "The picture of that girl, the fact that she had lived neighbor to that girl for twenty years, and had let her die for lack of life, was suddenly more than she could bear. "Oh, I *wish* I'd come over here once in a while!" she cried. "That was a crime! That was a crime! Who's going to punish that?" (378).

Again Martha Hale uses the term "death" to describe what Minnie's life has become, and she blames herself for having let Minnie "die." Her understanding of the crime is that Minnie has died and that physically and emotionally harsh living can indeed kill someone. In these terms, Minnie was already dead before she murdered her husband.

Martha Hale concludes, "I might 'a' *known* she needed help! I tell you, it's *queer*, Mrs. Peters. We live close together, and we live far apart. We all go through the same things—it's all just a different kind of the same thing! If it weren't—why do you and I *understand*? Why do we *know*—what we know this minute?" (378). The "we" in this passage can only be female, for it is evident in this story that the men are not "going through the same things" that their wives are. It is because women "all go through the same things—just a different kind of the same thing" that they understand what they do about Minnie Foster Wright. The sheriff and the county attorney and even farmer Lewis Hale do not understand the life of this house, and so they do not "know" and "understand" what Mrs. Peters and Mrs. Hale do. At this moment, Martha Hale understands the bonds that tie her to Minnie and to Mrs. Peters; what she understands as well is that their knowledge cannot be spoken aloud.

Their entire investigation—their coming to figure out how Minnie had been interrupted in filling her sugar bucket probably when Wright killed her bird; that then in anger she had killed him in a way that matched his strangulation of the canary (and his metaphoric "strangling" of her sing-ing, or the "life" in her); then had tried to calm herself by stitching on her log cabin quilt, producing the uneven stitches—has come about not through direct conversation and statement but rather through allusion and insinuation. Susan Lanser cites "A Jury of Her Peers" as an example of a text that demonstrates women's ability to speak in a "double voice," two women protecting a third "from a conviction for murder by communicating in 'women's language' under the watchful but unseeing eyes of the Law." [8]

In the following passage, Glaspell enacts her characters' "double voice" when Mrs. Peters points out to Martha Hale the badly stitched quilt block:

> "The sewing," said Mrs. Peters, in a troubled way. "All the rest of them have been so nice and even—but—this one. Why it looks as if she didn't know what she was about."
>
> Their eyes met—something flashed to life, passed between them; then as if with an effort, they seemed to pull away from each other. A moment Mrs. Hale sat there, her hands folded over that sewing which was so unlike all the rest of the sewing. Then she had pulled a knot and drawn the threads.
>
> "Oh, what are you doing, Mrs. Hale?" asked the sheriff's wife, startled.
>
> "Just pulling out a stitch or two that's not sewed very good," said Mrs. Hale mildly.
>
> "I don't think we ought to touch things," Mrs. Peters said, a little helplessly.
>
> "I'll just finish up this end," answered Mrs. Hale, still in that matter-of-fact fashion. (372)

The way they are acting and what they are saying are in direct opposition to the understanding they achieve when their eyes meet. Mrs. Hale is "mild" and "matter-of-fact" and just casually fixing a few stitches. What they both know is that she is destroying evidence and that she shouldn't be. Mrs. Peters, though not physically assisting, nevertheless colludes with this action, as her protestation is "a little helpless." Even the narrative voice averts its eyes, pretending not to see the action itself, when Mrs. Hale "had pulled" a knot and drawn the threads, the verb tense shifting from past tense to past perfect.

After they have found the bird the women have another of their coded talks:

> "I wonder how it would seem," Mrs. Hale at last began, as if feeling her way over strange ground—"never to have had any children around?" Her eyes made a slow sweep of the kitchen, as if seeing what that kitchen had meant through all the years. "No, Wright wouldn't like the bird," she said after that—"a thing that sang. She used to sing. He killed that too." Her voice tightened.

> Mrs. Peters moved uneasily.
> "Of course we don't know who killed the bird."
> "I knew John Wright," was Mrs. Hale's answer.
> "It was an awful thing was done in this house that night, Mrs.
> Hale," said the sheriff's wife. "Killing a man while he slept—slipping a
> thing round his neck that choked the life out of him."
> Mrs. Hale's hand went out to the bird-cage.
> "His neck. Choked the life out of him."
> "We don't *know* who killed him," whispered Mrs. Peters wildly. We
> don't *know*." (377)

When Mrs. Peters, here called "the sheriff's wife," protests that they
don't "know" who killed the bird or who killed Wright, she is speaking
in terms of the legal system. Of course, they have not actually witnessed
either event and so they do not technically, legally "know" for sure. But
they have witnessed the life in the house; Martha Hale's response that she
"knows" John Wright asserts her own intuitive interpretation of justice as
well as interposing her own sense of what it is to "know" something, as
when she asks, "Why is it we know what we know?" Mrs. Peters is "wild,"
of course, because she uses "know" in both senses, the double identification utterly upsetting her; what is at stake is the possibility that Minnie's
murder is justified.

In the same way that their investigation has proceeded by allusion,
their verdict is passed without words. What is interesting here is that
neither woman has ever stated the case directly: "Wright had been awful
to live with alone for twenty years, Minnie killed him, and the dead bird
is the evidence that would supply a motive and convict her for the crime.
We don't want her caught, therefore we will help her. What we are doing
is of course, illegal. Nevertheless, we are women, we understand this, we
too are guilty of letting life go untended. We will never tell what we
know." The most direct they have been with language is to ask: "*Why do
we know what we know?*"

Mrs. Hale and Mrs. Peters, married to the men they're married to, and
in the house for the purpose that they are—to gather evidence to convict
Minnie Foster Wright of murder—cannot speak what they know, for to
speak would move them into the discourse of a system of rules they are by
their silence and actions breaking. If they never say it aloud, then indeed, it
is not public fact that they know who killed John Wright. For them to
state explicitly what they know and what they could do would place them
in the realm of spoken, public discourse, the world of convention, the
patriarchal, male world. Further, they also do not dare to speak the truth

about the crime because to speak it would disqualify the alternative set of values they are using to judge the situation and decide upon the appropriate action. Speaking the truth would bring their intuitive and feminine understanding out into the world that is structured according to the male perspective and explained in the language that is used to maintain that structure. There is no room in the legal system, or in the patriarchal system of the world that has created that system, for justifying a woman's murder of her husband on the grounds of pet-ricide and neglect.

And yet the women, who have felt Minnie's life through identification and through what they know of their own lives, understand and exonerate her and take action to protect her by hiding the evidence. Their reading of this situation and their intended action make sense according to their shared values but fly in the face of conventional, patriarchal morals. To speak what they know would bring them face to face with the subversive nature of their withholding of evidence. They have been struggling with their consciences all along, and it is only when they recognize and acknowledge that their "we" knows and understands something that is at odds with the system of their husbands that they decide to take an action that unites them with each other and against the legal system. As long as they remain "silent" they remain in the female realm and are not bound by the justice system in the patriarchal land. Thus they use language indirectly, to imply and suggest; the real communication between them happens with their eyes, or through their bodies.

When Mrs. Hale and Mrs. Peters, relative strangers, are in the kitchen listening to Mr. Hale's descriptions of the day before and he excuses their concern for Minnie's frozen jam jars by saying, "Oh, well . . . women are used to worrying over trifles," Glaspell notes that "the two women moved a little closer together. Neither of them spoke" (366). This unconscious gesture physically allies the two women and prefigures the bond that will build between them as the story progresses.

Told to "look for clues" by the unseeing eyes of the law, the women always use their eyes to read the details of the situation. Martha Hale's "eye was caught" by a dishtowel on the table, and it is as if "her mind tripped on something (370); her "eye was held" by the half-filled sugar bucket (368); and Minnie's life becomes clear to her when "her eyes made a slow sweep of the kitchen" and it is as if she could "see what that kitchen had meant" through the years.

Mrs. Hale reads Mrs. Peters' reactions with her eyes as well. She notes that Mrs. Peters' eyes "looked as if they could see a long way into things" (369), and later, when they hear the men's footsteps above them, Martha

Hale notes that "that look of seeing into things, of seeing through a thing to something else, was in the eyes of the sheriff's wife now" (371). These two women use their eyes to understand what has happened, and they also use them to communicate what they are really thinking. They use verbal discourse to "tell it slant" or to disguise the truth they relay through their glances.

When they notice the irregular stitching on the quilt block, Glaspell notes that "their eyes met—something flashed to life, passed between them; then, as if with an effort, they seemed to pull away from each other" (372). When they find the mangled birdcage, "again their eyes met—startled, questioning, apprehensive. For a moment neither spoke nor stirred" (374). And when they come to realize that Wright killed Minnie's canary, Glaspell says, "again the eyes of the two women met—this time clung together in a look of dawning comprehension, of growing horror" (377).

In the same way that the two women move physically closer to each other in response to the men's derision early in the story, they move together through their gazes psychically and emotionally as they uncover Minnie's story. The language Glaspell uses to describe this collusion is nearly erotic. When their eyes meet, "something flashes to life between them" and it is "with an effort" that they "seem to pull away" (372). Later, when their eyes meet they "cling together" (376), and, when the men enter the room, the women's eyes "found one another" (379). The bonding that takes place between them goes beyond the battle-of-the-sexes taking of sides that initially delights us in this story. This is a profound reidentification process. Both these women cast their allegiance with another woman and with each other, implicitly breaking the bonds of loyalty they have had with their husbands.

In fact, it is at the end of the story when the county attorney (who had at the beginning called Mrs. Peters "one of us") suggests that she is "married to the law" that Mrs. Peters takes action to align herself with the other women, in effect divorcing the law. In prose that is rather more elegant than the rest of this farm-simple story, suggesting that the voice and point of view are Glaspell's rather than those of her characters, Glaspell describes their final decision:

> Again—for one final moment—the two women were alone in that kitchen.
>
> Martha Hale sprang up, her hands tight together, looking at that other woman, with whom it [their decision] rested. At first she could not see her eyes, for the sheriff's wife had not turned back since she turned away at that suggestion of being married to the law. But now

Mrs. Hale made her turn back. Her eyes made her turn back. Slowly, unwillingly, Mrs. Peters turned her head until her eyes met the eyes of the other woman. There was a moment when they held each other in a steady, burning look in which there was no evasion or flinching. Then Martha Hale's eyes pointed the way to the basket in which was hidden the thing that would make certain the conviction of the other woman—that woman who was there with them all through that hour. (380)

There has been no discussion about this between them, only this slow, tentative identification and bonding, signified by their gazes. The images of physical positioning and of eyes as emblematic of the female perspective come together in this final visioning of the truth. Mrs. Hale's eyes "make" Mrs. Peters turn to her, and in this moment "they held each other in a steady, burning look in which there was no evasion or flinching"; this is a depiction of rare honesty and truth and it certainly transcends the sense of "knowing" the women have with their husbands. If female connection is, as Gilligan suggests, the crucial element of women's psychology, then Minnie, the woman who was not there and yet who had been "there with them through that hour" becomes a third party to this intimate bonding.

It is then that Mrs. Peters decides to "do it"; she rushes forward and tries to put the box holding the dead bird into her handbag. When she discovers it won't fit, Mrs. Hale snatches the box from her as the men enter the room and places it safely in her coat pocket. At the story's end, the evidence showing motive has been hidden or destroyed, and presumably Minnie Foster Wright will go free. Nobody but them is any wiser. At the story's end, there are three men who are even more ignorant than they were at the beginning of the story, and there are three women who know everything. And one of them will go free—the woman who murdered her husband.

Overall, this seems a moment of triumph for the women. Some critics, however, disagree, casting it as a Pyrrhic victory, if any. Carolyn Heilbrun has commented that students reading this story in a class on women's narratives "saw the absence of any narrative that could take the women past their moment of revelation and support their bid for freedom from the assigned script."[9] Judith Fetterley also expresses the frustration that "the women are willing to let the men continue to control textuality in order to save the individual. . . . Minnie Wright is denied her story and hence her reality (What will her life be like if she does get off?), and the men are allowed to continue to assume that they are the only ones with stories. So haven't the men finally won?"[10]

Perhaps we should concede that in this case, male superiority and the presumptions of the patriarchy go unchallenged in any overt sense; the women keep silent about what they know. But that is within the level of the story of the text, and even there a murderess is going free. In the world outside the text, however, the story seems even more subversive because of this intact silence. The women in the story have not had to discuss their decisions, their reasoning, their rationale. They uncovered evidence, weighed it, and passed a sentence that exonerates Minnie, indicts the men's tradition of justice, and asserts the validity of their own assessments of their power. The women use the men's assumptions, their language, against them, to free one of their own, breaking marriage bonds and social convention.

The point of the story is not what the women know, but how they know it. It is not that the women knew to look in the kitchen and were able to find that misstitched quilt block, the canary with its broken neck, the half-mixed flour, nor is it merely that they can make the logical leap that a half-finished job indicates disruption, that faulty sewing indicates nervousness, and that the dead bird gives a reason for anger and retaliation. What they know is the thing they are referring to when they say "Why do we *know*—what we know?" (378). Mrs. Hale has exclaimed, "We all go through the same things—it's all just a different kind of the same thing! If it weren't—why do you and I *understand*?" (378).

They have brought to bear an identification based on similar experiences with Minnie Foster; the witness they bear is personal, experiential, culturally female. And further, they know that for all the not always exactly good-natured joking the men do about women's place, women's difference, they really don't know the half of it. The men in the story truly believe that a woman is married to the law, that *Mrs.* Hale and *Mrs.* Peters are essentially bonded to their husbands, and, through their husbands, will owe allegiance to the patriarchal structure of the world. All this is what the women have quietly turned upside down.

Fetterley has pointed out that Glaspell does not keep silent as her characters do, saying that "'A Jury of Her Peers' does not suppress, but, rather, tells the woman's story" and suggesting that it "is didactic in the sense that it is designed to educate the male reader in the recognition and interpretation of women's texts" (154). And it does, to the extent that all readers know what the men in the story do not: that official representatives of patriarchal justice in this text missed the evidence, the criminal, and the cover-up. The men in the story do not know, as the reader does, that there is a secret between the women. Given that the story stops there, though, the point is also that none of us knows where the women will go from here—what they will now do, knowing this secret, and knowing that they know it. At this moment Glaspell's female characters have a kind of power that is perhaps more subversive because it is circumscribed by the silence of women's shared knowledge. Nothing any of them has said is actionable. Nor, significantly, is anything the narrator has said.

The truly subversive nature of this text is not that it records the acts of the women, nor that it reveals their manner of acting without once uttering an incriminating word, but that Glaspell has used language to create the same collusive bond between her narrative and her readers; to the end, Glaspell's narrator has never admitted anything that the characters have not. In merely recording the enactment of this alternative form of justice, she shows a female shared experience that is not articulated, perhaps not articulable. What it is is the full resonance of their question: why do we know what we know?—which is of course in the text most immediately a question about knowing why Minnie has killed her husband. But as the story itself shows, there is a shared female experience of life that goes beyond the facts of spending more time in the kitchen than in the barn and knowing multiple methods of quilting. The shared experience is of living in a culture where those in power "laugh at the insignificance of kitchen things" and the question, "would women know a clue if they saw one?" brings a laugh.

Women reading the story, if they identify with the circumstances of the women's lives in the text, will share as well the insights of the characters about the bonds between women and their lariatlike facility with language and subtext. The story ends with a pun on the words "knot-it," which is the women's response to the attorney when he says "facetiously, 'at least we found out that she was not going to quilt it. She was going to—what is it you call it, ladies?'" (381).

The women intentionally call up the knot of Minnie's noose, which brings unnervingly to mind the image of all those farm women knotting hundreds of knots daily in the fabric of their lives (how many necks could those knots noose?) and is also a pun on "not-it." To the patronizing of the male legal authorities, to the daily strangulations of husbands, these women's actions shout, as do today's teenagers, "Not!" With this repudiation, they are restitching the faulty fabric of life, as Mrs. Hale explains, "replacing bad sewing with good" (372).

Notes

1. Susan Glaspell, "A Jury of Her Peers," in *American Voices, American Women*, ed. Lee R. Edwards and Arlyn Diamond, 363. All further references to this source will be cited parenthetically in the text.

2. Sandra M. Gilbert and Susan Gubar, *No Man's Land,* 1:91.

3. Annette Kolodny, "A Map for Rereading," 464.

4. Ibid., 463.

5. Lucy, Ethel, Ricky, and Fred were characters in "I Love Lucy," a television situation comedy popular in the United States from the early 1950s.

6. See Elaine Hedges, "Small Things Reconsidered."

7. Carol Gilligan, *In a Different Voice,* 43.

8. Susan S. Lanser, "Toward a Feminist Narratology," 618.

9. Carolyn G. Heilbrun, *Writing a Woman's Life,* 42.

10. Judith Fetterley, "Reading about Reading," 154.

ANN E. TRAPASSO

Returning to the Site of Violence: The Restructuring of Slavery's Legacy in Sherley Anne Williams's *Dessa Rose*

The number of contemporary slave narrative novels, most of which have been written by African American women, prompts Deborah McDowell to ask, "What personal need, what expressive function, does re-presenting slavery in narrative serve the twentieth-century black American writer?" She wonders if "the compulsion to repeat" is an issue of witnessing "from the 'safe' vantage point of distance" or of "attempt[ing] the impossible: to 'get it right' or 'set the record straight.'" Still, she remains "certain that these recent fictionalizations of slavery insert themselves, some by explicit design, into the store of warring texts, of conflicting interpretations of chattel slavery."[1]

In *Dessa Rose,* Sherley Anne Williams makes explicit the value of returning to the topic of slavery and situates her novel within a revisionist historical perspective. The Author's Note identifies her motives for writing while suggesting that the writing has been a vehicle for her own healing. The necessity of returning to the site of violence in order to heal is also enacted within the novel as those who have escaped slavery sell themselves back into it. Williams's return and the characters' return are returns with a difference, made after they have learned more about "the peculiar institution" and under the cloak of safety. Because Williams's commitment is to model healing from slavery's legacy, the novel sustains a delicate balance between representing the horrors and demystifying them.

An emphasis on healing is a defining characteristic of contemporary African American women's writing. Athena Vrettos says, "Through representations of healing, black women writers seek the inspiration and authority to heal, locating in language a new curative domain." She explains: "Only by invoking the origins of both injury and oppression can this act of healing begin. By thus turning to the past, by seeking that 'silver splinter' that obliterated a world, black women's narratives seek structures from which new worlds can emerge." [2] Indeed, Barbara Christian identifies a trend beginning in the 1980s toward historical novels that draw upon previous African American women's fiction and recent historical research on and by African American women and cites *The Color Purple, Dessa Rose,* and *Beloved* as illustrations.[3] She argues that recognizing African American women's experiences as integral to history "not only restores historical data, it frees the novelist from that data, to remember that which could not be precisely recorded but which continues to exist in storytelling, in cultural patterns, and in the imagination." Christian says that these novels "remind us that if we want to be whole, we must recall the past, those parts that we want to remember, those parts that we want to forget." [4]

By outlining her motives for writing in the Author's Note, Williams signals their importance. She says, "I admit also to being outraged by a certain, critically acclaimed novel of the early seventies that travestied the as-told-to memoir of slave revolt leader Nat Turner." [5] William Styron's *The Confessions of Nat Turner* (1967) so angered many that the year after it appeared a collection of essays entitled *William Styron's Nat Turner: Ten Black Writers Respond* criticized Styron for his portrait.[6] A primary source of Williams's anger is the violence being perpetuated by literature and history that misrepresent slavery. For Williams, Styron's *Confessions* is a contemporary manifestation of a written tradition that has kept African Americans at its "mercy," has "betrayed" them, and has denied them a "place in the American past [where they] could go and be free" (ix-x). In obscuring the horrors of slavery, as well as the community, agency, and resistance of African Americans, history and literature continue to violate their humanity.

Such violation "started [Williams] on the road to being a writer"; as a junior and senior high school student, she had difficulty finding books about African Americans that "transported" her and were useful. In particular, she wanted stories of "heroic young women who despite all they had to do and endure laughed and loved, hoped and encouraged, supported each other with gifts of food and money and fought the country that was quite literally, we were convinced, trying to kill us." [7] Like Toni Morrison, Williams has created for us the kind of book she wanted to read.[8]

While outraged at *Confessions,* Williams had access to sources that told a different story about slavery, in particular Angela Davis's "Reflections on the Black Woman's Role in the Community of Slaves" and Her-

bert Aptheker's *American Negro Slave Revolts*. In contrast to William
Styron's historical source, Stanley Elkins, Aptheker's 1943 pioneering
work on slave resistance argues that Nat Turner's revolt "was not an isolated, unique phenomenon, but the cumulation of a series of slave con-
spiracies and revolts which occurred in the immediate past." [9] Reading
Aptheker's book, Davis learned about women participating in rebellions
and performing acts of sabotage. Declaring in 1971 that "the paucity of
literature on the black woman is outrageous," Davis began "shattering"
those "reified images" of black women as aggressive matriarchs by re-
searching their "presumed historical inception" in slavery. She writes,
"Yet, a single theme appears at every juncture: the woman transcending,
refusing, fighting back, asserting herself over and over again against terrifying obstacles. . . . She fought alongside her man, accepting or providing
guidance according to her talents and the nature of their tasks. She was
in no sense an authoritarian figure." [10]

As a graduate student Williams went "looking for [her] history, to
learn the skills by which [she] would ferret it out from wherever white
folks had hidden it." [11] Reading Davis and Aptheker "marked a turning
point in her efforts to apprehend that other history." With new insights,
she was able to construct an alternate story of slavery, one that "eliminated neither heroism nor love" (x). In identifying her historical sources,
Williams establishes an intertextual relationship with scholarship, breaking the silence about the agency and resistance of those enslaved, both
men and women.

Williams makes it clear that "*Dessa Rose* is based on two historical
incidents." From her sources she learned of a pregnant black woman who
helped lead an 1829 revolt and a poor white woman who gave sanctuary
to runaways on her deserted farm in 1830. Feeling "sad . . . that these two
had never met," she recognizes unfulfilled possibilities and constructs a
fantastic story of the white woman joining the runaways in a selling scam
(ix). This creation of a past with a difference provides Williams with a
new reality: "Maybe it is only a metaphor, but I now own a summer in
the 19th century" (x). Though her ancestors were owned and could not
own anything, she is able through her imagination to reclaim this space
for us all. The past she offers is inscribed with more possibilities than
our "real" one. The suggestion lingers that if all this was possible in the
nineteenth century, then "more" is possible "for the children . . . who will
share in the 21st"—Williams's audience (x). As compelling in its own way
as the novel itself, the "Author's Note" suggests a process of healing from
the legacy of violence that involves expressing anger, educating oneself

about the institution, and then creating an alternative, a process that the characters will model for readers.

When Williams declares the novel to be "fiction," yet "as true as if I myself had lived it," she offers us insight into the way she sustains the balance between representing the horrors of slavery and demystifying them throughout the text (x). This both-and quality accurately describes the blending of fiction and truth, fantasy and realism. Throughout, the tension is between portraying what might have been and depicting what did happen during slavery. The novel offers both a realistic depiction of the violence and a spirited declaration of freedom from its effects.

Williams disrupts the realism of her text by creating a countercurrent in the three main sections of the novel, first of parody and then of increasingly fantastic possibilities. Deborah McDowell considers "The Darky" section "a veritable parody of the 'as-told-to' device of gathering empirical evidence and documenting events to construct historicist discourse." [12] The gravity of Dessa's imprisonment is mediated by Nehemiah's petty motives and concerns as he writes in hopes of being accepted by the plantation society. Though he has never owned a slave, he is heralded as "an expert on their management" because of his book, *The Masters' Complete Guide to Dealing with Slaves and Other Dependents* (25). Once Dessa escapes from slavery, Williams places her on the oasis of Ruth's farm, Sutton's Glen, where the social forces perpetuating slavery do not operate. The farm is managed by the runaways, who make the decisions about what to plant and when to harvest. Some social relations are reversed when Ruth serves as a wet nurse to Dessa's baby, and is jealous of the camaraderie and shared laughter of the African Americans. Such reversals question and then undermine historical power relations. The story becomes increasingly fantastic as the characters leave Sutton's Glen. By the middle of book 3, "The Negress," the plot resembles an adventure "as exciting as any in American lore" as the runaways turn the tables on the slave system by selling themselves back into slavery and then escaping with the profits.[13] At the close, Nehemiah is shown to have been driven crazy by his obsession to capture Dessa; his writing is reduced to "some scribbling" on paper that no one can read (255). The incorporation of a current counter to realism allows Williams to challenge historical relationships and signals her own agency as author of this novel.

Williams sustains both the realistic and the fantastic by portraying those who are enslaved as agents within a supportive community.[14] The prologue focuses on Kaine and Dessa's laughter and loving. The opening image reveals Kaine's vitality as he walks between the cabins "like he owned them" and laughs at Dessa's dread of his early arrival; he defies the rules with his good-spirited laughter. "Love suffuse[s Dessa]" as she looks into Kaine's eyes, which "were alive, gleaming with dancing lights . . . that turned their brown to gold" (1–3). Interspersed throughout the novel, Dessa's recollections of the Vaugham plantation reveal that African American men and women resisted slavery and supported each other in familial and communal relationships. The women rebelled against their role as breeders by using roots to dispel unwanted sexual advances and by practicing abortion and infanticide.[15] The prologue and epilogue, as well as the memory sections in italics within the chapters, portray the intimate lives of Dessa and her peers. These sections stand suspended outside the action of the novel, outside its chronological time. They assert the humanity and survival of the African American people despite the violence of the slave system.

The devastation is most poignantly illustrated by the fate of Dessa's sisters and brothers. Her mother, Rose, bore ten children: Little Rose who died when she was carrying Amos, Minta who died before the white folks could name her, Seth who was the first to live to go into the fields, Amos who died of diphtheria, (miscarriages before Bess), Bess who died, Jeffrey who died, Caesar who died, Carrie Mae who lives on the Vaugham plantation, Samuel or Jeeters who was sold away, and Dessa Rose who was sold away and then escaped. Rose tells her daughter that this litany is her heritage and asks her to repeat it "lest her poor, lost children die to living memory as they had in her world" (126). These sections keep the horrors of slavery present in our consciousness. At the same time, the movement of the text is toward healing Dessa and readers from slavery's legacy.

The novel draws upon tropes and incidents from the slave narrative tradition to educate readers about slavery, but the violence often remains in the background. Most of the violence Dessa and her peers have suffered has already happened when the novel opens, and direct narration of it is interspersed in brief passages. The reader is prepared for the most brutal scenes because they are alluded to, often several times, before they are depicted. For example, Dessa's scars are repeatedly referred to or described: "the horror that scarred her inner thighs, snaking around her lower abdomen and hips in ropy keloids that gleam with patent-leather smoothness" (56–57). Only after she is recovering from her imprisonment and childbirth in Ruth's bed do we learn the details of her punishment: the whipping, the sweatbox, and the coffle. In some cases, violence is acknowledged without direct representation, as in Dessa's reference to the rape of black women by white men: "Womens was subject to ravishment. . . . This the way it was during slavery. The woman was valued more because her children belong to the master" (210). The violence is mediated so that the agency of the central characters is not undermined.

Nehemiah's violence to Dessa is the only violence portrayed directly in the novel's present: he represents not only white male chroniclers of slavery such as Thomas Gray but also contemporary writers such as William Styron whose writings continue to violate the humanity of African Americans.[16] During the sessions in which he records Dessa's words, Nehemiah has the power, which he uses, to do physical harm and to order punishments such as no food and only saltwater to drink. Infuriated that she flickers her eyes at him "almost as though he had been a bothersome fly and her eyes a horse's tail flicking him away," Nehemiah strikes her so hard that he draws blood. Defining his striking of Dessa as "random violence," he considers it not as a perpetuation of white power under slavery but as an act that "lower[s him] almost to the same level . . . that characterized the actions of blacks among themselves" (24). Disassociating himself and other planters from the violence inherent in slavery, he locates it within the African Americans. By reading Dessa's scars as a sign of her "misconduct" and "savagery" rather than of the savagery of the system, he keeps the power to define those enslaved as subhuman creatures and to represent them as such to his readers (13).

However, Nehemiah's attempts to locate violence within those who are enslaved are undermined by the textual distinctions between anger as violence and anger as resistance. Nehemiah's anger in the scene described above springs from a desire to dominate, whereas Dessa's anger propels her toward actions that eventually lead to her escape from slavery. Dessa's anger comes to her in "flashes," suggesting a sudden, brief, and illuminating intensity of feeling: "Yes, I trembled; that feeling, that anger was like a bloodhound in my throat, a monster that didn't seem to know enemy or friend, wouldn't know the difference once it got loose" (199). The bloodhound simile, recalling the use of these animals to track down runaway slaves, suggests the focused intensity of Dessa's anger and also its potential destructiveness. The memory of strangling her mistress still exhilarates: "The four red welts in the suddenly pallid face, the white spot where her thumb had pressed at the base of the red neck filled Dessa with a terror and glee so intense they were almost physical." Unlike Nehemiah, she takes responsibility for her anger, recognizing it as a deep affirmation of self. She also has a greater understanding of what humanity entails: "Frightened at her own response, she was almost ashamed—not of the deed. No. Never that, but surely it was wrong to delight so deeply in anyone else's pain" (57). Similarly, when those enslaved fight to free themselves from the coffle they discover that "the actual deed there in the clearing was more frightening and more exhilarating than any of them had imagined" (60). The text distinguishes between anger that leads to actions that oppress and anger that leads to actions that liberate. The escapes and the journey at the close of the novel demonstrate that sustained resistance to oppression involves channeling collective anger.

Once Dessa escapes from slavery, the novel identifies what she must learn in order to be truly free, and it constructs Ruth's awareness of racist and sexist oppression as a process that frequently intersects with Dessa's own as they break down the dichotomies of black and white taught by the slave system. In "The Wench" and the first chapter of "The Negress," which are set on the deserted farm, Williams foregrounds the tensions among the characters. Confrontations occur between Ruth and Dessa over historical hurts between white and black women, such as the exploitation of the black mother and white women having sexual relationships with black men. Dessa and Ruth struggle over ownership of the name "mammy"; each tries to nullify the other's claim to this word in which the power relations of society are inscribed. With this name the white family can appropriate the black mother, while obscuring the fact that she is stolen from the black family. The narrative confirms that any further communication between black women and white women will be possible only after this issue is faced. Confrontations occur between Dessa and the men over the degradation of the black female as a mule and over Nathan's sexual relationship with Ruth. Each of these outbursts is followed by silent reflection, and sometimes further confrontation, which allows those involved to sort out their feelings and come to a better understanding of themselves and each other. Throughout, the novel emphasizes the importance of reflecting on the source of one's anger.

One sign of Ruth's growth is that she moves from an unfocused and displaced anger to a clearer understanding of racism and sexism. At first, her anger seems only a sign of her white woman's assumptions about what is owed to her as "mistress"; she is irritated and hurt that the runaways do not treat her with the proper respect. Jealous of their camaraderie and angry that Annabelle does not appreciate the superiority of her previous life, she lashes out: "Why—I'm telling you more joy and, and, happiness, yes! and excitement, too, than you can ever imagine in that paltry black hide. Nigger, you come back here" (102). Caught in white supremacist ideology, she cannot admit that she wants to share in their laughter. She also distrusts their stories about slavery. Believing that justice prevails, she insists that any punishments they received must have been deserved. After her confrontation with Dessa over the name "mammy," she talks with Nathan and reflects upon her past; she begins to see that her life has been built upon denial. Ruth's ignorance has made her complicitous with the slave system, for "she had accepted [the whippings] as long as she didn't hear the screams" (161). Dazed by these insights, she recognizes that she has been blinded to all that was around her and condemns herself: "She hadn't known [her husband] either, had purposefully kept herself from knowing him. . . . What else had she refused to see? she wondered bitterly" (166). Ruth's new understanding of how she has silently consented to the slave system propels her to examine what her relationship to the African Americans can be if they are not her slaves.

Dessa's isolation as a field hand has kept her from understanding the slave system: "This is what I hold against slavery. May come a time when I forgive—cause I don't think I'm set up to forget—the beatings, the selling, the killings, but I don't think I ever forgive the ignorance they kept us in" (227). Before the coffle, she had never been five miles from where she was born and had never seen more than four whites together. In Wilson's cellar she realizes that she lacks words to describe or interpret what has happened to her since the day Kaine was killed. Ironically, it is Nehemiah's questions that prompt her to comprehend how her identity has changed: "She saw the past as she talked, not as she had lived it but as she had come to understand it." She articulates what she has learned about white power and her own agency: "White men existed because they did; Master had smashed the banjo because that was the way he was, able to do what he felt like doing. And a nigger could, too. This was what Kaine's act said to her. He had done; he was. She had done also, had as good as killed Master" (56).

Whiteness has come to represent all that Dessa hates. When she awakens in Ruth's bed at Sutton's Glen, she literally sees white: a whitewashed ceiling, white walls, white light, and a white face. Aware that Ruth is nursing her baby, she prefers to "play possum" rather than consciously acknowledge this fact: "It went against anything she had been taught to think about white women but to inspect that fact too closely was almost to deny her existence" (123). Since she had thought of her existence as diametrically opposed to that of whites, changing her conception of whiteness threatens Dessa's very sense of self. The dichotomy between black and white that Dessa wishes to maintain is threatened by Nathan and Ruth's lovemaking and by the selling scam. Feeling betrayed and hurt by Nathan, and then confused and isolated as her peers ask her to apologize to Ruth and to accept Ruth's participation in the scheme, Dessa insists, "Miz Ruint wasn't no part of that knot [that bound Dessa and the men together]; the only way she could get in was to loosen it" (188). Though Dessa only reluctantly agrees to participate in the scheme, its success depends upon the characters' leaving individual conflicts and passions behind as they set out, and upon continuing the trust that has been developing over time on Sutton's Glen.

Planning the journey requires an imaginative leap for those previously enslaved because, as Dessa clarifies, the concept of a future was denied them during slavery when their future "belonged to [their] masters" (210). They dare to return to the institution of slavery because they know they can profit from it. The selling scam is perceived as "a good trick to pull on the white folks" and a just reversal: "Oh, I tell you, honey, slavery was ugly and we felt right to soak the masters for all we could get" (194, 226). Through this unlikely turn of the plot, Williams suggests that power can be attained by means of collective action.[17] Considering herself a political writer, Williams says, "I try to elucidate those elements in our lives on which constructive political changes, those that do more than blackwash or femalize the same old power structure, can be built.[18] Collective action is demonstrated throughout the rest of the novel as the characters work to protect themselves from rapists, robbers, Nehemiah, and other potential threats.

Midway through "The Negress," the plot increasingly resembles an adventure story as the characters escape detection and numerous threats. Their safety seems assured as the tone of the novel becomes lighter. Telling how they escaped armed robbers, Dessa concludes, "That's the way it was: bam, bam, bam, just like that, just like we'd done this a hundred times before." She explains, "We was feeling too good about ourselfs to take anything too hard," and "we'd come a long way from the time we'd watched Harker and Ned walk back into slavery. What we used to do with fear and trembling, we now did for fun. I told myself this was good, that it showed slavery didn't have no hold on us no more" (229, 233). Throughout the novel laughter has functioned as a sign of emotional well-being and of community. As Dessa explains, laughter is a cohesive force: "We had scaped, honey! And they'd come back for me and we'd scaped again. You didn't do this in slavery. We laughed about it—they teased me about the white man what 'kept company' with me while I was in that cellar; I said they'd been sparking the girls in the Quarters, that's what took them so long to see about me—but it was this that brought us close" (181). Discussing "the inflection of laughter [that] dominates Dessa's text," Deborah McDowell queries: "Am I suggesting something as out-landish (to say nothing of morally repugnant) as that Dessa's story would have us see that slavery was an institution to be laughed at, laughed about, laughed over? Clearly not." [19] Yet her very question suggests that it is not so clear. Indeed, it is Williams, not McDowell, who is offering this "out-landish" suggestion. The reason that laughter at slavery is not morally repugnant here is that it signals the triumph of survival and the recognition of new ways of being in the world, as indicated by Dessa's exclamation above about "scaping." Philip Sterling says: "Humor helped to make life in slavery liveable. . . . Laughter was an effective palliative for the injuries to body and psyche which bondage inflicted, and a medium for articulating hopes and fantasies of freedom." [20]

The novel reveals a progression as those previously enslaved move from laughing at slavery as a defense to laughing because they feel free. As they reenter society and the discourse of slavery, both Ruth and the African Americans gain greater insight into the institution and its effects upon them. When Ned is sent to the sheriff's office with a note asking that the bearer be whipped, he pays another slave to take the note for him. Dessa explains his action and their response: "This wasn't a nice trick but it was what slavery taught a lot of people: to take everybody so you didn't get took yourself. We laughed so we wouldn't cry; we was seeing ourselves as we had been and seeing the thing that had made us. Only way we could defend ourselves was by making it into some hair-raising story or joke" (228). Laughing at slavery signals that she and her peers are beginning to see more than just the horror; they are experiencing their own vitality, as well as acknowledging their complicity in harming others. The scam dramatizes that healing from slavery's legacy is facilitated by praxis, that is, using Paulo Freire's definition, "reflection and action upon the world in order to transform it." [21] Before the journey, escape from slavery was associated with "find[ing] someplace to go" (202). While traveling, Dessa comes to think of it as an internal feeling rather than a physical place. Articulating that her goal is "to have freedom in [her]," she considers it as a sense of inner well-being (244). Still, Dessa makes clear that healing is a long and private process, one that she will not share with Ruth: "But I wouldn't talk about Kaine, about the loss of my peoples; these was still a wound to me and remembrance of that coffle hurt only a little bit less" (237).

A balance between recognizing the horror and moving beyond it is sustained by the novel's two endings—of the plot and then the epilogue. The plot ends on a note of restrained triumph for all as Dessa escapes from Nehemiah and she and Ruth acknowledge their friendship: "We couldn't hug each other, not on the streets, not in Acropolis, not even after dark; we both had sense enough to know that. The town could even bar us from laughing; but that night we walked the boardwalk together and we didn't hide our grins" (256). In contrast, the epilogue says that Ruth went East, while the others went West. It emphasizes the pain and loss involved in sustaining a life in supposedly "free territory." Of her children, Dessa says, "I hope they never have to pay what it cost us to own ourselfs," and ends her narrative with this lament: "Oh, we have paid for our children's place in the world again, and again" (260). This profound pain balances the restrained triumph of the plot's conclusion. Dessa says in the epilogue that the laws and practices in the West are against Harker and Nathan so that "they walk such a tightrope, such a tightrope. This country have set us a hard task . . . give us so much hurt" (259). Dessa's comment can be read as a metacommentary on the tightrope Williams herself has walked in creating a text that offers us seemingly contradictory responses to slavery. We must never forget how horrible it was and we must also free ourselves from the horror so that we can move on.

Notes

1. Deborah E. McDowell, "Negotiating between Tenses," 144. For a list of contemporary slave narrative novels, see 161n.

2. Athena Vrettos, "Curative Domains," 456, 472.

3. Alice Walker's *The Color Purple* (1982), and Toni Morrison's *Beloved* (1987).

4. Barbara Christian, "'Somebody Forgot to Tell Somebody Something,'" 338, 341.

5. Sherley Anne Williams, *Dessa Rose*, ix. Subsequent page references to this work will be given parenthetically in the text.

6. Some of the criticisms of Styron's novel discussed in *William Styron's Nat Turner,* ed. John Henrik Clarke, are that the novel creates stereotypical and racist portraits of Blacks, portrays Turner as weak and irresolute, suggests that Turner is motivated by his desire for a white woman, and ignores the role of Turner's family and wife, and that it fails to put the rebellion in the context of the history of other uprisings.

7. These quotes are from an autobiographical introduction to Williams's novella "Meditations on History," in *Midnight Birds,* 195, 197. Sherley Anne Williams (born 1944) is a professor of literature at the University of California at San Diego. She has published two books of poetry, *The Peacock Poems* (1975) and *Someone Sweet Angel Chile* (1982), and a work of criticism, *Give Birth to Brightness: A Thematic Study in Neo-Black Literature* (1972).

8. See Jane Bakerman, "The Seams Can't Show: An Interview with Toni Morrison," 59. About her responsibilities as a Black writer, Morrison says, "At first, I didn't feel anything; I just thought that I wanted to write the kind of book that I wanted to

read. Later on it changed. There was also something else—I felt that nobody talked about or wrote about those Black people the way I knew those people to be."

9. Herbert Aptheker, *American Negro Slave Revolts,* quoted in Mae Henderson, "(W)riting the Work and Working the Rites," 634. Henderson says that in *Slavery: A Problem in American Institutional and Intellectual Life,* Elkins finds Turner's rebellion to be exceptional, "the only sustained revolt in the annuls of American Negro history."

10. Angela Davis, "Reflections on the Black Woman's Role," 3–4, 14.

11. Sherley Anne Williams, "Returning to the Blues," 820.

12. McDowell, "Negotiating between Tenses," 148.

13. Christian, "'Somebody Forgot to Tell Somebody Something,'" 339.

14. In "Negotiating between Tenses," 160, McDowell says, "Contemporary Afro-American writers who tell a story of slavery are increasingly aiming for the same thing: to reposition the stress points of that story with a heavy accent on particular acts of agency within an oppressive and degrading system."

15. For a discussion of such practices, see Darlene Clark Hine, "Female Slave Resistance."

16. Thomas Gray is the transcriber-editor of *The Confessions of Nat Turner . . . as reported by Thomas Gray* (1831). For an analysis of the correspondences between Gray, Styron, Williams, and Davis in Williams's novella "Meditations on History," which was written before the novel, see Henderson, "(W)riting the Work."

17. In *(Ex)tensions,* 149, Elizabeth A. Meese also notes that the novel "offers instruction in intragroup and intergroup coalition politics."

18. Williams, "Meditations on History," 198.

19. McDowell, "Negotiating between Tenses," 157, 159.

20. Philip Sterling, "Humor," 347.

21. *Pedagogy of the Oppressed,* 36.

S. LILLIAN KREMER

The Holocaust
and the Witnessing Imagination

Writing by Jewish American women focusing on women's Holocaust experience portrays Jewish women doubly cursed in the Nazi universe as racial pariahs and sexual victims, brutalized while the world remained silent. Although the primary motives of the Nazis' commitment to the destruction of the Jewish people were rooted in political, racial, and religious beliefs, women experienced the Holocaust in ways unique to their gender. Beyond the starvation, disease, hard labor, and physical violence endured by all victims, women were subject to gender-based suffering and degradation. They were sexually abused and subjected to medical experiments; pregnant women were killed or forced to undergo abortions; infants were systematically destroyed at birth; and young mothers were routinely murdered with their children rather than selected for slave labor. When the survivors returned to civilization, silence about their experience was often both internally and externally imposed. Some sought to still their voices to hasten recovery and quicken their adjustment to postwar society. Others, ready to testify, encountered indifference and at times hostility from those who did not want to know, from those who chose to evade the truth because of what it implied about the human condition, and from those who shrank from facing their own complicity. In the succeeding decades as Holocaust history and literature became more readily available, the experiences and perceptions of Jewish women were often obscured or absorbed into accounts and interpretations of male experience. However, significant writing by women survivors, scholars, and artists has appeared that gives voice to the experience of Jewish women under Nazi rule as well as to the postwar reactions of women survivors.

American novelists Cynthia Ozick and Norma Rosen had no direct Holocaust experience. They nevertheless felt compelled to write about the event that altered conventional thought about humanity, divinity, and social and political structure. In "Toward a New Yiddish," Ozick advocates an indigenous American Jewish literature, "centrally Jewish in its concerns."[1] Jewish history and the Holocaust, as the orienting event of the twentieth century, are moral and artistic imperatives for such a literature. Psychological, political, and theological consequences of the catastrophe find expression throughout Ozick's work.[2] The short story and novella collected in *The Shawl* focus on a woman who endures the agony of watching a guard murder her child in a Nazi camp and spends ensuing decades trapped by that memory. Norma Rosen, Ozick's colleague and friend, was profoundly moved by Emmanuel Ringelblum's *Notes from the Warsaw Ghetto* and by eyewitness testimony at the Eichmann trial. Rosen professes to be a "witness-through-the-imagination," a "documenter of the responses of those who 'had heard the terrible news.'"[3] Because the Holocaust is "the central occurrence of the twentieth-century . . . the central human occurrence," Rosen wrote *Touching Evil* to explore "what might happen to people who truly took into consciousness the fact of the Holocaust . . . the meaning to human life and aspiration of the knowledge that human beings—in great numbers—could do what had been done."[4] Both *The Shawl* and *Touching Evil* explore the violence perpetrated against Jewish women during the Holocaust, the responses of the victims and those who remember them, and the problematics of Holocaust transmission.

The title story of *The Shawl* marks the first instance in which Ozick locates her fiction directly in the lice-infested, disease-ridden, death-dominated world of the concentration camp. Its sequel, "Rosa," chronicles the postwar survivor syndrome of the title character nearly four decades after the events recounted in the first story. Unlike "The Shawl," Rosen's *Touching Evil* is removed in time and place from the historic concentration camp universe. The present tense of the novel is 1961, during the Eichmann trial; the place America; the major characters neither Jewish nor survivors of the Holocaust. Because Rosen perceives the Holocaust as a human rather than a Jewish problem, Jews appear only as the ghostly shadows of the documentaries, a somber reminder of the enormity of the Final Solution. The central characters of the novel are two gentile American women who learn of the horror through newspaper photographs of concentration camps and television coverage of the Eichmann trial. Their friendship is initiated and sustained by exposure to the concentration camp universe as they meet each day to view the trial. Past and present collide and merge as the novel alternates between 1944, the year Jean learned of the death camps, and 1961, the year of the Eichmann trial, which is the catalyst both for her rediscovery of the Holocaust's central significance to her life and for Hattie's initial Holocaust encounter. Moments of consciousness impinge on one another, varying in intensity from the fleeting to the all-consuming, and extend to penetrate the emotions and intellects of both women.

"The Shawl" begins dramatically with the central characters, Rosa, a young mother and her infant, Magda, and Rosa's fourteen-year-old niece, Stella, struggling to survive a death march to a concentration camp. Rosa confronts the choice many Jewish mothers suffered, whether to entrust her child to a stranger's goodwill or try to preserve its life herself. She considers passing her baby to a woman along the road, a choice fraught with danger for mother and child, since the penalty for stepping out of the line of march is death. There are other risks, too: the unexpected transfer might so startle the stranger that she would drop the bundle and injure the child, or if the stranger understood the Jewish woman's intentions, she might reject the child and denounce the mother.

Throughout the march and in the concentration camp, Ozick invests the shawl, which covers mother and child, with mystical power as an agent of its bearer's survival. The shawl provides Magda shelter, concealment, and nourishment. Ozick conveys the nurturing capacity of the shawl by juxtaposing the natural world with the unnatural Nazi universe. She describes the shawl-swaddled infant as "a squirrel in a nest"; the shawl forms a "little house" that hides her in the barracks when her mother stands outdoors for roll call.[5]

Ozick foreshadows the child's death by inverting normally joyous childhood milestones. The infant Magda's first tooth is described as "an elfin tombstone of white marble" (4), and her first steps are but a new source of terror for Rosa, who fears that a mobile but uncomprehending infant will stray into the sight of a German guard. When Stella usurps the shawl to warm her own frozen body, Magda toddles into the roll call area crying, uttering her first sounds since Rosa's breasts dried up. Uncertain whether to run for the shawl or to retrieve Magda without it and chance her continued screaming, Rosa runs for the shawl. But she is too late. As Magda reaches toward mother and shawl, a German guard sweeps her up and tosses her onto the electrified fence. The novelist gives life metonymically to the endangered Jewish woman and dead child by enumerating human parts, arms, legs, head, belly, to signify the valued lives. For the Nazis, she uses such metonyms as "helmet" and "boots," signifying their callousness and their disregard for Jewish life.

Nature imagery, pointedly contrasting Nazi-Jewish dichotomies, drawing attention to the discrepancy between the natural order and its German perversion, sharply heightens the intensity of the death scene. Ozick counterpoints plant and flower imagery suggestive of the world beyond the barbed wire with images of the human desecration of nature to convey the environment of the concentration camp and the transitory quality of life for the Jewish prisoners. Even the infant's journey to death is symbolically imbued with life as we follow her "swimming through the air . . . like a butterfly touching a silver vine" (9). The unnatural morbidity of the Nazi system and its environment is evoked in the humming of the electric fence and the "ash-stippled wind" (7). Butterflies yield to electrified fence as the Jewish reverence for life succumbs to the technologically charged carnage of the Nazis.

The text compounds the impact of the mother's pain by revealing her need to endure silently. With the electricity buzzing, Rosa suppresses her maternal instinct to scream and run to her child. She stifles the instinctive "wolf's screech" (10) ascending through her body. She must deny her body to save it; she must still her despairing voice and mute her grief, and she must stop her legs from running to the still child. Instead, she honors the survival instinct. To shriek and retrieve her baby's charred corpse would invite her own murder. As women have often responded to male violence with silence, so Rosa muffles her cry in the shawl, now *her* life preserver.

Although scenes of mothers witnessing the suffering and murder of their young children are a central feature of women's Holocaust writing, they are virtually absent in male Holocaust fiction, because children were segregated with women. Engaging reader sympathy through the evocation of the victimization of mothers and children is an essential feature in *Touching Evil* as well as in *The Shawl*. Norma Rosen's American women empathize with the women of the Holocaust: Jean, who expresses solidarity with the victims by remaining childless, and the pregnant Hattie, who identifies with women she learned of through the Eichmann trial: a pregnant woman on a forced march and another woman giving birth in typhus-lice-infested straw. Unlike the immediacy of the Holocaust universe in "The Shawl," Norma Rosen composes an indirect encounter, in which the characters witness the Holocaust through a fusion of documentary and art. Desire for respite from Eichmann trial testimony about the murder of mothers and children has brought the childless Jean and pregnant Hattie to the Museum of Modern Art to look at visions of holiness, statues of serene mothers surrounded by healthy, exuberant children. While the expectant mother gazes at the marble mother, a testament to human creative genius, she begins to read from a newspaper clipping covering trial testimony that shares with Ozick's portrait images of nurturing women trying, in vain, to bring some measure of relief to doomed children: "The children were covered with sores. They had diarrhea. They screamed and wept all night in the empty rooms where they had been put. There was nothing in the rooms but filthy mats full of vermin. Before dawn, our women crept among the children, trying to comfort and clean them. But there were no clean cloths, the water was icy cold. Terror had overcome them. The halls were a madhouse. When the orders were given to take the children to Auschwitz, it was as if they sensed what was in store. Then the police would go up and the children, screaming with terror, would be carried kicking and struggling to the courtyard."[6] Complementing the reported cries of the captive children is Jean's imagined hearing of a sound something like a great scream filling the silent sculpture hall and her imagined vision of the great goddesses "on broken toes with hands severed at the wrists" (223) suddenly struck blind, petrified by the testimony of human degradation. The children clinging to the mutilated marble figures now evoke Holocaust mothers and children. Rosen's integration of documentary detail and artistic empathy fuses the destructive and creative impulses of the twentieth century.

Both Ozick and Rosen make use of diction and image patterns to emphasize the gender-related suffering of the characters and their ways of coping. Ozick uses breast imagery to emphasize the female nature of women's Holocaust experience: Rosa, no longer able to nurse because of malnutrition, agonizes over her incapacity to provide nourishment for her infant. Anxiety about Magda's danger from starvation or electrocution is conveyed through references to teat and nipple: "Magda relinquished Rosa's teats . . . both were cracked, not a sniff of milk. The duct-crevice extinct, a dead volcano, blind eye, chill hole, so Magda took the corner of the shawl and milked it instead" (4) And when Magda walks into the roll call area, "A tide of commands hammered in Rosa's nipples" (8). Rosen's propensity for mixing Holocaust images with those of procreation and sexuality earned her Edward Alexander's condemnation for having "a womb's eye view" of the Holocaust and being "diverted by the temptations of analogy, of heavy symbolism, and feminist topicality."[7] Far from distracting, this rhetoric provides the authentic voice by which Rosen's women understand and claim the Holocaust. It is, indeed, through feminine language and imagery that Jean and Hattie connect humanely and elementally to their concentration camp sisters.

Like a number of other American writers who have not experienced the Holocaust directly, Rosen delineates the Holocaust sphere indirectly. Her American women respond to the victims' experiences through their own experience of pain. Hattie's childbirth and Jean's rape provide them with a means to imagine the pain and violation European Jewry suffered. Although Rosen deliberately removes her novel from the place and time of the Holocaust, the event is intended to be an experience that is felt, not an abstraction. Her language with its emphasis on sexuality and biology is intrinsic to her female characters' will to remember the suffering of women in the Holocaust. To suggest, as Nora Sayre does, that Rosen is making a feminist assertion that hospitals, or labor rooms in particular, are like concentration camps, is to ignore their role as objective correlative, as Hattie's postwar referent for the helplessness and vulnerability of the camp inmate.[8] Hattie's commiseration with a helpless patient subjected to the cruel indifference of an overworked inner-city hospital intern gains significance because it provides another connection with the Jewish woman who was completely powerless and humiliated, giving birth in a prison barrack beneath the gaze of a booted soldier of the "master race." The American patient's "unsightly genitals, bleeding, gaping, oozing" in the presence of and at the mercy of unsympathetic white, urban medical personnel in starched uniforms are Hattie's postwar link with the Eichmann trial account of the woman "who squeezed her baby out into a world of concrete, straw, and lice" (252). And it is Hattie's acknowledgment of the Holocaust legacy that is the source of her scream of outrage: "Cursed be the booted feet. Cursed be the legs that stood on them . . . Curse the Hun heart that shit on this grace" (252–53). In this cry, Hattie gives voice to the sexist nature of Nazi persecution of Jewish women and becomes a witness for the millions of Jewish women who did not live to testify to the devastation.

The violence the fictional women endure, whether Rosa's encounter with radical evil in the concentration camp or the emotional assault that the American women experience upon exposure to Holocaust history, becomes a constant element of their consciousness. In a sense, the American women, too, are survivors: Rosa is a physical survivor, but the Americans are psychological survivors. "Rosa," the long sequel to "The Shawl," deals with the title character at fifty-eight, decades after the events recounted in the first story, as it explores the long-term effects of Holocaust trauma. Measuring time and life by the Holocaust, Rosa identifies three ages of human experience: "The life before, the life during, the life after. . . . The life after is now. The life before is our *real* life, at home, where we was born" (58). "During" is, of course, the Nazi era. For Rosa, "Before is a dream. After is a joke. Only during stays and to call it a life is a lie" (58). Rosa is unable either to repress or to express Holocaust memories, and mourns perpetually for her lost child. Unlike parents who lose their children to natural causes or accident and are granted time to withdraw temporarily from routine activities, to grieve and express their anguish, Holocaust victims were imprisoned in silence.

Ozick dramatizes the severity of Rosa's lasting torment by contrasting her continued suffering with Stella's apparent recovery. Although Stella has no dramatic role in the narrative, she functions as Rosa's psychological foil. We do not know whether Stella is free of Holocaust trauma because she is kept offstage and we do not enter her thoughts and dreams, but we do get an inkling of her post-Holocaust adjustment in her letters to Rosa and in Rosa's commentary on them. In contrast to Rosa's fixation on the past, Stella focuses on school, career plans, and personal goals. Emblematic of their antithetical attitudes is Stella's gift of a striped dress to Rosa. Rosa, baffled and pained, concludes that Stella is acting "as if innocent, as if ignorant, as if *not there*" (33). To Stella, the dress is only an attractive garment; to Rosa, it is a direct link to the hated camp uniforms. Equally illustrative of their differences is Stella's embrace of English and Rosa's stubborn clinging to Polish. Rosa's faulty English, with its syntactical mis-structuring and fragmentation, evokes the Holocaust-wrought ruptures she endured. Increasingly tormented by the remembered loss of her child and frustrated by her customers' indifference on the rare occasions when she tries to communicate her feelings about the Holocaust, Rosa destroys her antique shop and is sent by Stella to recuperate in Florida. Her violent behavior abates, but there is little evidence of significant healing during the Florida respite. Mourning Magda's loss is Rosa's major preoccupation.

Rosa and Stella perceive each other as mentally ill. Their understanding of the shawl and of Magda's death could hardly be more different. For Rosa, the shawl is a holy emblem of her child; for Stella, it is Rosa's "trauma," "fetish," "idol," and she compares Rosa's adulation of the shawl to that of a benighted medieval worshiper of a false relic. Rosa pretends to accept Magda's death to appease Stella and convince her that she is sane. Yet her behavior reveals her delusion that Magda lives. Stella knows Rosa is trapped in the Holocaust and urges her to emerge from her self-imposed prison: "It's thirty years, forty . . . give it a rest" (31). In her letter chastising Rosa for worshiping the shawl, she warns, "One more public outburst puts you in the bughouse" (32–33). Stella's harsh words reinforce Rosa's charge of heartlessness, except in her last sentence, where she urges Rosa, "Live your life!" (33).

Rosa and Stella represent antithetical survivor roles. Rosa resembles survivors in the psychiatric literature who are plagued by associations and memories in their waking hours and by nightmares during sleep. Her survival is bitter: the hell of failed communication both with those who evade her Holocaust testimony and with those who would exploit her history; the hell of lost family, lost aspirations, lost language, lost life. Separated from the family she loved, the culture she loved, the language she loved, Rosa views life as a chain of dismal encounters that differ only in degree. She says, "Once I thought the worst was the worst, after that nothing could be the worst. But now I see, even after the worst there's still more" (14). From Rosa's perspective, Stella is free of Holocaust memories and anxieties because she consciously represses them and believes in the possibility of a new world. Rosa repudiates Stella's attitudes. In letters to the daughter she imagines is still alive, and in conversations with her Florida acquaintance, Persky, Rosa charges that "Stella is self-indulgent. She wants to wipe out memory" (58).

Ozick illustrates the survivor's tendency to experience postwar life through the Holocaust prism in a scene in which Rosa strays onto a private beach surrounded by a barbed wire fence. Rosa, like other survivors, experiences terror when encountering images that trigger Holocaust memories. She rebukes the hotel manager, insisting that barbed wire fences are inappropriate in American society. "'Only Nazis,'" she charges, "'catch innocent people behind barbed wire'" (51). When the manager treats her as a nuisance, she asks, "'Where were you when we was there?'" (51), challenging his ethics and, by implication, challenging others guilty of complicity whether by omission or commission.

Rosa's room and personal appearance reflect her unhealed trauma. She lives temporarily in a sparsely furnished unkempt hotel room described as "a dark hole" (13). The bed is unmade, "covers knotted together like an umbilical cord" (30) and the room smells of fish. A disconnected telephone attests to her alienation. Rather than taking meals at the oak table, she eats in bed or standing at the sink. Her diet, visually unappetizing and far from nutritious, is emblematic of self-imposed deprivation motivated by survivor guilt or remembrance of those who perished from starvation. Rosa's physical appearance complements her room and signifies her diminished interest in life. Hair askew, button missing from her dress, she is "the reflection of a ragged old bird with worn feathers.

Skinny, a stork" (22). Ozick dramatically contrasts Rosa's usually slovenly room and disheveled personal appearance to her frenzied, yet deliberate, cleaning of the room and donning of freshly laundered clothing in anticipation of a package from Stella containing Magda's shawl, behavior evocative of the sacred attitude she assumes toward her martyred child. That Rosa exists in the present but lives in the past is conveyed in letters to Magda and rare conversations with living acquaintances. "Without a life," Rosa says, "a person lives where they can. If all they got is thoughts, that's where they live" (27–28). Rosa's suffering may be related to Robert Jay Lifton's connection between survivor guilt and "death guilt." He argues that the guilt is a response to the question "Why did I survive, while others died?" Lifton contends: "Part of the survivors' sense of horror is the memory of their own inactivation—helplessness—within the death imagery, of their inability to act in a way they would ordinarily have thought appropriate (save people, resist the victimizers, etc.) or even feel the appropriate emotions. . . . Death guilt begins, then, in the gap between that physical and psychic inactivation and what one feels called upon to do and feel. That is one reason why the imagery keeps recurring, in dreams and in waking life."[9] Ozick's survivor portrait also embodies the findings of Jack Terry, who identifies unresolved mourning as a characteristic of traumatic Holocaust experience: "In concentration camps, mourning would have been impossible even if it had been permitted. Grief in itself threatens the integrity of the ego, and under circumstances in which the intensity of the affect is too great or the ego has been so weakened—both of which were the case in the Holocaust—mourning cannot take place. Thus, the attachment to the lost object remains unresolved."[10]

Henry Krystal's explanation of survivors engaging in "various forms of denial, idealization, and . . . 'walling off'" in response to inability to mourn the loss of a child finds expression in Ozick's Rosa.[11] Self-preservation demanded silence at the time of Magda's murder, and Rosa suffers the trauma of her infant's death decades later. Her denial of Magda's death and her invention of a mature Magda with a prosperous adult life epitomize the behavior chronicled in the psychiatric literature. In letters addressing Magda as "snow queen," "yellow blossom," "cup of sun," and "soul's blessing," vibrant language negating her child's terrible death, Rosa supplants reality with imagination. Three such restoration reveries reveal her desire for the life that should have been. She imagines Magda as a lovely young girl of sixteen at the threshold of adulthood; at thirty-one, a physician married to another physician with a large house in a New York suburb; and as a professor of Greek philosophy at a prestigious university. Because Magda's imagined lives are more real to Rosa than her death, Stella's insistence on Magda's death seems aberrant. But to placate Stella, Rosa "pretends" that Magda is dead. Her imagined constructions simultaneously address her need to deny Magda's murder and provide herself, in the imagined living daughter, with a nonjudgmental confidante to whom she can express post-Holocaust despair.

Psychological and psychiatric literature identify paranoia, suspicion, and emotional isolation and distance manifested by unwillingness to forge emotional connections as symptoms of survivor syndrome. Ozick dramatizes these responses by contrasting her survivor with a pre-Holocaust immigrant foil, Mr. Persky, whom Rosa meets in a Miami laundromat. Mr. Persky is socially engaged, trusting, at ease with his peers. Rosa has felt separate from Miami Jews, historically and socially alienated, convinced that, "Everything stayed the same for them: intentions, actions, even expectations" (28). Painfully aware of the gulf separating her from Persky, who emigrated from Warsaw decades before the Holocaust, she tells him, "'My Warsaw isn't your Warsaw'" (19). Not having known Poland in wartime, he cannot share Holocaust memories. Moreover, because his experience is limited to escape from nongenocidal Polish anti-Semitism and a circumscribed standard of living, he fails to understand the magnitude of Rosa's trauma. He exclaims: "'You ain't in a camp. It's finished. Long ago it's finished'" (58). But for Rosa it is not finished. Her pain endures. Profound lack of understanding, like Persky's, leads some survivors to fashion their own psychological prison, isolating themselves among their own kind, suspicious and distrusting of nonsurvivors.

Ozick, who believes in *t'shuva,* the redemptive Judaic faith in the individual's capacity to change, dramatizes in Rosa a dawning sense of this regenerative possibility. Herein lies our hope for Rosa. When Rosa discovers that she has wrongly suspected Persky of stealing her underpants in the laundromat, she forgoes detachment in favor of communication and begins to tell him her Holocaust history. Emblematic of Rosa's new trust is her order to reconnect her telephone, her call to Stella about returning to New York, and her reception of Persky as her guest. These small gestures suggest a turning point. More certain signs that healing is under way are Rosa's diminished interest in the shawl when it finally comes, and her realization that she is perpetuating a fantasy. When Persky arrives at her hotel, "Magda was not there. Shy, she ran from Persky. Magda was away" (70). Earlier in the novella, Rosa would have dismissed Persky rather than delay her imagined encounter with Magda. By the narrative's end, although she invites Magda's return, she responds to the immediate presence of the living. And in her willing social association with a person she had earlier disdained, she is on the road to a more complete recovery.

Jean, Norma Rosen's protagonist, is a survivor of a different sort, a psychological survivor who discovers that her life is radically altered by Holocaust knowledge: "Nothing of her life would, after she learned of the existence of the death camps, be as before." [12] For a considerable time, the mere mention of the words "concentration camps" was, Jean testifies, occasion for desolation. "My body and soul emptied out. I was ready to faint, to fall down. I marveled at anyone who remained standing" (77). At the end of the war, when others sought to return to prewar pursuits, Jean elected sacrifice: refusal to generate life in a universe of death. Marriage and motherhood no longer had meaning for her. That Jean's Holocaust epiphany occurred while making love and that her response is refusal to bear children is illustrative of her feminist political rebuttal to Holocaust history. Confronted by the reality of human evil, by the millions of gassed and burned bodies, the American woman shares the position of some survivors who refused to bring children into a Holocaust-corrupted world. In rejecting the maternal role for herself, Jean allies herself with her European sisters who lost their children and testifies to humanity's loss of Jewish progeny. Through this politically symbolic act, Jean makes the catastrophe her own.

The Eichmann trial serves as catalyst for Jean's reevaluation of her acceptance of the Holocaust as her own personal catastrophe. Despite considerable temporal distance from the event, she discovers that, contrary to expectations of release from Holocaust obsession, she is forcefully reclaimed by history. Sharing the trial with Hattie is for Jean a reiteration of her initial Holocaust despair. Her mind and heart are violated once more. Almost two decades after the initial trauma, Jean still feels surrounded by corpses. The horrors reappear, not instantaneously in a unified photographic composition, but piecemeal in daily doses of devastation: "machine guns punching bullet holes," "clubs beating against bone" (209), visions of the starving and screaming, bodies forever falling, piercing the psyches of heretofore immune Americans.

The Holocaust's continuing effect on future generations is conveyed through the fact that Hattie, too, becomes absorbed in the trial. As the trial progresses, the pregnant Hattie is at once physical foil and emotional double to the intentionally childless Jean. Astonished by the trial revelations, Hattie concurs with Jean's judgment that the Nazis defiled life itself, and she too expresses reservations about propagating the species. The trial is Hattie's initial Holocaust exposure, Jean's second exposure, and the author's affirmation that the Holocaust must not be conveniently put to rest for any of us.

An early title for this novel, *Heart's Witness,* reflects the importance Rosen assigns to the attestor role of the women. They are witnesses observing other witnesses who have come forward to testify in the Eichmann trial. Hattie's response to the television coverage of the trial echoes Jean's earlier reaction to postwar newspaper pictures of the camps. The younger woman absorbs the Holocaust experience, takes it thoroughly into her consciousness, into her body. "Hattie drinks in the words ... sucks up the images ... Her shoulders watch, her knees watch. Her fetus thrusts forward to watch" (68). For the Hatties and Jeans of the world, suffering will not heal with time; the dead will not depart from their thoughts, but burrow in.

Repudiation of God or, at the very least, anger for divine passivity in the face of absolute evil, is a characteristic response in Holocaust literature. Like the protesting Jews in the works of Elie Wiesel and I. B. Singer, Rosen's non-Jews agonize over God's responsibility for the six million. Jean Lamb offers vitriolic denunciation of the merciless God of Auschwitz: "God of the medical-experiment cell block ... God of the common lime pit grave ... God of chopped fingers ... of blinded eyes, God of electrodes attached at one end to a jeep battery and at the other to the genitals of political prisoners" (233). Countercommentary is used by Jewish writers to parallel liturgical and Holocaust disruption. Rosen echoes this technique with a prayer parody that replaces the traditional divine attributes of mercy and justice with diction connoting divine passivity in the face of Holocaust crimes. Hattie's transformation to nonbeliever is charted in her reactions in response to the trial: first personal relief, then an expression of doubt, and finally her identification with Holocaust horror: *"There but for the grace of God and there is no grace of God, we see that there is none — so I go sideslipping into the life of that woman who gave birth in the typhus-infected straw"* (131). And when Hattie asks whether God sees us, the older initiate responds, "It seems irrelevant ... Isn't it enough that we see each other? Witnessing and being witnessed without end?" (238).

Both Ozick and Rosen are concerned with the problems related to Holocaust remembrance and transmission. Expression of Holocaust memories and thoughts is difficult not only for its physical victims but also for those who choose to examine its relevance to the human condition. Sidney Bolkosky says that one problem that interviewers regularly encounter is the survivor's inability to find "proper words to express unimaginable and exhausting memories"; they describe the "paralyzing, dumbfounding difficulty: the poverty of language to convey emotion and unreal reality": "At the semantic . . . level lurk deeply hidden or repressed meanings; at the narrative level, the tone and style conceal complex emotions, memories, and associations. In the end, we must be resigned to the human inability to duplicate or assimilate those meanings and memories."[13] Sensitive to these difficulties, Cynthia Ozick dramatizes Rosa's reluctance and incapacity to communicate her Holocaust experience to strangers. The survivor knows that even those who invite her to speak are without the frame of reference to understand what she says. People sympathetic to survivors distress Rosa, for she believes that they perceive her one-dimensionally, as a refugee, "like a number—counted apart from the ordinary swarm. Blue digits on the arm" (36). Rosa's initial response to an American Jew's invitation to unburden herself is silence. She cannot communicate the incommunicable. Poverty of language is at the heart of Rosa's inexpressiveness. No satisfactory analogy exists. Driven inward, Rosa's authentic voice emerges in her Polish letters to her daughter conveying pre-Holocaust pleasure and plenty, Holocaust era deprivation and degradation, and post-Holocaust angst and anger.

Convinced that writers should make moral judgments, Ozick asserts the continuity of immorality by linking Polish disregard for Jewish suffering during the Holocaust with postwar American Holocaust amnesia. Rosa remembers, "The most ordinary citizens going from one section of Warsaw to another, ran straight into the place of our misery. Every day, and several times a day, we had these witnesses" (68). Similarly, American indifference to Holocaust history prompts Rosa to observe: "I wanted to tell everybody . . . Nobody knew anything. This amazed me, that nobody remembered what happened only a little while ago" (66).

That the Holocaust legacy continues is evidenced in Rosen's portrayal of characters immersed in the Eichmann trial two decades after the atrocities were committed, and in Hattie's bequeathing of this inheritance to her daughter and to her readers. In the scenario for the play she is writing, Hattie casts her daughter as the reincarnation of an infant victim among other young victims: "New children. . . . New births. . . . New joys. . . . Centuries and centuries and centuries of joyful births and terrible deaths" (237). Thus, the pattern of transmission is established for another generation; as it has been passed down from Jean to Hattie, so it will be from Hattie to her daughter. Each woman bears witness creatively, Jean in her diary-letters and Hattie in manuscripts for a play, a memoir, a novel.

Hattie's writing, incorporated as long italicized interludes in Jean's letters, becomes the life force of Jean's childless existence.

Holocaust images and references permeate the lives of Jean and Hattie, and Holocaust associations inform their thinking and their speech. Contemporary events, people, and conditions are correlated with Holocaust categories and definitions. A personal betrayal is "like telling the police where Anne Frank is hiding" (60); a person of ignoble behavior is described as "a gold tooth salvager" (60), or "an informer" (60). A skeletal Chinese laundryman is likened to "the near-corpses of last evening's televised trial" (43), and seen, in the mind's eye, stretched out on the freezing shelves with camp inmates whose will to live had been destroyed. Characteristic of Rosen's powerful merging of present experience with Holocaust perception is Jean's walk through the urban renewal project. As she stumbles over broken pavement, the trial legacy floods her consciousness and the walker through rubble becomes the digger through corpses. In this fleeting moment of free association, Rosen portrays the pervasive impact of the Holocaust on post-Holocaust sensibility. Jean, for whom the 1944 image of American soldiers evacuating "stick bodies, two and three to an armful" (78) initiated new consciousness, is the woman for whom the Vietnam era confirms that the evil of Nazism continues as an ever present specter.

That the Holocaust alarms so few people profoundly distresses Jean and her author as it does Ozick's Rosa. Jean had expected the Holocaust to evoke general horror comparable to that expressed in Picasso's *Guernica*. Instead, she discovered that there was virtual indifference to the destruction of European Jewry on her college campus, when the school president spoke of "troubled times," and campus life proceeded as usual. Representative of the larger world's apathy are the attitudes of the men most closely associated with Jean and Hattie. Hattie's husband, Ezra, is a photographer aesthetically distanced from flesh and blood, devoted instead to pleasing patterns. Jean's absent lover, Loftus, is (as his name suggests) above these concerns. When Hattie turns to him for an explanation of evil in the world, he brings the two women together to enable Hattie to get through the trial. Loftus, like most people who had lived through the Holocaust era, does not comprehend it any better as it is reiterated in the course of the Eichmann trial. His anxiety is not for the victims but for the sensibilities of a student who just might lose her joie de vivre if she succumbs to "the horrors of the monster's cave" (28). Yet it is, of course, through the clouded lens of the Holocaust that Ozick and Rosen insist we now must view human existence and measure radical evil.

Rosen forces her readers to consider the implications of the Holocaust for all of us. Like Jean before her, Hattie refuses to be lulled to indifference, to dismiss the Holocaust from her mind because it happened to other people. For Hattie, and others like her, the philosophical implications of the Holocaust remain. One cannot simply curse the Nazis and forget them: "Their possibilities are always with us" (84). Rosen poses the crucial question of our time: since the Nazis "passed for human beings, what does that say about human beings?" (84). Rosen's charge to her readers is that succeeding generations must encounter the consequences of Germany's legacy of shame: "A poison went into the atmosphere. Just as when an atomic bomb explodes. Each generation in turn will be sickened, poisoned with disgust for the human race" (84).

The moral injunction to remember collective history, central to Jewish thinking, is also central to Ozick's "Rosa." She not only confirms appropriate memory in Rosa's legitimate anger and healing sequences, but extends her commentary on Holocaust transmission and scholarship to condemn inappropriate transmittal. To convey the latter, she constructs a scathing satiric portrait of an unethical scholar who wants "to observe survivor syndroming within the natural setting" (38). In a jargon-strewn letter to Rosa, void of any sympathetic sensibility, Dr. Tree describes his interest in Rosa's camp experience for use in his study on repressed animation. Rosa sees him as a parasite and is offended at being addressed as a lab specimen. She is fully aware that Dr. Tree views her merely as a figure with "blue digits on the arm," and she condemns his intent to exploit her pain and is outraged by his assertion that he plans to write the definitive work on the subject, "to close the books so to speak on this lamentable subject" (36, 37). Tree's letter shows him to be insufferably arrogant, intellectually misguided, and insensitive. Although Rosa clearly wished to have an audience for her testimony, she refuses to dishonor that testimony by offering it to an inappropriate recorder whose misappropriation of Holocaust memory would be a disservice to history and Holocaust victims.

Holocaust transmission is a secondary theme in "Rosa," but it is of primary importance in *Touching Evil*. Rosen's narrative gives voice to Holocaust victims through survivor trial testimony and writing by American surrogate witnesses, Jean's letters and diary entries, and Hattie's journals, plays, and novel. The passage between receiving the news and making it one's own, between listening and telling, is traversed as Jean's memory is sparked by trial testimony. Acting both as Jean's foil and as her double, Hattie formally assumes the task of Holocaust transmission to the next generation. Transferal of the appalling tale leads to Rosen's narrative design of manuscript within manuscript within manuscript as readers experience Hattie's diary entries and writing strategies through the medium of Jean's letters.

A generation after the Holocaust, we possess a body of imaginative literature that struggles to comprehend an unparalleled evil. Cynthia Ozick and Norma Rosen have made significant contributions to that endeavor by demonstrating how lives are changed by the knowledge of Holocaust evil: Ozick through the survivor's voice and Rosen through the creation of American women who choose to bear "witness through the imagination." [14]

Notes

1. Cynthia Ozick, "Toward a New Yiddish," 174.

2. For a full analysis of Ozick's Holocaust works, aside from *The Shawl*, see S. Lillian Kremer, "The Dybbuk of All the Lost Dead."

3. Norma Rosen, "The Holocaust and the American-Jewish Novelist," 58.

4. Ibid., 57, 59. The Rosen sections of this essay are derived from S. Lillian Kremer, "The Holocaust in Our Time: Norma Rosen's *Touching Evil*."

5. Cynthia Ozick, "The Shawl," *The Shawl* (New York: Knopf, 1989), 4. Subsequent references to the two works in this collection will be given in parentheses in the text.

6. Norma Rosen, *Touching Evil* (New York: Harcourt, Brace, and World, 1969, rpt. Wayne State Univ. Press, 1990), 224. Subsequent references in the text are to the 1969 edition. This passage has much in common with a description of young French Jewish orphans being prepared for deportation from Drancy to Auschwitz in the historic account of the fate of French Jewry under Nazi occupation. See Claude Levy and Paul Tillard, *Betrayal at the Vel d'Hiv*, 157.

7. Edward Alexander, *The Resonance of Dust*, 132.

8. Nora Sayre, review of *Touching Evil*, 26.

9. Robert Jay Lifton, "The Concept of the Survivor," quoted in George Kren, "The Holocaust Survivor and Psychoanalysis," 70.

10. Jack Terry, "The Damaging Effects of the 'Survivor Syndrome,'" 145.

11. Henry Krystal, "Integration and Self-Healing in Post-traumatic States," 125.

12. Rosen, "The Holocaust," 58.

13. Sidney M. Bolkosky, "Interviewing Victims Who Survived," 34.

14. Rosen, "The Holocaust," 58.

VÈVÈ A. CLARK

Dangerous Admissions: Opening Stages to Violence, Anger, and Healing in African Diaspora Theater

> The constitution of a performance text, separate but equal to the written one, implies new dimensions in the co-production of the text. The importance of the author's intent gives way to the conditions of production and the composition of the audience in determining the meaning of the theatrical event. This implies that there is no aesthetic closure around the text, separating it from the conditions of its production. The performance text is constituted by the location of the theatre, the price of the ticket, the attitude of the ushers and the response of the audience as well as by the written dialogue and stage directions.
>
> —Sue-Ellen Case, *Feminism and Theatre*

Domination of any human being by another is a symptom of disease. From the era of colonialism, through capitalism to post–Cold War politics, some of us manage to survive unscathed in systems where the exercise of power among elites creates and condones the existence of a bottomless economic and emotional region filled with abuse, alienation, and self-hatred. I would argue that in such environments black women of the diaspora have been cast into the imperiled species category of the human. When women and men of the African diaspora speak publicly about the violence occurring around them, they become doubly victimized as messengers and for the indictments contained in the message. When the forum for disclosure is theater, there is "no aesthetic closure around the text," as Sue-Ellen Case suggests. Rather, revealing abuse in public endangers both creator and performer by subjecting them to hostile attacks by those seeking to maintain the dominance of a power structure that they mimic. To portray abusers symbolically on stage, without naming them directly as a form of agitprop might do, does not automatically protect playwrights or actors from censorship or reprisals. But display we must in order to reveal the contours of the malady. Ultimately, then, these admissions in performance allow the audience as well to take part in a process of healing.

Theater has remained a primal site of catharsis for millennia despite cultural differences and time frames. The genre is the quintessential medium for shedding light, literally, on the unspeakable; from *Oedipus Rex* to *Antigone in Creole,* traditions of representing silenced violence against the body and its politic persist.[1] Within French theater history alone, this truism displays a variety of perspectives and philosophies, beginning in the eighteenth century with theatrical street acts of terror during the French Revolution, leading in the twentieth century to Antonin Artaud's Theater of Cruelty from the 1930s and Jean Genêt's *Les Nègres* in 1958.[2] Within political theater, violence and anger appear as recurring themes and as modes of expression affecting the very structure of performance. Moreover, theoretical rereadings of classic and contemporary theater works in the late twentieth century have demonstrated the extent to which the very subject positions of these dramas have reproduced national, racial, class, and gender biases. Recent studies such as Sue-Ellen Case's *Feminism and Theatre* (1988), for instance, reveal how women have been silenced in theater but also how they have created ingenious methods for inserting their collective concerns onto the stages of the world.

Focusing on five theater works by authors from the African diaspora in the United States and the Caribbean, written between 1972 and 1987, I examine the range of themes and dramatic structures that have opened performance to representations of violence and anger within different New World black communities. From text to performance, methods of revealing anger evolve along a continuum of innovation in the following texts: Maryse Condé's *Dieu nous l'a donné* (God's Gift, 1972), Simone Schwarz-Bart's *Ton beau capitaine* (Your Handsome Captain, 1987), Frankétienne's *Kaselezo* (Womb Water's Breaking, 1987), Ntozake Shange's *For Colored Girls Who Have Considered Suicide / When the Rainbow Is Enuf* (1976), and Sistren's *Bellywoman Bangarang* (1978).[3] Incest, rape, adultery predominate as topoi seeking spaces for healing among the implied audiences of these works. These seemingly women-centered issues are set, nonetheless, within broader arenas of abuse occurring because of national, racial, or class background. Abuse is not gender specific; victimizers are not monolithic. As the twentieth century comes to a close, victims seem to be everywhere, and repressed anger is exploding daily into violent private and public acts approaching global anarchy.

Dangerous admissions in theater require that we name the violence publicly, inviting others to witness the display as a form of healing. Within the African diaspora, Haitians have had a long tradition of relying on drama rather than on other genres to portray in three dimension disturbing issues that might have aired elsewhere. In 1796 when a select group of mulattoes staged a private production of *La liberté générale* (General Emancipation in Cap-François), they were protesting French revolutionary efforts of 1794 to demolish the system of slavery. In their opinion, the legislation did not incriminate those Frenchmen who had profited from slave labor nor did it recognize that general emancipation would have restricted their already freed status by granting the same to the general populace of slaves in Saint-Domingue. By staging such a virulent indictment of the French absentee planter class and by publishing their audacious representation of reality as they saw it to be, they were talking back to an implied planter class of French readers who might have fathered them in the Caribbean.[4] As Jean Fouchard, the late Haitian theater scholar has noted, admission to performances of *La liberté* was restricted to the converted for fear of reprisals against the author and audiences alike in a problematic climate of revolution emerging in France's stellar colony. The sole copy of the text surviving in the Bibliothèque Nationale in Paris is signed anonymously by a certain "Citizen B."[5]

The threat of impending censorship of performances criticizing the status quo resurfaced during the 1930s and 1940s as a result of the American Marine occupation of Haiti from 1915 to 1934. Plays by Dominique Hippolyte, *Le forçat* (The Prisoner, 1929), and Roger Dorsinville, *Barrières* (Barriers, 1945), represented on stage the silenced public discourse on American racism during the occupation and color prejudices among the Haitian elite. As one might expect, the performances were suppressed.[6]

Censorship by government authorities plays only a small part in the silencing. Self-censorship continues among writers, among the oppressed, among women, perhaps because we have not identified those spaces where speaking, writing, performing, and healing violence might converge comfortably, at least in the initial stages of unsilencing. Among women, revealing abuse typically begins within close female friendships. We give voice first to those we trust, finding often in the process a shared set of experiences, a compassion for the hearing that lightens and illuminates the burden of pain and silence left over from childhood or young womanhood. Shange's *For Colored Girls* exemplifies the process of moving out of silence from private to public, from journal entries (the stand-in friend) to recitations, the Broadway stage, and finally to audiences of women who memorized those sections of the play that reflected their own anger. During the 1970s, *For Colored Girls* belonged to the consciousness-raising efforts of the American women's movement beyond the boundaries of class, race, and rage.[7]

Shange's play demonstrates two theoretical principles in feminist theater identified by Sue-Ellen Case in her chapter "Towards a New Poetics." Although Case questions the concept of feminine morphology or feminine form as an essentializing homogenization of women's experiences, she describes the circumstances when feminine morphology might be used or abandoned to raise consciousness.[8] Provocation and dialogue, both of which are present in *For Colored Girls*, are two strategies of communication that feminist playwrights and critics might employ within conservative academic environments or among the already converted:

> When used as a provocation, this morphological notion could invoke
> a defense of the traditional codes, raising questions concerning the
> canon and the structure of dramatic interpretation within the
> parameters of an alternative feminist tradition. Again, such a
> morphology might provide a way to push for a re-evaluation of
> women's work in the theatre, both by demonstrating the existence of
> a distinctively feminine form and by exposing the bastions of male
> privilege in the arts as political defenses against it. . . . On the other
> hand, in dialogue with feminists who valorize the gender inscription in
> the feminine morphology, the same critic might utilize the materialist
> analysis of form. In this case, she could raise the issues of race and
> class which are so important to the understanding and reception of
> works by women of color and working-class women, and which have
> such a strong bearing on their relationship to the theatre.[9]

In retrospect, I would suggest that *For Colored Girls* caused such a strong response because, theoretically, the text was double-voiced: it provoked a reassessment of black nationalist, male-centered dramas and films of the 1970s; it invoked feminist testimonies of love, lust, anger, and violence coinciding with one woman's response as a poet to Black Power ideology.

Both Shange and the Sistren Collective from Jamaica reformed their anger into rites of passage for actors and audiences alike. Their efforts to expose abuse publicly were not new. For centuries, women have gathered around the well or water spigot where these sanctioned areas of *commu-*

nitas allowed them space and time to express the unspoken in their private lives. Women have done so throughout the African diaspora knowing that their complaints might be told again behind the back. Jamaicans call this type of womanspeak *labrish* or gossip; among Haitians the term is *telediol (teleguele* in Creole), open to both women and men. In urban areas, the playground or neighborhood games and double Dutch rhymes have provided sites in which the unspeakable in children's lives emerges through improvisation, and new discourses enter into discreet traditions.

Unlike established rites of initiation in Africa, such as clitoridectomy or mutilation of a young girl's genitals, the games, codes, and signs displayed in these texts emerge as shared voices among age sets of the same generation horizontally, rather than from elderwomen who might have accepted the violence and repressed anger as their right to initiate and control the next generation of young women.[10] As contemporary texts move from provocation to dialogue to ritual, we learn that theater as a genre offers a unique place for women to transgress publicly against personal, collective, and symbolic violence. Repressed anger in drama appears in the Condé and Schwarz-Bart works; recipes for healing through collective creation, psychodrama, and oral histories are clearly represented by Frankétienne, Shange, and Sistren.

Where Are Women in the Texts? Condé and Schwarz-Bart

The plays by Condé and Schwarz-Bart, authors from Guadeloupe better known for their novels, share an ideology of provocation. Both present males as protagonists, thereby banishing female characters into the shadows of dramatic action. In the case of Condé's *Dieu nous l'a donné* (1972), the drama is a critique of the black nationalism emerging in the DOMS (Overseas Departments of France) during the 1970s and of histories of male-centered revolt from the Haitian revolution through Négritude and contemporary examples within the African diaspora. Schwarz-Bart's *Ton beau capitaine* (1987) addresses recent problems of immigration policies among men who migrate for better jobs from Haiti to the DOMS, and who must adapt to unexpected substandard labor conditions and extended separation from their families back home. The key word in each setting is "deplorable": morally corrupt in a small village; isolated deeply in one man's shack. The male protagonists, Dieudonné and Wilnor, are each separated from their original communities by choice, setting stages for tragic or ambivalent endings to their problems of resettlement. Each of these texts suggests that abuse of working-class black women in the emigration process is secondary as subject to male rebellion and exile.

Dieu nous l'a donné was Condé's second play, one of seven written between 1970 and 1989. *Dieu* belongs to the tradition of the Theater of Cruelty elaborated by Artaud in 1938.[11] Through the use of abrasive language, Condé illustrates torment among individuals residing in Grande Anse, an insulated village, an outpost to which the criminals and sexual deviants of nearby cities have been banished. Dieudonné, a physician returning home after ten years of study in France, chooses this village rather than his own town in which to practice medicine. He sees himself as a budding revolutionary, and yet he has not decolonized his mind or developed a personal morality befitting his return in order to minister as physician and leader to a chosen people who are and remain derelict and depraved. At moments in the drama, Dieudonné's actions remind us of the Black Muslims, Eldridge Cleaver, and the Black Panthers—combinations of naïveté and righteous zeal. Dieudonné is also the "been-to" revolutionary modeled on Frantz Fanon's biography and Jacques Roumain's protagonist in *Gouverneurs de la rosée* (Masters of the Dew, 1946). Condé's approach negates the optimism with which these earlier texts envisioned transformation of communities in pain. None of the redemptive qualities surviving Manuel's sacrifice in *Masters* appears in the text. Instead, Dieudonné is murdered as a matter of feeling at the end of this five-act drama, leaving the residents of Grande Anse as deeply ensconced in poverty and promiscuity as they were before his return to a modified version of Aimé Césaire's native land.

As Dieudonné seeks to lead a revolution among the disaffected with the assistance of the town's *quimboiseur* (healer), Mendela, he is compromised in his efforts by involvement in the very sexual license against which he preaches. Ignoring preexisting sexual relationships in the village, Dieudonné sleeps with Gastonia and reveals to her his plans to organize, against the power structure, workers exploited and left unemployed by the mayor, Laborderie. When Gastonia reveals her newest lover's secrets to her longtime paramour, Mayor Laborderie, her words upset the promise of revolution at its outset. By conflating sex with political action, Condé's text demonstrates how ill-prepared Dieudonné and the villagers are to decipher and execute strategies for social change.

Condé develops each of the major characters in depth, by depicting their emotional instabilities and rigid class biases. Psychological interpretations of this kind were unacceptable in Artaud's Theater of Cruelty because he associated such depictions with outmoded nineteenth-century forms typical of bourgeois playwrights. Condé's revisions of Artaud's theories are culture- rather than character-specific, drawing the reader into an insular, island mentality rarely exposed in twentieth-century drama. Moreover, her analysis of and descent into the personal avoids the didactic ethos surrounding Artaud's Theater of Cruelty. Ultimately, the drama invites us to identify with a collective story of deprivation, prostitution, and incest among the villagers of Grande Anse that offers little hope for substantial change.

But where are the women characters situated in the text? Given the significant roles of Gastonia and Maeva, as well as the constant references to absent mothers and surrogates, we might define Condé's depictions as peri-feminist, several beats away from the feminist movement as it was then developing in the United States. The violence inflicted upon Condé's women comes to us through the words of others; they do not speak directly of abuse. Rarely do these women appear on stage alone beyond the gaze of men. Guy Tirolien's comment in his introduction to the published version of the play about the "fundamental misogyny of the author" is in part accurate, although misguided in that he equates the messenger with the message.[12] Condé seems to be documenting the deep misogyny surrounding nationalist movements throughout the diaspora in the 1970s. Recent testimonies about the abuse of women by male members of the Black Panther Party in the United States substantiate the documentary and visionary statements in the text, because every character in *Dieu* is using someone else for her or his escape from reality or dreams of social mobility.[13] Women's bodies become resources for flirtation, copulation, incest, and all sorts of unrequited desires set within the context of a Caribbean nation still colonized, cannibalizing the women citizens of its body politic. In contrast to broader issues addressed in the drama, the style and structure of the play are insular and enclosed, more literary than performative and filled with allusions to Caribbean history and culture. It is difficult to imagine how a director might break through the walls of violence, anger, and silence submerged neatly in the text.

Writing fifteen years later, Simone Schwarz-Bart has left more space for a woman's voice to be represented, in this case, beyond the written word. Although she uses a documentary style reminiscent of Condé's approach in *Dieu,* she does so by combining two different performance modes that are realistic and symbolic. As a result, fact and fantasy portray simultaneously the lives of Haitian agricultural laborers residing in Guadeloupe. The realistic, even naturalistic, depictions of one worker's plight appear all the more paradoxical when the author's performance techniques rely on remembered Haitian cultural practices or the understatement of Japanese Noh drama.[14]

The problem of the play reflects the chasm existing between the political economies of Haiti and the DOMS through analysis of transnational migration and disrupted communication with one's homeland. Wilnor Baptiste, the handsome captain of the title, is alienated from the society of Guadeloupe, to which he has migrated to find work. He is a pariah whose sole means of communication with his family in Haiti is through audiotapes hand-delivered by fellow workers who can afford to travel back and forth. His despair and loneliness are represented in a minimalist, mimetic style: one act, one evening, a single character on stage, sparse setting. Wilnor's barren existence lends itself to Grotowski's "poor theater" techniques in which the world of work, of daylight interactions with boss, laborers, and friends is barely suggested. We meet Wilnor at night, a "husband" alone in his shack listening intently to one of the rare audiotapes he receives from his "cassette wife," Marie-Ange. Dialogue in the traditional sense is an illusion. In production, the drama is one long monologue between the voice of Marie-Ange in absentia and Wilnor's responses to her disturbing confessions on tape. Marie-Ange replies to Wilnor's fantasies of success in Guadeloupe by revealing the shame of seduction and adultery back home that have left her pregnant with another man's child.

Stylized Noh drama techniques and poor theater methods define Wilnor's migrant situation as a trope of litotes. By contrast, his fantasies of a new life are expressed through hyperbole. Beyond the ambiguities, physical separation from homeland and family are relieved momentarily through the memory of Haitian dances, drum rhythms, and songs mixed with postmodern synthesized music playing intermittently on Wilnor's cassette recorder. Productions of the play by the CAC in Guadeloupe, UBU Repertory Theatre in New York, and Rites and Reason at Brown University have captured the paradoxical uncertainty of Wilnor's emigrant status.

Like other migrant workers, Wilnor is obviously here and not there to protect his wife against a so-called friend's advances, the same person who delivered the tapes to Marie-Ange in Haiti. Wilnor is a man consumed by fantasies of a better life—new land, a cow, and a house with a veranda. Migration from Haiti to Guadeloupe creates a dream refracted and deferred. Desires sustained through physical deprivation, words spoken dishonestly, or honestly, into a talking box create an imaginary space that allows Wilnor and Marie-Ange to survive, though barely, the distance of their separation.

In the text of *Your Handsome Captain,* Schwarz-Bart has left space for reinterpretation in that Wilnor is all presence and Marie-Ange remains nothing more than a recorded voice. In the Brown University production, George Bass and Gilbert McCauley brought Marie-Ange's character on stage during a dream sequence, and though this was a departure from the written stage directions, it reminded those who knew the play how active Marie-Ange's perspective is in the text.[15] Her use of metaphorical language in her taped correspondence reshapes the passive role that women have accepted in the migration process when their men leave home. In Tableau I, Marie-Ange's voice evokes a newer world for wives abandoned and husbands wandering throughout the diaspora:

> Wilnor, I wish I were a boat sailing to Guadeloupe. Once there, you'd climb inside me, you'd walk on my decks, you'd place your hands on my frame, you'd explore me from stem to stern. And then you would set sail and I would take you to a country far, far, far away. (Pause). On the other side of the world perhaps, where people don't look at you as though you were less than nothing, dried-out coconuts. Wilnor, is there no country on earth where Haitians can work and send a little money home from time to time without being reduced to formless gusts of air? (Kourilsky and Temerson, 234)

Your Handsome Captain brings the abuse perpetrated against women to the foreground, albeit in a circuitous manner befitting the realities of migration and separation in contemporary Caribbean life and lore. The silence surrounding adultery is broken by Marie-Ange's cassette-letter and the consequences of a man leaving home refracted back across the Caribbean Sea. The "dialogue" between these characters reflects both the resentment of abandonment and the possibility of reconciliation suggested at play's end.

Who's Zoomin' Who? Negotiating Control in Theater Relationships: Fran
kétienne, Shange, Sistren

Three texts from Haiti, Afro-America, and Jamaica have represented some of the same issues addressed by Condé and Schwarz-Bart. Pregnancy and the feminist process of rebirthing the self preoccupy these dramas. Unwanted are these identities maturing into young womanhood as a result of racism, rape, abuse, or abandonment by a parent or mate. The three plays, written between 1974 and 1988, are deeply self-reflexive, concerned dually with control of women's bodies in real time and representations of abuse on stage.

As the abortion debates in the United States flowed outward into the

African diaspora during the 1970s, several performance artists depicted silenced anger using nonauthoritarian theater techniques. Collective creation was the means. Unlike the Condé and Schwarz-Bart texts, these are women-centered testimonies involving three or more actresses who tell all in Creole or versions of Black English. These dramas have demonstrated how we might transform suppressed anger in performance using as model collective creation techniques better known in Latin America.[16] The three plays belong to this tradition for several reasons, namely: commitment to representing silenced abuse of power; staging the case in a language of one's own; negotiating authorial control of the final production. When control is relaxed in collective creation dramas, theater becomes a forum for testimony.

As a consequence, the performances recreate *communitas,* as space where women feel free to recall and reenact the violence that they experienced in childhood or later. These revelations are dangerous admissions, however. Expressed publicly outside of the old, ritual venues, abuse is no longer protected by the privacy of gender-specific rituals—if such protection ever existed. The threat of male violence against women intrudes beyond performance into the arena of criticism and audience response.[17] Hostile reactions by postperformance detractors might seem to reimpose the victim role through their attempt to assert control in another form. But in Aretha Franklin's words, "Take another look baby, and tell me / Who's zoomin' who?"[18]

In collective creation theater, *problem* replaces *action* as the term describing the political intentions of the drama. The shift in terminology is not accidental because, as a subset of political theater, this tradition places violence and anger within the broader contexts of global abuse. In the case of these three texts, the violence is black-on-black, the victims are women, and rituals of healing created by the protagonists and authors are beyond the control of their abusers or therapists.

Frankétienne's *Kaselezo* (Womb Water's Breaking), originally written and performed in Creole, is a symbolic drama reminiscent of the foreboding ethos in Jean Giraudoux's works produced in pre–World War II France.[19] *Kaselezo* applies the metaphor of birthing to signs of deliverance on three different levels: the deliverance of peasant, working-class, and bourgeois women from the "mule duty" that they perform for their mates; the social deliverance of the Haitian landscape mutilated by political violence for three decades under the Duvaliers (1957–86); and deliverance of the human free spirit kept in bondage secretly by the *tonton macoutes* through greed and perversion. The play was first performed just before the overthrow of the Duvaliers, and for many audiences it was premonitory.[20] Problem here revolves around three characters: Mansya, the blind *mambo* or Vodoun priestess, and her two daughters, Benita and Amonise—all of whom have witnessed or experienced some form of male violence. The weight of criticism against such behavior is symbolized in the character of Amonise, who has been pregnant with pain for centuries, suffering for those who have turned their backs on the land. Repetition of *je m'échine* (to slave over a piece of work) permeates the dialogue just as the women set off on a Vision Quest seeking to uncover and heal gender and national torture. *Kaselezo* is a brilliant metaphor for revolt against dictatorship because it uncovers the subtext of misogyny inherent in such states of control. The list of abuses is staggering, from death in childbirth to various forms of punishments and beatings performed against young girls. The purpose of the drama is to give birth to a new understanding of the past, to children of the future who know their history unveiled:

> Mansya: Purify the soul
> Purify memory
> Cut skin and bones
> through to the source of light.
> Together we have woven our souls into
> a rainbow / necklace so that we will never forget.[21]

Although set in a different era and nation, *For Colored Girls* is also concerned with rebirthing the selves frozen "in postures of distress" at the very outset of the play.[22] These seven female characters, differentiated by the colors they wear (brown, yellow, red, green, purple, blue, orange), represent the urban rainbow of young colored women who have experienced violence in relationships, who are angry, too, because their racial status in American society has held back their development from the 1950s through the 1970s. The two arenas of political and interpersonal violence are interwoven. Rape and abortion hover at the corners of their consciousness. Prostitution within the black community and constraints placed on a young girl's education across the country define the madness of being a "colored me," as the lady in brown reveals in the opening monologue:

> somebody / anybody
> sing a black girl's song
> bring her out
> to know herself
> to know you
> but sing her rhythms

carin / struggle / hard times
sing her song of life
she's been dead so long
closed in silence so long
she doesn't know the sound
of her own voice
her infinite beauty
she's half-notes scattered
without rhythm / no tune
sing her sighs
sing the song of her possibilities
sing a righteous gospel
the makin of a melody
let her be born
let her be born
& handled warmly. (231–32)

Later in the play, the lady in green delivers a line that becomes the signature verse of these women's despair: "somebody almost walked off wid alla my stuff."

somebody almost walked off wid alla my stuff
not my poems or a dance i gave up in the street
but somebody almost walked off wid alla my stuff
like a kleptomaniac working hard & forgettin while
stealin
this is mine / this aint yr stuff /
now why don't you put me back & let me hang out in
my own self. (263–64)

This moment is the crossover point when the seven characters move from their individual testimonies toward the collective resolution of a common feeling of betrayal. Unlike the Vision Quest ending in *Kaselezo*, *For Colored Girls* leads to a "layin on of hands" (273) among the seven characters as they are drawn together in feminist solace beyond the control or comfort of a man or mother. In this respect, *For Colored Girls* was a premonitory text, projecting forward to a litany of healing that has appeared in other autobiographical and fictional works by women well into the 1990s: "i found god in myself / & i loved her / i loved her fiercely" (274).[23]

The Sistren group of Jamaica worked six years to create *Bellywoman Bangarang* (literally, "Pregnant Woman's Struggle" in Creole). It was presented in different versions in 1978 and again in 1982 within the anglophone Caribbean diaspora. *Bellywoman* was a unique theater enterprise combining the efforts and insights of a trained cultural worker, Honor Ford-Smith, and a collective of working-class Jamaican women new to theater and the written word.[24] Their testimonies in Creole about teenage mothering and the deliverance of young girls from working-class abuse are drawn from memories of the 1950s through the 1970s—the same time frame represented in Shange's drama—based on collective oral histories rather than on a single author's choreopoems. Testimony as embodied in *Bellywoman* emerged from therapeutic exercises in the collective creation process.

The setting of the play is a hospital emergency ward where four young teenage girls have come to deliver babies in the midst of a nurses' strike. But as the play demonstrates, the girls and their children have very limited futures. Neglect nationwide for those living in the *dungle* (urban ghettos) has eliminated the possibilities of proper prenatal care and employment; abuse by mates or female family members has simply compounded an already uneasy existence. The combined factors of neglect and abuse drew the original members of this group into a *sistren* of actors and characters courageous enough to reveal black-on-black violence in their own communities.

In a perceptive article, Rhonda Cobham identified the choral response "a wha kind a pen dis?" as the central metaphor describing the despair of containment embedded in their lives that developed among these women during the collective creation process.[25] The pen of indifference was a walled area of silence constructed by elders, including mothers, the parson, a shopkeeper, teachers, and the like. The final moments of the play bring the characters together in a chorus of solidarity similar to the resolutions in the two other texts from Haiti and the United States:

> Come forward, mothers
> Come forward, fathers
> Sisters and brothers
>
> We know our way from here
> We have conquered frustrations
> We have conquered tribulation
> Through all our ups and downs
> We've learned our lessons well.
>
> Sistren and Brethren
> Teenagers too
> Nurses and doctors
> We know our way from here.

Join hands together
Helping one another
Working together
On our way from here.

Come forward, mothers
Come forward, fathers
Working together
On our way from here. (54–55)

These works of collective creation theater, produced in different sites of
the African diaspora, have approached the subject of healing in similar
ways using metaphors of birthing and rebirthing as topoi of renewal.

Process and Practice

Beyond the provocation and dialogue model suggested by Case, beyond
the differences in context, class, and implied audiences, these three works
outline what we might call a black feminist morphology that developed
in theater during the 1970s and 1980s. By comparing them, we find na-
scent forms of feminist theater that, theoretically, have a common base in
African diaspora culture. Following the proposals of Honor Ford-Smith
and Rhonda Cobham, who recorded and analyzed Sistren's decade-long
experiments in educational theater, we might examine the commonalities
that exist among the three feminist dramas using process, practice, language and structure as measuring devices:

> Perhaps the most successful use of the play may be as a pattern for
> other productions which build as *Bellywoman* does on memories,
> shared rituals, and traditional resources. This is one of the reasons why
> so much time has been spent here talking about the problems of
> collective creation and mapping out the technical processes by which
> certain sequences and metaphors were developed. It is important for
> Sistren's work to be read and understood as a literary text. But we
> must also strive for ways of sharing the creative process by which this
> text is produced if Sistren is to break through the cycle of maverick
> achievement, dispersal, and amnesia which has characterized the
> process of collective creation in the work of other Caribbean groups.[26]

At the level of process, these three theater works cast women into
subject rather than object roles as authors, collaborators, and actresses.
They crossed gender lines and class barriers, negotiating control differently in each case. Frankétienne worked with the actresses to create dia-

logue based on an infrastructure of expression that he brought to rehearsals from January through March of 1985. Ntozake Shange credits dance instructors Raymond Sawyer, Ed Mock, and Halifu Osumare in the San Francisco Bay Area of the 1970s, faculty and students of the Women's Studies Department at Sonoma State College, and choreographer Paula Moss, among others, for the release and subsequent development of her own once-silenced voice. She acknowledges director Oz Scott as well for his guidance. Obviously, he helped Ntozake as poet-performer let go of her choreopoems so that they might be reinterpreted by others. Sistren collaborated with cultural workers from the Jamaican National School of Drama, including artistic director Honor Ford-Smith, playwright Dennis Scott, and choreographer Pam Reid. Together through theater exercises such as lifting and catching, they established a climate of trust among working-class women for whom the practice of unsilencing on stage was altogether new.[27] The *communitas* that developed in each of these experiments relied upon individuals and institutions already committed to negotiating collective control with cross-sections of "colored girls" within the diaspora.

Whether these similarities in process and practice result from intertextual relationships will require further research. Were the artistic directors of Sistren influenced by Shange after 1976? Did Franketienne hear of Sistren's work after 1982? To what extent did Shange rely for structure on scholarly research devoted to African diaspora rituals of healing revealed in women's studies programs throughout the 1970s? These three texts seem to suggest that a feminist theater morphology exists within the African diaspora. Although expressed differently, all three rely on children's tales, games, or riddles as a forum for recovering the silenced self. As the plays move into confrontation with male discourses of containment, the female characters find innovative devices for acting out the speech and gestures of their abusers: puppets worn overhead in the agitprop tradition become masks for actresses to imitate duplicitous male language (Franketienne); the "sorry raps" of African American men are repeated by their women in mock form (Shange); and through "male impersonations" actresses mimic shiftless behavior and deconstruct nationalist dread speech (Sistren).[28]

The structure of these texts begins with a diversity of voices: colored girls pluralized by location across the United States; Jamaican girls forced to give birth out of wedlock in a hospital room; biological sisters seeking a road to recovery initiated by their mother who is also a priestess willing to relinquish control. Each text ends by constructing a unit of healing, a feminist therapeutic site evolving from the release of anger and control in theater problem, process, and production.

In the latter decades of the twentieth century, the negotiation of control in relationships and in theater when women's pain is the subject demands that feminists must open their psyches to dangerous admissions subject to intense criticism by those males who recognize in the texts a part of their own behavior. Anyone adopting this type of feminist analysis must anticipate repercussions as an extension of the form. In climates of provocation and dialogue, we cannot expect to be liberated from negative responses that, ultimately, will follow the unsilencing of persistent violence in our relationships to entrenched power. But we can negotiate for respect as Aretha Franklin proclaims: "I'm in love under new management."

Notes

1. In 1953, the Haitian poet and playwright Félix Morisseau-Leroy wrote and staged *Antigone en créole* in response to Francophile Haitian intellectuals who believed that Creole speech could not communicate abstract thought or high dramatic action.

2. See James Heffernan, ed., *Representing the French Revolution.*

3. References to the five plays are drawn from published and unpublished sources as well as from translations from the French or Creole: Rhonda Cobham, ed., with Sistren and Honor Ford-Smith, "Bellywoman Bangarang"; Maryse Condé, *Dieu nous l'a donné;* Paul Carter Harrison, ed., *Totem Voices: Plays from the Black World Repertory;* Jean Jonassaint, ed., *Frankétienne, écrivain haitien;* Francoise Kourilsky and Catherine Temerson, eds., *Plays by Women;* Simone Schwarz-Bart, *Ton beau capitaine.*

4. VèVè A. Clark, "Haiti's Tragic Overture."

5. Jean Fouchard, *Le théâtre à Saint-Domingue,* 231–34.

6. VèVè A. Clark, "When Womb Waters Break."

7. Sue-Ellen Case, *Feminism and Theatre,* 95–111.

8. Ibid., 127–32.

9. Ibid., 131.

10. For readers unfamiliar with the practice of clitoridectomy, Alice Walker's novel *Possessing the Secret of Joy* and her list of selected readings are excellent beginnings.

11. Antonin Artaud, *The Theatre and Its Double.*

12. Condé, *Dieu,* 7.

13. See the memoirs of two former Black Panther Party members: Elaine Brown, *A Taste of Power,* and David Hilliard, *This Side of Glory.*

14. Schwarz-Bart, *Ton beau capitaine,* 7–8.

15. The Brown University production was staged Nov. 12–14, 1988, at Rites and

Reason Theatre in Providence. It was directed by George Houston Bass, and the roles of Wilnor and Marie-Ange were played, respectively, by Gilbert McCauley and Ramona Bass. Simone Schwarz-Bart and the translators were present in the audience at the Nov. 14 performance.

16. Claudia Kaiser-Lenoir, ed., *The New Theatre of Latin America,* special issue of *Theatre Research International* 14, no. 2 (1989).

17. Useful summaries of the critiques of *For Colored Girls* and *Bellywoman* appear in the following sources: Neal A. Lester, "Shange's Men"; and Cobham, ed., "Bellywoman," vii–viii, xxv–xxvi, xxxv–xxxvi.

18. From *Who's Zoomin' Who?* compact disc, Arista Records, 1985. The lyrics are by Narada Michael Walden and Preston Glass, the vocals by Aretha Franklin.

19. I am referring specifically to Giraudoux's *La guerre de Troie n'aura pas lieu* (1935), translated by Christopher Fry as *Tiger at the Gates.*

20. Yves Chemla, "*Kaselezo* de Franketienne," 171.

21. Jonassaint, "Franketienne," 162, translation by VèVè Clark.

22. Harrison, ed., *Totem Voices,* 231.

23. I am thinking here of works by black and white American feminists alike, from Alice Walker's *The Color Purple* (1982) through Gloria Steinem's *Revolution from Within* (1992).

24. Cobham, ed., "Bellywoman," xv–xxi.

25. Rhonda Cobham, "'A Wha Kind a Pen Dis?'" *Theatre Research International,* 1990.

26. Cobham, ed., "Bellywoman," xxxiv.

27. Ibid., xv–xvi.

28. Chemla, "*Kaselezo,*" 174–77; Harrison, *Totem Voices,* 265–68; Cobham, ed., "Bellywoman," xxx–xxxi.

PART FIVE

Revolting Texts:
Transgression (and) Transformation

ROSEANNE LUCIA QUINN

Mastectomy, Misogyny, and Media: Toward an Inclusive Politics and Poetics of Breast Cancer

> If "woman" is a fiction, a locus of pure difference and resistance to logocentric power, and if there are no women as such, then the very issue of women's oppression would appear to be obsolete and feminism itself would have no reason to exist (which, it may be noted, is a corollary of poststructuralism and the stated position of those who call themselves "post-feminists").
>
> —Teresa de Lauretis

The impetus for writing this essay comes from my own witnessing of and resulting anger at the misogynistic depiction of women with breast cancer in the media and at the brutal treatment of women in past and current oncological practice. I have not had breast cancer myself, but my mother has and so have millions of other women around the world. In one year, in the United States alone, 42,000 women died as a result of this disease. One such woman, of course, was Audre Lorde, who chronicled her fifteen-year battle first in *The Cancer Journals* (1980) and later in *A Burst of Light* (1988). At the heart of what is remarkable about her story is the courage it took for her to tell it. That courage, too, connects Lorde to every other woman, past and present, living and dead, who has struggled to bring to light the horror of her own experience—whether it was a story told over the telephone from mother to daughter, as my mother to me; or a poem, journal entry, personal narrative, or conversation written down on scraps of paper; or even prose and poetry published in anthologies, such as *Cancer as a Women's Issue: Scratching the Surface* (1991) and *Her Soul beneath the Bone: Women's Poetry on Breast Cancer* (1988).

For me, what has been most important in these women's words is their exposing of the particularity of their exploitation as women burdened with breast cancer in a sexist, racist, classist, ageist, homophobic society. Methodologically speaking, my own aim is to demonstrate what I would like to reinforce as the cornerstone of feminism: that "the personal is political." All women, sooner or later, in some way or another, will have to confront the existence of breast cancer. The women I discuss here are by virtue of their race, class, and sexuality at a disadvantage in that confrontation because they already occupy positions of marginality in society. In some cases, they are systematically denied medical care; in other instances, they are subjected to routine and unwarranted amputation of their breasts. What prevails is loss. Women lose their breasts and their lives: dismembered, disfigured, diseased, ignored, dismissed, disregarded, humiliated, abandoned, betrayed.

As I have attempted to contextualize the power inequalities in the medical establishment that have created so much women's suffering, I have witnessed in my own profession the disturbingly similar tendency to push out, silence, dismiss, ridicule, separate, and eliminate women who supposedly do not belong. Too often I have seen academic feminists participate in the dichotomization of what women do, say, think, and write into opposing and mutually exclusive camps of "theory" versus "practice." Such dichotomizers routinely devalue those women who do not think and write as they do. For this type of feminist, the words of many women of color, working-class women, and women outside the academy are dismissed because they are considered atheoretical.[1]

The keys to the theoretical kingdom seem to be held by those who delight in using inaccessible language and who continue to insist that Euro-male theorists such as Freud and Foucault (the former pathologizes women, the latter erases them) should be revered. A similarly disturbing dichotomization occurs between the poststructuralists who tend to devalue experiential knowledge and those feminists who still talk about women as having real lives, with real bodies. In her essay on the importance of Italian feminism, "The Essence of the Triangle or, Taking the Risk of Essentialism Seriously: Feminist Theory in Italy, the U.S., and Britain" (1989), Teresa de Lauretis offers this criticism of Chris Weedon's highly acclaimed book, *Feminist Practice and Poststructuralist Theory:*

> My quarrel with Weedon's book is about its reductive opposition—
> all the more remarkable, coming from a proponent of
> deconstruction—of a *lumpen* feminist essentialism (radical—liberal—
> separatist and American) to a phantom feminist poststructuralism
> (critical—socialist—psychoanalytic and Franco-British), and with the

byproducts of such a *parti-pris:* the canonization of a few (in)famous feminists as signposts of the convenient categories set up by the typology, the agonistic narrative structure of its account of "feminist theories," and finally to its failure to contribute to the elaboration of feminist critical thought, however useful the book may be to its other intended readers, who can thus rest easy in the fantasy that poststructuralism is the theory and feminism is just practice.[2]

Feminist political theory centered on identity politics calls into question the perpetuated fantasy that theory is somehow separate and elevated from practice, and that the reality of women's lives can be virtually theorized out of existence.

Specifically, the emergence of feminism formulated by women of color, emphasizing identity politics, has called attention to the universalist tendency within the mainstream women's movement to homogenize the particularity of women's lives and literatures by ignoring issues of race, class, and sexuality (Susan Faludi's best-selling *Backlash,* and Naomi Wolf's *Fire with Fire* leap to mind). Their lack of attention to forces that at once confer and reveal a kaleidescope of identities that distinguish women's differing privileged and disempowered positions leads mainstream writers to ignore women who do not fit into a white, middle-class, heterosexual model of patriarchal power relations.[3] Writers of the Combahee River Collective explain the importance of seeing through a personal yet prismatic methodological lens: "This focus upon our oppression is embodied in the concept of identity politics. We believe that the most profound and potentially most radical politics come directly out of our own identity, as opposed to working to end somebody else's oppression. . . . The major source of difficulty in our political work is that we are not just trying to fight oppression on one front or even two, but instead to address a whole range of oppressions."[4] Though written in 1977, and published as a pamphlet, the collective's position is neither outdated nor atheoretical; rather, it affirms that political oppression is based upon the very racist, sexist, and homophobic avenues through which identity is rendered in the first place.

In her essay "Notes toward a Politics of Location" (1984), Adrienne Rich writes that identity politics can be defined through the location of oneself and "naming the ground we come from."[5] Consider the women I focus on in the body of this essay, who are abused for the very act of "naming their grounds" even as they are enacting change for themselves and others. Rich reveals the complex ways in which human difference has been and continues to be patriarchally constructed. In my own practicing of feminist cultural criticism, such a focus enables me to place in the foreground the all-important difference that difference makes.[6]

> The mainspring of sex inequality is misogyny, and
> the mainspring of misogyny is sexual sadism.
> —Catharine A. MacKinnon

The photograph takes up the space of a full-page magazine advertisement. In muted tones of warm beige and bronze, a white woman with fine jewelry and bare shoulder is tilting her perfectly coiffed blonde head backward just a little and opening her lipsticked mouth ever so slightly. It is a familiar pose. It could be an advertisement for a new perfume designed to lead to seduction and an evening's worth of pleasure. Or perhaps the woman has just doubled the return on her personal CD account in a savings and loan that is promoting its financial stability.

Look more closely and you will notice, in the lower right-hand corner of the photograph, that the woman is having her left breast squeezed into a vise. Look further and in even paler hues, lurking in the background of the photograph, is the figure of a man wearing a tie and white doctor's coat and pressing his thumbs and forefingers firmly together. Although his face has been cropped out, he appears to be gazing at them: at the woman and her breasts. Get the picture? She is having a mammogram. She seems to be enjoying it. So does he. So, presumably, will you. At least that is what the picture, in the special Breast Cancer Awareness Month section of *Self* magazine, seems to intend to say to its viewer.[7]

Who is this woman, the letters "b-r-e-a-s-t" splayed across her chest, meant to represent? A woman with cancer, women who will likely get cancer, a woman with a left breast, Women? And who is the man in the photograph supposed to be? The radiologist? Because if he is then he is doing a damn-poor job, just standing there staring, leaving the smiling woman with her breast trapped in the X-ray machine. Even the speediest of magazine photographers (or radiology technicians) probably takes at least a minute or two to set up and snap the photo. How could he leave her there so long? How could she stand it? I've had a mammogram. It hurts. I could hardly stand still for five seconds, let alone the extended amount of time necessary to pose for *two* cameras.

This photograph is disturbing on several levels that are representative of the ways in which "breast cancer" gets constructed as a discursive category in the media as well as in medical literature and practice. As in this case, these popular and medical discourses are grounded in misogyny, pornography, and homogeny. The woman in the photograph is partly nude and centered for maximum viewing pleasure in front of the fully clothed man whose face we are not allowed to see. She is subordinated, in relation to him, by her vulnerable physical state (locked in a vise with, perhaps, a potentially fatal illness), her status within the medical establishment (she is a patient, not a doctor), and the fact that so much of her is shown. The man's identity is protected, and he is not rendered accessible in any of the ways that she is: he could be any man (or "Anyman"), a fact that makes it easy for a male viewer to identify with him and his function in the picture. The woman, on the other hand, has a clear set of identity markers. She is white, middle or upper class, and apparently heterosexual (or why else would she be posing for him?). For female viewers who are not racially, economically, or sexually privileged, it is not easy to identify with her. Why should this be problematic? Although this picture does not appear in the latest male-pornographic publication but in a well-known "woman's magazine," it nonetheless represents an intersection of pornography with medical practice, where the perhaps soon-to-be dismembered breast becomes the locus for pleasure, where the diagnostic equation (in the media and in actual practice) is too often: misogyny plus masochism equals mastectomy.

Similarly, medical literature by and large represents "women with breast cancer" in monolithic terms, with no allowance for differences of culture, class, age, race, sexuality, or even biology. In countless scientific studies women are lumped together symptomatically without controlling for variables in relation to the treatment prescribed, the treatment actually given or not offered, and responses to those courses of action. Given the sexist nature of the patriarchal health care system in the United States, all women face obstacles in seeking treatment for any medical problem. But those difficulties are particularly magnified for women who are already marginalized in mainstream society and whose needs are subsumed under dominant cultural imperatives. For women of color, working-class and economically impoverished women, lesbian and bisexual women, elderly women, women without medical insurance, and immigrant women, access to health care and the quality of treatment are often severely compromised under the interlocking oppressions of racism, classism, homophobia, ageism, and xenophobia. These injustices appear also in the research practices now commonly in place throughout the United States. It seems obvious that clinical trials without young women, without older women, without poor women, without women of color, without lesbian women (or those with women from these variable subgroups who are not studied distinctly from one another) lead to studies that lack comprehensive data, and this lack leads in turn to inadequate or unnecessary surgical practices and suspect (so-called) noninvasive treatment choices and opportunities.

Even the few recent studies that attempt to define women with breast cancer as a special category still fail miserably at the crucial stages of data collection and analysis. For example, consider the study entitled "Racial Differences in Survival of Women with Breast Cancer," published in the *Journal of Chronic Diseases,* which was "undertaken to evaluate racial differences in survival experience among women with breast cancer in a geographically defined population. . . . The demographic factors considered in this investigation were race (black vs white), age, marital status (married vs not married), and county of residence. . . . The final sample size of 2322 white females and 536 black females was obtained." [8]

The framework of the study is testimony to its false claims of inclusivity. First, not only is the category of race exclusionary, it is implicitly defined as an adversarial contest where the whites "win" from beginning to end not only because there are more of them but also because of their higher survival rates. Second, marital status itself is a sexist category having no scientific merit, and it is further applied in a racist way when the researchers comment that "the black subjects . . . were significantly more likely to be unmarried," and that the unmarried women of the total sample, marked "Other" in the appropriate chart of which black women form a "significant" number, are also less likely to survive breast cancer than their married counterparts. Finally, there is no explanation why, in a study undertaken in the Atlanta, Georgia, area, the sample of women with breast cancer contained almost five times as many white women as black women. On the contrary, it seems to be assumed that this is an unbiased sample because the women are drawn from the same Georgia counties. The study concludes, "The results of the present investigation lend further support to the notion that racial differences in survival from breast cancer are not attributable to the effects of SES [socioeconomic status]." [9] There seems to be no awareness on the part of the researchers that the whole study rests upon the consequences of the policies of our national health care system, which makes it difficult for women of color to gain access to any medical diagnosis in the first place: only black women who have broken through those barriers get "counted." Again, the message of this study is that it is mainly white women who get breast cancer, and white married women who survive it.

Patriarchal medical interpretations such as these, along with unnecessarily violent surgical practices, have the effect of predetermining many women's silent and virtually paralytic responses to their illness. In addition, many women become mired in the prevalent new age, quasi-medical, contradictory rhetoric that puts the burden of disease squarely on their shoulders. If women would only eat less, drink more, have sex at an early age, have sex at a later age, get pregnant, not take birth control pills, and eat all their vegetables then they would not have to worry about, in effect, "giving" themselves breast cancer. Feminist activist Jackie Winnow explains the absurdity of this "disease model":

> This form of thinking plays out the concept that we create our own reality, that we have ultimate freedom of choice and total control. Fuck the world around us, the people around us, the government and corporations, even our own biology. They don't exist. They don't affect us. There are no such things as sexism, homophobia, racism, anti-Semitism, capitalism, pollution, biology. . . . We live in a world with acid rain, with a hole in the ozone layer, where food is mass produced and picked early with no nutrients, where pesticides are sprayed on the workers and the food we eat, where the animals we eat are raised in a tortured environment and fed hormones and antibiotics; we live in a world that has chemical dumps under housing tracts, schools, playgrounds, with nuclear weapons and dumps, where winds spread radiation over all of us. This is labelled pollution when, in fact, it is invisible violence.[10]

A radical politics, and an accompanying body of literature by women such as the late Jackie Winnow, offer feminist poetical responses that directly counter the misogynist rhetoric and practices that serve to define and defile women with cancer. These women writers seek to make visible the fact that the daily "invisible" violences committed against them in the name of science and technology are part of a whole institutionalized model of oppression that operates within and outside the medical establishment. In foregrounding issues of race, class, sex, and sexuality, these writers articulate and underscore the multiplicities of diverse women's experiences of breast cancer as a means to combat medical violence and enforced silence.

In her poem entitled "A Woman Dead in Her Forties," Adrienne Rich politicizes her friend's death from breast cancer as a consequence of the brutal and sexist treatments she underwent through invasive modern medical practices, complicated by the silence around her illness and the nature of their relationship.[11] I used to teach this poem in my undergraduate American literature class. During poetry week every student was responsible for bringing one poem to class in order to read, explicate, and explain why she or he picked it. We would sit in a circle and I would begin. I used to read "A Woman Dead in Her Forties" out loud with perfect pitch and inflection. This would always be a successful class because I would be participating on an equal footing with my students and we would usually learn a lot about one another. Then, three years ago, my mother got breast cancer. I still continued having poetry week, but I was no longer an active participant. It became impossible for me to share *any* poem with my students because it became impossible for me to read "A Woman Dead in Her Forties." I could not face in the poem what my mother would have to endure in her life.

The violent, toxic treatments used to counteract Rich's friend's cancer only serve to disfigure and humiliate her. Through mastectomy and radiation, she is reduced to a

> scarred, deleted torso
>
> . . . . .
>
> till uncontrollable light began to pour
>
> . . . . .
>
> from every wound and suture
> and all the sacred openings.

Rich goes on to connect her friend's loss of dignity with respect to her own body to their mutual loss of the possibility of having access to each other's bodies through a shared sexual relationship. She recalls that their love only "took the form of jokes, and mute / . . . loyalty":

> we lied about our lives: I wearing
> the face of a proper marriage
>
> . . . . .
>
> you the face of the independent woman
> We cleaved to each other across that space.

Unable to cross boundaries of expected social and sexual behavior, they are forced to "cleave" to repressive religious and social mores as well as to heterosexual dictates: "We stayed mute and disloyal / because we were afraid." Despite the mutuality of their "muted" lives, Rich as speaker and poet lives on at the expense of the woman who is now dead though only in her forties.

Rich's legacy to her dead friend is this poem of regret, but her tone is accompanied by an anger directed at her friend's seeming passivity—"you who might have told me / *everything you feel is true.*" She elaborates on her disappointment:

I wish you were here tonight I want
to yell at you

Don't accept
Don't give in

. . . . .

I would have touched my fingers
to where your breasts had been
but we never did such things.

Here, Rich mourns the many kinds of prohibitive silences suffered between them: verbal and tactile. She writes in the conditional mode of how
silences could have (should have) been broken and how breaking silence
might have led to the conquering—or at least acknowledgment—of her
friend's breast cancer, and to a more honest and woman-identified relationship between them. Had she been able to admit her sexual love for
this woman, Rich says, she could have made her friend's life and death an
easier one; by breaking silence on this crucial front, she could also have
broken the silence that surrounded her friend's imminent death and, more
importantly, the nature of that death. The poem concludes: "In plain language: I never told how I loved you / we never talked at your death bed of
your death."

In *The Cancer Journals,* Audre Lorde writes from a place of already
exploded silence even as she pushes the boundaries of transformative language further from the place of lost opportunity and marginalization to
one of centrality and action. As a self-identified black lesbian feminist,
Lorde must negotiate the inhospitable terrain of institutionalized breast
cancer care as a triple outsider. None of the resources available to her
makes sense because they have nothing to do with who she is. A woman
from Reach for Recovery comes to visit Lorde in the hospital, offering
her a "pale pink breast-shaped pad" and extolling the virtues of breast
reconstruction as a marital aid. Implicit in that interaction is the assumption that Lorde can only be accepted as a survivor if she is coded as a
comfortably heterosexual, white woman. Lorde writes: "Off and on I kept
thinking. I have cancer. I'm a black lesbian feminist poet, how am I going
to do this now? Where are the models for what I'm supposed to be in this
situation? But there were none. This is it, Audre. You're on your own." [12]
Lorde's lonely battle culminates after she leaves the hospital, during the
postmastectomy stage of her treatment, when she refuses to wear a temporary prosthesis or have a surgical implant.

During a visit to her surgeon's office, Lorde is scolded by the "usually supportive and understanding nurse" for not wearing a prosthesis to the office. The nurse tells Lorde that it was "better than nothing," and coming in without one was "bad for the morale of the office." Trying to put this insulting encounter in perspective, Lorde writes that she "realized that the attitude towards prosthesis after breast cancer is an index of this society's attitudes towards women in general as decoration and externally defined sex object."[13] Certainly Lorde's analysis harkens back to the woman in the *Self* magazine photograph. Just as she is captured in a perpetual frozen moment that conflates everything about her body and her illness as sex object, so too does reconstructive care perpetuate that conflation.

The overarching ramifications of urging temporary prosthesis and permanent implant is to treat postmastectomy women as damaged goods. If the only good woman is a two-breasted one, then it follows that there is a ready-made circulation of capital to be gained when the prevailing medical procedure for women with breast cancer in the United States is still amputation. Moreover, as Lorde explains, "masking" mastectomy prevents individual women from recognizing others who have had breast cancer; in turn, that hiddenness eliminates the possibility for women to meet around a shared experience in order to connect with one another for individual support and community activism. She writes:

> If we are to translate the silence surrounding breast cancer into language and action against this scourge, then the first step is that women with mastectomies must become visible to each other. For silence and invisibility go hand in hand with powerlessness. By accepting the mask of prosthesis, one-breasted women proclaim ourselves as insufficients dependent upon pretense. We reinforce our own isolation and invisibility for each other, as well as the false complacency of a society which would rather not face the results of its own insanities. In addition, we withhold that visibility and support from one another which is such an aid to perspective and self-acceptance.[14]

In addition to making visible the ravaging of her body to amputation, her resistance is also a resistance to the erasure of her identity as a black lesbian. Once again, recalling the image of *Self* magazine, which does not allow for the presence of a nonwhite female, Lorde inserts the black body absent from popular and medical discourses. Her refusal to adorn herself with a pale pink breast-shaped pad meant to appeal to white men is a political stance by which she affirms her control over the scripting of her own body. In so doing, she makes the text of her body readable to other women as nonwhite, nonheterosexual, and non-bi-breasted. The companion processes of writing her journal as well as her body become a model for honoring her life that Lorde creates for herself in the absence of any other. Whether or not other women embrace Lorde's poetically rendered struggle, the act of writing itself serves as a tool for her own empowerment.

Similarly, Sandra Butler and Barbara Rosenblum write a collaborative account of their life together, from the moment of the diagnosis of Barbara's breast cancer to her untimely death, as a way to give voice to what is happening to them separately and as life partners. After Barbara's death at age forty-four, Sandy is left alone to compile their story for publication. In the process, she must "sift through scraps of paper, journal entries, recorded dreams, photographs, medical records." [15] From the very beginning of the resulting book, *Cancer in Two Voices* (1991), Sandy highlights just how many "texts" needed to be written and then reread in order for the full truth of their life to be told.

It is difficult for me to comment on *Cancer in Two Voices* in any way that feels traditionally academic. I need to validate the accessibility of Barbara and Sandy's narrative by not becoming inaccessible myself. There is also the frustration and anger I feel simply as a reader of Sandy and Barbara's story. Barbara's tumor was misdiagnosed "time after time" as benign, until it was too late for any medical professional to do anything to Barbara but amputate her breast, bombard her with toxic chemicals, and burn her with radiation to prolong her life for just three torturous years. [16]

Through her collaboration with Sandy, bringing their life public by telling their story, the traditionally rigid academic Barbara "learned the power of the spoken word . . . and began to write in a new style. . . . I no longer needed 'the data' to tell the story. I went inside myself and wrote about my life and my feelings" (54). This insistence on orality in Barbara's and Sandy's individual entries in their collaborative journal achieves the simultaneous effects of rendering their words both easily understandable and poetic. In addition, the fact that they are writing for each other cushions the impact of the daily manifestations of Barbara's impending death. It somehow does not feel like such a completely devastating loss to be told that, because she is in so much pain, they must stop having sex. For Barbara points out that there is a deeper intimacy that they have forged together, and that this is still possible between them through their writing itself. She says: "We have developed a new form that can accommodate our individual and unique voices into a dialogue. We write about things that are important to us. We make love at the typewriter, not in the bedroom" (132).

But communication was not always this easy for them. In the beginning of Barbara's breast cancer the two women became silent partners. Sandy, in particular, although she accompanied Barbara to various doctors' appointments and waited at the hospital while she had surgery, "[could] not imagine anything to say" (21). Sandy's inability to express herself surprises Barbara, who has known her to be a rather fearless public activist and counselor. Sandy's silence also surprises herself. Both women turn away from each other and toward their journals in an attempt to sort out their feelings. Here is what each woman writes:

> Sandy: I have spent the past ten years of my life writing and talking, training and facilitating so that women can speak and engage both politically and psychologically with all the forms of violence against women. Now, this violence against this woman leaves me frozen and silent. (26)
> Barbara: She and I are mute. Dumb. This woman of so many words, so many verbal styles, presentations, public speeches is mute with me. And that is how I know—in part—how deadly serious this is. We cannot use words to build bridges between us. . . . We are each trapped in our own terror and cannot find our way towards each other. (22)

Their "way towards each other" is also interrupted by differences between them of class and culture that come to the surface during their ordeal. Barbara, born of immigrant Jewish parents, grew up in a working-class home and never had access to private medical care. She becomes victimized by a public health care system that is too big, too busy, and too ill-equipped to attend adequately and responsibly to her medical needs. Despite what Barbara calls her "class travel," an academic job and dinners at nice restaurants, she "never had any idea what constituted a good doctor or good medicine" (30). Unfortunately, yet again, Barbara is an example of a woman taking responsibility for the incompetence of mass medicine. She concludes: "I will die an early death because I was not competent enough to discern and judge the incompetence of my doctors. . . . I never deeply understood that class was a matter of life and death. My class. My life" (24). It is Sandy, born of upper-class assimilated Jewish parents, who takes Barbara out of one economic class and into another. This life-saving medical class travel leads Barbara to private health care and an accurate diagnosis of her metastastic cancer.

What am I to learn from this mobility? My own mother is being treated by the very same health maintenance organization that misdiagnosed Barbara. And I am one of the 37 million people in the United States who cannot afford health insurance, so I paid for my last doctor's visit with a charge card. Even if a woman recognizes the incompetence of her physician, like my mother's oncologist offering her Valium instead of treating her postchemotherapy side effects, what can she do? Where can she travel without a first-class ticket?

Ironically, Barbara suddenly switches class roles with Sandy when she is awarded an out-of-court settlement for several hundred thousand dollars in her malpractice suit. Barbara calls this "blood money," and finds the award an insult to her life and oncoming death. However, she does need to decide how to bequeath her money, and she makes a will distributing her assets in similar amounts to her mother, father, sister, nephew, and Sandy. Sandy reacts angrily to Barbara's decision. She writes: "I recognized that I would not be 'well taken care of' in the distribution of her assets. . . . I had come to think of this as *my* blood money. My trade-off for the loss of my beloved partner. If I wasn't going to have Barbara, I wanted all the money that had come to represent her life" (89). Sandy's belief that she needs the money as a trade-off lies in the gap between each woman's cultural experience of Judaism. Sandy had been taught to assimilate and be " 'not too Jewish' " (4). She grows up being denied any sense of her cultural history and only begins to discover it herself as a thirty-five-year-old reentry student writing about the Holocaust. Her attraction to Barbara's family lies in their collective willingness to embrace their common Jewish heritage and bear witness to it daily: through food, expression of emotion, speaking in Yiddish, and rallying around Barbara in honest, loving ways. In this cultural sense, Sandy is the outsider who will not have an unassimilated Jewish identity and family to rely on after Barbara is dead.

Cancer in Two Voices concludes with Sandy living alone. It is a sad ending, made more tragic by Sandy's own cancer of the thyroid coming two and a half years after Barbara's death. Her fate seems unfair and horrible, for there is no Barbara to help Sandy cope. There is only Sandy, still sleeping on Barbara's side of the bed, with the need to heal her pain: "I move, unable to still myself, unable to feel, to believe this thing is happening. Write it down, I think to myself. Do what you have done. It works, I whisper to myself. Record this" (178).

> On the book of my body I have permanently inscribed a tree.
> —Deena Metzger

It is difficult for me to come to some sort of conclusion, or even a resting place. Writing this essay has not been restful, and I wonder myself what the implications are in what has been said. When I put the work aside, and sit quietly, I imagine a future not unlike that depicted in Lesléa Newman's short story "The World to Come." In her vision, all the women she has ever known join together in a circle and dance—in celebration of women's friendship, community, love, endurance, and triumph.[17]

I begin to think back to the Amazons of old, those misguided heroines who removed their right breasts in order to shoot their deadly bows and arrows with greater accuracy. Those images blur, and I see the Amazons of then and the women with cancer now, united: the grandmother, mother, daughter, sister, aunt, cousin, friend, lover, wife, girlfriend, warrior, woman, women. All those who have been cut, sliced, burned, poisoned, amputated. They, too, form a circle. The bows and arrows lie dusty, and in their place women are exchanging their stories, writing newsletters, marching on Washington, testifying before Congress, assisting in each other's child care, picketing the N.I.H., refusing mastectomy, demanding a cure.

As I, too, am called to join their circle, I hesitate, thinking that I don't really belong there. Not yet understanding how to deal with their pain and rage, I deny my own. As in Lesléa Newman's story, from the circle a woman emerges and walks toward me. She is someone I have never met, though she feels familiar nonetheless. She gives me advice: "Write it down, think about yourself. Do what you have done. It works. . . . Record this." As she turns to rejoin her comrades, I follow, finally seeing that I am not simply a guest in the world to come. I belong there, and so do you. And the time is now.

It is in the recording of women's histories, such as Adrienne Rich's, and Audre Lorde's, and Barbara Rosenblum's and Sandra Butler's; those being collected in anthologies like *Cancer as a Women's Issue: Scratching the Surface* and *Her Soul beneath the Bone: Women's Poetry on Breast Cancer;* and those in feminist journals such as *Bridges: A Journal for Jewish Feminists and Our Friends,* that a much needed countering of misogynist constructions of women and women with breast cancer is being written. As Audre Lorde reminds us: "Each of us is here now because in one way or another we share a commitment to language, and to the reclaiming of that language which has been made to work against us. In the transformation of silence into language and action, it is vitally necessary for each one of us to establish or examine her function in that transformation, and to recognize her role as vital."[18]

Notes

1. See, for example, Toril Moi: "Some feminists might wonder why I have said nothing about black or lesbian (or black-lesbian) feminist criticism in America in this survey. This answer is simple: this book purports to deal with the theoretical aspects of feminist criticism" (*Sexual / Textual Politics,* 86).

2. Teresa de Lauretis, "The Essence of the Triangle," 10.

3. Barbara Smith, "Foreword," *Combahee River Collective Statement,* 4.

4. *Combahee River Collective Statement,* 12, 14.

5. In Adrienne Rich, *Blood, Bread, and Poetry,* 219.

6. See Catharine A. MacKinnon, *Feminism Unmodified,* 8–9, 22–23.

7. "B-r-e-a-s-t" photograph taken by Max Aguliera Hellmeg. It appears in "Breast Cancer Breakthroughs," by Peter Korn, *Self,* October 1992, 148–52.

8. Raymond P. Bain, Raymond S. Greenbury, and J. Patrick Whitacker, "Racial Differences in Survival of Women with Breast Cancer," *Journal of Chronic Diseases* 39 (1986): 632.

9. Ibid., 633, 635, 639.

10. Jackie Winnow, "Lesbians Evolving Health Care," 32, 33–34.

11. Adrienne Rich, "A Woman Dead in Her Forties," in *Dream of a Common Language,* 53–58.

12. Audre Lorde, *The Cancer Journals,* 42, 28–29.

13. Ibid., 59, 60.

14. Ibid., 61.

15. Sandra Butler and Barbara Rosenblum, *Cancer in Two Voices,* 1. Subsequent quotations from this volume will appear in parentheses in the text.

16. Ibid., 18.

17. Lesléa Newman, "The World to Come," in Newman, *A Letter to Harvey Milk,* 163–69.

18. Lorde, *Cancer Journals,* 22.

MADELINE CASSIDY

"Love Is a Supreme Violence": The Deconstruction of Gendered Space in Etel Adnan's *Sitt Marie-Rose*

Etel Adnan's novel, *Sitt Marie-Rose,* is the story of a young Lebanese woman, the mother of three children, who was abducted, tortured, and executed by the Christian militia during the Civil War in Lebanon in 1975. Her "crime" was aiding the Palestinians. The struggle between Palestinian and Christian factions in twentieth-century Beirut is rooted in tribal allegiances that go back at least to the fifth century.[1] Adnan, a Lebanese poet, writer, and graphic artist who grew up in Beirut, portrays this tradition of exclusive tribal identity and conflict as an aspect of the marginalization, exclusion , and resulting dehumanization of the "other" that has led to the uninhabitable chaos and destruction of Beirut. The daughter of a Greek Christian mother and a Syrian Muslim father, Adnan was educated in France and the United States. She lived in and out of Beirut between 1972 and 1979, and now lives in California and Paris. Both her poetry and her prose, little known in the United States, stress the interconnectedness of all individuals with each other and with the physical universe throughout time, as well as the anguish and suffering that result from ideologies of domination and violence.[2]

The story of Marie-Rose is told through the alternating and disparate voices of characters both central and marginal to the actual drama of the execution. Each voice is separate, yet all are connected by the violence that surrounds and permeates their lives in Beirut. The important distinction among them lies in the point of view of each of the storytellers as each reveals an internal response to traditionally held concepts of identity, gender, and society. In the end, the apocalyptic horror that Adnan portrays demands a reexamination of the validity and viability of these traditional concepts and the ideology of violence that they generate.

These contrasting perspectives reflect the influence of a society delineated by discretely gendered spheres. In this society, the distinctly masculine sphere of hunting, war, commerce, and power is traditionally separated from the distinctly feminine sphere of nurturing, home, family, and subservience. The traditional masculinist perspective of the young men in the novel contrasts with the feminist perspective of the woman scriptwriter, who introduces the first section, "Time I." The film writer speaks from a perspective that encompasses both traditionally male and traditionally female attributes, such as power and sympathy. However, Adnan portrays the young men as speaking only from a perspective of power and dominance, immersed in a psychology of violence that is for them a way of life.

In the opening scenes, Adnan's imagery speaks for itself: "The sunset is marvelously intense. The hunters aim their rifles toward the sky like missile launchers. They laugh. They show their teeth, their vigor, their pleasure." [3] And then, "The synchronization is perfect. Tony shoots. A bird falls. Pierre shoots. A bird falls. Mounir shoots. A bird falls. Fouad shoots. A bird falls. All their faces glow. Except Fouad's. Fouad is the perfect killer. He suffers from never having killed enough. The bullet in the body of the bird sinks into something soft. It lacks that hard, dry satisfying contact" (2). But beyond this phallic imagery is the realization that these young men, who prefer the excitement of auto races and hunting expeditions to actual sexual encounters, are fixed in a state of adolescent sexuality, defining their manhood with the trappings of maleness and group machismo. Adnan portrays this "hypermasculine" mentality as competitive, destructive, mindlessly exploitive.

Through the eyes of her female characters, Adnan establishes two views. One is the traditional feminine perspective. The other is the feminist perspective. Yet among the multiplicity of storytellers no traditionally feminine voice is heard. The women enclosed within this sphere are silent. (This is particularly ironic in contrast to the deaf-mute children, who are endowed with a representative voice.) We get a glimpse of these women, gathered with the wife of one of the young men, to watch a film clip made during a hunting trip in the Syrian desert. They are fulfilling the traditional role, kept within the family circle, watching, admiring, supporting, reflecting the exploits and performance of the men, the doers, the hunters. There exists only an undercurrent of silent dissatisfaction. "One of the girls present is Tony's cousin, and she takes it all with a rather spiteful air. The 'men' refused to take her hunting in Turkey. They didn't want to be bothered" (2).

The woman scriptwriter, however, is portrayed by Adnan as straddling two worlds. She remains intellectually removed from this traditional position, while appreciating the irony of her own apparent participation in this role. She says, "We women were happy with this little bit of imperfect colored cinema, which gave, for twenty minutes, a kind of additional prestige to these men we see every day. In this restrictive circle, the magic these males exert is once again reinforced. Everybody plays at this game" (4).

The scriptwriter, as we come to know her, clearly views the world in a way different from either the passive women in Mounir's home or the phallocentric young men. In contrast to these women, she seems to define herself beyond the strictly gendered sphere of silence and passivity. Artistically, she speaks from a position that encompasses both the traditionally male and the traditionally female spheres while refusing to be limited by societal delineations of gender. She quite literally enters the male-dominated space of the construction site in order to gain a better understanding of the subject of the film script she is writing. Amid the dust and noise of cement mixers, she speaks directly with the Syrian workers, witnessing firsthand the backbreaking conditions of their labor. She demands that her ideas for the film be taken seriously. In effect, she breaks through the borders of gendered space and creates for herself a new space. According to theologian Mary Daly, "The new space is located always 'on the boundary.' Its center is on the boundary of patriarchal institutions, such as churches, universities, national and international politics, families. Its center is the lives of women, whose experience of becoming changes the very meaning of center for us by putting it on the boundary of all that has been considered central."[4]

But this new geography extends beyond the issue of gender and has implications, too, for strictly perceived distinctions among ethnic, religious, and cultural "spaces." The writer sympathizes with the aggrieved Syrian laborers. She wants the film she is writing to "say something," to speak for her interpretation. This creative approach is rooted in the feminist perspective, which requires that she both respond to and act in her world in a way that integrates and redefines traditionally perceived masculine and feminine territories. The new space she creates for herself is an ideological no-man's-land that exists wherever strict borders are obscured.

Marie-Rose and the film writer occupy a similar space, unbounded by delineations of gender, ethnicity, and class. In the process of defining themselves outside traditional masculine or feminine borders, the two women approach an authenticity and integrity unattainable within the traditional geography. And there is risk in the no-man's-land.

Marie-Rose exists very much "on the boundary," both literally and intellectually. She embraces both the cause of the Palestinians in the camps and the welfare of the deaf-mute children at the school she runs in the Christian sector. She has been raised in a Lebanese Christian tradition, but she loves a Palestinian man. Almost daily, she crosses between the Christian and Palestinian sectors of the city, choosing the risk of a life without borders; emotionally, as well, she embraces the two cultural perspectives. She embraces the humanity at the heart of both traditions and creates a personal identity in a new space, encompassing a transcendent moral ethic that extends beyond the framework of tribalism and factionalism.

Like the scriptwriter, Marie-Rose is an observer with an underlying concern for others. There is a significance in the particular children whom Marie-Rose embraces in her work. For these deaf-mutes are, like women in a man's world, outcasts. They have no place within the culture of militarized boys posturing as men. Like women, they exist mainly on the boundary; they are observers. Their vision is extra sharp. They do not hear, but they see and feel the violation of their world. They respond to love, and they are aware of the presence of death.

In contrast, the young hunters turned Phalangist militiamen hear, but do not listen. For them, talk is cheap. The only real currency is power. They think of the female only as not male: femininity denotes a void. To them, the "feminine" qualities such as love, forgiveness, gentleness, and respect for life are weak, outside the "masculine" consciousness. All their aspirations are toward power and dominance. In the process, these men severely limit their effectiveness as human beings. Adrienne Rich describes this process as a "dissociation of sensibility." She says, "Denying his own feminine aspects, always associating his manhood with his ability to possess and dominate women, man the patriarch has slowly, imperceptibly, over time, achieved a degree of self-estrangement, self-hatred, and self-mutilation which is coming to have almost irreversible effects on human relationships and on the natural world."[5] For in rejecting the "feminine" qualities within his own consciousness, each of Adnan's young men is not merely throwing aside an integral part of himself; he is also participating in a fundamentally exploitive and destructive way of life.

The dehumanization that allows these young men to justify the kidnapping, torture, and execution of Marie-Rose can be seen as a reflection of their hierarchical world view. Riane Eisler describes the distortions of this masculinist perspective as they manifest themselves in the "dominator solutions": "Be it rightist or leftist, Christian or Muslim, the totalitarian solution is nothing more nor less than an updating of the androcratic solution. Its basic premises are contempt for 'effeminate' or peaceful, approaches, a conviction that obedience to orders, be they divine or temporal, is the ultimate virtue, and a creed that—starting with male and female—divides humanity into in-groups and out-groups that must forever be at war."⁶ The limited perspective of Adnan's young men closely parallels the mentality that Eisler describes. Even the more sensitive Mounir, when confronted by Marie-Rose, says: "I only recognize the power of the State, even when that's based on nothing but violence. It's violence that accelerates the progress of a people" (55). And later, when Marie-Rose asserts her belief that the Palestinians and Christians are not enemies but brothers, he distances himself with the statement, "I represent legality" (57). His callousness is reminiscent of the Nazi obsession with the legality of unimaginable atrocities. Mounir substitutes "the law" for personal morality in order to dissociate himself from his decision to execute Marie Rose. It is only by hiding behind the authority of the State, denying the validity of her inclusive moral ethic, that he can ignore her impassioned confrontation.

It is Adnan's most extreme character, Fouad, who is the ultimate authoritarian, the ultimate fascist, the ultimate terrorist. His is a morality of total power: "I didn't position artillery on the hills of this city to get myself mixed up in some story about a woman. I did it to blow up things. A militia is a government without a governed. A militia is always right. . . . I am absolute order. I am absolute power. I am absolute efficiency. I've reduced all truths to a formula of life and death" (37). Fouad—whose name ironically means "heart"—represents the logical extension of the phallocentric mentality. He is desensitized to the complications of human compassion, having narrowed his perspective to allow only the most limited range of vision. In effect, his absolutism blinds him to the distractions of uncertainty, contradiction, and counterperspective. All truth is reduced to a hierarchy of power, in which dominance is the only logical motive for action. The ultimate solution is death. It is precisely this deadly perspective that Marie-Rose has risked confronting in order to define for herself an existence, a new space, that is not part of this morality of power. Unfortunately, the confrontation is ultimate; death is inevitable.

But it is in confronting the absolute power of death that Marie-Rose affirms and participates in the power of life, which is, in her words, "the love of the Stranger" (95). Whereas Mounir and his followers hide behind the rhetoric that simplifies the world into a division of "us" and "them," "our country" and "the enemy," Marie Rose affirms a morality that transcends such borders. And in her awareness of the authenticity of her position on the boundaries of her worlds, she is able to transcend her own victimization and her own cultural destiny. She says: "Morality is violence. An invisible violence at first. Love is a supreme violence, hidden deep in the darkness of our atoms. When a stream flows into a river, it's love and it's violence. When a cloud loses itself in the sky, it's a marriage. When the root of a tree splits open a rock it's the movement of life. When the sea rises and falls back only to rise again it's the process of History. When a man and a woman find each other in the night, it's the beginning of the end of the tribe's power and death itself becomes a challenge to the ascendancy of the group" (55).

In identifying morality as violence, Marie-Rose redefines violence as the crossing of the boundaries, or barriers, that define our individual existences, not with the force of destruction but with the force of creativity. This is the violence of Love, a healing violence that transcends the divisive boundaries of the physical universe and enters into the dynamism of the evolutionary process, the history and the future of all existence. It is within this "supreme violence" that we and the universe are one, and that life and death can be seen as a universal evolutionary process that makes the phallocentric principles of factionalism and tribalism ultimately meaningless.

In her personal confrontation with death, Marie-Rose embodies a moral conviction that gives both her life and her death a meaning and integrity that go beyond the isolation of her individual death. She becomes the embodiment of her definition of love. She says: "I know that the only true love is the love of the Stranger. When you have cut the umbilical cords that bind you together, you will at last have become real men, and life among you will have meaning" (95). These young men, bound together by their "umbilical cords," are like babies pretending to be men. They are constricted, their development bound by the umbilical cords of their tribalism and exclusive identity with the group. It is as if they have not separated from their mothers, still being nourished by the common blood, the exclusive bond that at once sustains them and entangles them in the mentality of the tribe. Marie-Rose challenges them to cut these cords of tribal dependency and confront the risk of entering the unbounded territory of an authentic human connectedness.

For Marie-Rose, love of the Stranger is the force that allows all humanity (both male and female) to become "real," fully human, and full participants in the process of creation. She has, in effect, become a Christ figure, dying for love of the Stranger, embodying the law of Love that transcends the law of men, that dissolves the barriers that divide us from each other and within ourselves. In this ultimate reconciliation of opposites, the final dissolution of the borders maintaining our internal and external separateness—us versus them, Christian versus Muslim, masculine versus feminine—her feminist ideology manifests its potential for evolutionary social change.

The image of Marie-Rose as the sacrificial victim provides a symbolic closure to the novel that allows the reader to extract meaning from an otherwise irreconcilable death, but the recognition of this symbolic paradox requires a considerable leap from the historical moment to the transcendent. The historical basis of the novel remains the torture, rape, and murder of an innocent woman. A major implication of this narrative would appear to be that to reject the phallocentric ideology, to embrace the Stranger and violate the boundaries of the patriarchal order, is to become its victim. We know historically that the borders separating human beings from each other as individuals and societies still prevail, and that the traditional order of ethnic, religious, and gender-based marginalization still predominates both in the political realities of the Middle East and in personal and cultural ideologies throughout the world.[7]

The feminist ideology that the novel articulates, in creating its own space and crossing the borders of traditionally defined cultural territory, would seem to invite and ultimately even to require a sacrificial resolution such as the martyrdom of Sitt Marie-Rose. Yet for her to become the scapegoat of the existing order seems only to confirm its deadly exaltation of power. In fact, the symbol of sacrificial violence remains central to phallocentric religious tradition. Margaret Whitford's discussion of the basis of religious sacrifice as interpreted by René Girard and shaped by Luce Irigaray demands a further consideration of Adnan's use of Marie-Rose as a sacrificial symbol. Girard "claims that the function of religion is to keep violence out of the community by means of the mechanism of the scapegoat, or a ritual that substitutes for it. For Girard, brotherhood, the pact between the brothers, does not lead to harmony; the regime of the Same produces conflict, because the brothers have the same desires, which they are unable to negotiate, except through the medium of a third party, a scapegoat, who insures their unanimity. Violence, then, can be temporarily expelled from the community, but only at the price of another violence, a sacrificial victim."[8]

According to Whitford, Irigaray agrees that religion serves the purpose of curbing societal conflict and unifying members within the masculinist social order. Yet she also notes the correspondence of sacrificial violence to the Freudian model of male sexuality as tension-discharge-homeostasis. Moreover, for Irigaray there is a prior, more fundamental sacrifice, that of the mother, which society does not recognize; and this primary devaluation, the refusal of society to validate this debt to the mother, results in a social impasse between men and women.

It would seem that for Irigaray the devaluation of the female in the masculine order represents an omission so fundamental as to invalidate the sacrificial symbol. She proposes that the Christian Eucharistic ritual partakes not of the body and blood of Christ, but of that of woman. Instead, Irigaray opposes the value of fertility to the masculine symbol of sacrifice. She links this new feminine valuation, or economy of fertility, with the adoption of social symbols or rituals that acknowledge and validate female experience and, more important, the utilization of linguistic symbols, words, to substitute for sacrificial violence in the mediation of societal conflict. For Irigaray, the God who requires sacrifice must be replaced with a God who is the word, or mediating symbol.[9]

Irigaray articulates the possibility of an existence in which mediation, the *word,* rather than sacrificial violence and death, catalyzes the transcendental "moment" of reconciliation. It becomes clear that the real significance of Adnan's novel is contained more in the healing violence of the words spoken by Marie-Rose to her captors than in the final violence of her death. Of this the narrator-scriptwriter says: "Like patients maintained with transfusions of blood and food, the Arab world lies on an operating table. The equipment should be removed, the respirator unplugged. The patient should be obliged to spit out, not the mucous, but the original illness, not the blood clogging his throat but the words, the words, the swamp of words that have been waiting there for so long" (100).

The patient represents not only the Arab world but patriarchal society as a whole. The throat-clogging mucus and blood are merely the symptoms of the underlying sickness. The "original illness" is the silence, the failure to speak, the stagnation and death of the *word* in the "swamp of words that have been waiting there for so long." By refusing to validate the "other," to "spit out" the stagnating swamp by uttering the words, even the angry words, of mediation and healing, the patient chooses to die.

Clearly, for Adnan, the only hope amid the chaos and sickness of society is the word, and the real danger, in the end, is silence. "Whether you like it or not, an execution is always a celebration. It is the dance of Signs and their stabilization in Death. It is the swift flight of silence without pardon" (104–5). Both in her life of compassionate commitment and in her *words,* the outward signs and symbols of her love of the Stranger,

Marie-Rose brings us closer to a realization of Adnan's message. The creative and dangerous violation of boundaries, the quiet rebellion in which she engaged every day, and the final, enraged penetration of the silence with her words of loving violence, are the medium of ultimate reconciliation.

Notes

1. For a brief history of the Lebanese Civil War, see Thomas L. Friedman, *From Beirut to Jerusalem,* 11–18.

2. Adnan's prophetic poem "The Beirut-Hell Express," written in English in 1970, is excerpted in Joanna Bankier and Deirdre Lashgari, eds., *Women Poets of the World,* 102–5.

3. Etel Adnan, *Sitt Marie-Rose,* 2. Subsequent page references to this work will be given parenthetically in the text.

4. Mary Daly, *Beyond God the Father,* 40–41.

5. Adrienne Rich, *On Lies, Secrets, and Silence,* 111.

6. Riane Eisler, *The Chalice and the Blade,* 180–81.

7. For a discussion of the ongoing ethnic marginalization of Palestinians in Israel and its implications, see Edward Said, "An Ideology of Difference."

8. Margaret Whitford, *Luce Irigaray: Philosophy in the Feminine,* 145. Whitford cites the following sources particular to this discussion: René Girard, *Violence and the Sacred;* and Luce Irigaray's *Ethique de la différence sexuelle,* "Women, the Sacred, and Money," and *Sexes et parentés.*

9. Whitford, *Luce Irigaray,* 145–47.

DEIRDRE LASHGARI

Disrupting the Deadly Stillness:
Janice Mirikitani's Poetics of Violence

> my poems
> strung like bloody beads across my throat,
> my disembowelment, my seppuku—
> scarlet entrails
> twisting from the open wound. . . .
>
> my unbeautiful hunger,
> this selfish desire to be loud, bigger
> than light, this longing
> for movement, my own.
>
> —Janice Mirikitani, "It Isn't Easy"

Janice Mirikitani's collection *Shedding Silence* is multigenre, incorporating poetry, short stories, and drama arising largely but not exclusively from the Japanese American experience.[1] In this volume she establishes a daring poetics of violence in which she appropriates—makes her own—what has been defined as taboo, inappropriate, improper. Here she speaks the unspeakable names of violence—against women, against Asians, against the planet. She gives voice to those who have been constrained into silence in the face of violation, thus shattering powerful gender- and culture-based injunctions to "keep still."

She reclaims her vision and her voice, and helps us reclaim ours, by creating an aesthetic counterviolence, violating boundaries, violating patriarchal assumptions, violating the reader's own resistances and silences. By peeling the ceremonial covering off the face of violence, she disrupts the deadly sameness, the status quo imposed by social constructs or literary genre. When she shocks, it is with purpose, a way of daring us past our squeamishness, shaking us into hearing, speech, and action.

Yet she is also remarkably gentle with her characters and poetic personae who are not yet capable of speech or action. In fact, whenever her writing seems to imply a binary opposition between us and them, or good and bad, she immediately deconstructs her own implied construction. Many of her poems cry out against the pain of externally or internally imposed silence. At the same time, she insists that we see what Western, and especially European American, feminists often miss, or mis-see—the complexity of the silences as well as the angers of people of color as they respond to multifaceted violence. She gives us no easy dichotomy between the traditional silent woman and the "modern" woman who has broken through her silence. Neither is "right." If we as readers fall momentarily into a polarized stance in relation to the world, we are never allowed to stay there.

This shifting awareness of ambivalence and ambiguity, of multifaceted experience, shapes the recurrences of one of the key images in the book. It is interesting that a work about silence and the rending of silence should begin with three poems in which a central image is the knife. For the silenced victim, the knife turns inward, against herself. But the corollary of this self-violation is the implied possibility of a move from silence to anger, turning the knife (literally or symbolically) against the victimizer instead of the victim, cutting through to truth.

For example, in the first poem of the book, "Without Tongue" (1), the character is initially described as "without tongue" because words would be powerless against her father's repeated sexual assault. Then she "lifts the rock where she had buried the knife, / afraid she would use it to kill her father." What follows is suggestive and ambiguous, leaving us unsure whether the purpose of the blade is to silence herself, definitively, or to cut through silence with contra-active violence: "Her tongue tastes its cold steel edge, / shrill like blood." After she makes and drinks (remembers drinking?) "shiso no ha" tea, "Chinese flowers bloom in her throat." [2] The poem ends with the line, "She cleans the blade and returns it to the drawer." Is she cleaning it of dirt? or of her own tongue's blood? Is it going back in the drawer to use again against herself? Or are the suggestions of self-inflicted violence only an unenacted undercurrent of threat beneath a surface threat against her father?

Because we don't know, the poem leaves us profoundly disturbed. Because the language is left deliberately unclear, we cannot wrap up the images in neat explanations, and they cling to us and haunt us, forcing us to circle back, as the character circles back to the knife. The poem's disturbing indeterminacy has enfolded us, implicated us. It does not so much give us meaning as impel us to make meaning, drive us into movement *through* the revolting images of a knife in the tongue or the heart of the father, into active revolt.

As we reread, the pivotal midlines of the poem take on new meaning, metaphorical. Blade of knife merges with blade of tongue. The "cold steel edge," the "shrillness," emerge from out of the rock she had turned herself into, buried herself under, to hide from the desire and terror of "killing daddy." ("Keep quiet. Don't tell anyone, or you'll be responsible for killing me.") At the end of the poem, the "blade" goes back into hiding—but nearer to hand, no more "under stone." "Chinese flowers bloom in the throat"; form and significance begin to emerge where before there was nothing.

The complex and disturbing indeterminacy of this first poem sets the tone for the rest of the first section (also entitled "Without Tongue"), and for the rest of the book as a whole. As we read further, what we have read accompanies us, continually shifting its face, its voice, surprising us.

The knife image reappears in the second and third poems. "Jade Junkies" describes a Japanese American woman who, "cut deep" when her G.I. lover abandoned her in the "middle of America," has now "carved out a place" for herself as owner-cook in a small town sushi cafe. Like her character, Mirikitani can "do anything with a knife" (3). She takes the image of "cutting" through a virtuoso multiplicity of variations, the metaphorical implications dancing in and out of the literal, revealing the human vulnerability under the tough image of the poem's persona. She could

> dice
> an onion before a tear
> could slide.
> Make cucumber history
> each stroke quick
> like a blink
> thinner than your skin. (3)

As the knife slices vegetables, it at the same time slices through her customers' (and former lover's) racist reduction of her to exotic sexual prey. In an unnervingly deft reversal of the power imbalance, the character "skins" her customers (as she later "slips fish from scale to skin") making *them* "crave," redefining the sexism and racism they can't even see. She can't change their flawed perceptions of her, but because she is aware as they are not, she can protect herself from them.

In the third poem of the book, "Prisons of Silence," the image of the "knife in the tongue" becomes explicit as embodiment of the self-destructive power of silence. This poem carries further the technique of split focus that we saw in "Jade Junkies," where the lines blur between the literal description of food being cut and the"cuts" of emotional pain. Here, Mirikitani violates the boundaries between personal and political—or rather, crossing back and forth, she makes us know the two realms were never separate. Part 2 of the poem speaks the tenderness and passion of the love between the speaker and her husband "before the war." Part 4 speaks of his death and the distance now between them, the "walls of silence." Part 6 speaks "containment" and "burial," and describes how "I rebuilt my life / like a wall, unquestioning" (8).

Indented, encased by the personal walls, is the larger history the speaker has tried to bury in silence. This history—of racism, internment, humiliation, and the silence not just of one person but of a community—threatens to burst through the speaker's carefully built walls. It is as if another self lives within her, blurting out what she has tried to hide.

> Who lives within me? . . .
>
> Go home, Jap!
> Where is home?
>
> A country of betrayal.
> No one speaks to us.
>
> We would not speak to each other. (6)

The lines "Who lives within me?" and "Where is home?" weave through the personal love story and the public history it encloses, until by part 6 the formal separation between them disappears. "Their laws" and "their crimes" worm their way into the personal voice, until finally

> He awakens from the tomb
> I have made for myself
> and unearths my rage.
>
> I must speak. (8)

As the language here obliterates the distinction between political and personal, it also blurs the distinction between the speaker and the man she loved and still loves. Syntactically, the "tomb" is his, and hers. It is he who lives, she who is interred. "He" (alive in her love for him) "unearths [her] rage," which she now knows to be no other than her love.

That other self within her, that "stranger with knife in her tongue /

and broken wing" (7), is no longer a stranger but her (now multiple) selves:

> 9.
> . . . We heal our tongues. . . .
>
> We give testimony.
>
> Our noise is dangerous.
>
> 10.
> We beat our hands
> like wings healed.
>
> We soar
> from these walls of silence. (9)

There is a psychological violence in the very process of breaking through silence. To see, to acknowledge, to speak— this is dangerous to political and ideological structures. But in not speaking, one violates one's self, as the violence of Mirikitani's images in "Breaking Silence" suggests: "Pride has kept my lips / pinned by nails" (35).

The anger that fuels the act of breaking through silence need not express itself explicitly in words. The mother's testimony before the 1981 "Commission on Wartime Relocation and Internment of Japanese American Civilians" is restrained. And in the short story "Tomatoes," the deadly threat of Hanako's rage is clothed, but by no means hidden, in words of oblique action and seeming quiet politeness.

Hanako understands, suddenly, that the neighbor Mr. Haufmann has defined her young daughter as sexual target, "there for the picking," as he lifts her "high in the air, her skirt flying above her panties," "gave [her] pears and figs . . . ripe and sweet," and "let [her] stand on his shoulders so [she] could reach the top branches" (37–40). Without raising her voice, without being explicit about her understanding of Mr. Haufmann's designs on the child, Hanako reverses the power relationship, redefining his implicit definition of woman and girlchild as "tomatoes," "pickings." Shifting the locus of implicit violence from them to him, she lets him know that she will stop at nothing to protect her daughter. She inquires politely about Mr. Haufmann's wife and sons. At the same time,

> Hanako's hoe high in the air, whacked like a sword through a ripe tomato, juices springing up, smearing the soil
>
> > There's nothing we won't do
> > to insure their happiness, is there?

her voice low and glinting now like her blade as she whacked off the
head of another tomato smearing the handle red. (39–40)

She speaks her meaning without words, and is understood. The young
child Lisa stands, "her eyes wide and instantly older, seeing Haufmann
wilting shriveled in sweat and the wrinkles of his wet shirt" (40). Mirikitani here redefines the gaze, now as the female power to annihilate patriarchy's deadly threat of appropriation. In violating the "appropriate," she
reclaims her anger and her proper, or own, dynamic being.

One of the polarities Mirikitani denies us is the easy division between
women (certainly the principal focus of this book) and men. Part 1 of the
book ends with "Slaying Dragon Ladies" (with the epigraph "On seeing
the movie 'The Year of the Dragon'"), a harsh and jolting poem that plays
menacingly with popular Western stereotypes of the "Asian woman":

> My fingernails
> are long, steel tipped,
> sharp as stilettos
> to more easily pluck
> your eye,
> cleanly sever it from its nerve,
> roll it in my palm.
> We believe the eye
> brings luck, health.
> Seasoned with shoyu,
> sucked like embryos from eggs.
> Ahhh. the nourishment. (43)

The tone of the poem seems parodic one moment, genuinely angry the
next, as if the silenced woman were "putting on" the costume of the stereotype as a way of claiming her valid rage, much as the narrator of Kingston's *The Woman Warrior* clothes her timid social persona in the secret
cloak of the avenging woman warrior, Fa Mu Lan. She is also "putting
on" the reader, trapping us in a "no-man's land" in which we can neither
take the speaker's stance seriously nor dismiss it. Thus the reader, male or
female, is backed into a binary corner in which repudiation of the patriarchy seems to include men as well. Read in isolation, the poem dares us
to respond, "Ok, now we've got her figured! She has it in for men."

Of course, whenever we have anything "figured," Mirikitani trips us
up. The next section, "It Isn't Easy," begins with three tender and empathetic love poems to men: "In Remembrance" for her uncle Minoru,

framed by two poems for her husband.³ "In Remembrance" reminds us that it is not only women who respond to the unspeakable pain of "unjust punishment, racism, and rejection sharp as blades" by silencing themselves (53). Echoing the way the earlier poems played with multiple connotations of "knife," the speaker shifts the focus from victim to agent of transformation as she shifts the implied definition of "blade." She vows to speak out—"she" multiplied—what her uncle could not speak: "Our tongues are sharp like blades / we overturn furrows of secrecy" (54).

Then, quite abruptly after this tender section, we are hit with the terrifying short story "Spoils of War," in which a young Asian American woman is brutally raped, murdered, and mutilated by a soldier back from Vietnam. Again, it would be tempting to see this story in terms of a polarization between the vulnerable woman and the male "enemy." Paradoxically, what prevents a binary opposition is the split narrative structure, in which the point of view alternates between that of the young woman, Violet, and that of the unnamed Vietnam vet.

The story opens with Violet jogging on a running path in the hills above the campus in Berkeley, thinking of her European American lover, their involvement in protests against the Vietnam War, her parents' distancing from her because she was not born a son. Suddenly, without warning, we realize we are no longer in her mind but in someone else's—a consciousness that assaults us with its increasingly psychopathic violence and brutally sexual and racist language. By violating the boundaries between the characters, between the sympathetic "hero" and the "villain," Mirikitani makes it impossible to maintain a good-bad, us-them split in our response. In fact, she suggests that encapsulating the evil in the person of a polarized "enemy" only covers it over and makes real healing impossible, in the way that an abcess hides and protects the deep infection.

By denying us any neat polarization, by simultaneously repelling us, confusing us, disturbing us, she also makes it impossible for us to keep the horror of the story at arm's length, separate from our own safe lives. As the crazed violence of the veteran overflows the boundaries of the young woman's life, so violence on a national and international scale overflows the neat protective walls we have put up around our lives.

We are repulsed by the mind of the veteran; and we are at the same time forced to understand the influences that have brought him here: the horror of the war that the draft and the economy threw him into, the racist and sexist ideologies inculcated by military training and the daily hell of combat, the way the imperatives of killing have violated the borders between here and there, now and then, in his mind, so that he can no longer distinguish between his flashbacks of war and the reality of the present.

Juxtaposing the thoughts of the rapist and those of the victim both domesticates and universalizes his violence. The narrative cannot be kept within the "box" of aberrant pathology, seen as the story of an individual rapist. The narrative structure brings the man out of the box, out from under the label. It places him in a human context, and therefore in a larger context. The rapist is not simply this man; he-it is the whole interlocking system of sexism, racism, and military-sanctioned violence in our society that seeps into our "safe" doings and thinkings.

Mirikitani's use of imagery reinforces this violating of boundaries between the "good guys" of the private world and the "bad guys" who threaten it. Thinking of her parents' grief over the death of their infant son when she was a child, and how they have used that unforgiving grief to wall her out, Violet envisions their silence as being "like blades beneath their tongues" (58). Parents as well as soldiers may carry weapons that can kill; the rapist is not the only one who is poisoned with sexism. And at the end of the story, in a terrifying confluence of the rapist's violence and the tenderness of a father at home, the text reads: "Gently he wraps the arm in his flak jacket. Carries it like a child to his van and leaves" (62).

In obliterating boundaries, freeing the narrative from a definitive past into a never resolved, never finished present, the story does not minimize the horror of the rapist's act; on the contrary, it increases and multiplies it. We feel horror not only at the loss of Violet's young life, but also at the violation of the soldier's humanity through all the larger structures of violence in our society. As we see in the soldier's monologues, the distinction blurs between Violet and Vietnamese women—or populace, or land—as part of the "spoils of war." The war is not just "over there"; life here is also being "spoiled." The author is demanding that we, confronted with these widening circles of violence, move from a polite and distancing silence to an anger capable of making changes.

Mirikitani sets herself a difficult task: to get us to face the manifestations of violence in our world, not to turn away but to act. The question is, how to get us to see what we would rather not see. A writer may "slap us upside the head" to get us to pay attention, assaulting us, for example, with "inappropriate" language or images. But it is not easy to sustain that technique effectively because before long it ceases to jolt us and begins to numb and desensitize. Mirikitani avoids that numbing through a use of paradox and contradiction that keeps us from reducing the pain to the frames of a narrative, or a snapshot.

In the first lines of the poem "Shadow in Stone," Mirikitani deflects our tendency to distance the unspeakable and unbearable horror of atomic war. Confronting the impossibility of making the horror felt to us, her readers, now, she opens the poem in a touristy tone, as if the speaker were writing a postcard home from Hiroshima 1984, recounting the "August heat," the museum visited, the park.

Then the tone shifts with the double-edged words "I come to you late"—late in the year, and thus in weather that is too hot; and too late to see, hear, feel the horror of the bombing. She breaks the silence of the touristlike distance that separates us from the horror—the distance in time, the distance of our resistance to hearing—by giving voice in turn to the river, to a person whose shadow burned into the stone, to the bowl from which an old man fed his dying daughter. Mouth to mouth, the mute witnesses speak through her.

Only the first voice, that of the river, attempts to speak the horror directly, remembering

> bodies
> leaping into my wet arms
> their flesh in flame, and the flies
> that followed
> maggots in the bloated sightless waste,
> skin rotting like wet leaves.
> My rhythm stifled, my movement stilled. (29–30)

By the end of this passage, this direct voice is also stilled, in part by the inadequacy even of these appalling words, in part by the excess of the words, which threaten to make us shut down because it hurts too much to let them in. "Photographs remind us of a holocaust / and imagination stumbles, beaten, aghast" (31).

The voices that follow—that of the shadow in stone and of the disfigured bowl—do not assault us through the brutality of their images. They reach us instead through the banality of horror, the sheer mundane everyday simplicity of their language and imagery. Mirikitani skillfully juxtaposes the common noun, unadorned ("teacup," "iron," "coins," "bowl") with an accompanying adjective, the imagination's attempt to see ("distorted," "crippled," "melted," "disfigured"). Often, though, the lines are stark in their simplicity.

The woman behind the shadow had always seen the sun as "a kind friend who has gently pulled / my rice plants skyward." Describing the day of the bombing, she says, "No, I did not see the sun." The voice of the bowl describes how the old man fed his daughter "droplet by droplet / into the crack of her mouth" and "rocked her still body / watching the red sunset" (31). Mirikitani knows when to give her readers space to breathe, to be still, to watch. She understands that the silences in and between words are also necessary if we are to hear the experiences of others, the human heartbeat, the breathing in and out.

In the narrative poem "Assaults and Invasions," Mirikitani brings us into the work through a deft manipulation of repeated images and phrases, moving from being to acting, from hearing to demanding to be heard. By mixing genres and points of view (or vantage points), she prevents the reader once again from keeping "dirty problems" wrapped in discrete—or discreet—packages. Domestic and international assaults and invasions alike are brought into open view, out of the closet, off the television screen. Moving in and out of the two perspectives, she forces us to see them as intimately connected issues of power and control.

The narrative presents an account of Linette, whose husband beats, rapes, and slices her up. Lest we recoil, or frame this horror in a "domestic violence" box, Mirikitani interposes passages of poetry into this story in which she implicitly draws the analogy between domestic and foreign violence, other "assaults and invasions." And in the process of transgressing boundaries of genre, she erases other boundaries. We begin by individualizing Linette's story, personalizing her pain. But the interposed text forces us also to see her story as part of a much larger picture. If we care personally and passionately about this particular woman, we are also asked to care about our government's assaults and invasions against other countries, which the media too often allow us to generalize into safe abstraction. Moreover, the text demands that we see not only the analogies and the connections but also our own responsibility for this whole configuration of violence—and that we *do* something.

Linette is caught in a classic double bind. "He said she wasn't any good, dumb and weak even for a woman" (80). Yet when she takes action (moving, calling the police, begging "the courts to restrain him"), he becomes "enraged by her acts of defiance." Whether silent or angry, she "deserves" to be beaten. The analogy with Grenada suggests that small Third World countries, too, are "asking for it" if they seem "dumb and weak"; and if they resist, take a stand against the abuser, they define themselves as the enemy and "deserve" to be destroyed.

The language in this piece is hard to take. After Linette has moved out, reported her husband, tried to get protection, he finds her: "When she wouldn't whimper or cry or open her thighs this time, he with his razor began to slice small slivers of flesh from her breasts, her crotch, her belly, like scaling a fish, until her body bubbled like a red carp. Her mouth so thick with pain, she could hardly scream stop it. stop it. stop it" (80). The reader wants to cry to Mirikitani, "Stop it. Stop it." The pain is too much. The language is too much. Not good art. Too ugly. Too explicit.

Mirikitani here challenges the assumption that literature must be "discreet," "within bounds," that it must not be "political," or angry, or take a position. Mirikitani's work suggests that everything we write is political and positioned. If we are never angry, it can only be because we have walled ourselves off from truth and refuse to see the daily violences that assault our fellow human beings on this planet. There is no such thing as "inappropriate language" if it communicates effectively the truth it carries. On the other hand, whitewashing truth, falsifying language into teatable politeness, *is* inappropriate. In this piece, the speaker-narrator asks, "So why do I think of this woman on the day of the invasion of Grenada?" The text answers through its interwoven repetitions: "flesh," "slivers," "thick with pain," "scream," "stop it."

> Her mouth so thick with pain, she could hardly scream
> stop it. stop it. stop it. (80)
>
> . . . we want to scream, stop it. (80)
>
> We beat our fists against the windows, weeping in the
> passageways . . . stop it. (81)
>
> . . . surprise that she had made him stop it. (81)
>
> We cannot catch our breath, our tongues too thick with
> rage, beating our fists against windows. (81)

Linette, despite her pain, does manage to scream, to take action to stop the violence. As the text increasingly implicates us in the scream, it also moves us out of the impotent and inarticulate rage that keeps us isolated, enclosed, unable to breathe, toward a collectively empowered voice that can end the violence, both at home and abroad. Unlike Linette and others for whom no effective action seems possible except a contra-active violence, we do have options. We can still act by being heard.

> We must breathe deeply.
> Escape through the windows.
> We must gather, find each other.

Hear the heartbeats, the power in our veins.
We must clear our voices,
take action to make ourselves known.
We must stop it
stop it
stop it. (81)

We do not have the luxury of the aesthetic "propriety" that shuts out the unaesthetic, uncomfortable sounds of pain. Once we hear these cries, we can no longer turn away. Moreover, we do not have the luxury of immobilizing and ineffectual anger. We must find in ourselves and in each other an anger with the transforming power to heal. In the passage above, the final period suggests that our voices, energized by creative anger, *can* stop the violence.

Yet in the structure of the whole book, as in individual sections and pieces, we are not permitted any cathartic certainties or resolutions. The ambiguities and contradictions remain, still murky, demanding that we enter into the frame of the work, unraveling what we can. We are left with the task of speaking out the truths we think we understand, and acting collectively out of our passionately individual perceptions.

In this never finished task, we are not alone. The book ends with the long play "Shedding Silence," from which the book takes its title. A central motif in the play is the continued sniping hostility between Jadine, the "big mouth" rebel, and her conservative and patriarchal brother Russell. At the end of the play, the mutual misunderstandings in the family as a whole persist, but with a blurring of the lines of division. The tone now is gentler, less hostile. A healing has taken place, a reaffirmation of the community within the family despite—or rather, with—all their differences.

In terms of plot, of the actual interactions among the characters, there is no apparent justification for this perceived movement toward healing. To understand this shift, we need to imagine the reader-audience as part of the cast. The impression we get of a healing among the characters is actually a reflection of our response to the play's deconstructing of its initial binary oppositions: rebel-conservative, idealist-pragmatist, mother-daughter, father-son, brother-sister, male-female.

What has happened? Again and again, the play moves characters out of their locked opposing pairs. The sexism of the men is contextualized as we are allowed to hear their voices when they are not locked in polarization and can admit to each other their confusion, insecurities, childhood pain. The mother's hostile opposition to Jadine is deflected by Uncle

Tosh and the grandmother. Tosh dares to break the sentimentalized silence the parents have woven to protect them from the truth about their grown retarded son, Hiro. The grandmother, outside the circle of family warfare, shifts the locus of conversation to Hiro's difficult birth in the internment barracks. As the rest of the family is drawn into memories of the camps, breaking the taboo against mentioning them, they indirectly validate Jadine in her work to obtain reparations for internees. The splits and polarizations have blurred as the complexities of each person are spoken and heard.

The play ends with images suggestive of healing and community. Tosh says, "Let's all have a drink"; and the family members "gather at the table to toast and feast." The spirits of the dead, Grandfather and Chieko, "float off stage, singing" (162).

Yet there is no easy closure. Even here, the discord seeps past the boundaries of the play, the section, the book, demanding to be acknowledged. Beneath Tosh's call to drink and toast is our, and his family's, awareness of his alcoholism; beneath the sibling teasing lies real hurt and difference. And the songs of Grandfather and Chieko carry reverberations of the stories they have told us: of Grandfather's rage at the guards for starving the internees, a rage that almost got him killed; of the racism involved in Chieko's failure in the theater and her white ex-G.I. lover's betrayal.

As Mirikitani shows in the early poem "Generations of Women," the paradoxes and contradictions are inseparable from the movement toward community.

> Mother, grandmother
> speak in me. . . .
>
> Generations of yellow women
> gather in me. . . .
>
> We will come like autumn shedding sleep
> a sky about to open with rage,
> thunder on high rocks. (15)

In form as in content, Mirikitani does violence to conventional definitions of the proper, crossing boundaries, continually unraveling our comforting either-or polarities. She mixes genres within a work, shifts voice and point of view, establishes tone and patterns of imagery only to undermine them, and merges disparate realms of significance, transgressing the expected. In the process of violating formal expectations, she also violates our discrete ground as readers, sucking us into the work through the holes she has knocked in our defenses, through the fissures in its surface and the indeterminacies in its meaning. She refuses to let us off the hook. She not only shatters her own silences and the multiple silences of her characters; she also demands that we participate in the continually unfinished process of disrupting the "is" and breaking through to an empowered "becoming."

Notes

1. Janice Mirikitani, *Shedding Silence* (Berkeley, Calif.: Celestial Arts, 1987). (Citations to this text are hereafter given by page number only.) Previous works include an earlier volume of poetry, *Awake in the River* (1978), and an edited collection entitled *Time to Greez! Incantations from the Third World*. Her work has also been published widely in journals and anthologies.

2. *Shiso no ha* is an herb the leaves of which are used in preparing pickled plums. Tea made from this plant is believed to be good for anyone who is feeling unwell or is suffering from a sore throat. (Thanks to Doris Okada for this information.)

3. Mirikitani's husband, Cecil Williams, is the African American minister of San Francisco's Glide Memorial Church. Mirikitani has played a leading role in Glide's multiethnic social justice and community-building work.

ANN E. REUMAN

"Wild Tongues Can't Be Tamed": Gloria Anzaldúa's (R)evolution of Voice

> But it was the glint
> of steel at her throat
> that cut through
> to her voice.
> She would not be
> silent and still.
> She would live,
> arrogantly.

—Lorna Dee Cervantes, Emplumada

As it is for the Chicana poet Lorna Dee Cervantes in the epigraph above, so it is for her contemporary Gloria Anzaldúa, that the glint of steel at her throat does not cut her voice, but cuts through *to* her voice. Living on the border between Texas and Mexico, Anzaldúa finds herself in a land annexed by violent conquest, where the prominent features are hatred, anger, and exploitation.[1] As a twentieth-century Chicana *tejana* feminist poet and fiction writer, she realizes that little has changed since the middle of the nineteenth century when Mexican Americans, particularly women, had little voice. Alienated from both the Mexican and the American cultures, which find no room for lesbian, working-class writers of color, Anzaldúa acknowledges in *Borderlands / La Frontera: The New Mestiza* (1987) that "this is her home / this thin edge of / barbwire," and painfully recognizes that the dividing line is a wound that "splits me splits me" (2). Significantly, though, Anzaldúa does not let the wound destroy her. Rather, through her writing she heals the wounds, locating the points of pain, re-membering the discarded fragments of herself, and creating from the spaces between the different worlds she inhabits a new, affirmative, feminist landscape (20).

Anzaldúa is, as she writes in her preface to *Borderlands / La Frontera*, "a border woman," one who lives at the juncture of cultures and struggles to keep intact her shifting and multiple identities. Coeditor with prominent Chicana feminist Cherríe Moraga of the groundbreaking anthology *This Bridge Called My Back: Writings by Radical Women of Color* (1981), published author of poetry and prose, university instructor of Chicano studies, feminist studies, and creative writing, and political activist, Gloria Anzaldúa is an important voice in the literary world today. She understands the power of words and of collective voice and urges validation of a new mestiza language and way of life. In reappropriating the marginalized, she has found strength in her place of contradictions, has organized with other Third World feminists to resist divisive oppressions, and urges self-reconstruction and cultural synergy based on dialogic polyvocality, transformative crossings, and affirmative indeterminacy.

Retelling the story of the Alamo from the Mexican point of view, Anzaldúa exposes the violence enacted by white supremacists against Mexican citizens cut off from their country by the overnight erection of the border fence in 1848, and she tells the story of a people appropriated along with the land: "The Gringo, locked into the fiction of white superiority, seized complete political power, stripping Indians and Mexicans of their land while their feet were still rooted in it. *Con el destierro y el exilo fuimos desuñados, destroncados, destripados*—we were jerked out by the roots, truncated, disemboweled, dispossessed, and separated from our identity and our history" (7–8). The annexation of Chicanas that Anzaldúa addresses in her writings, however, is not just geographical and historical: it is cultural; it is literary; and it is personal. As a poor Mexican-American, a woman, a lesbian, and a writer, Anzaldúa faces intense and unrelenting threats of violence. If she does not renounce herself in favor of the male, she is considered selfish. If she does not marry and have children, she is a failure as a woman. If she rebels, she is a *mujer mala*. If she admits sensing the spiritual in the body, she is dismissed as "pagan," "superstitious," "irrational," or "mad." If she speaks bilingually or with a Chicana accent rather than keeping her English and Spanish separate and proper or untainted, she is ignored or invalidated. If she speaks of her difference, she is gagged, caged, and bound. If she questions the dominant paradigms, she is beaten or maligned. And if she names the violences done her, she can expect her tongue to be torn out by being "edited" or not published. The risks of being a woman (particularly a woman of color) are little different from those faced for speaking against violences done one as a woman: being battered, lynched, raped, sterilized, sold into prostitution. Individual annihilation, if not cultural genocide, threatens any of the marginalized if she presumes to challenge or defy white, patriarchal control.

Anzaldúa makes the brutal violence against women, workers, and people of color explicit in "We Call Them Greasers," a poem written from the point of view of a white man raping the Mexican wife of a share-cropper. Linking women to the land, both of which to his mind are made for seminal penetration and his exploitation, the rapist in this poem "plow[s]" into the woman, unmoved by her "whimpering" and "flailing." When he senses the woman's husband watching the rape and hears him "keening like a wild animal," he caps violence with racist disgust for the woman he has victimized:

> in that instant I felt such contempt for her
> round face and beady black eyes like an Indian's.
> Afterwards I sat on her face until
> her arms stopped flailing,
> didn't want to waste a bullet on her.

In "A Sea of Cabbages," Anzaldúa shows through the image of a land-owner "rooting" in a sea of female field workers that this is not an isolated incident but a rape that marks a history of violence. His inheritance a "thick stained hand / rooting in the earth," the man in this poem "tears" the cabbages from their nests, and "rips" the sexualized outer leaves until he reaches the more tender leaves at the core. Significantly, though, Anzaldúa subtly subverts male power in this poem, writing at the heart of it that, although this violence against women (and perhaps, more metaphorically, this violence against women of color who write, and write radically) happens "century after century," it is the man, not the women, who here is "flailing" and unleafed. In the last two stanzas, it is his mouth from which spume froths as the earth slams his face, his eyes that congeal in the baking sun, and his "broken shards" that are swept up by the wind; for as Anzaldúa insists, "He cannot escape his own snare."

In "Holy Relics," another poem in the collection, Anzaldúa extends her protest, and writes not just of the brutal dismemberment of women by patriarchal society as shown in the sanctified violence of "the good Father," but also of the accountability of women who acquiesce in such rituals of violation. Tellingly, Anzaldúa locates her poem in a feminized space identified by muteness, womblike enclosure, and experience outside patriarchal language: a town situated in a "silent landscape," in a "bricked-up place in the wall" from which "issued a sound to which they could give no name." Here, the "good father Gracian," in secret, by the light of torches held by cloistered nuns, exhumes the holy relics of Saint Teresa, entombed, significantly enough, nine months. The coffin "pulled" from the cavern, the lid "broken," the nuns scrape the earth clinging to the woman's skin, look their fill, then swaddle her in clean linen. Birthed into violence violently, women in patriarchal societies, Anzaldúa suggests, are reified and abused, made object and spectacle, open prey to religious gazers and collectors. Worship and dismemberment are synonymous: the Father approaches the saint, lifts her hand as if to kiss it, and instead with a knife severs her wrist from her arm. Then, as if embracing a gruesome newborn, the inevitable offspring of such violent appropriation, he hugs her cleaved hand to his body. Two years later, another priest disinters the saint to claim her body for the town of Avila, cuts off her truncated arm and flings it to the nuns of Alba "as one would a bone to a dog," and gallops off through the streets with the corpse of the saint. Though the woman's mouth is tightly shut and cannot be opened and her face is a little darker this time ("because the veil [of silence?] became stuck to it"), and though of course she is missing an arm, the rest of her body is intact. Returned to her grave by Pope's decree (prompted by assumption of ownership rather than by respect for her remains), she is again exhumed, this time surrounded by a crowd coveting her body, and pieces of her flesh are pinched off by ardent fingers: the priest snaps off two fingers from her remaining hand, another severs her right foot from her ankle, a third plucks three ribs from her breast, another gouges out an eye, and the rest auction off the scraps of her bones. Three centuries later, prying at the edges of the wound where her heart had been ripped out—the edges charred "as though by a burning iron,"—physicians examine "the remains of a woman."

At issue, quite literally here, is women's integrity, the constant struggle particularly of women of color to keep their bodies, their selves, intact against the ravages of the privileged. Power, Anzaldúa avers, lies in passing on what we have learned, in refusing what feminist poet and essayist Audre Lorde calls "historical amnesia" and in demanding accountability for the violences done women.[2] Personal and societal healing and survival depend on re-membering: facing the "residues of trauma" (70), naming the violences against women of color, and acting for change.

Anzaldúa knows the silencing forces surrounding her. "Who gave us permission to perform the act of writing?" she asks in her essay "Speaking in Tongues: A Letter to 3rd World Women Writers." She writes: "The voice recurs in me: *Who am I, a poor Chicanita from the sticks, to think I could write?* How dare I even considered becoming a writer as I stooped over the tomato fields bending, bending under the hot sun, hands broadened and calloused, not fit to hold the quill, numbed into an animal stupor by the heat."[3] And even if she finds the strength to legitimize her writing, who hears her? As Anzaldúa also notes: "Unlikely to be friends of people in high literary places, the beginning woman of color is invisible both in the white male mainstream world and in the white women's feminist world, though in the latter this is gradually changing. The lesbian of color is not only invisible, she doesn't even exist. Our speech, too, is inaudible. We speak in tongues like the outcast and the insane."[4] Yet if she *is* heard, she faces the threat of violent silencing: by invalidation of her voice as "too angry," "too harsh," or "too strident" (read "too political"); by "invitations" to blanch representations of her culture, her language, and her sexuality; or by figurative-literal mutilation. The societal expectations and implicit threat for transgression are clear: "The white man speaks: Perhaps if you scrape the dark off of your face. Maybe if you bleach your bones. Stop speaking in tongues, stop writing left-handed. Don't cultivate your colored skins nor tongues of fire if you want to make it in a right-handed world."[5]

In the section of *Borderlands / La Frontera* entitled "How to Tame a Wild Tongue," Anzaldúa describes a literal and forceful invasion of female space that speaks as much about patriarchal numbing of the bilingual as of the female voice: " 'We're going to have to control your tongue,' "the dentist says as he cleans out her roots and caps her teeth; " 'I've never seen anything as strong or as stubborn.' And I think, how do you tame a wild tongue, train it to be quiet, how do you bridle and saddle it? How do you make it lie down?" (53) Equally destructive for Anzaldúa were the warnings of her mother to eradicate what Morrison in *The Bluest Eye* calls "funkiness"; to stay out of the sun lest her skin darken, to wrap her budding breasts in tight cotton girdles lest she betray her sexuality, to clip her accent.[6] As Anzaldúa writes about her parents in her poem *"Cihuatlyotl, Woman Alone"*: "as I grew you hacked away / at the pieces of me that were different." Yet even more insidious than her parents' pressure to assimilate is Anzaldúa's own excision of her darker selves, which she represents variously as an animal, an intruder, a "dark shining thing." And when it is not a part of herself that she alienates or denies, it is a part "lovingly" put to death, as in her poem "Cervicide" (a title that conjures images of the uterus as much as of a deer) where the penalty for being caught in possession of a deer (symbolic of women's Self, Anzaldúa notes) prompts Prieta ("the dark-skinned one") to crush the skull of her beloved pet before the game warden does. "It is our custom," she writes in "The

Cannibal's *Cancion*," another poem in the collection, "to consume / the person we love." Every motion to speak battles heavy cultural encouragement to kill off the female, the sexual, the bilingual, the nonwhite, the non-Anglo parts of herself; to split body and spirit; to hold her tongue or lose it.

Crucially, though, Anzaldúa resists injunctions to silence herself. Though "annexed," she is not conquered: "Wild tongues can't be tamed, they can only be cut out" (54). [Rather than bury her rage in static and impotent bitterness or internalized contempt, she transforms it into poetry. Rather than transfer blame onto her mother for being embedded in the same oppressive society Anzaldúa resists, she takes responsibility for her own complicitous rejection of socially unapproved parts of herself and learns to mother herself.[7] Audre Lorde sees this self-mothering as the power of the erotic, an "assertion of the lifeforce of women; of that creative energy empowered," a springboard for change: "Mothering. Claiming some power over who we choose to be and knowing that such power is relative within the realities of our lives. Yet knowing that only through the use of that power can we effectively change those realities. Mothering means the laying to rest of what is weak, timid, and damaged—without despisal—the protection and support of what is useful for survival and change, and our joint explorations of the difference."[8] It is finding "the *yes* within ourselves."[9] In *This Bridge Called My Back*, Anzaldúa says: "I write to record what others erase when I speak, to rewrite the stories others have miswritten about me, about you. To become more intimate with myself and you. To discover myself, to preserve myself, to make myself."[10] And a "protean being" (41), Anzaldúa makes herself into the many things she is. In her poem "*Cihuatlyotl,* Woman Alone," she writes:

> Raza.   I don't need to flail against   you.
> Raza *india mexicana norteamericana,*   there's no-
> thing more you can chop off   or graft on me that
> will change my soul.   I remain who I am, multiple
> and one   of the herd, yet not of it.   I walk
> on the ground of my own being   browned and
> hardened by the ages.   I am fully formed   carved
> by the hands of the ancients,   drenched with
> the stench of today's headlines.   But my own
> hands whittle   the final work   me.

For Anzaldúa as for feminist theorist bell hooks, speech is not just an expression of creative power; it is, hooks writes in *Talking Back*, "an act of resistance, a political gesture that challenges politics of domination that would render us nameless and voiceless."[11] Refusing to be discarded as the remains of a woman, Anzaldúa collects the bits and pieces of writing—parts of herself—strewn across her room ("my fragments on the floor"), and confronts her demons.[12] Fearful yet fascinated by the "wild animal kicking at its iron cage," she recognizes herself: "It had been my footsteps I'd heard" (167–69). She writes: "It was then I saw the numinous thing / it was black and it had my name / it spoke to me and I spoke to it" (172). It took her forty years, she reports in the section of her book entitled "Entering into the Serpent," to "acknowledge that I have a body, that I am a body and to assimilate the animal body, the animal soul" (26). Wrestling her own denials as well as cultural pressures to conform, she finally (though not without constant grappling) accepts and integrates "that dark shining thing" and the serpent-sexuality that are parts of herself; and she sees the vital importance of this naming and reclamation: "I know it's come down to this: / *vida o muerte*, life or death" (172). Anzaldúa chooses life. And she recognizes that this choice necessitates coming to terms with her anger.

In *Sister Outsider*, Lorde writes that "women responding to racism means women responding to anger; the anger of exclusion, of unquestioned privilege, of racial distortions, of silence, ill-use, stereotyping, defensiveness, misnaming, betrayal, and co-optation."[13] In the poem "*El sonavabitche*," Anzaldúa expresses the rage that has choked her for years:

> brown faces bent backs
> like prehistoric boulders in a field
> so common a sight no one
> notices
> blood rushes to my face
> twelve years I'd sat on the memory
> the anger scorching me
> my throat so tight I can
> barely get the words out.

Anzaldúa does get the words out, and she uses that speech to fight further colonization of her voice. It is a struggle, she realizes, that reaches beyond a merely personal need. "Waging war is my cosmic duty," she writes in *Borderlands / La Frontera* (31). She will no longer veil the Chicana in her, nor will she repress her sexuality, or write conventional narratives, or append glossaries to her work. She will not stand quietly by as "pseudo-liberal[s] . . . who suffer from the white woman's burden" attempt to talk *for* her: "This act is a rape of our tongue and our acquiescence is a complicity to that rape. We women of color have to stop being modern medusas—throats cut, silenced into a mere hissing."[14] She will speak; she will speak for herself; and she will speak in her own language: "Until I am free to write bilingually and to switch codes without having always to translate . . . and as long as I have to accommodate the English speakers rather than having them accommodate me, my tongue will be illegitimate. I will no longer be made to feel ashamed of existing. I will have my voice: Indian, Spanish, white. I will have my serpent's tongue—my woman's voice, my sexual voice, my poet's voice. I will overcome the tradition of silence" (59). And her affirmation extends the invitation-imperative to other women of color to write, and to write radically: "Write with your eyes like painters, with your ears like musicians, with your feet like dancers. You are the truthsayer with quill and torch. Write with your tongues of fire. Don't let the pen banish you from yourself. Don't let the ink coagulate in your pens. Don't let the censor snuff out the spark, nor the gags muffle your voice. Put your shit on the paper."[15]

Yet even as she claims that as poets-writers, "we wield a pen as a tool, a weapon, a means of survival," Anzaldúa acknowledges the self-doubts, fears, and pain inherent in such writing.[16] "*Escribo con la tinta de mi sangre.* I write in red. Ink. Intimately knowing the smooth touch of paper, its speechlessness before I spill myself on the insides of trees. Daily, I battle the silence and the red. Daily, I take my throat in my hands and squeeze until the cries pour out, my larynx and soul sore from the constant struggle" (71–72). The power of writing, she insists, resides in transforming such pain: "Writing is dangerous because we are afraid of what the writing reveals: the fears, the angers, the strengths of a woman under a triple or quadruple oppression. Yet in that very act lies our survival because a woman who writes has power. And a woman with power is feared."[17] Evolution of her voice from throttled murmurings to defiant cries and articulate self-affirmation begins with each piece of writing, each effort to transmute pain into power, each woman's battle against silence: "The revolution begins at home."[18]

That the war against silencing is also a process toward healing is clear in Anzaldúa's writing. In fact, it is such "talking back" that bell hooks places at the core of self-recovery: "Moving from silence into speech is for the oppressed, the colonized, the exploited, and those who stand and struggle side by side a gesture of defiance that heals, that makes new life and new growth possible."[19] It is her calling, Anzaldúa says, to "traffic in images" (70), a calling that transmutes anger and pain into a "numinous experience" (73). Yet this transformation, she insists, is not simple, quick, or miraculous: it is, rather, deliberate, physical, and wrenching. She states:

"When I don't write the images down . . . I get physically ill . . . Because some of the images are residues of trauma which I then have to reconstruct, I sometimes get sick when I *do* write. . . . But in reconstructing the traumas behind the images, I make 'sense' of them, and once they have 'meaning' they are changed, transformed. It is then that writing heals me" (70). Like defanging a cactus, living in a borderland and writing about the experience takes patience and the ability to endure intense pain: "Living in a state of psychic unrest, in a Borderland, is what makes poets write and artists create. It is like a cactus needle embedded in the flesh. It worries itself deeper and deeper, and I keep aggravating it by poking at it. When it begins to fester I have to do something to put an end to the aggravation and to figure out why I have it. I get deep down into the place where it's rooted in my skin and pluck away at it, playing it like a musical instrument—the fingers pressing, making the pain worse before it can get better. Then out it comes. No more discomfort, no more ambivalence. Until another needle pierces the skin. That's what writing is for me, an endless cycle of making it worse, making it better, but always making meaning out of the experience, whatever it may be" (73). "Making the pain worse before it can get better," Anzaldúa presses herself to get beneath the surface, to dig out poisonous barbs embedded in her flesh.

In "Cultures," Anzaldúa locates the beginnings of such healing in discovering her buried culture. Directed, significantly enough, by her mother to turn the soil below the clothesline for a garden, the speaker in this poem picks at the "hard brown earth" with an axe, "disinter[s]" a tin can, and "unmould[s]" a shell from a "lost" ocean, the bones of an "unknown" animal. Her sweat dripping on "the swelling mounds," she uncovers the remnants of a distinctly female culture, bred in a modern, seemingly sterile junk heap, nettled and variegated, but nevertheless alive. She rakes up "rubber-nippled" baby bottles, cans of Spam with "twisted umbilicals"; she "overturn[s] the cultures / spawning in Coke bottles / murky and motleyed." Significantly, her tilling of the mother-soil is done independently, without the help of any man. In her autobiographical essay "La Prieta" she makes this explicit:

> Nobody's going to save you
> .   .   .   .
> There is no one who
> will feed the yearning.
> Face it. You will have
> to do, do it yourself.[20]

Yet while there is no princely rescue, there is a feminist redemption. The effort to remember, as hooks asserts, is "expressive of the need to create spaces where one is able to redeem and reclaim the past, legacies of pain, suffering, and triumph in ways that transform present reality."[21] Out of the discarded, the marginalized, and the dispossessed, Anzaldúa creates a new landscape, a synergy of cultures; a place, as hooks phrases it, "where one discovers new ways of seeing reality, frontiers of difference."[22] In *Borderlands / La Frontera*, Anzaldúa names this enlightened way of seeing a "new *mestiza* consciousness": "At the confluence of two or more genetic streams, with chromosomes constantly "crossing over," this mixture of races, rather than resulting in an inferior being, provides hybrid progeny, a mutable, more malleable species with a rich gene pool. From this racial, ideological, cultural and biological cross-pollinization, an "alien" consciousness is presently in the making—a new *mestiza* consciousness, *una conciencia de mujer*. It is a consciousness of the Borderlands" (77).

The mestiza of which Anzaldúa speaks is both literal and figurative: it is the borderland between Mexico and the United States, a land cast aside by patriarchal governments as a part of neither country, a wasteland, even as both cultures strive to master with rules and laws those whom they have alienated; and it is a space reclaimed by the Chicana and recreated as the intersection of several heritages, a female space of confluence and power. In Anzaldúa's reenvisionment of this borderland, the mestiza is a space for a new and richer race, a mixed race made stronger by its crossings over. "If going home is denied me," Anzaldúa continues, "then I will have to stand and claim my space, making a new culture—*una cultura mestiza*—with my own lumber, my own bricks or mortar and my own feminist architecture" (77).

It is in this new space that Anzaldúa locates her lesbianism, her most pronounced resistance to colonization. By her own choice, she is "two in one body," an "entry into both worlds" (19), a crosser of unnatural boundaries. "For the lesbian of color," Anzaldúa writes, "the ultimate rebellion she can make against her native culture is through her sexual behavior. She goes against two moral prohibitions: sexuality and homosexuality. . . . The choice to be queer . . . is a path of knowledge—one of knowing (and of learning) the history of oppression of our *raza*. It is a way of balancing, of mitigating duality" (19). Perhaps most importantly, it is understanding her oppression as a lesbian that helps her to reconnect with her mother. Cherríe Moraga's words in "La Güera" seem to share meaning for Anzaldúa, her coeditor of *This Bridge Called My Back*. Moraga writes: "It wasn't until I acknowledged and confronted my own lesbianism in the flesh, that my heartfelt identification with and empathy for my mother's oppression—due to being poor, uneducated, and Chicana—was realized. My lesbianism is the avenue through which I have learned the most about silence and oppression." [23] It does not seem accidental that both lesbianism and the Mother become Anzaldúa's symbols of the new mestiza, "the coming together of opposite qualities within" (19).

More than mere resistance to patriarchal society, then, Anzaldúa envisions movement toward a new world of female possibility where personal and political healing begins with retrieval of her cultural myths as they were before the Conquest. It is a vision of return to the mother: one who is a balance of many differences, a crossroads, a bridge. She writes in "*La conciencia de la mestiza*": "As long as woman is put down, the Indian and the Black in all of us is put down. The struggle of the *mestiza* is above all a feminist one. As long as *los hombres* think they have to *chingar mujeres* and each other to be men, as long as men are taught that they are superior and therefore culturally favored over *la mujer,* as long as to be a *vieja* is a thing of derision, there can be no real healing of our psyches. We're halfway there—we have such love of the Mother, the good mother. The first step is to unlearn the *puta/virgen* dichotomy and to see *Coatlapopeuh-Coatlicue* in the Mother, *Guadalupe*" (84).

In *Borderlands / La Frontera,* Anzaldúa reconnects upperworld (light) *Tonantsi* with the underworld (dark) and sexualized *Coatlicue-Tlazolteotl-Cihuacoatl* from whom she had been split by the Spaniards and their Church after the Conquest, and retrieves *Guadalupe,* by Indian name *Coatlalopeuh,* who traces back to, or is an aspect of, earlier Mesoamerican fertility and Earth goddesses. That is, she resexes the virginized *Guadalupe.* The "synthesis of the old world and the new," *Guadalupe* "mediates between the Spanish and the Indian cultures . . . and between Chicanos and the white world. She mediates between humans and the divine, between this reality and the reality of spirit entities." Indeed, she is "the symbol of ethnic identity and of the tolerance for ambiguity that . . . people of mixed race . . . by necessity possess" (30). Importantly, though, *Guadalupe* is one of three mediators for Anzaldúa's people. She is joined by two other women of Aztec origin, *La Chingada* and *La Llorona.* History traditionally names the former *La Malinche,* cast off as the traitor woman who aided Cortés in his conquest of her people and condemned (by the culture that forced her into slavery and concubinage) as whore or mother of a bastard race of mestizos, a symbol of deviance and infection.[24] Anzaldúa, however, redefines her as *La Chingada,* "the raped mother whom we have abandoned" (30). Similarly, Anzaldúa alters the negative representations of *La Llorona* as a woman who transgressed her proper roles as mother, wife, and patriot.[25] Anzaldúa claims her as "the mother who seeks her children" (30), who laments her lost Chicanos-mexicanos (38).

Through these three women, "Our Mothers" (31), Anzaldúa rejoins long obscured parts of herself; and this reconnection allows her to be many things at once:

> You say my name is ambivalence? Think of me as Shiva, a many-armed and legged body with one foot on brown soil, one on white, one in straight society, one in the gay world, the man's world, the women's, one limb in the literary world, another in the working class, the socialist, and the occult worlds. A sort of spider woman hanging by one thin strand of web.
>
> Who me confused? Ambivalent? Not so. Only your labels split me.[26]

Anzaldúa resists attempts to label her what literary critic Mary Dearborn in *Pocahontas's Daughters* refers to as a cultural schizophrenic, and claims a new literature, more Indian in its roots than English.[27] Native American critic and novelist Paula Gunn Allen speaks of such literature in *The Sacred Hoop:* persons reared in traditional American Indian societies, she says, "do not organize perceptions or external events in terms of dualities or priorities. This egalitarianism is reflected in the structure of American Indian literature, which does not rely on conflict, crisis, and resolution for organization, nor does its merit depend on the parentage, education, or connections of the author. Rather, its significance is determined by its relation to creative empowerment, its reflection of tribal understandings, and its relation to the unitary nature of reality."[28]

For Anzaldúa, reconnection with her history is crucial to her healing, for, as she says, "by taking back your collective shadow the intracultural split will heal" (86). And such reconnection is at the core of her power. "I write the myths in me, the myths I am, the myths I want to become" (71). Grounding a new culture in the remains of the past, she creates a stronger species with "skin tone between black and bronze" who, survivors of a Fire Age, are "alive *m'ijita,* very much alive":

> Yes, in a few years or centuries
> *la Raza* will rise up, tongue intact
> carrying the best of all the cultures.
> That sleeping serpent,

rebellion-(r)evolution, will spring up.
Like old skin will fall the slave ways of
obedience, acceptance, silence.
Like serpent lightning we'll move, little woman.
You'll see. (203)

In finding her mouth, her "motherlode" (53), Anzaldúa makes of herself a bridge, huge and powerful, that spans abysses.[29]

The landscape of myth and "reality," of light and dark, of the many-legged spider woman, is not just abstraction: it is a borderland for each of us to live in, and a new literary terrain. This new mestiza speaks, for instance, for rediscovery and validation of writing based on difference. Protesting a patriarchal, exploitative history of literature that elevates "art for art's sake," "purity" of form, academic distancing, elitism, and individualism, Anzaldúa rejects that "sacred bull" and validates in its stead social art, mixed genres, multilingualism, writing that is simple, direct, immediate, and inclusive.[30] Writing, for her, is an enactment, a "performance," a "who" as much as a "what." Like the totem pole, it is an art form that merges the sacred and the secular, the artistic and the functional, art and everyday life (66). It is communal, inclusive, accessible to the common person, meant to be shared. It insists on going public. For, as literary critic Trinh T. Minh-ha suggests in *Woman, Native, Other,* "publication means the breaking of a first seal, the end of a 'no admitted' status, the end of a soliloquy confined to the private sphere."[31] Such writing, Anzaldúa asserts, celebrates open vistas; it finds its own voice, it speaks confidently, it encourages interchange, and it sees beyond itself. It is not a conquered thing.

In this new mestiza, Anzaldúa validates her voice as a first-generation writer and lesbian of color, saying that she will not be ashamed of her difference, she will not be invisible, she will not be inaudible, she will not speak in one tongue. She will speak as a woman and as a lesbian. She will write bilingually, speak with an accent. She will reflect her color loud and clear. And she will talk back: "I am possessed by a vision: that we Chicanas and Chicanos have taken back or uncovered our true faces, our dignity and self-respect. It's a validation vision" (87).

With this vision, Anzaldúa replaces barriers with bridges, urges a "crossing over," and opens up a new world of possibility for women of color who want to speak: "It was only when I looked / at the edges of things," she writes in her poem "Interface," that "where before there'd only been empty space / I sensed layers and layers." The cost of speech is clear; yet greater is the cost of silence. The personal, Anzaldúa recognizes with Lorde, is political: "I change myself, I change the world" (70).[32] The hope in Anzaldúa's catalytic writing is that other women of color will discover in it their own courage to heal, that they will dare to speak, and that others will listen. In the words of bell hooks: "The struggle to end domination, the individual struggle to resist colonization, to move from object to subject, is expressed in the effort to establish the liberatory voice—that way of speaking that is no longer determined by one's status as object—as oppressed being. That way of speaking is characterized by opposition, by resistance. It demands that paradigms shift—that we learn to talk—to listen—to hear in a new way."[33]

Notes

1. Gloria Anzaldúa, *Borderlands / La Frontera: The New Mestiza* (San Francisco: Spinsters-Aunt Lute, 1987), preface. Unless otherwise noted, all references to Anzaldúa's writing are to this edition and will be cited parenthetically in this text.

2. Audre Lorde, *Sister Outsider,* 117.

3. In Cherríe Moraga and Gloria Anzaldúa, eds., *This Bridge Called My Back,* 166.

4. Ibid., 165.

5. Ibid., 166.

6. Ibid., 198–99.

7. Anzaldúa's rejection of socially unapproved parts of herself calls to mind Cherríe Moraga's story "La Güera" in which, in reference to having disowned her language, Moraga writes that she "cut off the hands" of her gesticulating mother and aunts in her poems. Moraga and Anzaldúa, *Bridge,* 31.

8. Lorde, *Sister Outsider,* 173–74.

9. Ibid., 57.

10. Moraga and Anzaldúa, eds., *Bridge,* 169.

11. Bell hooks, *Talking Back,* 8.

12. Moraga and Anzaldúa, eds., *Bridge,* 171.

13. Lorde, *Sister Outsider,* 124.

14. Moraga and Anzaldúa, eds., *Bridge,* 206.

15. Ibid., 173.

16. Ibid., 163.

17. Ibid., 171.

18. Ibid., xxiv.

19. Hooks, *Talking Back,* 9.

20. Moraga and Anzaldúa, eds., *Bridge,* 200.

21. Bell hooks, *Yearning,* 147.

22. Ibid., 148.

23. Moraga and Anzaldúa, eds., *Bridge,* 28–29.

24. Alfredo Mirandé and Evangelina Enríquez, *La Chicana,* 24.

25. Ibid., 33.
26. Moraga and Anzaldúa, eds., *Bridge,* 205.
27. Mary V. Dearborn, *Pocahontas's Daughters,* 20.
28. Paula Gunn Allen, *The Sacred Hoop,* 59.
29. Moraga and Anzaldúa, eds., *Bridge,* 209.
30. Ibid., 167.
31. Trinh T. Minh-ha, *Woman, Native, Other,* 8.
32. See also, Lorde, *Sister Outsider,* 11.
33. Hooks, *Talking Back,* 15.

Works Cited
Contributors
Index

Works Cited

Abel, Elizabeth. *Virginia Woolf and the Fictions of Psychoanalysis.* Chicago: Univ. of Chicago Press, 1989.

———, ed. *Writing and Sexual Difference.* Chicago: Univ. of Chicago Press, 1982.

Adnan, Etel. "The Beirut-Hell Express" (1970). Excerpt in *Women Poets of the World,* ed. Joanna Bankier and Deirdre Lashgari, 102–5. New York: Macmillan, 1983.

———. *Sitt Marie-Rose.* Sausalito, Calif.: Post-Apollo, 1982.

Ajala, John D. "*The Beggars' Strike:* Aminata Sow Fall as a Spokeswoman for the Underprivileged." *Collections littératures africaines (CLA Journal)* 34, no. 2 (1990).

Alarcón, Norma. "The Theoretical Subject(s) of *This Bridge Called My Back* and Anglo-American Feminism." In *Making Face, Making Soul / Haciendo Caras: Creative and Critical Perspectives by Women of Color,* ed. Gloria Anzaldúa, 356–69. San Francisco: Aunt Lute, 1990. Rpt. in *Criticism in the Borderlands: Studies in Chicano Literature, Culture, and Ideology,* ed. Hector Calderón and José D. Saldivar, 28–39. Durham, N.C.: Duke Univ. Press, 1991.

Alexander, Edward. *The Resonance of Dust: Essays on Holocaust Literature and Jewish Fate.* Columbus: Ohio State Univ. Press, 1979.

Allen, Paula Gunn. *The Sacred Hoop: Recovering the Feminine in American Indian Traditions.* Rev. ed. Boston: Beacon Press, 1992. "Sky Woman and Her Sisters." [Excerpt from *The Sacred Hoop.*] *Ms. Magazine,* September-October 1992, 22–26.

———. *The Woman Who Owned the Shadows.* San Francisco: Aunt Lute, 1983.

Alleyne, Mervyn. *Comparative Afro-American: An Historical Comparative Study of English Based Afro-American Dialects of the New World.* Ann Arbor: Karoma Publishers, 1980.

Alloula, Malek. *The Colonial Harem* (Le Harem colonial). Trans. Myrna Godzich and Wlad Godzich. Minneapolis: Univ. of Minnesota Press, 1986.

Andrade, Susan Z. "Rewriting History, Motherhood, and Rebellion: Naming an African Woman's Literary Tradition." *Critical Theory and African Literatures.* Special issue of *Research in African Literatures* 21, no. 1 (1990): 91–110.

Angel, Albalucía. *Misiá señora.* Barcelona: Argos Vergara, 1982.

Annas, Pamela. "A Poetry of Survival: Unnaming and Renaming in the Poetry of Audre Lorde, Pat Parker, Sylvia Plath, and Adrienne Rich." *Colby Literary Quarterly* 18, no. 1 (1982): 9–25.

Anzaldúa, Gloria. *Borderlands / La Frontera: The New Mestiza.* San Francisco: Spinsters-Aunt Lute, 1987.

———. "Speaking in Tongues: A Letter to 3rd World Women Writers." In *This*

Bridge Called My Back: Writings by Radical Women of Color, ed. Cherríe Moraga and Gloria Anzaldúa, 165–74. New York: Kitchen Table—Women of Color Press, 1981.

Aptheker, Herbert. *American Negro Slave Revolts.* 1943. Rpt. New York: International Publishers, 1963.

Arkin, Marian, and Barbara Schollar, eds. *Longman Anthology of World Literature by Women, 1875 -1975.* New York: Longman, 1989.

Armstrong, Louise. *Kiss Daddy Goodnight: A Speak-Out on Incest.* New York: Hawthorn, 1978.

Artaud, Antonin. *The Theatre and Its Double (Le Théâtre et son double).* Trans. Mary Richards. New York: Grove Press, 1958.

Ashcroft, Bill, Gareth Griffiths, and Helen Tiffin. *The Empire Writes Back: Theory and Practice in Post-Colonial Literatures.* London: Routledge, 1989.

Bâ, Mariama. *Un chant écarlate: roman.* Dakar: Nouvelles Editions Africaines, 1984.

———. *Une si longue lettre.* Dakar: Nouvelles Editions Africaines, 1987. Trans. as *So Long a Letter* by Modupe Bode-Thomas. Oxford: Heinemann, 1989.

Baetz, Ruth. "The Coming-Out Process: Violence against Lesbians." In *Women-Identified Women,* ed. Trudy Darty and Sandee Potter, 45–50. Palo Alto, Calif.: Mayfield, 1984.

Bain, Raymond P., Raymond S. Greenbury, and J. Patrick Whitacker. "Racial Differences in Survival of Women with Breast Cancer." *Journal of Chronic Diseases* 39 (1986): 632–39.

Bakerman, Jane. "The Seams Can't Show: An Interview with Toni Morrison." *Black American Literature Forum* 12 (1978): 56–60.

Bakhtin, M. M. *Art and Answerability: Early Philosophical Essays.* Ed. Michael Holquist and Vadim Liapunov; trans. Vadim Liapunov and Kenneth Brostrom. Austin: Univ. of Texas Press, 1990.

———. "Discourse and the Novel." In *The Dialogic Imagination: Four Essays,* ed. Michael Holquist; trans. Caryl Emerson and Holquist. Austin: Univ. of Texas Press, 1981.

Bambara, Toni Cade. *The Salt Eaters.* New York: Vintage, 1981.

Bankier, Joanna, with Thomas D'Evelyn. "Greece of Antiquity." In *Women Poets of the World,* ed. Joanna Bankier and Deirdre Lashgari, 136–41. New York: Macmillan, 1983.

Bankier, Joanna, et al., eds. *The Other Voice: Twentieth-Century Women's Poetry in Translation.* New York: Norton, 1976.

Bankier, Joanna, and Deirdre Lashgari, eds. *Women Poets of the World.* New York: Macmillan, 1983.

Barthes, Roland. *Mythologies* (1959). Trans. Annette Lavers. New York: Hill & Wang, 1972.

Bass, Ellen, and Laura Davis. *The Courage to Heal: A Guide for Women Survivors of Child Sexual Abuse.* New York: Harper & Row, 1988.

Bateson, Gregory. *Steps to an Ecology of Mind: Collected Essays in Anthropology, Psychiatry, Evolution, and Epistemology.* New York: Ballantine, 1972.

Baym, Nina. "Melodramas of Beset Manhood: How Theories of American Fiction Exclude Women Writers." *American Quarterly* 33 (1981): 123–39.

Bedlington, Stanley S. *Malaysia and Singapore: The Building of New States.* Ithaca, N.Y.: Cornell Univ. Press, 1978.

Bell, Quentin. *Virginia Woolf: A Biography.* New York: Harcourt Brace Jovanovich, 1972.

Benstock, Shari, ed. *The Private Self: Theory and Practice of Women's Autobiographical Writings.* Chapel Hill: Univ. of North Carolina Press, 1988.

Bernabé, Jean, Patrick Chamoiseau, and Raphaël Confiant. *Eloge de la créolité.* Paris: Gallimard, 1989.

Beverley, John. "Introducción." *Revista de crítica literaria latinoamericana* (Lima) 18, no. 36 (1992): 7–18.

———. *La voz del otro: Testimonio, subalternidad y verdad narrativa.* Lima (Peru): Latinoamericana Editores, 1992.

Bhabha, Homi, ed. *Nation and Narration.* New York: Routledge, 1990.

Bickerton, Derek. "The Nature of a Creole Continuum." *Language* 49 (1973): 640–69.

Blair, Dorothy S. *Senegalese Literature: A Critical History.* Boston: Twayne, 1984.

Bolkosky, Sidney M. "Interviewing Victims Who Survived: Listening for the Silences That Strike." *Annals of Scholarship* 4, no. 1 (1987): 33–51.

Bonder, Gloria. "Women's Organisations in Argentina's Transition to Democracy." *Women and Counter-Power,* ed. Yolande Cohen, 65–85. Montreal: Black Rose, 1989.

Bourdieu, Pierre. "Marriage Strategies as Strategies of Social Reproduction." In *Family and Society, Selections from the Annales—Economies, Societies, Civilizations,* ed. Robert Forster and Orest Ranum, 117–45. Trans. Elborg Forster and Patricia M. Ranum. Baltimore: Johns Hopkins Univ. Press, 1976.

Bourne, Jenny. "Homelands of the Mind: Jewish Feminism and Identity Politics." *Race and Class* 29 (1987): 1–24.

Bousquet, Jean-Pierre. *Las locas de Plaza de Mayo.* Buenos Aires: El Cid, 1983.

Brewster, Anne. "Post-colonial and Ethnic Minority Literatures in Singapore and Malaysia: A Cultural Analysis." Diss. Flinders University of South Australia (Adelaide), 1989.

———. *Toward a Semiotic of Post-colonial Discourse: University Writing in Singapore and Malaysia, 1949–1955.* Singapore: Heinemann for the Centre for Advanced Studies, 1988.

Brittin, Alice A., and Kenya Carmen Dworkin. "Rigoberta Menchú: 'Con quien nos comunicamos?'" Interview with Menchú, including her poem "Patria abnegada." *Lucero: A Journal of Iberian and Latin American Studies* 3 (Spring 1992): 1–10.

Brontë, Charlotte. *Shirley.* 1849. Rpt. New York: Penguin, 1974.

Brown, Elaine. *A Taste of Power: A Black Woman's Story.* New York: Pantheon, 1992.

Brown, Lloyd W. *Women Writers in Black Africa.* Westport, Conn.: Greenwood Press, 1981.

Brown, Lyn Mikel, and Carol Gilligan. "Meeting at the Crossroads: Women's Psychology and Girls' Development." *Feminism and Psychology: An International Journal* 3, no. 1 (1993): 11–35.

Brown, William Wells. *Clotel or, The President's Daughter.* 1853. Rpt. New York: Carol Publishing Group, 1969.

Browning, Christine. "Changing Theories of Lesbianism: Challenging the Stereotypes." In *Women-Identified Women,* ed. Trudy Darty and Sandee Potter, 11–30. Palo Alto, Calif.: Mayfield, 1984.

Butler, Sandra. *Conspiracy of Silence: The Trauma of Incest.* San Francisco: New Glide, 1978.

Butler, Sandra, and Barbara Rosenblum. *Cancer in Two Voices.* San Francisco: Spinsters, Ink, 1991.

Carby, Hazel. *Reconstructing Womanhood: The Emergence of the Afro-American Woman Novelist.* New York: Oxford Univ. Press, 1987.

Case, Sue-Ellen. *Feminism and Theatre.* New York: Routledge, 1988.

Castro-Klarén, Sara, Sylvia Molloy, and Beatriz Sarlo, eds. *Women's Writing in Latin America.* Boulder, Colo.: Westview Press, 1991.

Certeau, Michel de. "History: Ethics, Science, and Fiction." In *Social Science as Moral Inquiry,* ed. Norma Haan, Robert Bellah, Paul Rabinow, and William Sullivan, 125–52. New York: Columbia Univ. Press, 1983.

Cervantes, Lorna Dee. *Emplumada.* Pittsburgh: Univ. of Pittsburgh Press, 1981.

Césaire, Aimé. *The Collected Poetry.* Trans. Clayton Eshleman and Annette Smith. Berkeley: Univ. of California Press, 1983.

Chemla, Yves. "*Kaselezo* de Frankétienne." In "*Frankétienne, écrivain haitien,*" ed. Jean Jonassaint. *Dérives* 53–54 (1986–87).

Cheung, King-kok. "'Don't Tell': Imposed Silences in *The Color Purple* and *The Woman Warrior.*" PMLA 103 (1988): 162–74. Rpt. in *Reading the Literatures of Asian America,* ed. Shirley Geok-lin Lim and Amy Ling , 163–90. Philadelphia: Temple Univ. Press, 1992.

Child, Lydia Maria. *Fact and Fiction: A Collection of Stories.* New York, 1847.

Chinweizu; Onwuchekwa Jemie; and Ihechukwu Madubuike, eds. *Toward the Decolonization of African Literature.* Washington, D.C.: Howard Univ. Press, 1983.

Christian, Barbara. "The Race for Theory." In *Making Face, Making Soul: Haciendo Caras,* ed. Gloria Anzaldúa, 335–45. San Francisco: Aunt Lute, 1990.

———. "'Somebody Forgot to Tell Somebody Something': African-American Women's Historical Novels." In *Wild Women in the Whirlwind: Afra-American Culture and the Contemporary Literary Renaissance,* ed. Joanne M. Braxton and Andrée Nicola McLaughlin, 326–41. New Brunswick, N.J.: Rutgers Univ. Press, 1990.

"Citizen B." *La liberté générale* (General Emancipation). In *Le Théâtre à Saint-Domingue,* ed. Jean Fouchard. Port-au-Prince, Haiti: Editions Henri Deschamps, 1988. Ms. (1955) in the Bibliothèque Nationale, Paris.

Cixous, Hélène. "The Laugh of the Medusa" ("Le Rire de la Méduse"). In *New French Feminisms,* ed. Elaine Marks and Isabelle de Courtivron, 245–64. New York: Schocken Books, 1981.

Cixous, Hélène, and Catherine Clément. *The Newly Born Woman.* Trans. Betsy Wing. Mineapolis: Univ. of Minnesota Press, 1986. First published as *La Jeune née,* Paris: Union Générale d'Editions, 1975.

Clammer, John. *Singapore: Ideology, Society, Culture.* Singapore: Chopman, 1985.

Clark, VèVè A. "Haiti's Tragic Overture: (Mis)Representations of the Haitian Revolution in World Drama (1796–1975)." In *Representing the French Revolution: Literature, Historiography, and Art,* ed. James Heffernan. 237–60. Hanover, N.H.: University Press of New England, 1992.

———. "When Womb Waters Break: The Emergence of Haitian New Theater, 1953–1987." *Callaloo* 15 (1992): 778–86.

Clarke, John Henrik, ed. *William Styron's Nat Turner: Ten Black Writers Respond.* Boston: Beacon Press, 1968.

Cobham, Rhonda. "'A Wha Kind a Pen Dis?': The Function of Ritual Frameworks in Sistren's 'Bellywoman Bangarang.'" *Theatre Research International* 15, no. 3 (1990): 233–49.

———, ed., with Sistren and Honor Ford-Smith. "Bellywoman Bangarang," by Sistren Collective. Unpublished ms.

Cohen, Andrew. "Some Scenes from an Intervention." *The Nation,* Feb. 8, 1993, 160–65.

Condé, Maryse. *Dieu nous l'a donné* (God's Gift). Paris: Editions Pierre Jean Oswald, 1972.

Connelly, Bridget. "The Arab World." In *Women Poets of the World,* ed. Joanna Bankier and Deirdre Lashgari, 88–92. New York: Macmillan, 1983.

Costa, Emilia Viotti da. "Slave Images and Realities." In *Comparative Perspectives on Slavery in New World Plantation Societies,* vol. 292, ed. Vera Rubin and Arthur Tuden, 293–310. New York: New York Academy of Sciences, 1977.

Daly, Mary. *Beyond God the Father.* Boston: Beacon Press, 1971.

Daneshvar, Simin. *Savushun: A Novel about Modern Iran.* Trans. M. R. Ghanoonparvar. Washington, D.C.: Mage, 1990.

Davis, Angela Y. "Reflections on the Black Woman's Role in the Community of Slaves." *Black Scholar* 3, no. 4 (1971): 2–15.

———. *Women, Race, and Class.* New York: Vintage Books, 1981.

Dearborn, Mary V. *Pocahontas's Daughters: Gender and Ethnicity in American Culture.* New York: Oxford Univ. Press, 1986.

de Lauretis, Teresa. "The Essence of the Triangle, or Taking the Risk of Essentialism Seriously: Feminist Theory in Italy, the U.S., and Britain." *Differences: A Journal of Feminist Cultural Studies* (1989): 3–37.

———, ed. *Feminist Studies, Critical Studies.* Bloomington: Indiana Univ. Press, 1986.

DeSalvo, Louise. *Virginia Woolf: The Impact of Childhood Sexual Abuse on Her Life and Work.* Boston: Beacon Press, 1989.

DeShazer, Mary K. "'Nothing but Myself? . . . My Selves': The Communal Muse of Adrienne Rich." In DeShazer, ed., *Inspiring Women: Reimagining the Muse,* 135–69. New York: Pergamon Press, 1986.

Diehl, Joanne Feit. "'Of Woman Born': Adrienne Rich and the Feminist Sublime." In Diehl, ed., *Women Poets and the American Sublime,* 142–68. Bloomington: Indiana Univ. Press, 1990.

Diop, Birago. *Les Contes d'Amadou-Koumba.* Paris: Fasquelle, 1947.

Diop, David. *Hammer Blows and Other Writings*. Bilingual with English trans. by Simon Mpondo and Frank Jones. Bloomington: Indiana Univ. Press, 1973.

Donaldson, Laura E. *Decolonizing Feminisms: Race, Gender, and Empire-Building*. Chapel Hill: Univ. of North Carolina Press, 1992.

Dorsinville, Roger. *Barrières* (Barriers). Haiti: H. Deschamps, 1945; English trans., 1946.

DuPlessis, Rachel Blau. "The Critique of Consciousness and Myth in Levertov, Rich, and Rukeyser." In DuPlessis, *Writing beyond the Ending: Narrative Strategies of Twentieth-Century Women Writers*, 123–41. Bloomington: Indiana Univ. Press, 1985.

Edwards, Lee R., and Arlyn Diamond, eds. *American Voices, American Women*. New York: Avon, 1973.

Eisler, Riane. *The Chalice and the Blade: Our History, Our Future*. San Francisco: Harper & Row, 1988.

Ekpenyong, Rosaline. "Women's Role in the New Age." Paper presented at the New Age Symposium, Univ. of Maiduguri, Nigeria, Mar. 12, 1978.

Elkins, Stanley. *Slavery: A Problem in American Institutional and Intellectual Life*. Chicago: Univ. of Chicago Press, 1959.

Ellis, Sarah. *The Daughters of England: Their Position in Society, Character, and Responsibilities*. New York: Appleton, 1844.

Eltit, Diamela. *Lumpérica*. Santiago, Chile: Las Ediciones del Ornitorrinco, 1983.

Fall, Aminata Sow. (1979). *The Beggars' Strike, or The Dregs of Society (La Grève des battu, ou Les Déchets humains.)* Trans. Dorothy S. Blair, London: Longman, 1981.

———. *Le Jujubier du patriarche*. Dakar: C.A.E.C. Khoudia Editions, 1993.

Faludi, Susan. *Backlash: The Undeclared War against American Women*. New York: Crown, 1991.

Fanon, Frantz. *Black Skin, White Masks (Peau noire, masques blancs)*. (1952). Trans. Charles Lamm Markmann. New York: Grove Press, 1967.

———. *The Wretched of the Earth*. Trans. Constance Farrington. New York: Grove Press, 1963.

Feijoó, María del Carmen. "The Challenge of Constructing Civilian Peace: Women and Democracy in Argentina." In *The Women's Movement in Latin America: Feminism and the Transition to Democracy*, ed. Jane S. Jaquette, 72–94. Boston: Hyman, 1989.

Felman, Shoshona, and Dori Laub. *Testimony: Crises of Witnessing in Literature, Psychoanalysis, and History*. New York: Routledge, 1992.

Fernando, Lloyd. *Cultures in Conflict: Essays on Literature and the English Language in South East Asia*. Singapore: Graham Brash, 1986.

Fernea, Elizabeth Warnock, and Basima Qattan Bezirgan, eds. *Middle Eastern Muslim Women Speak*. Austin: Univ. of Texas Press, 1977.

Ferré, Rosario. *Maldito amor*. Rio Piedras: Ediciones Huracán, 1988. English ed. trans. by the author as *Sweet Diamond Dust*. New York: Available Press-Ballantine, 1991.

———. *Papelas de Pandora*. Rios Piedras, Puerto Rico: Ediciones Huracán, 1991 (1976).

Fetterley, Judith. "Reading about Reading: 'A Jury of Her Peers,' 'The Murders in the Rue Morgue,' and 'The Yellow Wallpaper.'" In *Gender and Reading: Essays on Readers, Texts, and Contexts,* ed. Elizabeth A. Flynn and Patrocinio P. Schweickart, 147–64. Baltimore: Johns Hopkins Univ. Press, 1986.

Fielaux, Michèle. "'Femmes invisibles' et 'femmes muettes': A propos des événements Ibo de 1929." *Cahier des Etudes Africaines* 17, no. 1 (1977): 189–94.

Foster, David William. *Gay and Lesbian Themes in Latin American Writing.* Austin: Univ. of Texas Press, 1991.

Foster, Frances. *Witnessing Slavery: The Development of Ante-Bellum Slave Narratives.* Westport, Conn.: Greenwood Press, 1979.

Foucault, Michel. *The Archaeology of Knowledge* (L'Archéologie du savoir) (1969). Trans. A. M. Sheridan Smith. New York: Pantheon, 1972.

Fouchard, Jean. *Le Théâtre à Saint-Domingue.* 1955. Rpt. Port-au-Prince, Haiti: Editions Henri Deschamps, 1988.

Fox-Genovese, Elizabeth. *Within the Plantation Household: Black and White Women of the Old South.* Chapel Hill: Univ. of North Carolina Press, 1988.

Frankétienne. "Kaselezo" (Womb Water's Breaking). In Jean Jonassaint, ed., *Frankétienne, écrivain haitien. Dérives* (Montreal) 53–54 (1986–87): 126–63.

Franklin, Aretha. *Who's Zoomin' Who?* (compact disc). Lyrics by Narada Michael Walden and Preston Glass. New York: Arista Records, 1985.

Freire, Paulo. *Pedagogy of the Oppressed* (Pedagogia del oprimido). Trans. Myra Bergman Ramos. New York: Herder & Herder, 1970.

French, Marilyn. *Beyond Power: On Women, Men, and Morals.* New York: Ballantine Books, 1985.

Friebert, Lucy M., and Barbara A. White. *Hidden Hands: An Anthology of American Women Writers, 1790–1870.* New Brunswick, N.J.: Rutgers Univ. Press, 1987.

Friedman, Ellen. "Where Are the Missing Contents? (Post)Modernism, Gender, and the Canon." *PMLA* 108 (1993): 240–52.

Friedman, Thomas L. *From Beirut to Jerusalem.* New York: Doubleday, 1989.

Furst, Lilian R., and Peter W. Graham, eds. *Disorderly Eaters: Texts in Self-Empowerment.* University Park: Pennsylvania State Univ. Press, 1992.

García Pinto, Magdalena. *Women Writers of Latin America: Intimate Histories.* (Historias intimas). Trans. Trudy Balch and Magdalena García Pinto. Austin: Univ. of Texas Press, 1991. First published as Hanover, N.H.: Ediciones del norte, 1988.

Gates, Henry Louis, Jr. *Signifying Monkey: A Theory of African-American Literary Criticism.* Baltimore: Johns Hopkins Univ. Press, 1989.

———. ed., *The Classic Slave Narrative.* New York: Mentor, 1987.

———. *"Race," Writing, and Difference.* Chicago: Univ. of Chicago Press, 1986.

Genêt, Jean. *Les Nègres* (The Blacks). 1958. Rpt. Paris: Barbezat, 1963.

Giddings, Paula. *When and Where I Enter: The Impact of Black Women on Race and Sex in America.* New York: Bantam Books, 1985.

Gilbert, Sandra M., and Susan Gubar. *The Madwoman in the Attic: The Woman Writer and the Nineteenth-Century Literary Imagination.* New Haven, Conn.: Yale Univ. Press, 1979.

———. *No Man's Land: The Place of the Woman Writer in the Twentieth Century.* Vol. 1. New Haven: Yale Univ. Press, 1988.

Gilligan, Carol. *In a Different Voice: Psychological Theory and Women's Development.* Cambridge: Harvard Univ. Press, 1982.

Gilman, Charlotte Perkins. *The Yellow Wallpaper.* Boston: Small, Maynard, 1899. Rpt. in *The Charlotte Perkins Gilman Reader: "The Yellow Wallpaper," and Other Fiction,* ed. Ann J. Lane, 3–20. New York: Pantheon, 1980.

Girard, René. *Violence and the Sacred* (La Violence et le sacré). Trans. Patrick Gregory. Baltimore: Johns Hopkins Univ. Press, 1977.

Giraudoux, Jean. *La guerre de Troie n'aura pas lieu.* 1935. Rpt. in *Théâtre complet.* Paris: Gallimard, 1982: 1490–1526. Trans. Christopher Fry as *Tiger at the Gates.* New York: Oxford Univ. Press, 1955.

Glaspell, Susan. "A Jury of Her Peers." 1917. Rpt. in *American Voices, American Women.* ed. Lee R. Edwards and Arlyn Diamond, 359–81. New York: Avon, 1973.

Goldman, Renitta L., and Virginia R. Wheeler. *Silent Shame: The Sexual Abuse of Children and Youth.* Danville, Ill: Interstate, 1986.

Gordon, Lyndall. *Virginia Woolf: A Writer's Life.* New York: Norton, 1984.

Gordon, Mary. *The Company of Women.* New York: Random House, 1980.

———. *Final Payments.* New York: Ballantine, 1986.

———. *Men and Angels.* New York: Ballantine, 1985.

———. *Temporary Shelter.* New York: Ballantine, 1988.

Gray, Thomas R., trans. and ed. *The Confessions of Nat Turner . . . voluntarily made to Thomas [R.] Gray.* Salem, N.H.: Ayer, 1861. (Baltimore, 1831).

Grotowski, Jerzy. *Towards a Poor Theatre.* New York: Simon & Schuster, 1970.

Gwin, Minrose. *Black and White Women of the Old South.* Knoxville: Univ. of Tennessee Press, 1985.

Hacker, Marilyn. Review of Adrienne Rich, *Time's Power. The Nation,* Oct. 23, 1989, 464–67.

Hafez, Sabry. "Intentions and Realization in the Narratives of Nawal El Saadawi." *Third World Quarterly* 11, no. 3 (1989): 188–98.

Handler, Richard, and Daniel Segal. *Jane Austen and the Fiction of Culture: An Essay on the Narration of Social Realities.* Tucson: Univ. of Arizona Press, 1990.

Harris, Wendell. "Canonicity." *PMLA* 106 (1991): 110–21.

Harrison, Paul Carter, ed. *Totem Voices: Plays from the Black World Repertory.* New York: Grove Press, 1989.

Hedges, Elaine. "Small Things Reconsidered: Susan Glaspell's 'A Jury of Her Peers.'" *Women's Studies* 12 (1986): 89–110.

Heffernan, James, ed. *Representing the French Revolution: Literature, Historiography, and Art.* Hanover, N.H.: Univ. Press of New England, 1992.

Heilbrun, Carolyn G. *Writing a Woman's Life.* New York: Ballantine Books, 1988.

Henderson, Mae G. "(W)riting the Work and Working the Rites." *Black American Literature Forum* 23 (1989): 631–60.

Herman, Judith Lewis, with Lisa Hirshman. "Father-Daughter Incest." *Signs* 2 (1977): 735–56.

———. *Father-Daughter Incest.* Cambridge: Harvard Univ. Press, 1981.

The Hikayat Abdullah. Trans. with notes by A. H. Hill. New York: Oxford Univ. Press, 1970.

Works Cited

Hilliard, David. *This Side of Glory: The Autobiography of David Hilliard and the Story of the Black Panther Party.* Boston: Little, Brown, 1993.

Hine, Darlene Clark. "Female Slave Resistance: The Economics of Sex." *Western Journal of Black Studies* 3, no. 2 (1979): 123–27.

Hippolyte, Dominique. *Le Forçat* (The Prisoner). 1929. Rpt. Paris: Jouve & Cie, 1933.

Hirsch, Marianne. *The Mother-Daughter Plot: Narrative, Psychoanalysis, Feminism.* Bloomington: Indiana Univ. Press, 1989.

Hogue, W. Lawrence. *Discourse and the Other: The Production of the Afro-American Text.* Durham, N.C.: Duke Univ. Press, 1986.

Homans, Margaret. " 'Her Very Own Howl': The Ambiguities of Representation in Recent Women's Fiction." *Signs* 9 (1983): 186–205.

Hooks, Bell. *Ain't I a Woman? Black Women and Feminism.* Boston: South End Press, 1981.

———. *Talking Back: Thinking Feminist, Thinking Black.* Boston: South End Press, 1989.

———. *Yearning: Race, Gender, and Cultural Politics.* Boston: South End Press, 1990.

Humm, Maggie. "Adrienne Rich." *Feminist Criticism: Women as Contemporary Critics,* ed. Teresa de Lauretis, 177–87. New York: St. Martin's Press, 1986.

Hurston, Zora Neale. "What White Publishers Won't Print." *Negro Digest* 8 (April 1950): 85–89; rpt. in *I Love Myself When I Am Laughing and Then Again When I Am Looking Mean and Impressive: A Zora Neale Hurston Reader,* ed. Alice Walker, 169–73. Old Westbury, N.Y.: 1979.

Hussey, Mark. *Woolf and War: Fiction, Reality, and Myth.* Syracuse, N.Y.: Syracuse Univ. Press, 1991.

Irigaray, Luce. "La Différence sexuelle." In Irigaray, *Ethique de la différence sexuelle.* Paris: Minuit, 1984. Trans. Seán Hand as "Sexual Difference" in *French Feminist Thought: A Reader,* ed. Toril Moi, 118–30. Oxford: Blackwell, 1987.

———. *Sexes et parentés.* Paris: Minuit, 1987. Trans. Gillian C. Gill as *Sexes and Genealogies.* New York: Columbia Univ. Press, 1993.

———. "Women, the Sacred, and Money." Trans. Diana Knight and Margaret Whitford. *Paragraph* 8 (October 1986): 6–18.

Jacobs, Harriet. *Incidents in the Life of a Slave Girl.* New York: Harcourt Brace Jovanovich, 1973. Ed. Jean Fagin Yellin. Cambridge: Harvard Univ. Press, 1987. Orig. ed. Maria Lydia Child, 1861.

James, Ibrahim. "The Four-Stage Revolution." New Age Symposium, Univ. of Maiduguri, Nigeria, Jan. 12, 1978.

JanMohamed, Abdul R. "The Economy of Manichean Allegory: The Function of Racial Difference in Colonialist Literature." In *"Race," Writing, and Difference,* ed. Henry Louis Gates, Jr., 78–106. Chicago: Univ. of Chicago Press, 1986.

Johnson, Kay. *Women, the Family, and Peasant Revolution in China.* Chicago: Univ. of Chicago Press, 1983.

Jonassaint, Jean, ed. "Frankétienne, écrivain haitien." *Dérives* (Montreal) 53–54 (1986–87): 126–63.

Jones, Gayl. *Corregidora.* New York: Random House, 1975.

Joubert, Elsa. *The Long Journey of Poppie Nongena.* (*Die Swerfjare van Poppie Nongena*). Trans. Elsa Joubert. London: J. Ball, with Hodder and Stoughton, 1980 (1978). American ed., *Poppie Nongena: A Novel of South Africa,* trans. Joubert. New York: Holt, 1987.

Julien, Eileen. *African Novels and the Question of Orality.* Bloomington: Univ. of Indiana Press, 1992.

Kader, Soha Abdel. *Egyptian Women in a Changing Society, 1899–1987.* Boulder, Colo.: Lynne Rienner, 1987.

Kaiser-Lenoir, Claudia. "Nicaragua: Theatre in a New Society," 122–31, and "Argentine New Theatre: The Coming of Age of Popular Tradition" 165–74. In *The New Theatre of Latin America,* ed. Claudia Kaiser-Lenoir, special issue of *Theatre Research International* 14, no. 2 (1989).

Kane, Hamidou. *Ambiguous Adventure.* (1969). Trans. from the French by Katherine Woods. New York: Collier Books, 1974.

Kathigasu, Sybil. *No Dram of Mercy.* (1954). Singapore: Oxford Univ. Press, 1983.

Keckley, Elizabeth. *Behind the Scenes; or, Thirty Years a Slave and Four in the White House.* New York: Arno, 1968 (1868).

Keene, Carolyn. *The Secret at Shadow Ranch.* Nancy Drew Mystery Series. New York: Grosset & Dunlap, 1931.

Keene, Donald. *No and Bunraku: Two Forms of Japanese Theatre.* New York: Columbia Univ. Press, 1990.

Kilmer, Anne Draffkorn. "Sumero-Babylonia." In *Women Poets of the World,* ed. Joanna Bankier and Deirdre Lashgari, 111–13. New York: Macmillan, 1983.

Kingston, Maxine Hong. *The Woman Warrior: Memoirs of a Girlhood among Ghosts.* 1976. Rpt. New York: Vintage International, 1989.

Koh Tai Ann. "Biographical and Literary Writings and Plays in English by Women from Malaysia and Singapore: A Checklist." *Commentary* 7, no. 2–3 (1987): 94–96.

Kolodny, Annette. "A Map for Rereading: Or, Gender and the Interpretation of Literary Texts." *New Literary History* 11 (1980): 451–67.

Korn, Peter. "Breast Cancer Breakthroughs." *Self,* October 1992, 148–52.

Kourilsky, Françoise, and Catherine Temerson, eds. *Plays by Women: An International Anthology.* New York: UBU Repertory Theater, 1988.

Kremer, S. Lillian. "The Dybbuk of All the Lost Dead: Cynthia Ozick's Holocaust Fiction." In Kremer, *Witness through the Imagination: Jewish American Holocaust Literature,* 218–78. Detroit: Wayne State Univ. Press, 1989.

———. "The Holocaust in Our Time: Norma Rosen's *Touching Evil.*" *Studies in American Jewish Literature* 3 (1983): 212–22.

Kren, George. "The Holocaust Survivor and Psychoanalysis." In *Healing Their Wounds: Psychotherapy with Holocaust Survivors and Their Families,* ed. Paul Marcus and Alan Rosenberg, 3–21. New York: Praeger, 1989.

Kristeva, Julia. "Stabat Mater." *Poetics Today* 6, no. 1–2 (1985): 133–52. Trans. Toril Moi. Rpt. in *The Kristeva Reader,* 160–86. New York: Columbia Univ. Press, 1986.

Krystal, Henry. "Integration and Self-Healing in Post-traumatic States." In *Psy-*

choanalytic Reflections on the Holocaust: Selected Essays, ed. Steven A. Luel and Paul Marcus, 113–33. New York: KTAV Publishing House, 1984.

Lanser, Susan S. "Toward a Feminist Narratology." *Style* 20 (1986): 341–63. Rpt. in *Feminisms: An Anthology of Feminist Literary Criticism,* ed. Robyn R. Warhol and Diane Price Herndl, 610–29. New Brunswick, N.J.: Rutgers Univ. Press, 1991.

Lashgari, Deirdre. "Africa," "Iran," and "Native American." In *Women Poets of the World,* ed. Joanna Bankier and Deirdre Lashgari, 271–76, 66–72, 401–10. New York: Macmillan, 1983.

———. "What Some Women Can't Swallow: Hunger as Protest in Charlotte Brontë's *Shirley.*" In *Disorderly Eaters: Texts in Self-Empowerment,* ed. Lilian R. Furst and Peter W. Graham, 141–52. University Park: Pennsylvania State Univ. Press, 1992.

Laye, Camara. *L'Enfant noir.* Paris: Librairie Plon, 1953. Trans. James Kirkup and Ernest Jones as *The Dark Child.* New York: Noonday Press, 1954.

Lazarus, Neil. "Africa." In *Longman Anthology of World Literature by Women, 1875–1975,* ed. Marian Arkin and Barbara Schollar, 1061–72. New York: Longman, 1989.

Le Guin, Ursula. "The Hand That Rocks the Cradle Writes the Book." *New York Times,* Jan. 22, 1989, sec. 7, pp. 1, 35, 36.

Lee, Mary Paik. *Quiet Odyssey: A Pioneer Korean Woman in America.* Ed. Sucheng Chan. Seattle: Univ. of Washington Press, 1990.

Lee Chin Koon. *Mrs. Lee's Cookbook.* Singapore: Eurasia Press, 1974.

Lenta, Margaret. "Independence as the Creative Choice in Two South African Fictions." *Ariel: A Review of International English Literature* 17 (1986): 35–52.

Leong Liew Geok. "Literature from History: Perspectives of the Pacific War in Malaya and Singapore." Paper presented at the New Directions in Asian Studies Conference, Singapore, 1989.

Lerner, George. "Nawal El Saadawi." Interview. *The Progressive* 56 (April 1992): 32–35.

Lessing, Doris. *The Diaries of Jane Somers.* New York: Vintage, 1984.

———. *The Four-Gated City.* New York: Knopf, 1969.

———. *Martha Quest.* St. Albans, Eng.: Panther, 1973.

Lester, Neal A. "Shange's Men: *For colored girls* Revisited, and Movement Beyond." *African American Review* 26, no. 2 (1992): 319–28.

Levy, Claude, and Paul Tillard. *Betrayal at the Vel d'Hiv.* Trans. Inea Bushnaq. New York: Hill & Wang, 1967.

Lifshitz, Leatrice H., ed. *Her Soul beneath the Bone: Women's Poetry on Breast Cancer.* Urbana: Univ. of Illinois Press, 1988.

Lifton, Robert Jay. "The Concept of the Survivor." In *Survivors, Victims, and Perpetrators: Essays on the Nazi Holocaust,* ed. Joel Dimsdale, 113–26. New York: Hemisphere, 1980.

Lim, Janet. *Sold for Silver: An Autobiography.* Singapore: Oxford Univ. Press, 1985; Cleveland: World Publishing, 1958.

Lim, Shirley Geok-lin. "The English-Language Writer in Singapore." In *Management of Success: The Moulding of Modern Singapore,* ed. Kernial Singh Sandhu and Paul Wheatley, 552–62. Singapore: Institute of Southeast Asian Studies, 1989.

Lim, Shirley Geok-lin, and Amy Ling, eds. *Reading the Literatures of Asian America.* Philadelphia: Temple Univ. Press, 1992.

Lim, Shirley Geok-lin, and Norman A. Spencer, eds. *One World of Literature.* Boston: Houghton Mifflin, 1993.

Lipking, Lawrence. "Aristotle's Sister: A Poetic of Abandonment." *Critical Inquiry* 10 (1983): 61–81.

Litmus One (Selected University Verse, 1949–57). Singapore: Raffles Society, 1958.

Lorde, Audre. *A Burst of Light: Essays.* Ithaca, N.Y.: Firebrand Books, 1988.

———. *The Cancer Journals.* San Francisco: Spinsters-Aunt Lute. 1980.

———. *Sister Outsider: Essays and Speeches.* Trumansburg, N.Y.: Crossing Press, 1984.

Lyman, Peter. "The Politics of Anger: On Silence, Resentment, and Political Speech." *Socialist Review* 11 (1981): 55–74.

Lyotard, Jean François. *The Differend: Phrases in Dispute.* Minneapolis: Univ. of Minnesota Press, 1988.

MacKinnon, Catharine A. *Feminism Unmodified: Discourses on Life and Law.* Cambridge: Harvard Univ. Press, 1987.

Madubuike, Ihechukwu. *The Senegalese Novel: A Sociological Study of the Impact of the Politics of Assimilation.* Washington, D.C.: Three Continents Press, 1983.

Mahdi, Muhsin. Foreword. *Middle Eastern Muslim Women Speak,* ed. Elizabeth Warnock Fernea and Basima Qattan Bezirgan. Austin: Univ. of Texas Press, 1977.

"Major Long-term Aim: To Preserve Asianness." *Straits Times,* Weekly Overseas Ed., Oct. 6, 1990, 9.

Marcus, Jane. *Art and Anger: Reading like a Woman.* Columbus: Ohio State Univ. Press for Miami Univ., 1988.

———. *Virginia Woolf and the Languages of Patriarchy.* Bloomington: Indiana Univ. Press, 1987.

Margolies, Liz, Martha Becker, and Karla Jackson-Brewer. "Internalized Homophobia: Identifying and Treating the Oppressor Within." In *Lesbian Psychologies: Explorations and Challenges,* ed. Boston Lesbian Psychologies Collective, 229–41. Urbana: Univ. of Illinois Press, 1987.

Marquard, Jean. "Poppie." *English Studies in Africa* 28, no. 2 (1985): 135–41.

Masiello, Francine R. "En breve cárcel: La producción del sujeto." *Hispamérica: Revista de literatura,* August 1985, 103–12.

Mathabane, Mark. *Kaffir Boy: The True Story of a Black Youth's Coming of Age in Apartheid South Africa.* New York: Macmillan, 1986.

McClintock, Anne. " 'The Very House of Difference': Race, Gender, and the Politics of South African Women's Narrative." In *The Bounds of Race: Perspectives on Hegemony and Resistance,* ed. Dominick LaCapra, 196–230. Ithaca, N.Y.: Cornell Univ. Press, 1991.

McDowell, Deborah E. "Negotiating between Tenses: Witnessing Slavery after Freedom—*Dessa Rose.*" In *Slavery and the Literary Imagination,* ed. Deborah E. McDowell and Arnold Rampersad, 144–63. Baltimore: Johns Hopkins Univ. Press, 1989.

McIntosh, Peggy. "White Privilege: Unpacking the Invisible Knapsack." *Peace and Freedom* (July-August, 1989): 10–12. Excerpted from "White Privilege and Male Privilege." Working Paper no. 189. Wellesley, Mass.: Wellesley College Center for Research on Women Publications Department, 1988.

Meese, Elizabeth A. *(Ex)Tensions: Re-Figuring Feminist Criticism.* Urbana: Univ. of Illinois Press, 1990.

Menchú, Rigoberta. *Me llamo Rigoberta Menchú y así me nació la conciencia.* Ed. and intro. by Elisabeth Burgos-Debray. Barcelona: Argos Vergara, 1983; Madrid: Siglo Veintiuno Editores, 1985. Trans. Anne Wright as *I, Rigoberta Menchú: An Indian Woman in Guatemala.* New York: Verso, 1983.

———. "Patria abnegada" (poem). In "Rigoberta Menchú: 'Con quien nos comunicamos?'" Interview with Alice A. Brittin and Kenya Carmen Dworkin in *Lucero: A Journal of Iberian and Latin American Studies* 3 (Spring, 1992): 1–10.

Metzger, Deena. "I Am No Longer Afraid." In *Her Soul beneath the Bone: Women's Poetry on Breast Cancer,* ed. Leatrice H. Lifshitz, 71. Urbana: Univ. of Illinois Press, 1988.

Milhaven, Annie Lally. "Interview with Mary Gordon." In *The Inside Stories: Thirteen Valiant Women Challenging the Church,* 101–18. Mystic, Conn.: Twenty-third Publications, 1987.

Miller, Harry. *Menace in Malaya.* London: George G. Harrap, 1954.

Miller, Nancy K. "Changing the Subject: Authorship, Writing, and the Reader." *Feminist Studies / Critical Studies,* ed. Teresa de Lauretis, 102–20. Bloomington: Indiana Univ. Press, 1986.

Miller, Randall M., and John David Smith, eds. *Dictionary of Afro-American Slavery.* New York: Greenwood Press, 1988.

Minai, Naila. "Women in Early Islam." In *Women in Islam: Tradition and Transition in the Middle East,* 3–24. New York: Seaview Books, 1981.

Mirandé, Alfredo, and Evangelina Enríquez. *La Chicana: The Mexican-American Woman.* Chicago: Univ. of Chicago Press, 1979.

Mirikitani, Janice. *Awake in the River.* San Francisco: Isthmus Press, 1978.

———. *Shedding Silence: Poetry and Prose.* Berkeley, Calif.: Celestial Arts, 1987.

———, ed. *Time to Greez! Incantations from the Third World.* San Francisco: Glide Publications, 1975.

Moi, Toril. *Sexual / Textual Politics: Feminist Literary Theory.* London: Routledge, 1985.

Molloy, Sylvia. *En breve cárcel.* Barcelona: Seix Barral, 1981. Trans. Daniel Balderston with the author as *Certificate of Absence.* Austin: Univ. of Texas Press, 1989.

———, ed. *At Face Value: Autobiographical Writing in Spanish America.* New York: Cambridge Univ. Press, 1991.

———. *Las letras de Borges.* Buenos Aires: Sudamericana, 1979.

Montenegro, David. "Interview with Adrienne Rich." *American Poetry Review,* January-February 1991, 7–15.

Montero, Oscar. "*En breve cárcel*: La Diana, la violencia y la mujer que escribe."

In *La sartén por el mango: Encuentro de escritoras latinoamericanas,* ed. Patricia Elena González and Eliana Ortega, 111–18. Puerto Rico: Huracán, 1984.

Moraga, Cherríe. "From a Long Line of Vendidas: Chicanas and Feminism." In *Feminist Studies / Critical Studies,* ed. Teresa de Lauretis, 173–90. Bloomington: Indiana Univ. Press, 1986.

———. "La Güera." In *This Bridge Called My Back: Writings by Radical Women of Color,* ed. Cherríe Moraga and Gloria Anzaldúa, 27–34. New York: Kitchen Table, Women of Color Press, 1981.

Moraga, Cherríe, and Gloria Anzaldúa, eds. *This Bridge Called My Back: Writings by Radical Women of Color.* New York: Kitchen Table–Women of Color Press, 1981.

Morisseau-Leroy, Félix. *Antigone en créole.* Pétionville, Haiti: Morne-Hercule, 1953.

Morrison, Toni. *Beloved.* New York: Knopf, 1987.

———. *The Bluest Eye.* New York: Simon & Schuster, 1970.

———. "Unspeakable Things Unspoken: The Afro-American Presence in American Literature." In *Toni Morrison* (Modern Critical Views series), ed. Harold Bloom, 201–30. New York: Chelsea House, 1990.

Morsy, Soheir A. "Sex Differences and Folk Illness in an Egyptian Village." In *Women in the Muslim World,* ed. Lois Beck and Nikki Keddie, 599–616. Cambridge: Harvard Univ. Press, 1978.

Mortimer, Mildred. *Journeys through the French African Novel.* Portsmouth, N.H.: Heinemann, 1990.

Mukherjee, Bharati. "Betrayed by Blind Faith." Review of Nawal el Saadawi's *God Dies by the Nile. New York Times Book Review,* July 27, 1986, 14.

Muñoz, Susana, dir. *Las madres de Plaza de Mayo* (film). Direct Cinema Ltd., Los Angeles, 1985.

———, dir. *Susana* (film). Women Make Movies, New York, 1980.

Newitt, Hilary. *Women Must Choose: The Position of Women in Europe Today.* London: Gollancz, 1937.

Newman, Lesléa. *A Letter to Harvey Milk.* Ithaca, N.Y.: Firebrand, 1988.

Newman, Naomi. *Snake Talk: Urgent Messages from the Mother.* Unpublished one-woman theater piece. 1988.

Newton, Judith Lowder. *Women, Power, and Subversion: Social Strategies in British Fiction, 1778–1860.* Athens: Univ. of Georgia Press, 1981.

Nichols, Margaret. "Lesbian Sexuality: Issues and Developing Theory." In *Lesbian Psychologies: Explorations and Challenges,* ed. Boston Lesbian Psychologies Collective, 97–125. Urbana: Univ. of Illinois Press, 1987.

Norat, Gisela. "Four Latin American Writers Liberating Taboo: Albalucía Angel, Marta Traba, Sylvia Molloy, Diamela Eltit." Ph.D. diss., Washington University, 1991.

Norfolk, Lawrence. Review of Adrienne Rich, *Time's Power. Times Literary Supplement,* Sept. 15, 1989, 1000.

Nye, Andrea. "Woman Clothed with the Sun: Julia Kristeva and the Excape from / to Language." *Signs* 12 (1987): 664–86.

O'Ballance, Edgar. *Malaya: The Communist Insurgent War, 1948–60.* Hamden, Conn.: Archon Books, 1966.

Olsen, Tillie. "Women Who Are Writers in Our Century" (1972). Rpt. as "One Out of Twelve: Women Who Are Writers in Our Century" in Olsen, *Silences,* 22–46, New York: Delacorte Press-S. Lawrence, 1978.

———. "Silences" (1965). Rpt. as "Silences in Literature" in Olsen, *Silences,* 5–21. New York: Delacorte Press, 1978.

Ong Song Siang. *One Hundred Years' History of the Chinese in Singapore.* Singapore: Univ. of Malaya Press, 1967.

Ostriker, Alicia. "Her Cargo: Adrienne Rich and the Common Language." *American Poetry Review,* July-August 1979, 6–10.

Oyono, Ferdinand. *Une vie de boy.* Paris: Julliard, 1956. Trans. John Reed as *Boy!* New York: Collier, 1970 (1966).

Ozick, Cynthia. *The Shawl.* New York: Knopf, 1989.

———. "Toward a New Yiddish." In Ozick, *Art & Ardor: Essays,* 151–77. New York: Knopf, 1983.

Parini, Jay. Review of *Time's Power. New York Times Book Review,* Oct. 22, 1989, 16.

Patmore, Coventry. *The Angel in the House.* 1856. 3d ed. 2 vols. London: Parker & Son, 1960.

Patterson, Tiffany R., and Angela M. Gilliam. "Out of Egypt: A Talk with Nawal El Saadawi." *Freedomways* 23, no. 3 (1983): 186–94.

Poole, Roger. *The Unknown Virginia Woolf.* 3d ed. Atlantic Highlands, N.J.: Humanities Press International, 1990.

Pratt, Mary Louise. "Scratches on the Face of the Country; or, What Mr. Barrow Saw in the Land of the Bushmen." *Critical Inquiry* 12, no. 1 (1985). Rpt. in *"Race," Writing, and Difference,* ed. Henry Louis Gates, Jr., 138–62. Chicago: Univ. of Chicago Press, 1986.

Pres, Terrence des. "Adrienne Rich, North America East." In des Pres, *Praises and Dispraises: Poetry and Politics, the 20th Century,* 187–223. New York: Penguin, 1989.

Prince, Mary. *The History of Mary Prince, A West African Slave.* 1831. Rpt. in *The Classic Slave Narrative,* ed. Henry Louis Gates, Jr., 183–242. New York: Mentor, 1987.

Pye, Lucien. *Guerrilla Communism in Malaya.* Princeton, N.J.: Princeton Univ. Press, 1956.

Renan, Ernest. "What Is a Nation?" In *Nation and Narration,* ed. Homi Bhabha, 8–22. New York: Routledge, 1990.

Rich, Adrienne. *An Atlas of the Difficult World: Poems 1988–1991.* New York: Norton, 1991.

———. *Dream of a Common Language: Poems 1974–1977.* New York: Norton, 1978.

———. Interview by David Montenegro. *American Poetry Review,* (January-February 1991), 8.

———. "Notes toward a Politics of Location." Talk delivered at conference on Women, Feminist Identity, and Society in the 1980's, Utrecht, June 1984.

Printed in Rich, *Blood, Bread, and Poetry: Selected Prose, 1979–1985.* New York: Norton, 1986.

——. *On Lies, Secrets, and Silence: Selected Prose, 1966–1978.* New York: Norton, 1979.

——. "Sliding Stone from the Cave's Mouth." *American Poetry Review,* September-October, 1990, 11–17.

——. *Time's Power: Poems 1985–1988.* New York: Norton, 1989.

——. *What Is Found There: Notebooks on Poetry and Politics.* New York: Norton, 1993.

——. *Your Native Land, Your Life.* New York: Norton, 1986.

Rich, Evelyn. *Memorandum on the Aba Women's Riot.* New York: African American Institute, 1975.

Ringelblum, Emmanuel. 1958. *Notes from the Warsaw Ghetto.* Ed. and trans. Jacob Sloan. Rpt. New York: Schocken, 1974.

Robertson, Claire, and Iris Berger. *Women and Class in Africa.* New York: Africana, 1986.

Robinson, Sally. *Engendering the Subject: Gender and Self-Representation in Contemporary Women's Fiction.* Albany: State Univ. of New York Press, 1991.

Rodney, Walter. *How Europe Underdeveloped Africa.* Washington, D.C.: Howard Univ. Press, 1982.

Rose, Phyllis. *Woman of Letters: A Life of Virginia Woolf.* New York: Harcourt Brace Jovanovich, 1978.

Rosen, Norma. "The Holocaust and the American-Jewish Novelist." *Midstream* 59 (October 1974): 54–62.

——. *Touching Evil.* New York: Harcourt, Brace, and World, 1969. Rpt. Wayne State Univ. Press, 1990.

Roumain, Jacques. *Gouverneurs de la rosée.* Paris: Editeurs Français Réunis, 1946. *Masters of the Dew.* Trans. Langston Hughes and Mercer Cook. New York: Collier Books, 1971.

Rush, Florence. *The Best Kept Secret: Sexual Abuse of Children.* Englewood Cliffs, N.J.: Prentice Hall, 1980.

Russell, Diana. *The Secret Trauma.* New York: Basic Books, 1986.

Saadawi, Nawal el. "Arab Women and Western Feminism: An Interview with Nawal El Saadawi." *Race and Class* 22, no. 2 (1980): 175–82.

——. "Creative Women in Changing Societies: A Personal Reflection." *Race and Class* 22, no. 2 (1980): 160–73.

——. *The Fall of the Imam* (Suqut al-Imam). Trans. Sherif Hetata. London: Methuen, 1988.

——. *God Dies by the Nile* (Mawt al-rajul al-wahid ala al-ard). Trans. Sherif Hetata, London: Zed Books, 1985. Beirut, 1974.

——. *The Hidden Face of Eve: Women in the Arab World.* Trans. Sherif Hetata. London: Zed Press, 1980. Boston: Beacon Press, 1980.

——. *Al-Insan* (The People). Cairo: Maktabat Madbuli, 1982.

——. *Al-Marah wa-al-jins* (Women and Sex). Cairo: Al-Nashirun al-Arab, 1971.

———. *Memoirs of a Woman Doctor* (Mudhakkirat tabibah). Trans. Catherine Cobham. London: Saqi Books, 1988.

———. "Nawal El Saadawi." Interview with George Lerner. *The Progressive* 56 (April 1992): 32–35.

———. "The Political Challenges Facing Arab Women." In *Women of the Arab World*, ed. Nahid Toubia. London: Zed Books, 1988.

———. *Two Woman in One* (Imraatan fi imraah). Trans. Osman Nusairi and Jana Gough. London: Saqi Books, 1985.

———. *Woman at Point Zero*. Trans. Sherif Hetata. London: Zed Books, 1983.

Saadawi, Nawal el, Fatima Mernissi, and Mallica Vajarathon. "A Critical Look at the Wellesley Conference." *Quest* 4, no. 2 (1978): 101–8.

Said, Edward N. "An Ideology of Difference." In *"Race," Writing, and Difference,* ed. Henry Louis Gates, Jr., 38–58. Chicago: Univ. of Chicago Press, 1986.

Sandahl, Stella. "India." In *Women Poets of the World*, ed. Joanna Bankier and Deirdre Lashgari, 49–52. New York: Macmillan, 1983.

Sandoval, Chela. "Feminism and Racism: A Report on the 1981 National Women's Studies Association Conference." Oakland, Calif.: Center for Third World Organizing, 1982. Rpt. in *Making Face, Making Soul,* ed. Gloria Anzaldúa, 55–71. San Francisco: Aunt Lute, 1990.

———. "U.S. Third World Feminisms: The Theory and Method of Oppositional Consciousness in the Postmodern World." Talk presented at the Claremont Colleges, Claremont, Calif., 1991.

Sayre, Nora. Review of *Touching Evil* by Norma Rosen. *New York Times Book Review,* Sept. 14, 1969.

Scarry, Elaine. *The Body in Pain: The Making and Unmaking of the World*. New York: Oxford Univ. Press, 1985.

Schwarz-Bart, Simone. *Ton beau capitaine* (Your Handsome Captain). Paris: Editions du Seuil, 1987.

Segal, Daniel, ed. *Crossing Cultures*. Tucson: Univ. of Arizona Press, 1992.

Sembène, Ousmane. *Les Bouts de bois de dieu: Banty Mam Yala*. Ibadan: Heinemann, 1960; Paris: Libre Contemporain, 1982. Trans. as *God's Bits of Wood* by Francis Price. Ibadan, Nigeria: Heinemann, 1962; rpt. 1970.

———. *Xala*. Paris: Présence Africaine, 1973. Trans. Clive Wake. Westport, Conn.: Hill, 1976.

Senghor, Léopold Sédar, ed. *Anthologie de la nouvelle poésie nègre et malgache de langue française*. 1948. Rpt. Paris: Presses Universitaires de France, 1969.

Shange, Ntozake. *For Colored Girls Who Have Considered Suicide When the Rainbow Is Enuf: A Choreopoem*. New York: Macmillan, 1977.

Shaw, Robert. Review of Adrienne Rich, *Time's Power*. *Poetry* 156 (1990): 166–68.

Short, Anthony. "Communism and the Emergency." In *Malaysia: A Survey*, ed. Wang Gungwu, 149–60. New York: Praeger, 1964.

Showalter, Elaine. "Feminist Criticism in the Wilderness." In *Writing and Sexual Difference*, ed. Elizabeth Abel, 9–35. Chicago: Univ. of Chicago Press, 1982.

Shteir, Rachel. "Breaking the Silence: Nawal Assadawi's *Al-Insan*." *Theater* 20, no. 1 (1988): 47–50.

Works Cited

Shulman, Alix Kate. "Lost Women Writers II: Far from Home." *PEN Newsletter* 71 (Spring 1990).

Silko, Leslie Marmon. *Ceremony.* 1977. Rpt. New York: Penguin, 1986.

Silver, Brenda. *Virginia Woolf's Reading Notebooks.* Princeton, N.J.: Princeton Univ. Press, 1983. (Includes index to the manuscripts.)

Singer, Isaac Bashevis. *Enemies, a Love Story.* New York: Farrar, 1972. 1st published in the *Jewish Daily Forward* in 1966 as "Sonim, di Geshichte fun a Liebe."

Sistren Collective. "Bellywoman Bangarang." Ed. Rhonda Cobham and Honor Ford-Smith with Sistren. Unpublished ms., 1990.

Slowik, Mary. "The Friction of the Mind: The Early Poetry of Adrienne Rich." *Massachusetts Review* 25, no. 1 (1984): 142–60.

Smith, Barbara. "Foreword." *The Combahee River Collective Statement.* New York: Kitchen Table–Women of Color Press, 1985.

Smith, S. J. "Social Geography—Patriarchy, Racism, Nationalism." *Progress in Human Geography* 14, no. 2 (1990): 261–71.

Smith, Sidonie. *A Poetics of Women's Autobiography: Marginality and the Fictions of Self-Representation.* Bloomington: Indiana Univ. Press, 1987.

Smith, Valerie. *Self-Discovery and Authority in Afro-American Narrative.* Cambridge: Harvard Univ. Press, 1987.

Sommer, Doris. "Sin secretos." *Revista de crítica literaria latinoamericana* (Lima) 36 (1992): 135–54.

Spiegelman, Willard. " 'Driving to the Limits of the City of Words': The Poetry of Adrienne Rich." In Spiegelman, *The Didactic Muse: Scenes of Instruction in Contemporary Poetry,* 147–91. Princeton, N.J.: Princeton Univ. Press, 1989.

Spillers, Hortense J. "Interstices: A Small Drama of Words." In *Pleasure and Danger: Exploring Female Sexuality,* ed. Carole S. Vance, 73–100. Boston: Routledge and Kegan Paul, 1984.

Spivak, Gayatri Chakravorty. *In Other Worlds: Essays in Cultural Politics.* London: Routledge, 1988. (Contains the essays "French Feminism in an International Frame" and "A Literary Representation of the Subaltern: A Woman's Text from the Third World.")

Starhemberg, Fanny, Princess. Propaganda issued by Starhemberg as Nazi Women's Leader of Austria; transcribed by Hilary Newitt. In Newitt, *Women Must Choose: The Position of Women in Europe Today.* London: Gollencz, 1937.

Starzecpyzel, Eileen. "The Persephone Complex." In *Lesbian Psychologies: Explorations and Challenges,* ed. Boston Lesbian Psychologies Collective, 261–82. Urbana: Univ. of Illinois Press, 1987.

Steedman, Carolyn. *Landscape for a Good Woman: A Story of Two Lives.* New Brunswick, N.J.: Rutgers Univ. Press, 1987.

Steinem, Gloria. *Revolution from Within.* Boston: Little, Brown, 1992.

Steiner, George. *After Babel: Aspects of Language and Translation.* New York: Oxford, 1975.

Stemerick, Martine. "Virginia Woolf and Julia Stephen: The Distaff Side of History." In *Virginia Woolf: Centennial Essays,* ed. Elaine K. Ginsberg and Laura Moss Gottlieb, 51–80. Troy, N.Y.: Whitston, 1983.

Stephen, Julia. *Stories for Children; Essays for Adults.* Ed. Diane F. Gillespie and Elizabeth Steele. Syracuse, N.Y.: Syracuse Univ. Press, 1987.

Sterling, Dorothy. *We Are Your Sisters.* New York: Norton, 1984.

Sterling, Philip. "Humor." In *Dictionary of Afro-American Slavery,* ed. Randall M. Miller and John David Smith, 347–48. New York: Greenwood Press, 1988.

Stimpson, Catharine. "Adrienne Rich and Lesbian / Feminist Poetry." *Parnassus* 12–13 (1985): 249–68.

Stoll, David. "*I, Rigoberta Menchú* and Human Rights Reporting in Guatemala." Paper presented at the Conference on "Political Correctness" and Cultural Studies, Western Humanities Institute, Univ. of Calif., Berkeley, Oct. 20, 1990.

Styron, William. *The Confessions of Nat Turner.* New York, Random House, 1967.

Swigart, Rob. "Japan." In *Women Poets of the World,* ed. Joanna Bankier and Deirdre Lashgari, 29–34. New York: Macmillan, 1983.

Takaki, Ronald T. *Iron Cages: Race and Culture in Nineteenth-Century America.* New York: Knopf, 1979.

Terry, Jack. "The Damaging Effects of the 'Survivor Syndrome.'" In *Psychoanalytic Reflections on the Holocaust: Selected Essays,* ed. Steven A. Luel and Paul Marcus, 135–48. New York: KTAV Publishing House, 1984.

Thiam, Awa. *La Parole aux négresses.* Paris: Denoel / Gonthier, 1978.

Thumboo, Edwin. *The Second Tongue: An Anthology of Poetry from Malaysia and Singapore.* Singapore: Heinemann, 1976.

Tirolien, Guy. Introduction to Maryse Condé's *Dieu nous l'a donné.* Paris: Editions Pierre Jean Oswald, 1972.

Traba, Marta. *Conversación al sur.* Coyoacán, Mexico: Siglo Veintiuno, 1981. English trans., Jo Labanyi, *Mothers and Shadows.* New York: Readers International, 1986.

Trinh T. Minh-ha. *When the Moon Waxes Red: Representation, Gender, and Cultural Politics.* London: Routledge, 1991.

———. *Woman, Native, Other: Writing Postcoloniality and Feminism.* Bloomington: Indiana Univ. Press, 1989.

Trombley, Stephen. *"All That Summer She Was Mad": Virginia Woolf and Her Doctors.* London: Junction Books, 1981.

Turner, Nat. 1831. *The Confessions of Nat Turner . . . voluntarily made to Thomas [R.] Gray.* Rpt. Salem, N.H.: Ayer, 1861.

Valverde, Mariana. *Sex, Power, and Pleasure.* Toronto: Women's Press, 1985.

Vrettos, Athena. "Curative Domains: Women, Healing, and History in Black Women's Narratives." *Women's Studies* 16 (1989): 455–73.

Walker, Alice. "Beauty: When the Other Dancer Is the Self." 1974. Rpt. in *In Search of Our Mothers' Gardens,* 361–70. San Diego: Harcourt Brace Jovanovich, 1983.

———. *The Color Purple.* New York: Harcourt Brace Jovanovich, 1982.

———. "In Search of Our Mothers' Gardens." 1974. Rpt. in *In Search of Our Mothers' Gardens,* 231–43. San Diego: Harcourt Brace Jovanovich, 1983.

————. *Possessing the Secret of Joy.* New York: Harcourt Brace Jovanovich, 1992.

Walker, Barbara G. *The Woman's Encyclopedia of Myths and Secrets.* San Francisco: Harper & Row, 1983.

Wang Gungwu. *Pulse.* Singapore: Beda Lim, 1950.

————. "Some Suggestions for Malayan Verse Written in English." *New Cauldron* (Singapore), November 1958, 26–28.

————. "Trial and Error in Malayan Poetry." *Malayan Undergraduate* (Singapore), 1958, 6–8.

Wee, Vivienne. "The Ups and Downs of Women's Status in Singapore: A Chronology of Some Landmark Events (1950–1987)." *Commentary* 7, no. 2–3 (1987): 5–12.

Weedon, Chris. *Feminist Practice and Poststructuralist Theory.* New York: Blackwell, 1987.

Welz, Dieter. *Writing against Apartheid: Interviews with South African Authors.* Grahamstown: National English Literary Museum Press of South Africa, 1987.

Wesleyan Methodist Missionary Society (London) Archive. *China: Women's Work Collection.* Zug, Switzerland: Inter Documentation Co., 1982 or 1983 (*sic*).

Whitford, Margaret. *Luce Irigaray: Philosophy in the Feminine.* New York: Routledge, 1991.

Wiesel, Elie. *Night.* Trans. from the French by Stella Rodway. New York: Hill & Wang, 1960. Orig. published in Yiddish in an expanded version entitled *Un di velt hot geshvign.*

Williams, Sherley Anne. *Dessa Rose.* New York: Berkley, 1987.

————. *Give Birth to Brightness: A Thematic Study in Neo-Black Literature.* New York: Dial, 1972.

————. "Meditations on History." In *Midnight Birds: Stories by Contemporary Black Women Writers,* ed. Mary Helen Washington, 200–248. Garden City, N.Y.: Anchor, 1980.

————. *The Peacock Poems.* Hanover, N.H.: Univ. Press of New England, 1975.

————. "Returning to the Blues: Esther Phillips and Contemporary Blues Culture." *Callaloo* 14 (1991): 816–28.

————. *Someone Sweet Angel Chile.* New York: Morrow, 1982.

Winnicott, D. W. *Home Is Where We Start From.* New York: Norton, 1986.

Winnow, Jackie. "Lesbians Evolving Health Care: Our Lives Depend on It." In *Cancer as a Women's Issue: Scratching the Surface,* ed. Midge Stocker, 23–35. Chicago: Third Side Press, 1991.

Wittgenstein, Ludwig. *Philosophical Investigations.* Trans. G. E. M. Anscombe. New York: Macmillan, 1953.

Wolf, Margery. "Women and Suicide in China." In *Women in Chinese Society,* ed. Margery Wolf and Roxane Witke, 111–42. Stanford, Calif.: Stanford Univ. Press, 1975.

Wolf, Naomi. *Fire with Fire: The New Female Power and How It Will Change the 21st Century.* New York: Random House, 1993.

Woolf, Virginia. *Between the Acts.* London: Hogarth, 1941. New York: Harcourt Brace, 1941.

Works Cited

———. *The Death of the Moth and Other Essays*. 1942. Rpt. San Diego: Harcourt Brace Jovanovich, 1970.

———. *The Diary of Virginia Woolf, Vol. V: 1936–1941*. San Diego: Harcourt Brace Jovanovich, 1984.

———. *Holograph Reading Notes*. Vols. 21 and 26. Henry W. and Albert A. Berg Collection, New York Public Library. (Contains Woolf's citations from Benito Mussolini, Princess Fanny Starhemberg, and other sources connecting patriarchy and fascism. See "Brenda Silver" for index to the *Reading Notes*.)

———. *Moments of Being: Unpublished Autobiographical Writings*. 1976. Ed. Jeanne Schulkind. 2d ed. London: Hogarth Press, 1985.

———. *Mrs. Dalloway*. London: Hogarth Press, 1925.

———. *A Room of One's Own*. London: Hogarth Press, 1929; New York: Harcourt, Brace & World, 1929. Rpt. San Diego: Harcourt Brace Jovanovich, 1957.

———. "A Sketch of the Past." *Monk's House Papers*. (Manuscript: MH/ A.5c). Publ. in *Moments of Being*, ed. Jeanne Schulkind, 64–159. 2d ed. London: Hogarth Press, 1985 (1976).

———. *Three Guineas*. London: Hogarth, 1938. San Diego: Harcourt Brace, 1938.

———. *To the Lighthouse*. New York: Harcourt Brace, 1927.

———. "22 Hyde Park Gate." In Woolf, *Moments of Being*, ed. Jeanne Schulkind, 164–76. 2d ed. London: Hogarth Press, 1985 (1976).

Wynter, Sylvia. "History, Ideology, and the Reinvention of the Past in Achebe's *Things Fall Apart* and Laye's *The Dark Child*." *Minority Voices* 2 (1978).

Yamamoto, Gloria. "Something about the Subject Makes It Hard to Name." In *Making Face / Making Soul*, ed. Gloria Anzaldúa, 20–24. San Francisco: Aunt Lute, 1990.

Yarbro-Bejarano, Yvonne. "Cultural Influences: Chicana." In *Women Poets of the World*, ed. Joanna Bankier and Deirdre Lashgari, 342–46. New York: Macmillan, 1983.

Yeats, William Butler. "The Mother of God." In *The Selected Poems and Two Plays of William Butler Yeats*, ed. M. L. Rosenthal, 133. New York: Collier Books, 1962.

Yellin, Jean Fagin. "Text and Contexts of Harriet Jacobs' *Incidents in the Life of a Slave Girl: Written by Herself*." In *The Slave's Narrative*, ed. Charles Davis and Henry Louis Gates, Jr., 262–82. New York: Oxford Univ. Press, 1985.

Yúdice, George. "Testimonio y concientización." *Revista de crítica literaria latinoamericana* (Lima) 18, no. 36 (1992): 207–27.

Zevy, Lee, and Sahli A. Cavallaro. "Invisibility, Fantasy, and Intimacy: Princess Charming Is Not a Prince." In *Lesbian Psychologies: Explorations and Challenges*, ed. Boston Lesbian Psychologies Collective, 83–94. Urbana: Univ. of Illinois Press, 1987.

Zwerdling, Alex. *Virginia Woolf and the Real World*. Berkeley: Univ. of California Press, 1986.

Contributors

MADELINE CASSIDY is a writer of fiction currently raising two children while completing her graduate studies in English at Sonoma State University in California. She has delivered papers on Etel Adnan's work at the National Association of Ethnic Studies Conference and at the annual meeting of the Philological Association of the Pacific Coast.

VÈVÈ CLARK is associate professor of African and Caribbean literatures in the African American Studies Department at the University of California, Berkeley. She is a specialist in African diaspora literatures, theater, and folklore, and African-American dance theater. She is coeditor of *The Legend of Maya Deren,* a multivolume account of the life and work of the independent filmmaker. Her publications in theater include work in the journal *Callaloo* and in *Representing the French Revolution: Literature, Historiography, and Art.*

MICHAELA COOK teaches composition at Chaffey Community College, Alta Loma, California. She has published work on Samuel Richardson, Harriet Beecher Stowe, and Anzia Yezierska, and she is currently coediting a collection of interviews with Muslim women in the United States.

ANNE B. DALTON is assistant professor of English at Reed College. She has published articles on Djuna Barnes and T. S. Eliot in such journals as *Women's Studies, Mosaic,* and the *Review of Contemporary Fiction.* She is currently completing a book-length work on slavery and subjectivity in nineteenth-century African American women's narratives.

KRISTI DALVEN is a poet and writer of fiction. She is concurrently completing a Master of Fine Arts degree in fiction at Columbia University and a Master of Arts degree in English, specializing in twentieth-century fiction, at California State Polytechnic University, Pomona, where she also teaches introductory literature and composition.

SHERRI HALLGREN is the director of the graduate creative writing program at Saint Mary's College, Moraga, California. She is managing director of the Napa Valley Writer's Conference and a regular reviewer of new fiction for the *San Francisco Chronicle.* Her short stories have been awarded the Eisner Prize for Literature. She is now working on a collection of short fiction.

GEORGE B. HANDLEY is completing his doctoral dissertation in comparative literature at the University of California, Berkeley, with an emphasis on the work of Caribbean American writers. He has published work on Cervantes and Homi

Contributors

Bhabha. At the Modern Language Association conference in Toronto (1993) he delivered a paper on Rosario Ferré as part of a session on Historicity in Latin American Literature.

JANE HOOGESTRAAT is assistant professor in the graduate program at Southwest Missouri State University, Springfield. Her poetry has been widely published in *Yarrow, Southern Review,* and *High Plains Literary Review,* and she has published articles on poetry in such journals as *English Literary History.* She is completing a collection of essays on silences in poetry by American women.

S. LILLIAN KREMER is assistant professor of English at Kansas State University, where she also teaches courses in ethnicity and gender in Jewish American literature in the Women's Studies and American Ethnic Studies programs. She is author of *Witness through the Imagination: Jewish-American Holocaust Literature;* and essays by her on Saul Bellow, Cynthia Ozick, Chaim Potok, Norma Rosen, and women and the Holocaust have appeared in several collected volumes, including *Saul Bellow and the Struggle at the Center, Jewish American Women Writers,* and *Holocaust Studies Annual.*

DEIRDRE LASHGARI is associate professor of English at California State Polytechnic University, Pomona, where she specializes in world literatures. She is coeditor of two international anthologies of poetry by women, *The Other Voice* and *Women Poets of the World;* a third volume on contemporary women poets of the world is in progress. She spent a year in Iran on a Fulbright Fellowship doing work on modern Iranian poetry, and she has translated and written on Iranian literature and film as well as British and American women writers.

SHIRLEY GEOK-LIN LIM is professor of English and Women's Studies at the University of California at Santa Barbara. Her poetry has been widely published in the United States and abroad. She is coeditor of *One World of Literature* and *Reading the Literatures of Asian America,* and editor of the Modern Language Association's *Approaches to Teaching Kingston's "The Woman Warrior."* In addition to writing extensively on English-language authors in Singapore and Malaysia, she edits *Asian America: Journal of Culture and the Arts.*

MADHUCHHANDA MITRA is assistant professor of English at the College of Saint Benedict, Saint Joseph, Minnesota, where she specializes in postcolonial theory and literatures and Third World women writers. Her writings include "The Discourse of Liberal Feminism and Third World Women's Texts: Some Issues of Pedagogy," with Indrani Mitra and, also with Indrani Mitra, a book in progress on four Indo-English women writers.

GISELA NORAT is assistant professor of Spanish at Agnes Scott College in Georgia. She has published articles on fiction, poetry, and drama by Latin American women writers in journals such as *Lingüística y literatura, Essays in Literature, Hispanic Journal,* and *Phoebe: An Interdisciplinary Journal of Feminist Scholarship, Theory and Aesthetics.* An essay on Carlos Fuentes is forthcoming in *Chasqui.*

Contributors

MERRY M. PAWLOWSKI is assistant professor in the English and Communications Department at California State University, Bakersfield, where she specializes in modern and contemporary British literature and writing by women. Her work on Virginia Woolf includes a forthcoming essay interrogating fascism and male modernism. She is also completing an advanced textbook in critical theory.

ROSEANNE LUCIA QUINN teaches courses on women and literature at the University of Iowa, where she is completing a doctoral dissertation in English on the subject of color, class, and sexuality in literature by multigenerational Italian- and Sicilian-American women. An essay is forthcoming in *Forum Italicum*.

ANN E. REUMAN is completing her Ph.D. in English at Tufts University with a dissertation on the subject of feminist dialogics and narrative strategies in works by contemporary American women writers. She has taught seminars on the American Renaissance, with an emphasis on women and African American writers, and on Native American literatures. An article on Kafka and O'Connor is forthcoming in *Papers on Language and Literature*.

RUTH O. SAXTON is associate professor of English and Dean of Letters at Mills College. She edits the *Doris Lessing Newsletter* and has written on undergraduate archival research as well as on Lessing, Anne Tyler, and Virginia Woolf. Her current work focuses on female dress, the body, and mothers and daughters. She is coeditor of a collection of critical essays entitled *Virginia Woolf and Doris Lessing: Breaking the Mold*.

PAMELA SMILEY is assistant professor of English at Carthage College, Kenosha, Wisconsin, where she teaches courses in the novel and gender in contemporary literature as well as on woman as cultural symbol and contemporary women artists. She has written on the gaze in *The Ancrene Riwle* and incest in the writing of Joyce Carol Oates, and is completing a book on the influence of Roman Catholicism on contemporary American women authors.

ANN E. TRAPASSO is completing her doctoral dissertation in African American literature at the University of North Carolina, Chapel Hill, where she has taught courses in the English and Women's Studies departments in composition, introduction to fiction, contemporary literature, and racism and sexism. Her publications include work on Georgia Douglas Johnson, Audre Lorde, and Gertrude Stein.

DOROTHY DAVIS WILLS is associate professor of anthropology at California State Polytechnic University, Pomona, where she teaches courses on Africa, the Middle East, language and culture, international development, and culture, environment, and waste management. She served as the International Center's coordinator for Program Development and Women in Development, and contributed to the award-winning film *Keepers of the Flame,* about the Yanomami people of the Amazon. She is currently completing a book based on the six years she spent working in Senegal and Nigeria.

Index

Abel, Elizabeth, 108, 109
Adnan, Etel, 5, 194; *Sitt Marie-Rose,* 16, 282–90
Allen, Paula Gunn, 316; novels of, 20
Anzaldúa, Gloria, 11, 19, 305–19; *Borderlands / La Frontera,* 17, 81, 315
Aptheker, Herbert, 220–21
Artaud, Antonin, 248, 252, 253
Atwood, Margaret, 81
Austen, Jane, 141

Bâ, Mariama, 5, 15; *The Beggars' Strike,* 158–60, 162–64, 166–70
Baetz, Ruth, 112, 114
Bakhtin, M. M., 11, 17–18, 70
Ballantyne, Sheila, 141
Bambara, Toni Cade, 11
Barthes, Roland, 17
Bell, Quentin, 98, 109
Benstock, Shari, 108
Berger, Iris, 156
Beverley, John, 69
Bezirgan, Basima Qattan, 189
Bolkosky, Sidney, 242–43
Brent, Linda, *see* Jacobs, Harriet
Brontë, Charlotte: *Jane Eyre,* 141; *Shirley,* 20
Brontë, Emily, 53
Brown, John, 29
Brown, William Wells, 61
Browning, Elizabeth Barrett, 195
Burgos-Debray, Elisabeth, 7, 67
Butler, Sandra, 277–79, 280

Camus, Albert, 78
Carby, Hazel, 39, 41, 59
Case, Sue-Ellen, 247, 248, 250, 260
Cassatt, Mary, 126
Certeau, Michel de, 62
Cervantes, Lorna Dee, 305
Césaire, Aimé, 158, 252
Chase-Riboud, Barbara, 58
Child, Lydia Maria, 38; "The Quadroons," 61
Chodorow, Nancy, 135
Christian, Barbara, 199, 220
Christie, Agatha, 204

Cixous, Hélène, 27, 32
Clammer, John, 176, 185
Cleaver, Eldridge, 252
Clement, Catherine, 116
Cobham, Rhonda, 259, 260
Columbus, Christopher, 65
Condé, Maryse, 248, 251, 252–53, 255
Costa, Emilia Viotti da, 78

Daly, Mary: space on the boundary, 9, 11, 17, 284
Daneshvar, Simin, 5; *Savushun,* 16, 190–99
Davis, Angela Y., 54, 220–21
de Lauretis, Teresa, 267, 268
Dearborn, Mary V., 316
Derrida, Jacques, 32; view of language, 26
DeSalvo, Louise, 108
Dickens, Charles, 136
Diop, Birago, 158
Diop, David, 158
Donaldson, Laura E.: "Miranda effect," 10
Dorsinville, Roger, 249
Douglass, Frederick, 59
Duckworth, George, 98, 104, 108–9
Duckworth, Gerald, 98, 104–5, 108
Duckworth, Stella, 98
Duvaliers, the (Papa Doc, Baby Doc), 256, 257

Eisler, Riane, 285–86
Eliot, George, 136
Elkins, Stanley, 221
Ellis, Sarah: *The Daughters of England,* 20
Erdrich, Louise, 20

Fall, Aminata Sow, 5, 15; *Such a Long Letter,* 158–60, 162–64, 166, 168–70
Faludi, Susan, 269
Fanon, Frantz, 252; *The Wretched of the Earth,* 17
Felman, Shoshona, 63, 72
Fernea, Elizabeth Warnock, 189
Ferré, Rosario, 14; *Sweet Diamond Dust,* 3, 63, 65, 72–77
Fetterley, Judith, 215, 216
Ford-Smith, Honor, 259, 260, 261
Foster, Frances, 53

349

Index

Foucault, Michel, 249, 268
Fox-Genovese, Elizabeth, 65, 66
Frank, Anne, 244
Franketienne, 248, 251, 255, 256–57, 260, 261
Franklin, Aretha, 256, 262
Freire, Paulo, 228
French, Marilyn, 189–90
Freud, Sigmund, 43, 116, 268; model of male sexuality, 288
Friedman, Ellen, 76

Gaskell, Elizabeth, 136
Gates, Henry Louis, Jr., 77
Genêt, Jean, 248
Gilbert, Sandra M., 41, 135, 204
Gilligan, Carol, 135, 209–10, 215
Girard, René, 288
Giraudoux, Jean, 256
Glaspell, Susan: "A Jury of Her Peers," 16, 203–18
Goldman, Renitta L., 118
Gordon, Mary: Final Payments, 134; interview with Annie Milhaven, 134; Men and Angels, 15, 124–34
Gray, Thomas R., 224
Gubar, Susan, 41, 135, 204
Gwin, Minrose, 58

Hacker, Marilyn, 33
Hafez, Sabry, 157
Heilbrun, Carolyn G., 215
Herman, Judith Lewis, 59
Hippolyte, Dominique, 249
Hirsch, Marianne, 132
Hogue, W. Lawrence, 17
Homans, Margaret, 28
hooks, bell, 1, 310, 312, 314, 318
Hussey, Mark, 108

Irigaray, Luce, 88, 288

Jacobs, Harriet (pseud. Linda Brent), 14, 38–61
JanMohamed, Abdul R., 3, 88, 89
Jemie, Onwuchekwa, 186
Jones, Gayl, 61
Joubert, Elsa, 14, 80–91

Kader, Soha Abdel, 156
Kane, Hamidou, 158
Kathigasu, Sybil (Daly), 6, 173–78, 183, 185
Keckley, Elizabeth, 60
Kingston, Maxine Hong, 141, 296
Kinkaid, Jamaica, 141–42

Kolodny, Annette, 204
Kristeva, Julia: "Stabat Mater," 43, 125, 130
Krystal, Henry, 239

Lacan, Jacques, 126
Laub, Dori, 63, 72
Laye, Camara, 158
Lee Chin Koon, Mrs., 183
LeGuin, Ursula, 136
Leong Liew Geok, 178
Lessing, Doris, 140–43

Lifton, Robert Jay, 239
Lim, Janet, 6, 173–74, 175–76, 178–85
Lorde, Audre, 192, 267, 275, 280, 308, 318
Lyman, Peter, 133
Lyotard, Jean-François, 63, 67, 68

Madubuike, Ihechukwu, 158, 186
Mansfield, Katherine, 141
Marcus, Jane, 108
Marquard, Jean, 83
Marshall, Paule, 141
Mathabane, Mark, 85
McDowell, Deborah E., 219, 228
McIntosh, Peggy, 8
Menchú, Rigoberta, 7, 14; autobiography, 63, 65, 66–72, 78–79; interview with Alice Britton and Kenya Dworkin, 79; "Patria abnegada," 79
Mernissi, Fatima, 156
Milton, John, 197; "Aeropagitica," 11; Miltonic myths, 42
Minai, Naila, 190
Mirikitani, Janice, 9; Shedding Silence, 17, 291–304
Molloy, Sylvia: Certificate of Absence, 15, 111–23
Moraga, Cherrie, 7, 20
Morrisseau-Leroy, Félix, 262
Morrison, Toni, 58, 141; on the canon, 6; "funkiness," 309; interview with Jane Bakerman, 220, 229–30; the "not not-there," 4; "unspeakable things unspoken," 6; Song of Solomon, 189
Muñoz, Susana: the film Susana, 111; the film Las madres de Plaza de Mayo, 122
Mussolini, Benito, 99, 107

Newitt, Hilary, 99–100
Newman, Leslea, 280
Newman, Naomi: "Snake Talk," 21
Newton, Judith Lowder, 20
Nichols, Margaret, 120

Index

Norfolk, Lawrence, 34
Nye, Andrea, 26

O Hehir, Diana, 141
Olsen, Tillie: "One Out of Twelve," 136; "Si-
    lences," 1
Ostriker, Alicia, 35
Oyono, Ferdinand, 158
Oz, Amos, 18
Ozick, Cynthia, 16, 231–41, 242–46

Parini, Jay, 28
Patmore, Coventry, 136
Poole, Roger, 108
Pratt, Mary Louise, 3
Prince, Mary, 60

Renan, Ernest, 72
Rhys, Jean, 141–42
Rich, Adrienne, 12, 14, 280, 285; critique of
    the dominant language, 27; interview
    with David Montenegro, 26; "Notes
    toward a Politics of Location," 269;
    Time's Power, 25–37; Your Native
    Land, Your Life, 28
Ringelblum, Emanuel, 232
Robertson, Claire, 156
Robinson, Sally, 9
Rosen, Norma, 16, 231–36, 241–46
Rosenblum, Barbara, 277–79, 280
Roumain, Jacques, 252
Rush, Florence, 41
Russell, Diana, 47

Saadawi, Nawal el, 156, 165, 190; God Dies
    by the Nile, 15, 147–57
Sandoval, Chela, 18
Sayre, Nora, 236
Scarry, Elaine, 70; the "unsharability of
    pain," 64
Schulman, Alix Kate, 173
Schwarz-Bart, Simone, 248, 251, 253–55,
    263
Sembene, Ousmane, 158–59, 170; Xala, 163
Senghor, Léopold Sédar, 158
Shange, Ntozake, 248, 250–51, 255, 261
Silko, Leslie Marmon, 5; novels of, 20
Singer, Isaac Bashevis, 242
Sistren Collective, 248, 250–51, 255,
    258–61
Siyavesh, Savushun, 197–98
Smith, Sidonie, 108
Smith, Valerie, 59
Sommer, Doris, 65

Spillers, Hortense J., 43
Spivak, Gayatri Chakravorty, 89
Starhemberg, Fanny, Princess, 100
Starzecpyzel, Eileen, 117; "Persephone com-
    plex," 119
Steinem, Gloria, 263
Stemerick, Martine, 108
Stephen, Julia, 97–98, 100–101, 104, 107–8
Stephen, Leslie, 101–4, 107–8
Stephen, Vanessa, 103, 106
Stoll, David, 67, 69
Stowe, Harriet Beecher, 81, 194
Styron, William, 220–21, 224, 229–30

Takaki, Ronald T., 78
Teresa, Saint, 308
Terry, Jack, 239
Thackerkay, William Makepeace, 136
Thiam, Awa, 165
Tirolien, Guy, 253
Traba, Marta, 122–23
Trinh T. Minh-ha, 3–4, 9–12, 89–90, 317
Tubman, Harriet ("Moses"), 30
Turner, Nat, 220–21, 229–30

Vajarathon, Mallica, 156
Valverde, Mariana, 115

Walker, Alice, 57, 136, 262–63
Wang Gungwu, 173–74
Weedon, Chris, 268
Wheeler, Virginia R., 118
Whitford, Margaret, 288
Wiesel, Elie, 242
Williams, Sherley Anne, 16, 58, 219–30
Winnow, Jackie, 273
Wittgenstein, Ludwig, 77
Wolf, Naomi, 269
Woolf, Leonard, 98, 100, 109
Woolf, Virginia, 15, 141, 194; Mrs. Dallo-
    way, 98; "Professions for Women," 135,
    137, 141, 143; A Room of One's Own,
    136; "A Sketch of the Past," 95–110;
    Three Guineas, 99, 102, 107; To the
    Lighthouse, 124, 136, 137, 138, 139,
    140, 142–43
Wynter, Sylvia, 17

Yamamoto, Gloria, 87
Yeats, William Butler, 60
Yezierska, Anzia, 194
Yudice, George, 70, 78

Zwerdling, Alex, 108

Feminist Issues: Practice, Politics, Theory
Alison Booth and Ann Lane, Editors

Carol Siegel, *Lawrence among the Women: Wavering Boundaries in Women's Literary Traditions*

Harriet Blodgett, ed., *Capacious Hold-All: An Anthology of Englishwomen's Diary Writings*

Joy Wiltenburg, *Disorderly Women and Female Power in the Street Literature of Early Modern England and Germany*

Diane P. Freedman, *An Alchemy of Genres: Cross-Genre Writing by American Feminist Poet-Critics*

Jean O'Barr and Mary Wyer, eds., *Engaging Feminism: Students Speak Up and Speak Out*

Kari Weil, *Androgyny and the Denial of Difference*

Anne Firor Scott, ed., *Unheard Voices: The First Historians of Southern Women*

Alison Booth, ed., *Famous Last Words: Changes in Gender and Narrative Closure*

Marilyn May Lombardi, ed., *Elizabeth Bishop: The Geography of Gender*

Heidi Hutner, ed., *Rereading Aphra Behn: History, Theory, and Criticism*

Peter J. Burgard, ed., *Nietzsche and Feminism*

Frances Gray, *Women and Laughter*

Nita Kumar, ed., *Women as Subjects: South Asian Histories*

Elizabeth A. Scarlett, *Under Construction: The Body in Spanish Novels*

Pamela R. Matthews, *Ellen Glasgow and a Woman's Traditions*

Mahnaz Afkhami, *Women in Exile*

Deirdre Lashgari, ed., *Violence, Silence, and Anger: Women's Writing as Transgression*